THE GERMAN REVOLUTION OF 1918

D1326978

Kameraden! Arbeiter!

Die Regierung Ebert - Scheidemann hat sich unmöglich gemacht. Sie ist von dem unterzeichneten Revolutionsausschuss als Vertretung der revolutionären sozialistischen Arbeiter und Soldaten (Unabhängige sozialdemokratische Partei und kommunistische Partei) für abgesetzt erklärt.

Der unterzeichnete Revolutions-Ausschuss hat die Regierungsgeschäfte vorläufig übernommen.

Kameraden! Arbeiter!

schliesst Euch den Massnahmen des Revolutions-Ausschusses an.

Berlin, den 6. Januar 1919

Der Revolutions - Ausschuss

i. V. Ledebour,   Liebknecht,   Scholze

Manifesto of the Revolutionary Committee of January 1919, signed by Liebknecht, Scholze, and by Liebknecht on behalf of the absent Ledebour (see p. 201).

THE GERMAN
REVOLUTION OF 1918

A Study of German Socialism in War and Revolt

BY

A.J.RYDER

Lecturer in History at St David's College, Lampeter

CAMBRIDGE UNIVERSITY PRESS

CAMBRIDGE
LONDON · NEW YORK · MELBOURNE

Published by the Syndics of the Cambridge University Press
The Pitt Building, Trumpington Street, Cambridge CB2 1RP
Bentley House, 200 Euston Road, London NW1 2DB
32 East 57th Street, New York, NY 10022, USA
296 Beaconsfield Parade, Middle Park, Melbourne 3206, Australia

© Cambridge University Press 1967

Library of Congress catalogue card number: 67–10057

ISBN 0 521 06176 8

First printed in Great Britain
at the University Press, Cambridge
Reprinted in Great Britain by
REDWOOD BURN LIMITED
Trowbridge & Esher

To
KRYSTYNA

CONTENTS

CONTENTS

ILLUSTRATIONS

between pages 144 and 145

A reproduction of the Manifesto of the Revolutionary Committee of January 1919 will be found opposite the title page. (Reproduced by permission of Ullstein Bilderdienst.)

ACKNOWLEDGEMENTS

We should like to thank the following for allowing us to reproduce photographs: Bildarchiv der Österreichischen Nationalbibliothek for Plates 1a, b; Ullstein Bilderdienst for Plates 2a, b, 3b, 6a, c, 7b, 10a, b, 11a, b, 12a, b, 14b, 16a, b; the Radio Times Hulton Picture Library for Plates 3a, 4a, 5, 6b, 7a, 8, 14a; the Library of the Sozialdemokratischen Partei Deutschlands, Bonn, for Plate 4b. The Wiener Library kindly lent us the photographs for Plates 10a, b, 14b.

Plates 9a, b and 13 are taken from *Illustrierte Geschichte der deutschen Revolution* (Berlin, 1929); we are grateful to the Internationaal Instituut voor Sociale Geschiedenis for providing us with these photographs. Plates 15a, b are taken from *Zeitgeschichte in Wort und Bild* (Munich, 1931).

PREFACE

I became interested in the German revolution of 1918 while working in Germany between 1946 and 1956 in the education branch of the British Control Commission and its variously named successor bodies. I found that in trying to account for the collapse of the Weimar Republic, and more generally for the failure of German democracy, I was led to an investigation of the unsuccessful revolution which gave the republic its unpromising start. In Berlin, where I spent nearly four years, I was struck, as everyone must be, by the ideological wall (since reinforced by a concrete one) that splits the city, a small but particularly significant section of the great divide which now runs across the world. Western visitors to Berlin are likely to be puzzled, as I was, by the nomenclature which describes East Berlin as the Democratic Sector, and Soviet-occupied Germany as a Democratic Republic. The conflicting meanings attached to one word, democracy, stand for the difference between two ideologies, eastern and western socialism, for semantics, like other sciences, has been made the servant of politics. Yet both have, basically, a common origin, and their divergence dates mainly from the dissolution of the pre-1914 liberal–Marxist synthesis—a process begun by the first world war and completed by the revolutions in Russia and Germany. Thus an interest in Germany's recent past (the Weimar Republic) and present (the East–West confrontation) led me to their common source, the war and the upheavals to which it gave rise. Within the transformation of German socialism brought by the socialist split and the experience of revolution, the Independent Social Democrats as the 'centrist' party played a key part, and they naturally form the central strand of the story.

A grant from London University helped me to visit the International Institute of Social History at Amsterdam, where I was able to consult two important primary sources, the Kautsky Archive and the Minutes of the Central Council of the 'German Socialist Republic' for January 1919. The late Mr Werner Blumenberg, then head of the Institute's German Department, gave me most valuable advice and guidance, and I am grateful to the Institute for letting me make use of much published material not readily available elsewhere. In Berlin I benefited from the useful collection of pamphlets on the German revolution in the Library of the Free University. Dr G. Kotowski (now Professor Kotowski of the Otto Suhr Institute of the Free University of Berlin) kindly allowed me to read a part of the Memoirs of the Independent socialist leader Wilhelm Dittmann, which are to be published under his editorship in conjunction with the International Institute of Social History, to which they belong. My friend Douglas Blackett of the British Council, formerly Professor of English at the Technical University of Berlin, and his staff provided me with much appreciated secretarial assistance. In London I have received help from several libraries, including the Foreign Office Library (where I was able to see the German cabinet minutes from November 1918 to February 1919), the British Museum and the Institute of Historical Research. I am particularly grateful to the two institutions of which I have made most use: the Wiener Library, which has often let me keep books out for an unconscionable period; and the British Library of Political and Economic Science at L.S.E., whose resources were usually equal to the most exacting demands. I should like to thank the librarians of those two and of other libraries, named and unnamed, for assistance in many ways. It is a pleasure to record my indebtedness to the Library staff at St David's College, Lampeter.

I wish to express my appreciation of the advice, help and encouragement generously given over a lengthy period by Professor W. N. Medlicott of the London School of Economics and Political Science, under whose supervision I undertook the research from which this book has grown, and who kindly found time to read the finished product in typescript. Dr Curt Geyer, who before coming to England played a prominent part in German socialism and in the events described in this book, was also good enough to read and comment on the script; I have been fortunate in profiting from his unique knowledge of the subject. I am grateful to Professor C. D. Chandaman of St David's College, Lampeter, for his interest and counsel. Mrs S. Cox of Lampeter aided me greatly by typing out most of the text. I should like to thank the Pantyfedwen Fund Committee of St David's College for a much-valued grant towards publication. I am especially indebted to Dr Roger Morgan of the University of Sussex for his expert scrutiny of the script, and for suggesting improvements. Any remaining mistakes are, of course, my own. I desire to take this opportunity of thanking the editorial and other departments of the Cambridge University Press for their care, skill and forbearance in seeing the work through all stages of production. Finally, my wife has helped me in ways too numerous to mention; the dedication of this book to her is a token of my gratitude.

A. J. R.

LAMPETER AND ST JOHN'S WOOD
NOVEMBER 1966

ABBREVIATIONS

Ausschuss	*Protokolle der Sitzungen des Parteiausschusses der Sozial-demokratischen Partei Deutschlands* (Minutes of the S.P.D. Council), September 1914–June 1917.
Cabinet	*Protokolle der Kabinettsitzungen* (German Cabinet Minutes), November 1918–February 1919.
Congress	*Allgemeiner Kongress der Arbeiter- und Soldatenräte Deutschlands: Stenographischer Bericht* (Stenographic Report of the (first) Congress of German Workers' and Soldiers' Councils), December 1918.
K.P.D.	*Kommunistische Partei Deutschlands* (German Communist Party).
Prot. S.P.D.	*Protokoll über die Verhandlungen des Parteitages der Sozialdemokratischen Partei Deutschlands* (Minutes of S.P.D. conferences) followed by place and date.
Prot. U.S.P.D.	*Protokoll über die Verhandlungen des Parteitages der Unabhängigen Sozialdemokratischen Partei Deutschlands* (Minutes of U.S.P.D. conferences) followed by place and date.
Reichskonferenz	*Protokoll der Reichskonferenz der Sozialdemokratie Deutschlands* (Minutes of the national conference of German Socialists), September 1916.
Reichstag	*Verhandlungen des Deutschen Reichstages* (Reichstag Debates).
Reichstag Inquiry	*Die Ursachen des deutschen Zusammenbruches im Jahre 1918.* Vierte Reihe im Werk des Untersuchungsaus-schusses der Deutschen Verfassunggebenden Nationalver-sammlung und des Deutschen Reichstages, 1919–28 (Inquiry into the Causes of the German Collapse in 1918), 12 vols.
S.P.D.	*Sozialdemokratische Partei Deutschlands* (German Social Democratic Party).
U.S.P.D.	*Unabhängige Sozialdemokratische Partei Deutschlands* (Independent German Social Democratic Party).
Zentralrat	*Protokoll des Zentralrates der Sozialistischen Republik Deutschlands* (Minutes of the Central Council of the German Socialist Republic), vol. 1, 8–25 January 1919.

INTRODUCTION

Between the idea
And the reality
Between the motion
And the act
Falls the Shadow.   T. S. ELIOT

Among the revolutions known to history the German revolution of November 1918 occupies a modest place. Indeed some of its witnesses and commentators, though fewer of its chroniclers, would hardly disagree with Borkenau, the historian of the Third International, who doubted whether what then occurred in Germany deserved the name of revolution at all. The German revolution has been described as the mutiny of a defeated army (Rathenau), the product of sheer exhaustion (Friedrich Naumann), a revolution without ideas (Maximilian Harden), and a philistine affair without fire or inspiration (Bülow). All these judgements contain some truth; none is adequate, some are misleading. More apt would be Victor Hugo's description of the overthrow of Charles X's government in Paris in July 1830—a revolution which stopped half-way. Yet so far as any of the French revolutions offers a parallel to the German revolution of 1918–19, it is that of 1848. Berlin between November 1918 and the spring of 1919, like Paris between February and June 1848, experienced the sudden collapse of a discredited monarchy, the emergence of a republican government with a militant left wing, the election by manhood or universal suffrage of a constituent assembly with a non-radical or conservative majority, the dismissal or resignation of the left wing ministers followed by a revolt on the part of the discontented revolutionaries, and their suppression by the government with the help of the army. Berlin's Spartacus Week was the analogue of the June Days in Paris, and Noske the counterpart of Cavaignac. In both countries the attempt to turn the political revolution into a social one was defeated by the forces of order or reaction acting under the banner of parliamentary democracy. In France the counter-revolutionary wave brought to power a Bonapartist president who within four years made himself emperor; in Germany it was fourteen years before a much more ruthless adventurer acquired dictatorial power. In both countries the uncompleted revolution unleashed a bitter struggle between right and left as men realised that neither republic nor democracy provided an automatic solution of social problems. Indeed, Herzen's description of the shock caused by the June Days in France could well be applied to many German socialists after the suppression of the Spartacist revolts: 'Half of our hopes, half of our beliefs were slain; ideas of scepticism and despair haunted the mind and took root in it. One could never have supposed that, after passing through so many trials, ... we had so much left in our souls to be destroyed.'[1] There, however, the parallel ends.[2] Significant as the failure of the French revolution of 1848 was, its consequences can hardly be compared with those which followed the 'intermediate semi-revolution' as Trotsky called it of Germany in 1918–19. That an event or movement fails is, of course, no reason for a historian to neglect it, especially where its negative effects are of such fateful consequence as those which the German revolution bequeathed to the Weimar Republic. Still, in view of the transient and limited nature of that revolution, anyone who undertakes a study of it should perhaps begin by justifying his choice of subject.

The issues raised by the German revolution and the first world war from which it sprang were of far more than local or temporary importance. The war presented the socialist parties of Europe with their greatest challenge, for they had passionately believed both in the necessity of preventing a European conflict, the catastrophic scale and character of which they had been among the first to grasp, and in their ability to do so. Their failure to make good their anti-war pledges dealt the Second International a blow from which it never recovered. Ideologically the war divided the socialists into two camps; and under the impact of the Bolshevik revolution the division became permanent. Thus the first main theme of this book is the effect of the war on German socialism, and the transformation of what in 1914 was still a formally united and apparently flourishing party into two opposed groups, whose bitter rivalry survived the war. The second main theme is the revolution itself, which, in the eyes of the left wing intellectuals and their followers represented an attempt, the first of its kind, at the conquest of power by a Marxist party in a highly organised industrial country. The experiment was significant both in its geographical setting, since Germany was the focal point of the forces, ideological as well as military, contending for mastery, and in its timing, because it occurred during a uniquely crucial period, the last year and a half of the war.

In the war and the subsequent upheavals the three great formative influences of European history since the French revolution—nationalism, democracy and socialism—ran together to form an explosive mixture, and from their interaction the modern world was shaped. The war was a more destructive and traumatic experience than anything since the Thirty Years war, and its effects were incomparably wider. It rocked the political and social order as not even the French revolution had done. The first country to succumb was Russia, whose feeble autocracy proved incapable of mastering either its internal or its external enemies. As in 1905, revolution followed defeat, but

---

[1] Quoted in I. Collins, *The Age of Progress* (1964), p. 332.

[2] There is also a parallel between the German revolutions of 1848 and 1918. Of the former —another one which stopped half-way—Veit Valentin has written: 'A humane revolution is necessarily a semi-revolution' (*1848: Chapters of German History*, p. 447).

2

this time there was no respite for the Tsar. When in November 1917 the Bolsheviks seized power after a liberal interregnum, they proceeded to set up a new social order as the first stage of a world revolution in which Germany, with its trained proletariat and Marxist leadership, was to play the central part. At the same time as Russia, absorbed in its revolutionary experiment and paralysed by civil war, withdrew from Europe, America entered it for the first time as a belligerent and decisively tilted the balance of the war in favour of the Entente. In its final phase the war had a more pronounced ideological character, for although the Entente had all along declared that they were fighting for democracy, their alliance with the Tsar had made the claim unconvincing in many parts of Europe. The three powers, liberal America, Hohenzollern Germany and Bolshevik Russia embodied in varying degrees the forces at work. With Wilson's Fourteen Points inscribed on their banners the United States led a crusade for democracy. Under Lenin Russia carried the torch of revolutionary socialism. Germany represented authoritarian nationalism unrelated to any 'world historical' idea. Before the war reached its bloody climax on the battlefield, a struggle of ideas began above it which continued after the guns were silent and in one form or another has lasted ever since. The two super-powers of the future confronted each other across the world, champions of rival creeds. Lenin promised a millennium through revolution: Bolshevism would destroy the economic roots of war and inaugurate, after much turmoil, the reign of social justice and proletarian brotherhood. Wilson, the Presbyterian president of a bourgeois republic, offered popular government, the self-determination of peoples and a League of Nations to settle international disputes. Between them lay Germany, on whose downfall the realisation of all these plans depended. Germany had defeated Russia, and was reaping the benefits of that victory and of the Bolshevik revolution which she had helped to bring about. For over four years her armies had dominated Europe and defied the world. But in the late summer of 1918 the military collossus cracked. With their dwindling resources stretched to breaking-point, the German armies retreated after missing victory, it seemed, by the narrowest of margins, and as the reinforced Allies closed in, Germany's own allies surrendered. The shock of defeat caused the collapse of the Hohenzollern regime, which hitherto had appeared almost impregnable.

The collapse made the German revolution possible, but also ensured that it occurred in a way no one had foreseen. Beginning as a naval mutiny, it spread rapidly to the army and the factories. Spontaneous and locally organised, it soon acquired a national momentum. Within a few days Germany was covered by a network of hastily and informally elected bodies calling themselves soldiers' and workers' councils, and claiming to be the effective government. They acted as revolutionary state parliaments or town councils, usually leaving executive functions to the central or local government officials, who carried on under the supervision of their new masters. Abandoned by its civilian and military defenders, the legal government was powerless, and the Reichstag was ignored. The councils were a crude but workable form of democracy. But since they were, in the main, elected only by those who could be described as workers or their sympathisers, they represented also class rule. As such they were unacceptable as a permanent form of government, not only to the disfranchised classes, but also to the majority of socialists, who were not prepared to abandon their traditional belief in parliamentary democracy. This had (in theory) just been introduced by the Kaiser's last Chancellor, Prince Max of Baden, in whose government the majority socialists had sat. But the reforms, which had been stubbornly resisted by conservatives so long as Germany had a chance of winning the war, came too late to halt the revolutionary wave which brought the councils to power and threatened to sweep away parliament as well as the monarchy. The Kaiser was forced by public opinion to abdicate and a republic was proclaimed, while Prince Max gave way to an all-socialist government under Ebert. It was at this point that the divisions inside socialism which the war had developed proved fatal to the further progress of the revolution.

The split was complete by 1917, when the majority of the parliamentary socialists, keeping the name of S.P.D. and giving general though often critical support to the government's war policy were opposed by a minority, known as the Independent Social Democrats, who refused to vote for war credits or to support it on any major issue. The former represented the reformist and nationalist elements and conceived of socialism as a fairly remote objective, to be attained only after the transformation of Germany into a parliamentary state, itself an unlikely contingency before October 1918. The latter sought to uphold in very difficult circumstances the revolutionary and international principles of socialism enshrined both in dogma and in the programme of the party and the International. Under the martial law which prevailed during the war, anti-war activities such as strikes inevitably assumed a semi-revolutionary character. Thus while remaining a parliamentary opposition, the Independent socialists, especially on their militant industrial wing, were carried by their hostility to the war into a radical, subversive policy. The party as a whole did not, however, go far enough to satisfy the Spartacists, the small but fanatical revolutionary group which was organisationally linked to the Independents but doctrinally separate. The Spartacists operated clandestinely, and most of their leaders spent much of the war in prison.

When the November upheaval came, the majority socialist leaders, who did not want it, sought to contain and control it. The Independents, on the other hand, urged on by the militant Spartacists, tried to turn it into the full-scale socialist revolution proclaimed by Marx, interpreting the defeat of the Hohenzollern regime as the predicted collapse of capitalism; for imperialistic capitalism, seen as the ultimate cause of the war, had evidently reached its mortal crisis. Though co-operation between the two socialist parties was far from easy in view of these differences, for seven weeks they tried to find a common policy in an all-socialist coalition government that received its mandate from the workers' and soldiers' councils. But the attempt broke on the incompatibility of aims. Disappointed by the lack of revolutionary progress caused by the majority socialist leaders' marked distaste for radical changes and frustrated by formidable practical difficulties, the Independents resigned. Meanwhile the workers' and soldiers' councils, represented in an all-German congress, had voted for a speedy return to parliamentary government, but also for far-reaching reforms in the army (abolition of the officer's power of command) and in the economy (immediate socialisation). This was a policy which significantly fell between those of the two socialist parties.

The resignation of the Independents was the signal for the extreme left—the Spartacists and the revolutionary shop-stewards loosely attached to the Independent party—to rise in an ill-conceived and badly executed attempt to overthrow the government. So defenceless was the government, however, that it was able to suppress the rebels only with the help of the Freikorps, volunteer units commanded by anti-republican officers of the regular army, now in course of demobilisation, who took advantage of the plight of Ebert and his colleagues to establish themselves as a counter-revolutionary force. It was the Freikorps who, during the reprisals that followed the Berlin rising, killed the Spartacist leaders, Liebknecht and Rosa Luxemburg. When, three weeks later, the newly elected constituent assembly met at Weimar, appointed a new government and proceeded to draw up a new republican constitution, the revolutionary period was formally at an end. In fact the civil war, in the form of left wing risings and political strikes, continued. The failure of the two socialist parties, now more than ever at daggers drawn, to win a majority in the assembly put an end to immediate hopes of a radical policy. Exasperated by the revival of militarism embodied in the Freikorps and disillusioned by the compromises that followed the establishment of a mixed S.P.D.-bourgeois government at Weimar, many socialist voters now transferred their allegiance to the Independents, who remained in implacable opposition. Under pressure of these events, and with an eye on the apparently successful Bolshevik experiment in Russia, the Independent socialists adopted a more left wing policy. The party now abandoned, in stages, its cherished adherence to parliamentary democracy in favour of government by workers' councils which they recognised as the only means of preserving the revolutionary *élan* that the Weimar assembly conspicuously lacked. But the Independents' decision to demand proletarian rule, including eventually the dictatorship of a minority, carried the party far in the direction of the Communists, who, following the Russian slogan of all power to the soviets, advocated a soviet regime in Germany. As, however, not all the Independents were willing to adopt the Leninist formula for revolution and jettison the democratic principle, the party eventually split. The left wing merged with the much smaller Communist party and accepted Lenin's Twenty-One Conditions as the price of membership of the Third International, while the right later rejoined its parent body, the S.P.D. The significance of the Independent socialists is that they represented an attempt to bridge the gap between reformist and revolutionary socialism, between bourgeois democracy and proletarian dictatorship, which alone could have healed the socialist breach and might have reconciled the radically minded masses to the Weimar parliamentary regime. The party's failure had far-reaching implications for Marxist socialism in general as well as for German politics in particular. The regrouping of German socialists in the aftermath of the revolution, and more specifically the development and dissolution of Independent socialism, thus forms the final theme of this book. While the Independents were moving left, the majority socialists found themselves increasingly under attack from the thwarted revolutionaries on the one hand, and from the incorrigible anti-republicans, who were already accusing them of stabbing Germany in the back during the war, on the other. The unsolved problems of parliamentary democracy or proletarian dictatorship, of socialisation and 'demilitarisation' continued to divide the left, while the counter-revolutionary revival culminating in the Kapp Putsch threatened the life of the republic. The struggle between the three main blocs which emerged from the revolutionary period—the republican centre, including the majority socialists, the Communist left and the nationalist right—was the legacy of the revolution to the Weimar regime, which was thus largely preoccupied with settling the issues the revolution had raised.

It is in the light of these developments that one should consider the most serious charge brought against the German revolution—that it lacked genuineness. The charge is true if applied to the leaders of the majority socialists, such as Ebert and Scheidemann, who accepted the November upheaval as an accomplished fact, an unavoidable but temporary deviation from the constitutional course they were determined to follow. But among the rank and file of the party (and indeed among some of the leading members too) as well as among all sections of the Independents a different spirit prevailed. The spontaneity and breadth of the movement which gave rise to the workers' and soldiers' councils in small towns as well as big is evidence of a genuine revolutionary impulse, a popular upsurge which owed little to socialist doctrine, though something to the Russian precedent of the year before. The view of some scholars that the masses who made the November revolution wanted only peace, democracy and a republic contains a measure of truth,[1] but ignores the radical military and economic demands of the congress of workers' and soldiers' councils. As for the leaders of the militant left, the Independents Ledebour and Däumig with their shop-steward allies, and the Spartacists Liebknecht and Rosa Luxemburg, they were conscious revolutionaries in deed as well as in word. They were bent on using the opportunity presented by the fall of the Hohenzollern regime to set in motion the socialist revolution which they believed would carry them to power in place of Ebert as Lenin had displaced Kerensky. In Munich Eisner, a utopian rather than a Marxist, sought to apply socialist principles to foreign policy and to initiate a new era in international relations. Like Liebknecht and Luxemburg and many others, he paid for his intrepidity with his life. In different circumstances they might have accomplished something of their purpose; but the dice were loaded against them, and they were also victims of their miscalculations. Few possessed the qualities of a successful revolutionary leader. By common consent Rosa Luxemburg was the outstanding personality of the left, but her intellectual gifts and personal fanaticism were not matched by a grasp of reality. She was at heart a romantic, a visionary appearing in the garb of 'scientific socialism'. Liebknecht's courage could not make up for his lack of prudence. He and Ledebour were amateurs compared with Lenin, but this was a difference of training and technique rather than of attitude. The German revolution contained some moments of sham and farce, more of misplaced heroism and baffled idealism.

[1] For example, Erich Matthias in *Die deutsche Sozialdemokratie und der Osten* (Tübingen, 1954).

CHAPTER I

GERMAN SOCIALISM BEFORE 1914

Social Democracy was not a party in the usual sense of the word, but an Islam. MAXIMILIAN HARDEN in 1899

ORIGINS AND BACKGROUND OF GERMAN SOCIAL DEMOCRACY

No political development in Europe between the Franco-Prussian war and the first world war was more striking than the rise of German Social Democracy. It is difficult half a century later to realise the strength of the hopes and fears aroused by this party, which by 1890 received more votes than any other German party and was easily the largest socialist party in any country.[1] This success had been achieved in the comparatively short space of thirty years. It was in 1863 that the first German working-class party, the General German Workers' Union, was founded by the gifted and romantic Lassalle. Its aim was the establishment of a socialist society after the capture of political power by the workers. This was to be done through the vote—a task which must have seemed utopian indeed at a time when the Prussian parliament was being overborne by Bismarck, the same Bismarck who four years later introduced manhood suffrage into the German constitution. A rival radical party, also in Saxony (the most industrialised German state), was formed in 1869 by Wilhelm Liebknecht, a middle-class veteran of the 1848 revolution, and August Bebel, a carpenter. This party was influenced by Marx, whose International Working Men's Association had been formally constituted in London in 1864, in its acceptance of the class struggle and its denunciation of capitalism; but in other ways, such as its emphasis on a democratic, united Germany (as opposed to the Bismarckian, Prussian solution of the German problem) it was nearer the liberal–radical ideas of 1848. Despite Liebknecht's disparagement of the Reichstag (which he described as the figleaf of absolutism) his party too sought to achieve its ends by legal, evolutionary means, whereas in the *Communist Manifesto* and in many other writings Marx had proclaimed his belief that the existing social order must be overthrown by force.

In 1875 the Lassallean and Liebknecht–Bebel groups (Lassalle himself had been killed in a duel in 1864) met at Gotha and decided to merge. The new, enlarged party became known as the German Socialist Workers' party. The programme on which they agreed was an eclectic mixture of the

---

[1] C. Schorske, *German Social Democracy, 1905–17, The Development of the Great Schism* (1955), p. 3. Though the S.P.D. had more votes than any other party it did not have the largest number of seats because the distribution of seats did not reflect the post–1871 growth of population in the industrial districts.

ideas of both Lassalle and Marx, the former predominating. Unity was reached at the expense of clarity, for the two conceptions of socialism could hardly be reconciled. Typically Lassallean features that reappeared in the new programme were the demand for a free people's state (i.e. a democratic republic), the affirmation that power was to be won through the ballot box, acceptance of the claims of the national state (Lassalle had been a Prussian patriot and admired Bismarck) and an emphasis on practical reform.[1] This remained the Socialist Workers' party programme for the next sixteen years.

Not surprisingly, the Gotha programme was subjected to scathing comment from Marx and Engels, who, from their exile in London, followed, critically but not unhopefully, the progress of German socialism.[2] For them the people's state was a petty bourgeois heresy. Marx's censure would not, however, have carried so much weight had the Gotha conference not been followed three years later by the period of persecution initiated by Bismarck's anti-socialist law of 1878. For twelve years all socialist activity in Germany was banned except for the appearance in the Reichstag of the handful of socialist deputies. Despite this handicap the party's popularity grew, and its vote rose from 312,000 in 1881 to nearly 1,500,000 in 1890. To the socialist leaders the Bismarckian persecution revealed the reactionary character of the German government and thus served to vindicate the views of Marx, who, in contrast to Lassalle, held that the state was an instrument of class oppression. Revolutionary thinking among socialists was strengthened, and the demand was made for a more radical policy.[3] The result was the adoption, at a party congress held in 1891, of a new, almost wholly Marxist programme. At the same time a new name, the *Sozialdemokratische Partei Deutschlands* or S.P.D., was adopted. By this time William II was on the throne, Bismarck had fallen, and the party was no longer proscribed. Hence the congress could be held in Germany, and the place chosen was Erfurt. The Erfurt programme was an important document; it was destined to stand for thirty years, including the first world war and the German revolution. Before considering this programme it is necessary to glance at the background influences without which the whole course of German socialism in this period cannot be understood.

Political life in Hohenzollern Germany revolved round two main institutions: the imperial government, embodying the autocratic principle, and the Reichstag or parliament, representing popular forces. The two were in no way integrated; constitutionally, in fact, members of the government were not allowed to belong to the legislature. The authority of the King of Prussia (who after 1871 was also German emperor), based on the army, the bureau-

---

[1] A. J. Berlau, *The German Social Democratic Party, 1914–21* (1949), p. 21. For German socialism before 1875 see also R. P. Morgan, *The German Social Democrats and the First International, 1864–1872* (Cambridge Univ. Press, 1965).

[2] Marx and Engels, *Selected Works*, II, 17 ff. (*Critique of the Gotha Programme*).

[3] *Die neue Zeit*, X, i, p. 582. For Lassalle's view of the state see Berlau, *op. cit.* p. 21

cracy and the landowning class of Junkers, had been raised by Bismarck to the strongest power in Europe. Its prestige, buttressed by its triumph over parliamentary liberalism between 1862 and 1866, had been greatly enhanced and consolidated by the victory over France and by the reconstruction of Germany under Prussian leadership. United Germany was in theory a federal state, with sovereignty vested in a federal council or *Bundesrat*. But since the *Bundesrat*, which was a gathering of state ministers rather than an upper house, was virtually controlled by Prussian votes, federalism did not in fact represent an effective brake on Prussian power. Moreover, within Prussia the autocratic regime was strengthened by a permanent conservative majority in the parliament or Diet, thanks to the three-class franchise which Prussia inherited from the counter-revolution of 1849 and was to keep until 1918. This franchise, which even Bismarck described as absurd and miserable[1] (though he never changed it) made a man's voting power depend on his wealth measured by direct taxation. The result was a distorted reflection of political feeling in Prussia, which contained three-fifths of Germany's population. It also affected national policy, because the imperial Chancellor, being also prime minister of Prussia, had to take the wishes of the Prussian Diet into account as well as those of the more liberal Reichstag. Under the imperial constitution the Chancellor was appointed and dismissed by the Kaiser, who had the power to declare war or peace.

In contrast to the Prussian Diet, the Reichstag, elected by equal manhood suffrage, gave a fairly accurate picture of the political views of the German people despite some anomalies in the electoral system. The Chancellor did not depend on the Reichstag in any formal constitutional sense, and if it rejected legislation he put before it, as occasionally happened, he was under no obligation to resign. Clearly, however, the smooth working of the constitution required the co-operation of the Reichstag, or rather of the parties commanding a majority in the Reichstag, with the Chancellor, and this was normally forthcoming. The Reichstag could have used its power over bills, especially finance bills, to coerce the government as the first step towards parliamentary control of the executive, but did not in fact do so. The lack of constitutional progress in Germany thus owed more to the acquiescence of the Reichstag in the prevailing system than to the system itself. Most of the party leaders were quite content to be critics of the government; they hardly aspired to be the government.[2] The notion that mere politicians were capable of ruling Germany seemed far-fetched to them, and they were satisfied to exercise limited influence without the burden of responsibility.

[1] E. Eyck, *Bismarck and the German Empire* (1950), p. 147.

[2] F. Stampfer, *Die ersten 14 Jahre der deutschen Republik* (1936), p. 11. A favourite way for ministers to crush opponents in the Reichstag was to ask them, ironically, to imagine themselves in the ministers' place. But the Chancellor did at times abandon bills unpopular with the Reichstag.

For this attitude there were several reasons. The majority of German liberals, organised in the National Liberal party, had become reconciled to the Hohenzollern empire in return for the undoubted blessings of unity, prosperity and national greatness. German liberalism was still suffering discredit from its failure in the 1848 revolution and its defeat at the hands of Bismarck.[1] Even those radicals who refused to accept the Bismarckian system were in no mood to risk a new challenge to a much stronger government. Moreover most middle-class politicians were afraid that parliamentary government would open the door to socialism because of the electoral strength of the S.P.D. Fear of the economic consequences of democracy outweighed their desire for democracy.[2] In the case of the Centre party, whose left wing had democratic leanings, there was the additional motive that as Catholics they were unwilling to do anything that might bring nearer the day when Germany would be governed by Marxists. Finally it was recognised by both liberals and socialists that any attempt to use the Reichstag's voting rights to force a parliamentary regime on the government would not only challenge the whole Bismarckian constitution but would precipitate a revolutionary crisis, for which few people were prepared.

The only major constitutional crisis of the pre-war years occurred in 1908 when the Kaiser came under heavy criticism from all parties in the Reichstag for some characteristically unwise remarks he made in an interview with the *Daily Telegraph*. Bülow, who as Chancellor was responsible for the published text, later resigned, and William made a vague promise to respect his constitutional obligations in future. The incident exposed the anomalous position of the Chancellor, who, dependent on the Kaiser by whom he was appointed, yet needed the confidence of the political parties. It indicated the limits of the Chancellor's power, if not of the Kaiser's, and could have been used, as the government's left wing critics wanted, to press the demand for parliamentary government. But since, for reasons already mentioned, the leaders of the Reichstag parties (apart from the socialists) were unwilling to take advantage of the crisis, the opportunity was allowed to pass.

Whatever the inadequacies of this system of government—and they were to be glaringly shown up during the war—the average German was made less aware of them by the excellence of his country's civil service; and he tended to make favourable comparisons between Germany's orderly and paternal administration and the turbulent democracy of France. Nor did Germany's

---

[1] Between 1874 and 1881 the National Liberal parliamentary party was reduced to a third of its original size, and liberalism as a whole was split into four smallish parties (K. D. Bracher, *Die Auflösung der Weimarer Republik* (1955), p. 10).

[2] *Reichstag Inquiry into the causes of the German Collapse* (henceforth referred to as *Reichstag Inquiry*), VIII, 370; P. Gay, *The Dilemma of Democratic Socialism: Eduard Bernstein's Challenge to Marx* (1952), p. 221. There was also the fear that any reduction of the power of the military state caused by constitutional reform would weaken Germany as a great power.

political backwardness sensibly slow down its economic progress. The industrial revolution started in Germany about two generations later than in Britain, but when it came its impact was sharp and swift. Between 1870 and 1914 Germany overtook Britain in the production of iron, steel and manufactures generally, and was rapidly catching up with British coal output. Between 1890 and 1914 German foreign trade trebled, and its competition was felt in every part of the world. German industry was noted for its careful planning and good equipment. It made greater use than British industry of scientific research and technical training; its managerial class was intelligent and enterprising, its workers skilful, industrious and thrifty. Insurance legislation had brought great benefits to the workers, whose trade unions had also done much to raise living standards, but relations between labour and capital were often tense and the workers resented the rather superior and patronising attitude of the employers. In a population which rose from forty-one million in 1870 to sixty-seven million in 1914 the number of large cities multiplied, and by 1910 three out of five Germans lived in towns.[1] Many of the new industrial proletariat were recent immigrants from the countryside and still felt uprooted. The rapid social and economic changes consequent upon industrialisation favoured the growth of a large-scale socialist party.

Politically as well as geographically Germany occupied an intermediate position between France and Russia. By comparison with France, with its revolutionary traditions and parliamentary radicalism, Germany was 'eastern'. By comparison with Russia, with its obscurantist Tsars and ignorant depressed peasantry, it was 'western'. Technologically and culturally Germany compared favourably with its western as well as with its eastern neighbours; but the frontier between democracy and autocracy ran along the Rhine, not along the Niemen. It was the paradox of Hohenzollern Germany that its well educated society and rapidly expanding economy had to operate within a political system that paid scant regard to the needs and aspirations of an industrial community and whose values were derived from Prussia's feudal, agrarian and military past.

These special features of Germany's development were reflected in the policy and outlook of its socialists. Had Germany been without any parliamentary life its socialist party would no doubt have acquired the characteristics of a conspiratorial sect, as Social Democracy did in Russia. If, on the other hand, Germany had had a parliamentary regime, German socialists might well have adopted a policy of collaboration with the radicals, as the Millerand socialists did in France at the time of the Dreyfus Affair; and gradually shed their revolutionary ideology. The German socialist party showed that it could capture millions of votes, but it could hardly climb to power through an alliance with the left wing liberals, for the latter, organised

---

[1] K. S. Pinson, *Modern Germany: its History and Civilisation* (1954), p. 221.

as the Progressive party, were not strong enough to give them and the S.P.D. together a majority in the Reichstag. The number of Progressive seats actually fell from seventy-six in 1890 to forty-two in 1912. The Progressives were the only party, apart from the S.P.D., which unequivocally wanted parliamentary government, so that the task of fighting for it fell mainly on the socialists, who were thus heirs of the democrats of 1848 as well as of Marx. Yet the weakness of liberalism, especially in Prussia, favoured the survival within the S.P.D. of a hard core of anti-parliamentary feeling. In face of the strong, autocratic state there was little reason to reject Marx's belief that only through revolution could the proletariat seize power in Germany. At the same time the country's social and economic progress acted as a disincentive to revolutionary sentiment among the working classes. These divergent trends within the S.P.D. came to the fore during the period that followed the adoption of the Erfurt programme in 1891.

MARXISM IN THE LIBERAL ERA: THE ERFURT PROGRAMME

The Erfurt programme consisted of two parts.[1] Part 1 outlined the party's long-term objective of the socialist transformation of society that was to follow the breakdown of capitalism. This breakdown, the programme asserted, was as inevitable as a law of nature (it was not for nothing that Marx compared himself with Darwin as a discoverer of the laws of social evolution), and would be preceded by pauperisation of the masses and by increasingly severe crises. Socialism would be the achievement of the working class alone, for all other classes, despite the conflict of interests between them, were bound to private property and thus to support the existing social order. A corollary of this was that socialists should not enter into alliance with bourgeois parties: thus the policy of 'Millerandism', as it became known, was condemned in advance. The programme implied that the conquest of power by the proletariat would be possible through the vote. It is hardly surprising that the word revolution, which might well have provoked the authorities to renew their ban on the S.P.D., did not appear in the programme. Nor was any reference made to the other concept with which in Marx's writings the revolution is coupled: the dictatorship of the proletariat. (Significantly enough, only in Russia was this aim included in the programme of the Social Democratic party.)[2]

The second part of the Erfurt programme—the practical as contrasted with the theoretical part—described the short-term objectives which could be striven for within the existing capitalist system. They included such things

[1] The text of the Erfurt programme is in the Report of the S.P.D. congress of 1891 (*Prot. S.P.D.*, Erfurt, 1891).
[2] E. H. Carr, *The Bolshevik Revolution* (1950), p. 28. L. Schapiro, *The Origin of the Communist Autocracy* (1955), p. 350.

as votes for women, proportional representation, biennial parliaments, direct election of civil servants, democratic government at all levels, secular education, a national militia instead of a standing army, and the eight-hour day. The programme also called for the settling of international disputes by arbitration (thus anticipating the League of Nations) and the abolition of capital punishment. Many of these demands were radical not socialist and represented the unfulfilled aspirations of 1848.

This programme was ingeniously designed to appeal to all shades of socialist opinion. Doctrinaire Marxists could reassure themselves with the affirmation in Part I of the ultimate transformation of society and the firm rejection of any tactical compromise. Those who attached more importance to immediate reforms could take comfort from the aims enumerated in Part II, the realisation of which would lighten the burdens of everyday life and would also appeal to radicals. The party's preoccupation with practical reforms and its relegation of the long-term objective to a possibly distant future seemed reasonable enough at a time when capitalism showed no sign of imminent collapse. Moreover the political atmosphere in Germany since the fall of Bismarck the year before had become less hostile to socialism. The new Kaiser, William II, was anxious to show good will and refused to start his reign by antagonising a large section of his subjects. Not only was the anti-socialist law discontinued, but, in contrast to Bismarck, the Kaiser allowed an international labour congress to meet in Germany. Despite his low opinion of socialists, it appeared for a time that the Kaiser was making a bid for working-class support. In 1891, a Workers' Protection Act was passed and industrial arbitration courts were set up (with S.P.D. approval) on the initiative of the Prussian minister of trade.[1] This was in keeping with the prevailing social trend; the famous Papal Encyclical, *Rerum Novarum*, was issued in the same year.

Engels, since Marx's death in 1883 the undisputed leader of revolutionary socialism, in an article published in 1892 approved of the Erfurt programme to the extent that it was based on Marx and eradicated the heresies of Lassalle, though he noted that, somewhat inconsistently, the S.P.D. was bringing out a new edition of Lassalle's works.[2] What the programme did not reveal was the extent to which Lassalle's influence remained in the party, particularly among the rank and file. Lassalle had indeed had several advantages over Marx: his influence had been felt first, his personality and oratory gave him a personal magnetism which Marx, coldly intellectual and geographically distant, notably lacked, and his ideas, less abstract and more instinctive, were easier to grasp and had more popular appeal. However, as has been seen, Bismarck's persecution of the socialists seemed to justify Marx's concept of

---

[1] Balfour, *The Kaiser and his Times* (1964), pp. 129, 172.
[2] *Die neue Zeit*, x (1892), i, p. 582.

the state as against Lassalle's, and the Erfurt programme now gave orthodox Marxism the seal of party approval. The emphasis on practical reforms might have been held to weaken the grip of revolutionary doctrine, but this was specifically denied.[1] Concessions won in the day-to-day struggle were dubbed 'payments on instalment', and it was recalled that Marx had welcomed the Ten Hours Act in England. In fact German experience was to show that improvements in the worker's standard of living tended to reduce his enthusiasm for the revolution. Yet even this argument was not conclusive to those doctrinaire Marxists who inherited the master's belief in the inevitability of the collapse of capitalism.

The Erfurt programme made two assumptions. One was that the S.P.D. was capable of gaining a majority of seats in the Reichstag. This assumption was supported by election results between 1891 and 1912; for apart from the election of 1907, fought on a colonial issue in an atmosphere unfavourable to socialism, the party's share of the vote rose steadily. The culmination of this process was the general election of 1912, when the S.P.D. polled four and a half million votes, representing a third of the nation, and won 110 seats out of 397. Its triumph was even greater than it appeared, for the distribution of seats did not take into account recent population shifts, and the urban areas, where socialism was strong, were under-represented. Membership of the S.P.D. was for the first time over a million. Since the working class (urban and rural) formed the majority of the population, many socialists expected that the gaining of a socialist majority in the Reichstag was only a matter of time.[2] The flaw in this reasoning was that many Catholic working men, and, as elections from 1919 onwards were to show, still more of their wives, voted for the Centre party, whose left wing had strong industrial roots.

More questionable, from the perspective of 1891, was the second assumption of the Erfurt programme: that if the S.P.D. secured a majority in the Reichstag it would be able to use its power to make Germany a parliamentary democracy. This point was not lost on Engels, who criticised the authors of the programme for not explicitly demanding the concentration of all power in the hands of a national parliament.[3] The reasons why the Reichstag made no significant progress in this direction have already been referred to. Among them was the negative attitude of the National Liberals, which was to be strikingly exhibited in 1912. In that year the S.P.D. managed to persuade the National Liberals and Progressives to support a socialist bill for equal franchise in Prussia. But at the last moment, the National Liberals, under the

---

[1] Marx's *Communist Manifesto* had included a number of practical reforms as well as long-term aims.

[2] P. Scheidemann, *Der Zusammenbruch* (1921), p. 1. 'The results of the 1912 elections were a sure indication that in a relatively short time the great majority of the German people would support Social Democracy.'

[3] *Die neue Zeit*, xx (1902), i, p. 9. This article was published ten years after it was written.

influence of their right wing, backed out, and the project fell through.[1] If liberals showed so little enthusiasm for reform, the stubbornness with which the ruling conservatives in Prussia resisted demands for constitutional change is understandable. The historian Hans Delbrück once admitted that the Prussian Officers' Corps would never tolerate the introduction of a parliamentary regime except after defeat—a judgement that was to be borne out by events.[2] In postulating a peaceful transfer to power from the executive to the Reichstag the S.P.D. was being unrealistic; and it is somewhat surprising that Engels, who had no illusions about where power lay in Germany, should have built so many hopes on the potentialities of a massive socialist parliamentary party.

ENGELS AND THE ABANDONMENT OF REVOLUTIONARY TACTICS

The adoption of the Erfurt programme coincided with the beginning of a new phase in the history of German social democracy. Europe was in the heyday of liberalism. The period of revolutions, which had spanned the middle decades of the nineteenth century, was over, the Paris Commune of 1871 being its last manifestation. Thereafter (except in Russia) political conflicts took on a more or less peaceful character. This was possible because after 1870 almost every state in Europe except the Russian and Ottoman empires had some form of constitution;[3] and even Russia had felt the reforming hand of Alexander II. Governments became less arbitrary, even autocratic countries introduced manhood suffrage, the press became freer, human rights were acknowledged, discrimination against minorities was on the decline. Even where, as in Germany, political parties lacked power, they could develop considerable influence through parliament. The German socialists were active in state legislatures and in municipalities as well as in the Reichstag in promotion of their social policies, and there were even town councils with socialist majorities.[4] Whereas the socialists of Marx's day had been small, obscure groups of extremists whose only hope of attaining power was as the left wing of a bourgeois liberal revolution, those of the 1890s were a large, recognised parliamentary party, equal or superior to the liberals in numbers and organisation. Meanwhile, however, the revolution foretold by Marx had not come about, and its arrival, in an unrevolutionary era, seemed increasingly improbable. How was a party which, at least in theory, was committed to a revolutionary policy, to behave under these circumstances, so different from those postulated by Marx? Engels set himself to answer this

[1] Schorske, *op. cit.* p. 240.
[2] H. Delbrueck, *Regierung und Volkswille*, p. 136, quoted in Braunthal, *In search of the Millennium* (1945), p. 94. Bülow's view was that parliamentary government would be the ruin of Germany.
[3] C. J. H. Hayes, *A Generation of Materialism* (1941), p. 51.
[4] W. H. Dawson, *The Evolution of Modern Germany* (1908), p. 133.

question in a special Introduction, published in 1895, to Marx's study of French politics in 1848–50, *The Class Struggles in France:* 'Rebellion in the old style,' wrote Engels, 'street fighting with barricades, which decided the issue everywhere up to 1848, was to a considerable extent obsolete [even by 1871]...The time of surprise attacks, of revolutions carried out by small conscious minorities at the head of unconscious masses, is past.'[1] The ballot box was the weapon which would bring victory in future.

The significance of what Engels intended as a tactical reappraisal of the socialist campaign appears by comparison with what he and Marx had written earlier, and particularly with their emphasis on the need for revolution. The *Communist Manifesto*, published on the eve of the fall of the July monarchy in February 1848, was an appeal to the proletariat of all nations to unite and prepare for an uprising. Yet outside England and certain industrial pockets in Belgium and Germany the industrial proletariat hardly existed. Marx's revolutionary zeal did not spring from the sufferings of the proletariat, of which he knew little in 1843 when his revolutionary beliefs crystallised. Pragmatically the young Marx became a revolutionary because he was convinced that only in that way could backward and reactionary Germany escape from its past and join the ranks of the advanced countries like France and England, both of which had experienced revolution. Philosophically Marx became a revolutionary under the influence of Hegel as interpreted by the radical Young Hegelian school. Marx believed that philosophy should be a guide to action, but for this to happen a material instrument was needed.[2] Marx found this instrument in the proletariat, which was to play the dynamic part within the Hegelian scheme and to realise the aims of philosophy. The proletariat, however, could act only according to the rules of history: that is, it must wait until the bourgeoisie, the class which it was destined to overthrow, had established its own victory over autocracy and feudalism. The *Communist Manifesto* declared that a bourgeois revolution in Germany was imminent, and that it would be almost immediately followed by a proletarian revolution. The first prophecy was soon to be fulfilled, though it was to end in failure. The German middle class proved less ambitious and less militant than the French bourgeoisie in 1789, and such proletariat as existed in Germany never really had a chance to seize power.

Yet Marx's revolutionary optimism survived the crushing defeat of the Paris proletariat in the June Days of 1848 and the triumph of counter-revolution in France and in the rest of Europe. He expected that despite or rather because of the rise to power of Louis Napoleon a new revolution was

---

[1] Marx and Engels, *op. cit.* I, 120, 123.

[2] 'Philosophy cannot be realised without the abolition of the proletariat; the proletariat cannot abolish itself without realising philosophy', wrote Marx in his essay on Hegel's *Philosophy of Right*, which appeared as 'Zur Kritik der Hegelschen Rechtsphilosophie' in *Deutsch-französische Jahrbücher* for February 1844.

17

possible. It would take place, he wrote, only after a new crisis, but it was just as certain as that crisis. A 'real revolution' could occur, however, only when the 'modern productive forces' and the 'bourgeois productive forms' collided.[1]

This is an anticipation of the argument developed at much greater length in *Capital* that the proletarian revolution would result from the incompatibility of capitalist economic production with the needs of society. But the breakdown would be the consequence of contradictions which would reveal themselves only in capitalism's maturity. In 1848, however, French capitalism was in its infancy. Nor was the French proletariat strong enough in numbers (as *a fortiori* the failure of the Paris Commune was to show) to carry out a nation-wide revolution. Thus the pre-conditions of success were lacking in 1848. Why then did Marx advocate a proletarian revolution in France at that time? The answer he gave himself was that the proletariat would not stand alone: the peasants, petty bourgeoisie and even the 'middle classes in general' would ally with the workers against the dictatorship of Louis Napoleon, 'grouping round the proletariat as the decisive revolutionary power'.[2] Marx had to admit that the French peasants had used the franchise given them by the revolution to vote against it. Still, he claimed that they were being quickly disillusioned, and were finding their 'natural ally and leader' in the urban proletariat, whose task was the overthrow of the bourgeois order. The conservative peasants, Marx explained, represented the peasant's superstition, not his enlightenment; the past, not the future. The peasant of the future would be revolutionary.[3]

In fact, the French peasants did not become revolutionary, as Marx later recognised. Electorally they behaved as the property owners they were. The middle classes were terrified of a return of the 'red republic'; as for the urban proletariat as a whole, all likelihood of revolution vanished in the industrial boom of the 1850s. Yet neither failure of the revolutionary movement nor realisation that the conditions of 1848 would not recur was a reason for Marx to despair of revolutionary prospects; for by linking the revolution firmly to the predicted collapse of capitalism, he was giving it a new basis of economic determinism. At the same time the growth of capitalism, by increasing the numbers of the proletariat to the level where they would form the majority of the population, would for the first time make a revolution politically feasible. This was a point taken up by Engels in his Introduction to

[1] Marx and Engels, *op. cit.* I, 210.
[2] *Ibid.* p. 201.
[3] In the original text of his *Eighteenth Brumaire of Louis Bonaparte* Marx wrote that the French peasant would cease to believe in his small holding and that in consequence 'The proletarian revolution will obtain that chorus without which its solo song becomes a swan song in all peasant countries' (Marx and Engels, *op. cit.* p. 308). Since this passage was omitted from the 1869 edition of the *Eighteenth Brumaire* it is a reasonable deduction that by the latter date Marx had changed his mind about the French peasants.

Marx's *Class Struggles in France*. He frankly admitted that he and Marx had been mistaken in their expectation of a proletarian revolution in 1848, mainly because of their miscalculation about the peasants:

History has proved us, and all who thought like us, wrong. It has proved that the state of economic development on the Continent at that time [1850] was not, by a long way, ripe for the elimination of capitalist production; it has proved this by the economic revolution which since 1848 has seized the whole of the Continent, and has caused heavy industry to take real root in France, Austria, Hungary, Poland and, recently, in Russia, while it has made Germany positively an industrial country of the front rank—all on a capitalist basis, which in the year 1848, therefore, still had great capacity for expansion.[1]

Engels went on to draw three conclusions from the quarter century that had passed since the defeat of the Paris Commune. First, the proletariat was now, thanks to industrialisation, strong enough in numbers and organisation to accomplish its revolutionary task. The revolution need not be, as it would have been in 1848, the work of a small minority. Secondly, Engels noted as a favourable omen the impressive growth of Social Democracy in Germany. Despite Bismarck's persecution, the party now had the backing of two and a quarter million voters:

If it [the S.P.D.] continues in this fashion, by the end of the century we shall conquer the greater part of the middle strata of society, petty bourgeois and small peasants, and grow into the decisive power in the land, before which all other powers will have to bow, whether they like it or not. To keep this growth going without interruption until it automatically gets beyond the control of the prevailing government system, not to fritter away this daily increasing shock force in vanguard skirmishes, but to keep it intact until the decisive day, that is our main task.[2]

One cannot read this passage without being struck by its similarity to Marx's optimistic prediction in his *Class Struggles in France:* both foresaw an alliance between the proletariat and other social classes, and it can hardly be coincidence that they used almost the same words. It seems not to have occurred to Engels that the very success of socialists at the polls might have the effect of driving the smaller property owners, such as peasants and small shopkeepers, into the arms of the political right. The attachment to the working-class party of discontented or impoverished members of the middle classes was for Marx and Engels the political result of the polarisation of society to be caused by the concentration of industry in fewer hands and the growth of monopolies. In fact, as will be shown, as capitalism matured it led to a diffusion as well as to a concentration of wealth. The political consequences were thus not those which Engels expected. And when, a generation later, the German middle classes were hit by economic catastrophe (the depression of 1929, following the war and inflation) it was not to the Social Democrats that they turned.

---

[1] Marx and Engels, *op. cit.* p. 115.   [2] *Ibid.* p. 124.

Engels showed more realism in the third conclusion he drew from recent developments: the impossibility of a successful barricade revolt in the style of 1848. Advances in military science (a subject on which Engels had expert knowledge) such as the breech-loading magazine rifle and the percussion shell gave any government an overwhelming advantage against rebels. But this need not cause despair, for what the proletariat had lost through changes in military technique was more than made up for by its increased electoral importance. The weapon that would emancipate the working class in the new age was the vote. It would be folly to throw away the gains acquired by the party's electoral success by toying with premature insurrection ('vanguard skirmishes'), though force would have to be used if the ruling classes ever resorted to violation of the constitution in order to crush socialism. Meanwhile, Engels continued, 'The irony of world history turns everything upside down. We the "revolutionaries", the "rebels"—we are thriving far better on legal methods than on illegal methods and rebellion. The parties of order, as they call themselves, are perishing under the legal conditions created by themselves.'[1] This essay by Engels was of great importance for the future of German socialism. It was reproduced in *Die neue Zeit*, the leading socialist weekly edited by Karl Kautsky, with omissions considered necessary for reasons of censorship. The passages omitted were those in which Engels referred to the possible use of force. The effect of the cuts was to lay undue emphasis on the argument that the party could achieve its aim through the vote. The article was seen as a renunciation of revolutionary tactics, and it gave powerful encouragement to those in the party who believed in reformist, not revolutionary socialism, and who attached more importance to the practical Part II of the Erfurt programme than to the doctrinaire Part I. After 1890 the S.P.D. was increasingly preoccupied with winning parliamentary elections, and Engels' advice—his last important piece of writing, for he died in the same year (1895)—confirmed a tendency that was already strong.[2]

BERNSTEIN AND REVISIONISM

One of Engels' friends and party associates in his later years was Eduard Bernstein, the founder of 'revisionism'. Bernstein, a journalist and scholar who had been forced to leave Germany during the Bismarckian persecution, had settled first in Zürich and later in London as a correspondent of socialist newspapers.[3] He became known in the 1890s as an exponent of reformist

---

[1] Marx and Engels, *op. cit.* p. 125.

[2] E. Prager, *Geschichte der U.S.P.D.* (1921), p. 16. 'The hour of revisionism, of reformism, had struck.'

[3] Eduard Bernstein, born in 1850, started his career as a bank clerk but changed to political journalism and became editor of *Der Sozialdemokrat* in Zürich and then in London. He remained in England, where he was influenced by the ideas of the Fabian Society, until 1901, when he returned to Germany, becoming a socialist member of the Reichstag for

socialism, and his best known book, *Die Voraussetzungen des Sozialismus und die Aufgaben der Sozialdemokratie*, was published in 1899. Bernstein's influence inside the S.P.D. began to be felt at a time when the party, while not repudiating the revolutionary legacy of Marx, had put it into cold storage. The revolution remained an article of belief, but was relegated in the minds of most people to a vague and distant future. Moreover the assumption underlying the Erfurt programme that the party might be able to attain power through the ballot box represented an important shift of emphasis in Marxist doctrine, for as far as Germany was concerned Marx had never admitted that socialism would be possible except through the dictatorship of the proletariat.[1] How far Engels in his last years had come to differ from Marx in this respect is debatable, but there is no doubt, as the quotations from his later writings have shown, that he was impressed by the possibilities of a peaceful transfer of power opened up by the electoral success of the German socialist party.

Bernstein, like Engels, was concerned with the adaptation of policy to the circumstances of the day, and particularly to the failure of the economic crisis foretold by Marx to materialise. But whereas Engels urged the use of parliamentary tactics without the abandonment of revolutionary theory, Bernstein was led, by an examination of Marx's writing in the light of subsequent developments, to an abandonment of the theory. He argued that if, as he claimed, the collapse of the capitalist economy was taking much longer than Marx had predicted, it would also assume a different form from what Marx had expected. Bernstein produced much evidence to show that social evolution was developing in such a way as to make the collapse of capitalism less likely than it had been in Marx's time. The masses were not becoming progressively poorer, economic crises were becoming less severe, the workers' standard of living was rising, not falling, and wealth, instead of being concentrated in fewer hands, was being distributed more widely, as was shown by the growing number of small businesses and small farms.[2] Bernstein did not deny that the workers were exploited, but he maintained that the element of exploitation was on the decline owing to the pressure exerted by socialists on the government and by trade unions on the employers. Factory and welfare legislation showed that progress was possible within the existing system. It was therefore no longer true, as Marx had claimed in 1848, that the worker had no country. The proletarian was becoming a citizen with the right to vote, with his health protected and his children educated by the state.

Breslau West in the following year. During the war he joined the Independent Socialist party, and during the revolution was a member of both socialist parties, whose reunification he supported. He died in 1932.

[1] Marx and Engels, *op. cit.* II, 30, 410.

[2] Bernstein, *Evolutionary Socialism* (edition of 1961), pp. 40 ff. (the English translation of his *Voraussetzungen des Sozialismus*).

It followed, in Bernstein's view, that German socialists should give up their traditionally negative approach to the state, and should make their principal aim the transformation of Germany into a parliamentary democracy. They should not passively wait for the promised catastrophe, or, in Bernstein's words, speculate on a great economic crash.[1] The idea of a dictatorship of the proletariat, which Marx had taken over from the French terrorist Blanqui, was out of date, and represented a survival within Marxism of the very utopianism which Marx derided. Bernstein, whose admiration for Marx was tempered with scrupulous regard for truth, described the master's work as a cross between scientific inquiry and a political tract. This was the crux of the matter.[2] Marx had claimed that his socialism alone was scientific: if so, it should be able to stand verification. Bernstein claimed to be ridding the political doctrine known as Marxism of its unscientific accretions.

All this was highly unpalatable to the leaders of the S.P.D., who regarded Marx as the last word, and ascribed to his writings the authority of holy writ. Bernstein made himself even more unpopular by rejecting the philosophy of dialectical materialism, the basis of 'scientific socialism', as itself unscientific. He thus deprived socialism of its determinist basis, and freely admitted that while socialism was desirable, it was not inevitable. The agent of progress in Bernstein's eyes was the human will, and this will was ethical. He denied that ideas were in the last analysis simply the reflex of social and economic forces. Kant, not Hegel, was his philosophic guide, and his pragmatic, idealistic form of socialism was to be attained through democracy. Bernstein applied his considerable learning and powers of observation and analysis to undermine the main structure of Marxist dogma, and he further shocked the party faithful by asserting that for him the ultimate aim of socialism was nothing and the movement everything.[3]

This was a dangerous heresy. The task of refuting it naturally fell to Kautsky, the intellectual leader of German socialism after the death of Engels and editor of the party's most influential periodical, *Die neue Zeit*.[4]

---

[1] Bernstein, *Evolutionary Socialism*, p. xv.
[2] *Ibid.* p. 209.   [3] *Ibid.* p. 202, and Gay, *op. cit.* pp. 131 ff.
[4] Karl Kautsky, born in Prague in 1854, was a member of the Austrian Social Democratic party before devoting himself to the work of the S.P.D. Active as a socialist journalist in exile (Zürich and London), during the Bismarck period he founded *Die neue Zeit* in 1883 and remained its editor until 1917. After returning to Germany he worked for some time in Stuttgart before moving to Berlin in 1897. A prolific writer on many subjects, and the author of the authoritative book *The Road to Power* (1909) as well as of the Erfurt programme, Kautsky was the most influential intellectual socialist of his time and perhaps the most typical representative of the generation of the Second International. Attacked by Lenin for his anti-Bolshevist views from 1917 onwards, Kautsky lost much of his standing in the divided socialist party, but his short period of office in the ministry for foreign affairs during the German revolution was notable for his publication of official documents seeking to prove the war guilt of the Kaiser's government. Later Kautsky returned to Vienna, until, to escape from Hitler, he fled first to Czechoslovakia and then to Amsterdam, where he died in 1938.

He was the principal author and expositor of the Erfurt programme, and the outstanding representative of the orthodox middle group in the party leadership known as the Marxist centre. Kautsky tried to disprove Bernstein's contention that capital was being more widely diffused, by showing that larger firms were growing more rapidly than small ones. He agreed with Bernstein that a new salaried middle class was coming into existence, but whereas Bernstein believed that the workers would become bourgeois in time, Kautsky thought that the salaried people would be proletarianised. Kautsky stuck to the belief that capitalism would collapse, though he refused to say when. Tactically the most important disagreement between the two men was that while Bernstein wanted democracy to precede socialism, Kautsky declared that 'the victory of the proletariat is the pre-condition of democracy'.[1] (Much later Kautsky was to agree with Bernstein.) Kautsky also argued that where, as in Germany, political power was concentrated, it could not be conquered piecemeal.[2] (Yet in 1912 Kautsky was in favour of the S.P.D.'s pact with the Progressives.) Kautsky often found himself relying on Marxist texts to refute Bernstein's facts, and became involved in over-subtle exegesis as well as in inconsistencies of the kind just mentioned.[3]

Revisionism was officially rejected by the S.P.D. at its annual conference in 1903, held that year at Dresden. But owing to a misunderstanding, the large majority against it included many revisionists, so that the victory of the orthodox was to a great extent illusory.[4] And despite this formal rejection, revisionist ideas penetrated the party's thinking, and still more its actions, at all levels. This was especially true of south Germany, where the absence of Prussian and Junker influence made possible a much less hostile relation between socialists and other parties. In the south German states the local S.P.D. defied official party policy by regularly voting for the budget and 'going to court'. In Baden, the most progressive German state, the socialists made a political pact with the liberal parties against the Centre.

[1] This remark, made at the S.P.D. congress of 1898, is quoted in Gay, *op. cit.* p. 64.

[2] Kautsky at the S.P.D. congress of 1903, quoted in Berlau, *op. cit.* p. 62.

[3] It is hardly surprising that during the war Kautsky became involved in further degrees of inconsistency. In 1907 he had expressed the view in a pamphlet, *Patriotism and Social Democracy*, that proletarian and bourgeois patriotism were unlikely to unite to protect popular liberty. He told the S.P.D. congress in the same year that in case of a war between France and Germany the proletarian cause would not be furthered by the victory of either. In October 1914, however, he wrote that, war having broken out, each nation must try to save its skin, and socialists must do their duty like other people. His argument, which was reiterated in an article published in *Vorwaerts* in 1916, that defence against invasion was the one case in which all classes of the population should rally to save their country, assumed that Germany was threatened by Russia in August 1914—which she was, but because of German weakness in the east caused by the Schlieffen Plan (see Frölich, *10 Jahre Krieg und Bürgerkrieg*, pp. 133–4, and Kautsky Archive, A. 64; also pp. 70–1 below). Rosa Luxemburg ridiculed Kautsky for admitting that the Socialist International was ineffective in time of war (*The Crisis in the German Social Democracy* (written in 1915), p. 10). [4] Gay, *op. cit.* p. 266.

Other influences moved the party in the same direction. The trade unions, which had grown rapidly with the expansion of industry, were decidedly pragmatic and reformist in outlook. Carl Legien, who became chairman of the largest trade union organisation, the General Commission of Trade Unions, in 1890, followed a policy of wresting piecemeal concessions from the capitalists and firmly opposed the use of extremist methods favoured by the left such as the political mass strike.[1] Connections between the unions and the S.P.D. were close. Legien himself was a member of the S.P.D. executive and for many years a member of the Reichstag. In 1914 about a third of the socialist parliamentary party in the Reichstag were union officials.[2] By that time about one industrial worker in three was in a union, and the unions had built up a massive organisation with considerable funds. The more they had to lose, the less inclined the union leaders were to provocative tactics.

Secondly, there was the rise within the S.P.D. of a new generation of party managers whose abilities lay in organisation and who by temperament and training were averse to extremism. Ebert, the future president of the German republic, was the outstanding example of this type of socialist: practical, shrewd, sober, and patriotic, he was a striking contrast to the 'revolutionary romantics' of the left.[3] Like many of the party leaders who came from the working classes—Scheidemann and Noske were other examples—Erbert was little interested in the Marxist theory which meant so much to middle-class intellectuals.[4] As secretary of the S.P.D. from 1905 to 1913 Ebert was in

[1] Berlau, *op. cit.* p. 68; Schorske, *op. cit.* pp. 257 ff. At a congress of trade unions in 1919, the new name *Allgemeine Deutsche Gewerkschaftsbund* was adopted. Legien remained chairman, but died late in the following year.

[2] H. J. Varain, *Freie Gewerkschaften, Sozialdemokratie und Staat* (1956), p. 45. Membership of the free trade unions rose from 1 million in 1902 to 2·5 million in 1913, *ibid.* p. 35.

[3] Friedrich Ebert, born in 1871, was a saddler by training who worked as an S.P.D. journalist before becoming a party secretary, first in Bremen, later in Berlin. His promotion was rapid; elected to the Reichstag in 1912, he became co-chairman of the party (with Haase) in the following year. In February 1919 he was elected president of the German republic, a post he held until his death in 1925. His health was undermined by the attacks of his nationalist critics, who never forgave him for taking part in the big strike of January 1918 (see p. 117 below); while the left reproached him for not having used the revolution to establish democracy on firmer foundations (see ch. 12 below).

[4] The memoirs of both Noske and Scheidemann show that Marxism played little part in shaping their socialist beliefs. Noske refers to it as an 'occult science', adding: 'I do not believe that I have ever spoken of Marxism in a speech or article' (*Aufstieg und Niedergang der deutschen Sozialdemokratie* (1947), p. 27). Noske, born in 1868, was originally a woodworker who entered S.P.D. politics, like many of his colleagues, via journalism, and became a member of the Reichstag in 1906. Having helped to contain the sailors' mutiny at the beginning of November 1918, Noske emerged in the following months as the strong man of the republic against the forces of the left, and was, among large sections of the population, the most hated man in Germany. In 1920 he left politics to become *Regierungspräsident* of Hanover, but was deposed by the Nazis, who later imprisoned him as a suspect in July 1944 and would have executed him had the Allied armies not arrived in time to liberate him. He died in 1946 after writing a second volume of memoirs. Scheidemann, born in 1865, was a printer who became a socialist journalist. Elected to the

a key position, and the secretariat exercised a conservative influence on party policy despite the fact that the party's official leader until his death in 1913, Bebel, was traditionally a man of the left. But Bebel, who had been a member of the North German Reichstag of 1867, and belonged to a revolutionary generation, was pretty cautious in practice.

The third influence was nationalism. As Bernstein pointed out, it was right and proper for a worker who had a stake in his country to feel a patriot. However true Marx's dictum that the proletarian had no fatherland may have been in an economic sense it was probably psychologically false even in 1848. It would have been strange if the upsurge of national feeling in Germany, which had gripped the middle classes, should have had no effect on the artisans and workers. The problem of reconciling the internationalism preached by Marx with the demands of nationalism was first faced by the S.P.D. on the outbreak of the Franco-Prussian war. Then the Lassalle group in the North German Reichstag voted for war credits and the Bebel–Liebknecht group abstained. Later, however, after the defeat of Napoleon III at Sedan, both groups voted against the continuation of the war on the grounds that it was not in the interests of the German proletariat. Both Bebel and Liebknecht were charged with high treason, condemned and sent to prison. The question how the party would behave in a future war began to exercise people's minds in the 1890s, when the Franco-Russian alliance confronted Germany with the prospect of a war on two fronts. Though France was Germany's irreconcilable opponent, the German left saw the main enemy in Tsarist Russia; and on ideological grounds the defence of Germany against Russia became a socialist's duty. This anti-Russian orientation, which was characteristic of nineteenth-century European radicalism, had the full approval of Engels, whose optimistic estimate of the future prospects of German socialism reinforced his belief that against Tsarist Russia even Hohenzollern Germany stood for progress and enlightenment.[1] Patriotism, of which Engels certainly had a share, was even stronger among the younger German socialists. Vollmar, a Bavarian socialist leader who was also an ex-officer, denied at a meeting of the Second International that being international meant being anti-national: 'It is not true that we have no country.'[2] He was, in effect, answering the Kaiser's earlier gibe that socialists

Reichstag in 1903, he was one of the two co-chairmen (Haase being the other) of the S.P.D. parliamentary group at the beginning of the war. Second in importance within the party only to Ebert, Scheidemann was the first socialist to become a senior minister (in October 1918) and during the revolution was one of the three S.P.D. People's Commissars. In February 1919 he became prime minister of the first regular republican government in Germany, but resigned over the Versailles treaty in June, and afterwards retired from politics to become mayor of Kassel. He died in exile in 1939, having survived an attack on his life in 1922. For his memoirs see the bibliography.

[1] *Die neue Zeit*, x, i, p. 580.
[2] Heidegger, *Die deutsche Sozialdemokratie und der nationale Staat, 1870–1920*, p. 56.

were an 'unpatriotic crew'. Thus anti-Tsarist sentiment, nationalism and a desire, often subconscious, to lose their outsider status and find full acceptance within the German community all helped to make socialists less revolution-minded. Bernstein, who was far from being a chauvinist (his enemies accused him of being too Anglophile) defended the German government's acquisition of Kiao-Chow in China, and David, a leader of the reformist group, spoke in favour of German interests in the Baghdad railway.[1] Noske was one of those who defended the German claim to colonies, and a book he wrote on the subject received favourable comment in the non-socialist press. Despite the anti-militarism which was traditional in the S.P.D., socialists began to take an interest in the armed forces, arguing that as Germany obviously needed an army and navy, they should be as efficient as possible.[2] Noske was prominent in debates on the services, and was the first socialist member of the Reichstag to be invited to visit the naval dockyards. There is little doubt that, had the authorities conceded the socialist demand for equal franchise in Prussia, they would have fostered a spirit of national unity, and have given more encouragement to the somewhat frustrated patriotism of German socialists. Even so, the strength of this patriotism was to be strikingly demonstrated in August 1914.

ROSA LUXEMBURG AND THE NEW CHALLENGE FROM THE LEFT

Although the S.P.D.'s Erfurt programme remained unchanged, its day-to-day interpretation shed a good deal of the doctrinaire orthodoxy to which the party still paid lip service. But the growth of reformism in the party in its turn provoked an opposing reaction from the left, the guardians of the revolutionary tradition. If the challenge to the party centre from the right was based on a reappraisal of revolutionary theory in the light of the relative stability and prosperity of capitalist society, the challenge from the left was based on belief in a new period of crises marked by the Russian revolution of 1905 and the deterioration in the international situation. The intellectual leader of the left was Rosa Luxemburg, who in a few years established for herself a formidable reputation in German socialism.[3] She combined a forceful and

---

[1] Bernstein, *op. cit.* p. 173.

[2] Noske, *Aufstieg und Niedergang*, pp. 33 ff. 'There was no sphere of practical politics in which the views of the S.P.D. had not undergone considerable change in the course of time.'

[3] There are two useful studies of Rosa Luxemburg by her contemporaries. One is by Paul Frölich, a leader of the extreme left wing group at Bremen and also the author of one of the main source-books on the revolutionary period, *10 Jahre Krieg und Bürgerkrieg*. Frölich co-operated with the Spartacists during the war and was a founder member of the German Communist party, in which he played a leading part before his expulsion as a right wing deviationist after 1928. His book on Luxemburg is a valuable political biography apart from its complete lack of criticism. The other study, by Rosa Luxemburg's close friend, the Dutch woman socialist Henriette Roland-Holst, is both more personal

incisive mind with artistic sensibility and an ardent revolutionary temperament. Born of a middle-class Jewish family in Russian Poland in 1871, she had studied economics in Switzerland before coming to Germany to throw herself into the work of the S.P.D. Though never a member of the Reichstag, she exercised considerable influence as a speaker, writer and teacher. She was one of the few who have made an original contribution to Marxist thought, and her study of imperialism in her *Accumulation of Capital*, which appeared in 1913, extended Marxist analysis to the colonial and undeveloped territories. She brought to the somewhat prim and reformist German socialist party a faith in 'direct action' and an impatience with parliamentary and gradualist tactics characteristic of the socialists of eastern Europe. As a member of the more left wing of the two Polish socialist parties, Rosa Luxemburg took part in the Warsaw rising of 1905, and she hailed the Russian revolution, of which it was part, as the beginning of a new, revolutionary era for the whole of Europe. This was a miscalculation, for the conflict of social forces unleashed in Russia was not paralleled anywhere in central or western Europe. The threat of a general war, however, was brought nearer by the Morocco crisis, which was a crisis of imperialism. Imperialism for Rosa Luxemburg was inspired by capitalism, which, faced with falling profits and over-production at home, prolonged its life by competing for the raw materials, cheap labour and markets of the rest of the world. On this view the scramble of the European powers for colonies was a symptom of the economic contradictions postulated by Marx and could be ended only by the forcible overthrow of the capitalist system. Meanwhile the carving up of Africa and other continents among the powers accelerated the arms race and increased the number of points of tension, so adding to the danger of global war. Despite differences in economic analysis between Luxemburg's book and Lenin's later work *Imperialism, the Highest Stage of Capitalism*, the political implications of both were similar. So while Bernstein, looking at the domestic scene, foresaw a further fruitful period of parliamentary activity for the S.P.D., Rosa Luxemburg, looking at the darkening international scene, urged the adoption of a crisis policy.

The German working class, she believed, as the largest and best organised in Europe, ought to take the lead and have recourse to what she saw as the decisive weapon of the twentieth-century revolution, the mass strike. In Belgium, Austria and Italy, mass strikes had been successfully used to wrest from the government political concessions such as an extension of the franchise. Prussia should follow this example. But in prevailing conditions the mass strike, as the first step towards the seizure of power by the proletariat,

in its approach and more critical. An East German book on Luxemburg by Fred Oelssner (1951) is also referred to in the bibliography. The new two-volume biography of Rosa Luxemburg by J. P. Nettl (Oxford Univ. Press, 1966) came out after this book had gone to press.

must be used not for reasons of internal politics but to meet the challenge of war and imperialism: the party's internal tactics must be determined by the needs of the international situation.

The questions of militarism and imperialism [she wrote in 1912] form the central axis of political life; in them, and not in questions of ministerial responsibility and other purely parliamentary demands, lies the key to the political situation.[1]

She was critical of the passivity of the party's leaders as well as of the Revisionist right wing:

Leaders who hang back will undoubtedly be pushed to one side by the advancing masses...to wait first patiently for this definite sign that the situation is ripe may be all right for a lonely philosopher, but for the political leadership of a revolutionary party it would spell moral bankruptcy. The task of Social Democracy and its leaders is not to let themselves be dragged along in the wake of events but deliberately to forge ahead of them, to foresee the trend of events, to shorten the period of development by conscious action and to accelerate its progress.[2]

In this very characteristic passage Rosa Luxemburg revealed her impatience with the party leadership and her belief—which events were not to justify—in the revolutionary spirit of the rank and file, those 'masses' whose reactions to crises, such as that of August 1914, were to prove so incalculable. She was right in seeing the approaching war as the decisive factor in European politics, even if she was wrong in attributing too much responsibility for it to economic causes. She was also mistaken in thinking that the 1905 revolution in Russia would have a marked effect on socialist parties elsewhere. Her failure to persuade the S.P.D. leaders to agree to the aggressive use of the mass strike marked the limitations of her influence.

Between the revisionists, reformists and trade unionists on the right, and the militant radicals on the left, the middle of the road leaders or 'Marxist centre' were in an embarrassing position, both logically and tactically. Kautsky, who had spent his earlier years refuting Bernstein, now turned his guns on Rosa Luxemburg. As the exponent of the Erfurt programme he had to keep a balance between the party's final revolutionary goal and the reformist needs of the moment. The right policy, Kautsky held, was one of attrition. Capitalism was doomed, but no one could say exactly how or when the end would come. Kautsky even persuaded himself that reforms would hasten not retard the coming revolution. But he explained that a revolution

need not necessarily be connected with violence and bloodshed. There have already been cases in world history in which the ruling classes were especially sensible, or especially weak and cowardly, so that they abdicated voluntarily in the face of compulsion. A social revolution need not be decided at one blow...Revolutions are prepared in political and economic struggles lasting years and decades and take

---

[1] Luxemburg, *Gesammelte Werke*, III, 527 quoted in Schorske, *op. cit.* p. 243.
[2] Frölich, *Rosa Luxemburg* (English edn. 1940), p. 168.

place during constant shifts and fluctuations in the power relations of different classes and parties, often interrupted by setbacks of long duration (periods of reaction).[1]

Thus Kautsky was able to offer his followers the prospect of a bloodless seizure of power, satisfying those who would be content with nothing less than a revolution as well as reassuring those who feared the loss of hard won gains and other unpleasant consequences of violence. In his interpretation of Marxism revolutions occurred only when the social and economic conditions were ripe; they could not be 'made'. In practice, however, the party could not remain inactive. Both right and left wings were pressing for action of different kinds. Sometimes Kautsky was driven to making unrealistic distinctions: the S.P.D., he wrote in 1909, was a revolutionary but not a revolution-making party.[2] He had always counted as a man of the left, especially in his dispute with Bernstein but in 1910 he broke with Rosa Luxemburg when he opposed her demand for a mass strike in favour of Prussian suffrage reform. On the issue of imperialism too Kautsky could no longer agree with the left. By 1912 he was writing that, while there was a close connection between capitalism and the arms race, yet capitalism was also capable of peaceful development.[3] The more far-sighted capitalists realised, according to Kautsky, that war, with its crushing financial burdens, was not in their interests. The great powers might even agree on a policy of cartels and abolish the arms race. This new phase would have its dangers for the proletariat, but not the danger of war. Tactically, too, Kautsky now supported the pact with the Progressives which he had formally opposed.[4] He continued to uphold the necessity of flexibility, by which he meant that the S.P.D. should be ready to revert to revolutionary methods if the situation called for them. By this date (1912), however, the party was so far committed to parliamentary tactics that a switch to revolutionary ones was not a practical possibility.

In the following year the ascendancy of reformism provoked a reaction from the party's moderate left as well as from its extreme left. The new alignment was seen at the annual conference, held at Jena. Two resolutions were introduced by the left wing radicals: one demanding the offensive use of the mass strike, the other opposing a measure to enlarge the German army known as the Military Tax Act for which the S.P.D. had voted in the Reichstag.[5] The centre as well as the right rejected the mass strike as certain to provoke reprisals, while they accepted the Military Tax Act as justified by the recent French decision to extend military service from two years to three years. The new law was made palatable to the S.P.D. by being financed through a capital levy and a tax on property. The significance of this move was that the

---

[1] Kautsky, *Das Erfurter Programm* (1892), pp. 106–7.

[2] Kautsky, *The Road to Power* (1909), p. 50.

[3] *Die neue Zeit*, xxx, ii, pp. 97 ff, and xxxii, ii, pp. 917 ff.

[4] Frölich, *op. cit.* p. 200.   [5] Schorske, *op. cit.* p. 263.

S.P.D. appeared to be abandoning its traditional anti-militarism in return for a progressive tax. The logic of the party's parliamentary activities had led to this bargain with the government—a bargain struck in terms of financial not constitutional policy. But now at Jena a group of left-centre socialists headed by Haase revolted. Haase, a lawyer from East Prussia, was a member of the Reichstag and co-chairman of the S.P.D., and the decision of him and his friends to side with the extreme left against official party policy was a significant sign.[1] For it was substantially this group of Reichstag deputies who a year later were to register the first protest against war credits in August 1914 and four years later were to found the Independent Social Democratic party. The pattern of disunity which was to lead to the party's disruption during the war was already taking shape. No one can say with certainty how much longer, had the peace lasted, formal unity could have been preserved; but that the reformist and revolutionary wings could not have remained in the same party indefinitely can hardly be doubted.

Thus in the years immediately preceding the outbreak of war German socialism presented a diverse picture. On the one hand the party's spectacular growth, culminating in the electoral triumph of 1912, seemed to be both a measure of strength and a reason for continued confidence. In numbers, organisation and discipline the S.P.D. had no rival among socialist parties, and observers as different as Viktor Adler and Trotsky considered it *the* party of the Second International. The S.P.D. was unquestionably rich in talent: a party which contained a leader like Bebel and intellectuals of the calibre of Bernstein, Rosa Luxemburg and Kautsky was certainly outstanding. Even the fact that, especially in Prussia, the socialists were officially ostracised was a handicap which they turned to advantage by developing to a remarkable extent their own resources. Against a hostile environment socialism became a kind of secular church, providing the faithful with an ideal and a philosophy of life and looking after their mental and physical well-being from the cradle to the grave. 'From the workers' co-operative he acquired his first toothbrush, from the workers' library he borrowed his first book', wrote an Austrian of his youth in the Austrian socialist party, which had learnt much from the S.P.D.[2] Not only co-operatives and libraries, but party schools,

---

[1] Hugo Haase, born in 1863, was elected member of the Reichstag for Königsberg in 1897. He made a name for himself by defending socialists at political trials, notably during the 1905 revolution in Russia, when a number of German socialists were charged with having helped the revolutionaries across the border. At the beginning of the war Haase was chairman of the S.P.D. Reichstag *Fraktion* as well as of the whole party. As the parliamentary leader of left wing opposition to the S.P.D.'s war policy Haase laid down these offices and became in succession leader of the rebel *Arbeitsgemeinschaft* (1916) and chairman of the Independent Social Democratic party (1917). He was co-chairman (with Ebert) of the all-socialist Council of People's Commissars in November–December 1918. He was assassinated towards the end of 1919, a victim of one of the many political murders which disfigured the early history of the Weimar Republic.

[2] Quoted in Joll, *The Second International* (1955), p. 191.

lecture courses, workers' theatres, concerts, sport and weekend excursions were among the activities run by the party. Moreover a member of the movement enjoyed a sense of brotherhood with the rest of humanity through the links between German socialism and other parties in the International.

Yet despite its obvious strength and formidable talents the German socialist party suffered from a serious weakness: the growing divergence between its revolutionary belief and its reformist practice. Bernstein's attempt to modify theory to bring it into line with practice was rejected, as was Rosa Luxemburg's attempt to make the party revolutionary in deed as well as in thought. As we have seen, the socialist leaders received little or no encouragement from the German government to modify or abandon the revolutionary creed they inherited from Marx; yet there was in their unwillingness to admit changes an element of self-deception. The left wing French socialist Hervé, on a visit to Stuttgart in 1907, noticed that despite their Marxist phraseology the German proletarians he saw in the street were in reality good and contented bourgeois. That many members of the party were unhappy about the widening gap between belief and practice is shown by the efforts of both right and left to change the party's orientation as well as by the attempts of the central leadership to reconcile differences.

It was another French socialist, Jaurès, who put his finger on this weakness of the S.P.D. during a policy debate at the Amsterdam congress of the Second International in 1904. Jaurès, whose criticism carried weight because he was an experienced socialist leader and thinker as well as a Germanophile, was stung by his German colleagues' doctrinaire condemnation of 'Millerandism'. He resented their cavalier attitude to human rights, the defence of which had in Jaurès' view justified the French socialists' decision to join a non-socialist cabinet in a crisis of the republic. When Kautsky quoted Marxist texts to refute this policy, Jaurès exclaimed:

You are a great and admirable party, but you still lack two essentials: revolutionary action and parliamentary action. You were granted universal suffrage from above, and your parliament is but a half-parliament...Yours will be the only country in which the socialists would not be masters even if they were to obtain the majority in the Reichstag...You hide your weakness and your impotence by trying to dictate to everybody else.[1]

Jaurès was really warning the S.P.D. that they might achieve success neither as the revolutionary party they were in theory nor as the reformist party they were in reality. He urged them to pay less attention to Marx and more to the practical problems of winning power in a non-parliamentary state. His criticism of the German socialists' inability to act, which he said was concealed by the inflexibility of the theoretical formulas with which their 'excellent comrade' Kautsky would supply them to the end of his days, was

---

[1] Quoted in Gay, *op. cit.* p. 269.

to be verified by events.[1] In one sense, of course, Jaurès' criticism applied to all the socialist parties of Europe: when war broke out in August 1914 hardly any of them[2] acted in accordance with the anti-war resolutions to which they had solemnly pledged themselves at successive meetings of the Socialist International. But in the western democracies the socialist parties were invited, during the war, to join their respective governments (France already had a socialist premier) and thus derived some advantage from their parliamentary allegiance; while at the other end of the spectrum the Bolsheviks ultimately reaped the benefit of their revolutionary intransigence. It was the tragedy of German socialists that because of the exclusive nature of the German political system before the revolution and because of their internal disunity during and after the revolution they were unable to gain power commensurate with their promise or potential.

[1] Quoted in Joll, *op. cit.* p. 102.   [2] For the exceptions see p. 59 below.

CHAPTER 2

THE OUTBREAK OF THE FIRST WORLD WAR

The international idea has been forced into the background for a long
time to come by the reality of a national workers' movement.

LUDWIG FRANK in 1914

SOCIALIST ATTITUDES TO WAR

It was the custom for German Social Democrats at their annual May Day
rallies to drink a toast to socialism as the liberator and reconciler of peoples.
They thus pledged themselves to a double task: the transformation of society
within the nation, peace between nations.

The Marxist ideology on which German socialism was based had always
been international in outlook. The *Communist Manifesto* asserted that with
the development of a world market and free trade the differences and antagon-
isms between nations were disappearing. Although this generalisation was
contradicted by the growing nationalism of Europe—to which, as a contemporary of Cavour and Bismarck, Marx was curiously blind—his rational,
essentially economic approach to political problems remained, and little
importance was attached by his followers to national idiosyncrasies. Moreover, just as the interests of the bourgeoisie were considered to be everywhere
in broad agreement, so were those of the proletariat. The well-known statement in the *Manifesto* that a worker had no country implied that he had no
interest in defending it. Thus socialists thought of themselves as joining
hands with their oppressed brethren in other lands in an international class
struggle against the capitalists. The first attempt at co-ordinating the workers'
efforts across national frontiers was marked by the setting up in 1864 of the
First International. It failed, but established a precedent; and in 1889, to
mark the centenary of the French revolution, a new initiative led to the foundation of the Second International, to which the various socialist parties and
groups, Marxist and non-Marxist, belonged. By that time socialist internationalism had come to mean not only the struggle for power, but also
co-operation against war.

This was a new emphasis. Marx and Engels were no pacifists, and both
accepted war as an instrument of policy. They judged the wars that occurred
in their lifetime according to whether they were in the interests of the proletariat, but they also took into account other criteria, such as what result
would be more favourable to the cause of democracy, and which side was the
aggressor. Thus they approved the Crimean war because it reduced the power

33

of Tsarist Russia, the bulwark of obscurantism and reaction, and the Franco-Prussian war (in its first phase) because Napoleon III had aggressive designs against Germany. After 1880, however, socialists realised that, partly because of the greater destructiveness of new weapons, partly because nearly all European states were involved in the alliance system and had conscript armies, a future war would be an unparalleled disaster. Engels, who was versed in military matters, predicted in 1887 that such a war would involve between eight and ten million soldiers, and would cause devastation equal to that of the Thirty Years war compressed into the space of three or four years and extending over the whole continent.[1] This remarkable prophecy painted a terrifying picture of famine, sickness, want, brutalisation of armies and populations, ruin of trade and general bankruptcy, collapse of the old state system with crowns rolling in the gutter, utter exhaustion on both sides, and finally the establishment of conditions for the final victory of the working class. The year 1918 was to see most of this prophecy fulfilled in eastern and central Europe.

Despite the prospect that such apocalyptic horrors might usher in the socialist age, no socialist could contemplate it with equanimity; and to use all its influence to prevent a European war breaking out became the main aim of the socialist International. Many socialists were by conviction or temperament pacifists, and inherited from liberalism its belief in international arbitration of disputes, arms limitation and the abolition of standing armies. Certainly the German socialists, especially in an age when imperialism created new rivalries between nations on a global scale, could not believe that real or lasting peace was possible as long as capitalists ruled the world, but meanwhile they were determined to do their utmost to prevent the capitalists dragging the proletariat into war.

One of the first acts of the Second International was to pass a resolution condemning war as the evil product of economic circumstances and claiming that it would disappear only when the capitalist mode of production had been superseded by the international triumph of socialism. Another resolution demanded the replacement of standing armies by popular militias on the Swiss model.[2] The object of this was to make war less likely by eliminating the influence of aggressive professional officers and substituting for them peace-loving civilians. This demand also formed part of the S.P.D.'s Erfurt programme. Nor could German socialists forget that the Prussian army had been used (in 1848), and might be used again, as the Kaiser had warned, to suppress the revolution.

After 1904 fear of war increased. One international crisis succeeded another, and the arms race became more intense. The Moroccan war scare of 1905

[1] From Engels' Introduction to a pamphlet by S. Borkheim quoted in Kautsky, *Sozialisten und Krieg* (Prague, 1937), p. 250.　　　　　[2] *Ibid.* p. 298.

forced socialists to consider practical steps to preserve peace. The left wing favoured the use of the mass strike, the success of which in coercing a government for revolutionary ends was demonstrated in the Russian revolution of 1905. Even right wing and centre socialists felt that their movement was now strong enough to frustrate the secretive diplomats and reckless militarists who were leading Europe to catastrophe. As Bebel put it, 'Only the fear of Social Democracy has so far prevented the ruling classes from making a European war'.[1] But this boast was soon to be belied by events.

Differences between socialists on how to deal with the war problem came to a head at the congress of the Second International in 1907, held that year at Stuttgart. Among the French delegates, the fiery Gustave Hervé took up the extreme position that the working class should not take part even in a defensive war. Under the slogan of 'Plutôt l'insurrection que la guerre' Hervé advocated a policy of military strike against any war, regardless of its causes. Jaurès, however, introduced a rival resolution which, while refusing to denounce a defensive war, made it the duty of socialists, in the event of a threat of war, to do everything in their power, from action in parliament to a general strike and open insurrection, to stop it. Even this went too far for Bebel, the leader of the S.P.D. delegation, who feared reprisals from the German government if his party supported Jaurès' resolution. Bebel accordingly introduced a milder resolution which limited the duty of socialists in such a situation to moral protest. This was much too timid for the left. Finally a compromise was reached in a resolution stating that in case of a threat of war, it would be the duty of the working class to do everything to stop war by whatever means seemed most effective. Should war break out nevertheless, socialists would be obliged to strive for its speedy termination and to work with all their power to use the economic and political crisis caused by the war to hasten the abolition of capitalist class rule.[2] The sponsors of this resolution were Lenin, one of the Russian delegates, and Rosa Luxemburg, who represented the Polish socialists: both on this occasion played the unusual role of mediator. The resolution was vague enough not to alarm the right, yet capable of a revolutionary interpretation and therefore acceptable to the left. It was however a solution in words only, as the events of August 1914 were to show. In particular the latter part of the resolution was to prove unrealistic, for once war broke out socialists lost their freedom of action.

The Stuttgart resolution was reaffirmed at the next congress of the International held at Copenhagen in 1910, and again at a special congress at Basle in 1912. The background to the Basle congress was the first Balkan war

---

[1] Bebel's remark, made at the Stuttgart congress of the Second International (1907), is quoted in M. Fainsod, *International Socialism and the World War* (Harvard Univ. Press, 1935), p. 15.

[2] Kautsky, *op. cit.* pp. 336 ff.

which, following the Agadir crisis and the Italian seizure of Tripoli, was seen as making a general war more likely. Yet Jaurès remained optimistic, and the success of the S.P.D. in the 1912 election was a hopeful sign. There was a moving scene at a socialist peace rally in Paris in March of that year, when Jaurès embraced Scheidemann on the platform and both French and German socialists swore to fight together to uphold peace.[1] Next year at Whitsun a meeting of French and German parliamentarians was held at Berne with the object of reaching an understanding and halting the trend to war. Of the 155 persons who took part, 121 were French and only 34 German. On the French side more than half belonged to non-socialist parties, whereas of the German delegates all but six were socialists. The lack of support shown by the German middle-class parties for this attempt at Franco-German understanding prompted Scheidemann to the reflection that most German liberals were now imperialists.[2] Another gathering of French and German parliamentarians took place at Basle in the summer of 1914. It reaffirmed resolutions passed by the Berne conference in favour of a cessation of chauvinism, limitation of arms and arbitration of international disputes by the International Court of Justice.[3] Ironically, such meetings not only totally failed to avert the threatened war, but even built up a mood of false optimism among socialists and led to an overestimate of their ability to keep the peace. Bebel spoke at times as if the working class were powerful enough to make war impossible, and Jaurès was sure that this was no idle boast. He told a friend in the spring of 1914: 'Don't worry, the socialists will do their duty. Four million German socialists will rise like one man and execute the Kaiser if he wants to start a war.'[4]

As the Stuttgart congress showed, the socialist position was not free from ambiguity. The Stuttgart resolution made no direct reference to defensive war, and it was assumed that socialists would take part in no other. Yet it was on this point that socialist opinion was divided,[5] and these divisions were to persist until 1914. While in the S.P.D. the right wing accepted the necessity of fighting a defensive war—which in Germany was always conceived of as a war against Tsarist Russia—the left denied that in the age of imperialism a war fought by a great power could ever be justified. The centre, which denounced imperialism in general but found mitigating circumstances in particular cases, preferred to judge each situation on its merits.

Another source of ambiguity in socialist policy on war and peace was the S.P.D.'s attitude to the armed forces. The party's traditional line was that not a man or a penny should be voted to the 'system', and for this reason socialists

---

[1] Scheidemann, *Memoirs of a Social Democrat* (1929), I, 176.　　[2] *Ibid.* p. 178.
[3] C. Grünberg (ed.), *Die Internationale und der Weltkrieg*, p. 399.
[4] Quoted in Joll, *The Second International*, p. 157.
[5] In 1907 Noske, then a new S.P.D. member of the Reichstag and on the right wing of his party, told the Reichstag that if Germany were attacked the S.P.D. would co-operate with other parties to defend her. Bebel gave qualified approval. Kautsky, *op. cit.* p. 341.

refused to approve the national budget, civil or military. This attitude was stiffened by the party's genuine suspicion and dislike of standing armies in general and of Prussian militarism in particular. On the other hand, socialists could not be indifferent to the conditions under which they themselves, their relations and friends had to do military service. They used their influence in the Reichstag and elsewhere to humanise army regulations and reduce the number of harsh punishments. As we noticed in Chapter 1, some socialists went farther and made it their business to see that the armed forces were efficient. The S.P.D. electoral handbook demanded military training for boys of the age of eleven upwards.[1]

Thus controversy about the army tended to split the S.P.D. as much as controversy about war. At one end of the spectrum was Karl Liebknecht,[2] who in 1907 was sentenced to a year and a half in prison for writing an anti-militarist pamphlet considered treasonable; at the other end Noske, the future Reichswehr minister, who took a lively and informed interest in the army and navy and acquired a reputation as a jingoist. The Military Tax bill of 1913 also, as we have seen, caused a split in the party, a majority abandoning their traditional anti-militarism in return for a progressive tax. Behind all these particular problems was the general difficulty of reconciling the duty owed by a socialist to the state of which he was a subject with his pledges to the International. The incompatibility of these conflicting obligations was soon to be shown.

AUGUST 1914

Few people imagined, when they heard of the murder of the Archduke Franz Ferdinand and his wife at Sarajevo on 28 June 1914, that it would lead within six weeks to a general war. Admittedly few people, and least of all socialists, had any illusions about the precariousness of peace; as Scheidemann later wrote, Europe at this time was like a barrel of gunpowder. But this seemed no worse than the preceding international crises, none of which had actually led to war. At first sight there seemed no reason why the Austro-Serb clash too should not be settled by diplomacy, especially in view of the willingness shown by the powers of both alliances to align their policies during the Balkan wars. Moreover the Austro-Hungarian government seemed in no hurry to deal with Serbia: not until 23 July was the fatal ultimatum dispatched. From 6 to 27 July the German Emperor was peacefully cruising in the Baltic, clearly a reassuring sign, and in the course of July most of Germany's socialist leaders also went away on holiday. Among the few who stayed behind was Haase, one of the two chairmen of the S.P.D. and of the parliamentary party. Haase was

---

[1] Heidegger, *Die deutsche Sozialdemokratie und der nationale Staat, 1870–1920* (1956), p. 99.
[2] Born in 1871, a lawyer by profession, Karl Liebknecht, son of Wilhelm, was elected an S.P.D. member of the Prussian Landtag in 1908, of the Reichstag in 1912.

largely responsible for the vigorous socialist reaction to the Austrian ultimatum.[1] He did not doubt that in the quarrel with Serbia Austria was the aggressor, and he was mindful of the Stuttgart resolution requiring socialists to do all in their power to prevent war. Accordingly a manifesto issued by the S.P.D. on 25 July (the day when the Austrian ultimatum expired) condemned the 'frivolous war provocation' of the Austro-Hungarian government in strong language:

The class-conscious proletariat of Germany, in the name of humanity and civilisation, raises a flaming protest against this criminal action of the warmongers. It demands peremptorily that the German government use its influence on the Austrian government for the preservation of peace, and, should it not be possible to stop the infamous war, that it should avoid being involved in it in any way. No drop of a German soldier's blood must be sacrificed to the Austrian despot's lust for power, to imperialist commercial interests. Comrades, we call upon you to express immediately in mass meetings the unshakeable will to peace of the class-conscious proletariat...The ruling classes who in peacetime oppress you, despise you, exploit you, want to see you as cannon-fodder. Everywhere the cry must ring in the despots' ears: 'We don't want war! Down with war! Long live international brotherhood!'[2]

Vorwaerts, the leading socialist daily, wrote on the same date:

They want war, the unscrupulous circles who have the decisive influence on the Vienna Hofburg...They want war—the Austrian ultimatum makes it plain and declares it to the whole world...[3]

Next day (26 July) *Vorwaerts* insisted that it was the duty of German socialists to prevent their government from getting Austria out of its mess, and added shrewdly that there was a 'complete absence of direction' in the German government, which was also criticised for not supporting the British government's proposal for a four-power conference. There is no reason to doubt the sincerity of these statements, especially as they were followed by a number of mass meetings (twenty-seven in Berlin alone) at which the Austrian government was denounced and the German government called upon to abstain from military intervention. Socialist demonstrations of this kind took place all over Germany between 26 and 30 July.

Events took a still more serious turn on 28 July when Austria declared war on Serbia. The S.P.D. executive decided to meet, absent members being recalled to Berlin by telegram. By the time the meeting took place, 30 July, a general war seemed inevitable. It was clearly assumed that, in case of a vote in the Reichstag on war credits, the socialists would vote against them, and that the leaders would be arrested and the party declared illegal.[4] Hence the decision was made to send Ebert, the co-chairman, and Braun, the treasurer, to Switzerland with the party funds.

---

[1] Ernst Haase, *Hugo Haase, sein Leben und Wirken* (Berlin, n.d.), p. 24.
[2] *Ibid.* p. 24.
[3] Quoted in E. Bevan, *German Social Democracy during the War* (1918), p. 5.
[4] Scheidemann, *op. cit.* I, 193.

Meanwhile Haase, as a chairman of the S.P.D. parliamentary party, had gone to Brussels to attend a special gathering of the International Socialist Bureau (the secretariat of the Second International) which had been arranged for 28 and 29 July. Delegates from all the main European countries, including those about to fight each other, were present. The conference condemned Austria for making war on Serbia and expressed distrust of the policy of Russia and Germany. Jaurès declared that Germany's support of Austria endangered peace, and claimed, without contradiction, that his government was doing everything possible to preserve peace.[1] Haase rebutted the suggestion that the German workers were tied to Austrian diplomacy, rhetorically asserting that 'secret treaties do not bind the proletariat. The German proletariat declared that Germany must not intervene even if Russia intervenes...'[2] Even if the other delegates had been aware of the speed with which the final moves towards war were being made, they could hardly have known how little substance there was in Haase's words. The conference realised the gravity of the situation but not its urgency. Before dispersing, the delegates issued a message to the socialist parties of Europe calling on them to redouble their efforts to prevent war and assuring them that the German and French proletariats would press their governments to restrain Austria and Russia respectively,[3] and on a German suggestion it was agreed that a special international socialist congress that was to meet in Vienna on 25 August should be held instead in Paris on 9 August.

By the time the delegates reached home Europe was within hours of war. On 31 July Jaurès was murdered by a nationalist fanatic in a Paris café. In that tragic hour he was the most tragic figure. The war that was about to begin meant the ruin of his hopes for peace, socialism and the International; and also for the reconciliation between France and Germany which was so dear to his heart. His death symbolised the end of an epoch. He was the first victim of the war, and in some ways the most notable. News of his death caused consternation at home and abroad, not least in Germany, where Haase returned to find a dramatic change of mood. Reports of Russian mobilisation on 30 July dispersed the last gleams of optimism, for it was assumed that mobilisation was the prelude to war. The news acted as a spur to the German general staff, whose plans depended on their ability to strike while Russia's preparations were still incomplete. The new mood was reflected in a statement issued by the S.P.D. executive after a meeting held on the same day (30 July) which not only virtually admitted that war was now inevitable, but let it be seen that the party would take no drastic anti-war action. The statement breathed a spirit of resignation mixed with anxiety. Henceforth all socialist agitation against the German government's support of Austria ceased, and the tone of the party press altered abruptly.

[1] Kautsky, *op. cit.* p. 371.   [2] Bevan, *op. cit.* p. 9.   [3] Kautsky, *op. cit.* p. 373.

The new note was struck by *Vorwaerts* on 31 July: 'If the fateful hour strikes the workers will redeem the promise made by their representatives on their behalf. The "unpatriotic crew" will do their duty and will not be surpassed by any of the patriots...'[1] Next day the German government declared war on Russia.

The entire German press, including the socialist press, was now subject to censorship, and martial law was declared. Here and there an individual newspaper of the left followed the old anti-war line, but otherwise the change of policy was complete. Contrary to expectations, however, no special measures were taken against the S.P.D. The authorities had rightly judged that the socialists would not cause any trouble, though they could hardly have guessed from the anti-war demonstrations of late July how patriotic most of them were. As early as 26 July—before his visit to Brussels—Haase had been called to the Prussian ministry of the interior and asked not to allow anything to be said at his party's anti-war rallies that would make war more likely by exciting Pan-Slav sentiment in Russia. He was also told that if Russia attacked Austria, Austria would be supported by Germany. Haase answered that in the understanding of his party the German alliance with Austria was purely defensive and that a war begun by Austria could not be of that kind. The official reply was that this was not the view of the government or of any party in the Reichstag except the S.P.D.[2] Haase's answer (if any) is not recorded.

There is other evidence that the government did not take the S.P.D.'s protestations against war too seriously. The Chancellor, Bethmann Hollweg, who was also Prussian prime minister, assured the Prussian cabinet on 30 July (or 31 according to another account) that there was little to fear from Social Democracy and that neither strike nor sabotage was to be expected.[3] On the following day the Prussian minister of the interior sent a confidential message to all army commands that according to reliable information in the government's possession the socialists would do their duty like other Germans.[4] He may well have been influenced by a talk between Bethmann

---

[1] These words were written by Friedrich Stampfer, one of the leading patriotic socialist journalists and afterwards editor-in-chief of *Vorwaerts* (Prager, *Geschichte der U.S.P.D.* (1921), p. 22). The author of one of the standard histories of the Weimar Republic (*Die vierzehn Jahre der ersten deutschen Republik*), after 1933 Stampfer emigrated in succession to Prague, Paris and America. He returned to Germany after the second world war and died there in 1957. For his memoirs, see the bibliography. See also P. Frölich, *10 Jahre Krieg und Bürgerkrieg* (1924), p. 65. Yet on the same day (30 July) David wrote an article for the socialist press in which he invoked the authority of Bismarck to condemn German support for Austrian aggression in the Balkans. The article was never published. During the war David was to be one of the staunchest defenders of German policy, notably during the socialist peace talks at Stockholm in June 1917 (Kautsky, *op. cit.* p. 438).

[2] Bevan, *op. cit.* p. 25.

[3] Spartakus (pseudonym), *German Communists* (London, n.d.), p. 10.

[4] Frölich, *op. cit.* p. 65.

Hollweg and Südekum, a right wing member of the S.P.D. executive and Reichstag deputy, who assured the Chancellor that his party would not vote against war credits.[1] It appears that Südekum was sent for because Haase was in Brussels and most other members of the S.P.D. executive were also absent. Haase himself intended to oppose war credits, and had he been interviewed in place of Südekum he must have given a different impression of socialist policy. It was difficult in that time of great emotional stress to say where the party as a whole stood on this issue. According to Kautsky, as late as 31 July all the socialist deputies he spoke to said they would vote against war credits;[2] but it is fairly certain that opinion in the party was shifting rapidly to a pro-credits position.[3] It became evident that the choice now lay between voting for credits and abstention. The whole country had been gripped by war fever. Sensational reports were coming in hourly of mobilisation and the violation of frontiers. Press censorship and tendentious government statements made it difficult, if not impossible, to gain a clear and objective picture of the international situation, which was changing with bewildering rapidity as the ultimata ran out. Scheidemann wrote of this time: 'We all believed that Germany had been attacked—that the French had poisoned German water supplies and that French airmen had dropped bombs on Nuremberg and Fürth.'[4] It is hardly surprising that, in the excitement of the moment, the socialists gave credence to these reports, which were officially confirmed by Bethmann Hollweg in the Reichstag on 4 August. Another current rumour which was readily believed was that the Cossacks had crossed the East Prussian frontier. This story fitted conveniently into the government's contention that Germany was the victim of Russian aggression: a point of cardinal importance for its effect on socialist opinion.

Against this highly dramatic background, in which chauvinism and hysteria were mounting, the S.P.D. executive met on 2 August to consider their attitude to the war credits bill which the government was to introduce into the Reichstag on 4 August. Of the six members present, four favoured voting for credits, two (Haase and Ledebour) were for opposition.[5] Next day (3 August) the socialist parliamentary party met with Scheidemann in the chair to discuss the same problem. One question uppermost in their minds was what their colleagues, the socialists in France, were going to do. Hermann Müller, a member of the executive, had been sent to Paris to try and reach agreement with French socialists on common action in case of war. Müller did not reach Paris till 1 August, the day of the German ultimatum to France, but was nevertheless received with the same cordiality as in previous years.

---

[1] *Illustrierte Geschichte der deutschen Revolution* (various authors, Berlin, 1929), p. 96.
[2] Kautsky, *op. cit.* p. 438. Kautsky speaks of the 'spiritual torture' of those days (31 July–4 August).
[3] *Ibid.* p. 444.   [4] Scheidemann, *op. cit.* I, p. 203.
[5] Scheidemann, *Der Zusammenbruch* (1921), p. 7.

He had told the French that although the German socialists had not made up their minds about war credits, a vote for them was, he thought, out of the question: the choice lay between opposition and abstention. It was agreed that if both groups of socialists abstained, the two policies would be in alignment, but both sides recognised that the final decision would have to be made in the light of circumstances. Should France be attacked, the French told Müller, they would vote for war credits. Müller urged the French to make their government restrain Russia, so that a general war might still be averted.[1] The French socialists were convinced of their government's peaceful intentions (Viviani, the prime minister, was himself a socialist); and the order to the French army to withdraw ten kilometres from the German frontier to avoid incidents was further evidence of France's good faith. Müller returned, not without difficulty, to his own country, and arrived back in Berlin in time to report the result of his mission to his parliamentary colleagues.

Müller's report could hardly strengthen the hands of those German socialists who were determined to vote against war credits when the matter was debated by the parliamentary group. Kautsky, who was present by invitation, spoke in favour of abstention, the policy which Bebel and Wilhelm Liebknecht had followed in 1870. But it was generally felt that as the largest party in Germany, with 110 Reichstag seats compared with the two of 1870, the S.P.D. could not escape the responsibility of a decision. Then Kautsky made another proposal: to vote for war credits on condition that the government guaranteed that it had no aggressive war aims. This proposition too was unsupported, Karl Liebknecht pointing out that such a guarantee would have little value since it could always be repudiated. Liebknecht himself introduced a resolution condemning Austria's aggression, but this was not taken up, David saying that the question of Austrian aggression was too complicated to be decided by a simple negative vote. In the end when a vote was taken, only fourteen deputies (including Haase and Liebknecht) opted for opposing war credits; seventy-eight were for supporting them.[2]

The split in the party was a breach in the unity that was one of its most cherished traditions, and it was decided that, whatever internal differences there might be, a united front should be presented to the outside world. In the Reichstag the party would vote *en bloc*, but as a concession to the minority, the S.P.D. would accompany its vote for war credits with a statement taking into account the reservations of the credit opposers. The statement, which Haase, against his will, was persuaded to read in the Reichstag, declared that Germany was threatened with invasion by Russian despotism, that defeat by Russia would ruin much if not all that the S.P.D. held dear, and that while the party disclaimed all responsibility for the war, it would not leave the country in the lurch in the hour of danger. The statement demanded

---

[1] Scheidemann, *Der Zusammenbruch*, p. 12. [2] Kautsky, *op. cit.* pp. 461 ff.

that the war be ended 'as soon as the goal of security is reached and our opponents are inclined to peace'. As originally drawn up, it contained a further sentence which ran: 'As soon as the war becomes a war of conquest we shall oppose it with the most resolute means.' When the statement was shown to Bethmann Hollweg before it was to be read to the Reichstag, he persuaded the S.P.D. to omit the additional sentence on the grounds that it might upset public opinion in Britain, whose neutrality was still hoped for.[1]

It was in the Reichstag on that historic 4 August that Bethmann Hollweg announced the violation of Belgian neutrality: he admitted the wrong, which he said would be made good, and quoted the proverb that necessity knows no law. No reference was made to Belgium by the S.P.D., who added nothing to the prepared statement, as amended by Bethmann, and their vote for war credits was unanimous. A few hours earlier the Kaiser in a speech from the throne that was fervently applauded declared that henceforward he would know no parties any more, only Germans. Never, it seemed, had Germany been so united, and of that unity the Social Democrats, for better or worse, were irrevocably a part. It was a moment for most socialists of exultation and relief. The stigma of being unpatriotic had at last fallen from them, and the tension—to some, at least, hardly bearable—between their duty as socialists and their duty as Germans was ended. Not a few socialists were to look back on this day with embarrassment or shame, but for the moment the overwhelming majority did not doubt that they had done the right thing. On one point everyone was to agree: the vote of 4 August was a turning point in the history of their party.

The explanation of the abrupt change in the S.P.D.'s attitude since the last days of July can be summarised in one word: Russia. The party had gone on record as voting for a war of defence against the Tsar. (France came in simply as Russia's ally, though Bethmann Hollweg, by charging the French with violating German territory, could also present France as an aggressor.) Fear and hatred of Russia as the 'gendarme of Europe' was deeply rooted in German socialism; it had been fully shared by Marx and Engels, and since the early 1890s the Franco-Russian alliance had provided a military, as well as an ideological reason for Russophobia. People remembered an article which Engels had contributed to Kautsky's *Neue Zeit* in 1892 in which he had discussed the duty of a German social democrat in the event of war

---

[1] *Ibid.* p. 459. The S.P.D. attitude in August 1914, as revealed by the Reichstag statement with its final, omitted sentence, seems to echo that of the party in 1870, when the majority of German socialists abandoned their pro-government attitude on finding that Bismarck intended not just to overthrow Napoleon III but to go on to annex Alsace-Lorraine. This fairly explicit assumption in 1914 that history would repeat itself reflected the widespread belief that the war would be as short as that of 1870 (which makes the support of national governments by socialist parties easier to understand). It was also characteristic of the S.P.D.'s general, and in 1933 fatal, tendency to think in terms of comforting but misleading historical analogies.

between France and Russia on the one hand and Germany, Austria and perhaps Italy on the other.[1] In such a war, Engels wrote, every German socialist should take up arms against Russia and its allies, for a defeat of Germany would be a defeat of socialism. If France was a bourgeois republic, Germany, whose future masters would be the S.P.D., stood for the coming proletarian revolution. What Engels envisaged was that if Russia invaded Germany the German working class would rise against them in a revolutionary patriotic upsurge like that of the French *sans-culottes* in 1793. This was a highly fanciful vision on Engels' part: he underestimated the ability of the German ruling class to remain in power, and overestimated the revolutionary potentialities of the German workers. Nevertheless, a war with Tsarist Russia was the one war which most German socialists felt was compatible with their obligations to the Second International. The impression left by Engels' later writings is that had he lived in Germany in 1914 he would have voted for war credits. Bebel, too, had made no secret of his preparedness to fight if Germany was attacked by Russia.[2] The part played by Russia in the decisive shift of opinion inside the German socialist party in the critical few days before the Reichstag vote of 4 August was as important as the part played by the violation of Belgian neutrality in influencing British left wing opinion. It was the wrong done to Belgium which made British entry into the war intellectually defensible and emotionally acceptable to pacifists and neutralists and united the nation behind the government. The danger from Russia acted in very much the same way in rallying the German left behind its rulers. Liebknecht afterwards denounced the 'cunning stage management' with which the German government substituted Russia for Austria in people's minds as the disturber of the peace.[3] Fear of the Russian steamroller soon outweighed the scruples of German socialists about Austria's war guilt; and Russia's mobilisation was held up as the fatal act that made war inevitable.

In the excited state of public opinion the Social Democrats could hardly avoid voting for war credits. The atmosphere of those days is well conveyed in a letter written by a socialist member of the Reichstag to a colleague and subsequently published:

On August 3 Dittmann and I travelled from Dortmund to Berlin to attend the party meeting on that day, at which the question of voting the war credits was to be decided

---

[1] *Die neue Zeit*, x, i, p. 586. When the war was discussed by the S.P.D. council at the end of September, future differences inside the party were foreshadowed. Haase said that they did not regard the breach of Belgian neutrality as justified, but did not contradict the assertion of another speaker (Keil) that their tactics on 4 August had been approved by the overwhelming majority of socialist voters *Protokolle der Sitzungen des Parteiausschusses der Sozialdemokratischen Partie Deutschlands*, 27 September 1914, henceforth cited as *Ausschuss*).

[2] Bebel once confessed at an international socialist conference: 'When war comes, we Germans will not be able to do anything about it.' H. Roland-Holst, *Rosa Luxemburg, ihr Leben und Wirken* (1937), pp. 115–16.

[3] K. Liebknecht, *Klassenkampf gegen den Krieg* (Berlin, n.d.), p. 16.

...I shall never forget the crowded incidents of those days. I saw reservists join the colours and go forth singing Social Democratic songs. Some socialist reservists I knew said to me: 'We are going to the front with an easy mind, because we know the party will look after us if we are wounded, and that the party will take care of our families if we don't come home.' Just before the train started for Berlin, a group of reservists at the station said to me: 'König, you're going to Berlin, to the Reichstag; think of us there: see to it that we have all we need: don't be stingy in voting money.' In the train I told Dittmann what a deep impression all this had made on me. Dittmann confessed that things had happened to him, too, which affected him in the same way. For hours as the train carried us to Berlin, we discussed the whole situation, what our attitude should be to national defence, whether the party should vote the credits. We came to the final conclusion that the party was absolutely bound to vote the credits, that, if any differences came up at the meeting, that was the line we should have to take. Dittmann wound up by saying: 'The Party could not act otherwise. It would rouse a storm of indignation among men at the front and people at home against the Social Democratic Party if it did. The socialist organisation would be swept clean away by popular resentment.'[1]

There is plenty of other evidence that the public would simply have not understood or forgiven it if the S.P.D. had voted against war credits. Noske once told the Reichstag that his party had voted for the credits to avoid being beaten to death in front of the Brandenburg Gate.[2] Stampfer, later the editor of *Vorwaerts*, shared his view: the millions of socialist voters would have turned in rage against a party that refused supplies needed by their friends and relations in the army.

Socialists who, like Kautsky, were influenced less by practical considerations than by the desire to reconcile the pro-credits vote with the party's past policies and professions, afterwards explained that the issue on 4 August was not war or peace—that had already been decided—but victory or defeat. And Viktor Adler, leader of the Austrian Social Democrats and a veteran of the Second International, felt that this was the overriding issue for his party too:

Today we are not faced with the question of the Russian Revolution, but with the question whether the Russian armies will reach Brünn, Budapest or Vienna. In such a situation I cannot investigate whether a Russian victory might be favourable for the struggle of the Russian workers for liberation. If I feel the knife at my throat I have, first of all, to push away the knife.[3]

The socialists of Germany, like those of Austria, were in a dilemma from which there was no escape.

[1] Quoted in Bevan, *op. cit.* p. 15 and reprinted from the *Vossische Zeitung* of 5 May 1916.
[2] Quoted in Berlau, *The German Social Democratic Party, 1914–21*, p. 73, from Reichstag *Verhandlungen*, vol. 314, p. 6212.
[3] Quoted from V. Adler, *Aufsätze, Reden und Briefe*, IX, 106 ff., in J. Braunthal, *In search of the Millennium*, p. 148.

THE CIVIC TRUCE

The Kaiser's speech at the opening of the Reichstag on 4 August, a few hours before the war credits vote, in which he proclaimed the unity of all Germans as transcending political and confessional barriers was enthusiastically hailed as the beginning of a civic truce or *Burgfrieden*. The sentiment of unity was soon to evaporate, but at the time it was genuine enough. By identifying themselves, to the surprise of their opponents and indeed to many of themselves, with the national interest on what was seen as the supreme issue of Germany's survival, the Social Democrats had earned for themselves a new status and a new relationship with the government. Henceforth they were no longer treated as hostile to the state or as little better than social outcasts. Discriminatory restrictions, such as the ban on socialist newspapers in the armed forces, were abolished, and the Reich Association for combating Social Democracy was dissolved. The government's attitude changed from aloofness and suspicion to good will and even confidence. The Chancellor frequently consulted the socialist leaders before making statements in the Reichstag, and they were given inside information. Their services were used to combat anti-German feeling in neutral countries; Scheidemann, for example, was sent to Holland and Südekum to Italy on propaganda missions. Prominent socialists were invited to the front to investigate complaints and see conditions for themselves; there they would be wined and dined by the generals. Symbolic of the Social Democrats' new standing was their entry into the newly founded 1914 Society, to which many liberal-minded intellectuals belonged. A similar transformation took place in the relations between the government and the trade unions. Numerous strikes in the years immediately preceding the outbreak of war had led the Prussian authorities to consider actually dissolving the unions and introducing anti-union legislation. The union leaders did not, however, abandon their reformist brand of socialism; and their patriotic support of the German government was evident during the crisis which preceded the declarations of war. At a meeting on 2 August the unions agreed not to take any anti-war action, and Legien, the chairman of the General Commission of free Trade Unions representing 2½ million workers, seems to have decided on that policy as early as 25 July, at a time when the S.P.D. were still demonstrating against Austria. The unions also decided not to strike while the war was on.[1] For its part the government recognized the importance of the trade unions in maintaining morale and

---

[1] The attitude of the trade union leaders can be gauged from an extract from an article which appeared in *Correspondenzblatt*, the official organ of the General Commission of Trade Unions, in 1916: 'The policy of 4 August is the total expression of decades of work by the German Trade Unions, whose whole past was a struggle for the rise of the workers to achieve participation in a higher culture.' Quoted in Varain, *Freie Gewerkschaften, Sozialdemokratie und Staat*, p. 74.

increasing production, and more than once it was to pay tribute to their contribution to the war effort.[1]

Yet in hard political terms the S.P.D. had gained practically nothing; in fact it had lost. By its vote of 4 August the party identified itself with the government's war policy; it thus acquired responsibility without power. For the *Burgfrieden* meant the freezing of the *status quo* for the duration of the war. It is true that the Chancellor made vague promises of reform, speaking of a 'reorientation of internal policy' but it was clear that the reform which mattered in the eyes of the left, that of the Prussian franchise, would have to wait indefinitely. Bethmann Hollweg did not intend to provoke a crisis with the right (from which he was constantly under attack) by introducing a drastic change in the constitution in wartime.[2] The Social Democrats did not, to begin with, complain, for they regarded their vote of 4 August as a patriotic gesture to save the country rather than as a bargain from which they could expect a *quid pro quo*. They knew they had a stake even in Hohenzollern Germany, and they believed that it would become much larger: 'We are defending the fatherland', Scheidemann was to tell the Reichstag, 'in order to conquer it.'[3] Or as Haenisch, a former left wing journalist who became very nationalist during the war, put it: 'What the Junkers are defending is at most the Germany of the past, what the bourgeoisie are defending is the Germany of the present, what we are defending is the Germany of the future.'[4] If the deferment of Prussian franchise reform till after the end of a war which most people expected to be short seemed no great sacrifice, martial law and the press censorship, both administered by generals hostile to social democracy, were felt as a real hardship, especially by the left. Political activity outside the Reichstag and various Landtage was practically brought to an end, and this meant that war aims could not be freely discussed, however much, in the socialist view, the government might deviate from its professed policy of defence. The main problem for the S.P.D. became how, by disciplining its dissident left wing, it could maintain the *Burgfrieden* inside itself.

---

[1] A. Grzesinski, *Inside Germany* (1939), p. 34.

[2] Scheidemann, *Memoirs*, I, 243 ff.; *Reichstag Inquiry*, VIII, 69 ff., 372. The government's immediate object in promising 'reorientation' of domestic policy was to prevent the subject being debated by the Reichstag. The term was actually used by Delbrück, the Vice-Chancellor, in an address to party leaders. (*Der Interfraktionelle Ausschuss 1917–18* (of the Reichstag), Düsseldorf (1959), vol. I, p. xiii.)

[3] Stampfer, *Die ersten vierzehn Jahre der deutschen Republik*, p. 23.

[4] Quoted in Heidegger, *op. cit.* p. 102. The views of Haenisch on the war are given in a book published in 1916, *Die deutsche Sozialdemokratie in und nach dem Weltkriege*. After the war he became minister of education in Prussia.

CHAPTER 3

THE GROWTH OF OPPOSITION SOCIALISM

We are defending the fatherland in order to possess it.

SCHEIDEMANN in 1915

WAR AIMS AND ANNEXATIONS

The patriotic excitement which swept through Germany at the outbreak of war was kept alive for some weeks by news of the first victories in west and east. But gradually, as it became clear that the victories had not been decisive and that the war would not be over by Christmas, the intoxication, in which the working class fully shared, gave way to a more sober and critical mood. Socialists had time to reflect on the historic decision of 4 August. Some began to have doubts. Kautsky feared that the party had become the prisoner of the government;[1] Haase was remorseful that it had failed to register a protest against the violation of Belgium;[2] Bernstein, having studied the diplomatic events that led to war, came to the conclusion that the German government was not as innocent as it made out.[3] It was also remembered that the Stuttgart resolution required the S.P.D. to agitate and work for peace even after war had broken out, though any attempt to do so would obviously have been incompatible with the civic truce and would have invited reprisals from the government. Already on the evening of 4 August Rosa Luxemburg had gathered with a few left wing friends to form the nucleus of an opposition group, and they were soon joined by Liebknecht, who regretted having yielded to pressure and voted for war credits.[4] He knew quite well that the S.P.D. had won popularity by its vote, but he asked himself what it would profit the party if it gained the whole world and lost its own soul.[5] His fears that under the guise of fighting a defensive war the German government was really practising aggression were confirmed by the widespread demand for annexations which began to be heard after the German armies had occupied large areas of enemy territory.

[1] Bevan, *German Social Democracy during the War*, p. 30.
[2] *Ausschuss*, 27 September 1914.
[3] Bevan, *op. cit.* p. 36. As Bernstein was to point out to his party colleagues after the war: why, if Russia was the main enemy, was so much of Germany's military strength deployed in the west?
[4] Frölich, *Rosa Luxemburg*, p. 232. Rosa Luxemburg was so depressed by the outbreak of war that she almost took her own life. H. Roland-Holst, *Rosa Luxemburg, ihr Leben und Wirken*, p. 129.
[5] Frölich, *op. cit.* p. 232; Liebknecht, *Klassenkampf gegen den Krieg*, p. 72.

Before the end of August 1914 Liebknecht proposed to the S.P.D. executive that meetings be held in favour of peace without annexations.[1] The executive refused on the grounds that such meetings might be used to advocate annexations, an indication of the extent of annexationist sentiment among socialists. The views of the executive were not free from ambiguity: Ebert declared that though they opposed annexations, this was no time to start a campaign against them.[2] Liebknecht also embarrassed the leaders by writing articles for the foreign press in which he revealed the existence of an opposition group within the party.[3] In September he told the executive that his vote for war credits had been a mistake, for the war was the imperialist war which they had long resolved to oppose.[4] The executive rebuked him for speeches he had made in Holland and Belgium, but Liebknecht counter-attacked by asking why chauvinist speeches by right wing socialists had gone unchallenged. He denied that the war was a genuine crusade against Tsarism, and asserted that the German socialists were more to blame for voting war credits than the French socialists, who had done so only after the German occupation of Luxemburg and the first ultimatum to Belgium. He wanted the S.P.D. to recognise its responsibilities and take the lead in working for peace without territorial changes or humiliation of any nation.[5] He determined to vote against the next war credits bill which was due in the Reichstag on 2 December.

The attitude to be taken up on this occasion by the socialist parliamentary party was the subject of prolonged and heated argument. The party leaders warned the Chancellor on 21 November that they could not vote for the next war credits without adding an explanation. The Chancellor, worried by the damage to Germany's international reputation caused by the violation of Belgian neutrality and reported atrocities, begged the socialist leaders not to cause him further embarrassment by public criticism.[6] There was a general feeling, however, in the party that in giving the government further support they must make it clear that they were not sanctioning a war of conquest. It was accordingly agreed to issue a statement in the Reichstag: the difficulty was to find a form of words that would be acceptable to the government and yet satisfy all sections of the party. No less than three different drafts were prepared and discussed, while confidential talks were held with Bethmann Hollweg and other ministers. Haase was at first unwilling to modify the views of the left wing to suit the government, but allowed himself to be persuaded.[7] Ledebour wanted to insist that, in return for socialist support, the government abolish martial law and reaffirm that the war was purely one of defence. Liebknecht objected that martial law could easily be reimposed if necessary, and that a government declaration on war aims would be of no

---

[1] Liebknecht, *Klassenkampf*, p. 16.   [2] *Ausschuss*, 27 September 1914.
[3] Liebknecht, *Klassenkampf*, pp. 16–17.   [4] *Ibid.* pp. 18–19.
[5] *Ibid.* pp. 21–3, 26–7.   [6] Scheidemann, *Memoirs*, I, 273 ff.
[7] *Ibid.*

lasting value.[1] Some thirty deputies refused to give way and said they would vote against war credits in the chamber, but their courage failed them at the last moment, and in the end only Liebknecht did so. The party declaration which, like that of 4 August was read by Haase as chairman, justified the new vote, like the previous one, on the grounds that Germany was threatened by an aggressive coalition. It also expressed the hope that the censorship would be relaxed. In a reference to Belgium the statement saw no reason to dissent from the view taken by the Chancellor on 4 August, in which he had defended the violation of Belgian neutrality on the grounds of necessity. The omission of any censure of the government for the invasion of Belgium may appear somewhat surprising in view of the condemnation expressed by Haase at a meeting of the S.P.D. council on 27 September and since enough time had elapsed for the party to have second thoughts (as Bernstein had had) about the morality of the whole action. But there were many who did not share Haase's indignation about the wrong done to Belgium; there was a strong desire not to split the party and break the political truce; and even on the left there was a disposition to treat the Belgian issue as subsidiary to the general question of imperialism.[2] A good many socialists probably believed Bethmann Hollweg not only when he denied in the Reichstag that Belgium had been decisive in bringing Britain into the war, but also when he declared that evidence had been found proving Belgium's abandonment of neutrality before receiving the German ultimatum.

In a speech at the Berlin working-class suburb of Neuköln in January 1915 Liebknecht threw down the gauntlet to his party and defied the censorship by making his criticisms public. Replying to arguments used by S.P.D. leaders he denied that the war credits vote was for the country not the war, or that under the Bismarckian constitution the socialists could have any effective influence on policy. There could be no solution, he asserted, to an imperialist war other than international socialist action. As for the view of the moderate opposition, led by Ledebour and Kautsky, that peace should be made as soon as Germany was secure—as stated by the S.P.D. on 4 August—Liebknecht contended that imperial Germany would never feel secure unless she could expand in one direction or another, and that the restoration of the 'security' which Europe had in the three years before the war was meaningless. For socialism the only security worth having was that of the international brotherhood of workers, and this could be gained only through class war. Class war against imperialist war, or peace through revolution, was the slogan he now proclaimed and was to proclaim until the end of his life.[3]

Meanwhile rumblings of opposition had been heard in the party press.

---

[1] Liebknecht, *Klassenkampf*, pp. 34 ff. [2] Prager, *Geschichte der U.S.P.D.*, p. 45.
[3] Liebknecht, *Klassenkampf*, pp. 69–71.

The first protest came as early as 4 August when the editorial board of *Vorwaerts* wrote to the S.P.D. executive that the argument used to justify the war credits vote—that the war had already begun—could be used to justify almost any kind of war claims.[1] Among those who signed this letter were several future leaders of the Independent Social Democratic party. Because of its critical views, *Vorwaerts* was banned twice by the censor before the end of September. Socialist newspapers with left wing policies in other parts of Germany such as the *Bremer Bürgerzeitung* and the *Leipziger Volkszeitung* also took an independent line.[2] It was in Württemberg that opposition to the *Burgfrieden* policy was strongest. The Stuttgart *Schwäbische Tagwacht* attacked the S.P.D. leaders for supporting war credits and launched a campaign for peace without annexations. The Württemberg branch of the party hit back, and on 4 November dismissed the editorial staff of the *Tagwacht* and appointed a new staff. The dismissed editors thereupon started an opposition newspaper and organisation.[3] This was the beginning of a split that was in time to extend to the whole country. In Prussia it was marked by the refusal of five of the ten socialist deputies in the Diet to vote for war credits on 22 October, and soon the majority of the ten were in opposition.[4] They complained bitterly of difficulty in propagating their views, owing to the censorship (which applied to newspapers and public meetings) and the absence of normal opportunities for party debate. The party leaders discouraged discussion, and party conferences had been adjourned for the duration of the war. Driven underground, opposition was already beginning to undermine the party's organisational unity.

After Liebknecht's anti-credits vote of 2 December, the S.P.D. executive passed a resolution that members voting against measures approved by the party were guilty of a breach of discipline. Liebknecht admitted the breach, but told his leaders that he set his duty to the party programme and principles above disciplinary regulations. Two months later he was called up, and became a non-combatant soldier. He was allowed to keep his seat in both the Reichstag and the Prussian Landtag, but was otherwise barred from political activities.[5]

Loyalties were subjected to a further strain when in March 1915 the third war credits bill was introduced in the Reichstag. This time it formed part of the annual budget. By tradition the S.P.D. never voted for the budget; further, the immediate threat of a Russian invasion, the background to the 4 August vote, had now been removed. The party's parliamentary group met before the Reichstag debate but could not agree what to do. In the end thirty abstained from voting and two, Liebknecht and Rühle, voted against

---

[1] Prager, *op. cit.* pp. 30 ff.   [2] *Ibid.* p. 33.
[3] *Ibid.* pp. 39–40.   [4] *Ibid.* p. 41; Bevan, *op. cit.* p. 43.
[5] Liebknecht, *Klassenkampf*, pp. 41–2, 49 ff., 59.

the budget. During the debate the existence of an opposition within the S.P.D. was brought into the open by speakers who criticised the government for its treatment of national minorities, for using savage reprisals on the Russian front, and for discrimination against the left in the exercise of press censorship.[1] The official party leaders disowned these criticisms, which they found embarrassing. The vote for the budget marked another stage in the party's breach with its past. The 're-education' (*Umlernung*) of which David had spoken on 3 August was taking place, slowly but inexorably.[2]

The question of annexations continued to be hotly debated. Pressure was exerted on the government from all sides, particularly from the Pan-Germans, not to make peace without securing for Germany some compensation for the losses incurred in what was represented as a defensive war. Thus on 2 December 1914 all parties except the S.P.D. supported a vaguely worded resolution in favour of a peace which would indemnify Germany for its sacrifices and would also contain lasting guarantees against future aggression by foreign powers. The Chancellor did not endorse such claims, but neither did he specifically repudiate them. Occupation of nearly all Belgium and of a large and valuable area of northern France gave the German government solid assets with which to bargain when the time came for an international settlement, that, it was confidently expected, would leave the Reich stronger than before. Powerful economic groups led a campaign for acquisitions in west and east. In May 1915 six economic associations representing industry and agriculture presented a memorandum to the Chancellor urging the virtual annexation of Belgium and of a strip of north-east France as far as the Somme, Briey with its iron ore, and the two fortresses of Verdun and Belfort. The memorandum also demanded that Germany should annex from Russia the Baltic seaboard and an area farther inland.[3]

In June another memorandum on war aims was handed to the Chancellor, signed by a large number of professors, judges, lawyers, senior civil servants, clergy, members of the Reichstag and retired admirals and generals. It made the same territorial claims as the other and asked besides for more colonies in Africa for naval bases. The memorandum asserted that German culture could flourish only in a secure political and economic framework and would benefit from an extension of German power.[4] It demonstrated the support given by the nation's intellectual *élite* to the policy of expansion.

Annexations were debated in the Reichstag on 28 May, five days after Italy's entry into war. The Chancellor, who publicly did not agree with the

---

[1] Liebknecht, *Klassenkampf*, pp. 58–9.

[2] *Ibid.* p. 14. David had told the S.P.D. parliamentary party on 3 August 1914 that they must free themselves from out-of-date ideals and re-educate themselves for the new period that was beginning.

[3] Frölich, *10 Jahre Krieg und Bürgerkrieg*, pp. 164 ff.

[4] The text of the memorandum, known as the *Professoreneingabe*, is in R. Müller, *Vom Kaiserreich zur Republik*, I, 185 ff.

more extravagant demands, was sufficiently influenced by Germany's favourable military position to state that his object was to obtain 'guarantees'—a vague phrase which was interpreted as meaning annexations by the non-socialist parties and in the opposite sense by the socialists. The usual meaning of 'guarantees' at this time was that Germany would give up Belgium only on certain conditions, which, however defined, involved some diminution of Belgian sovereignty, the German aim being to make sure that Belgium should not become a British springboard or sphere of influence. But a Belgium subject to such guarantees would almost inevitably have become a German satellite. On 8 March Bethmann Hollweg had addressed the leaders of political parties, including Scheidemann and Haase, in the Reichstag in similar language, telling them that his aim was 'a guarantee, greater freedom of movement and opportunities for development of a bigger and stronger Germany'. Scheidemann construed this ambiguous statement as a renunciation of annexations; Haase, more realistically, disagreed.[1] Thus while most of the S.P.D. professed themselves satisfied with Bethmann's cryptic utterances, the smaller but growing opposition did not. The other parties did not disguise their desire for acquisition of territory; this was clearly stated in a resolution introduced in the Reichstag by Spahn, a leader of the Centre, on 9 December 1915 which was supported by all except the socialists.[2]

The reaction of the socialist opposition group to the Chancellor's statement of 28 May was conveyed in an Open Letter to the executive committees of the S.P.D. and of the parliamentary group signed by 11 members of the Reichstag, 100 well-known party members and some 1,400 others. The Letter bluntly asserted that by voting war credits unconditionally at the beginning of the war the party had failed in its duty and renounced its principles. The party should have insisted, in return for its support, on the abolition of martial law. Subsequently the party was to blame for acquiescing in the government's refusal to make peace on the basis of the pre-war *status quo*, and for not rousing the socialist masses against the war in accordance with the International's Stuttgart resolution. By accepting the government's vaguely annexationist policy the S.P.D. had abandoned its defensive posture of 4 August and come out in favour of an aggressive war. The S.P.D. must therefore reverse its policy of supporting the government, abandon the *Burgfrieden* and return to the former course of socialism and class war.[3]

The Open Letter was the work of Liebknecht, with some assistance from Stroebel, a journalist who had been on the staff of *Vorwaerts*, and of Mehring,

---

[1] Scheidemann, *Der Zusammenbruch*, pp. 23–4.

[2] According to a statement by the Conservative Schiele on 2 March 1917, the Conservatives, National Liberals, Centre and a part of the Progressive party wanted to keep Belgium economically, militarily, and politically in German hands (Reichstag, *Verhandlungen*, vol. 309, p. 2494, quoted in Berlau, *The German Social Democratic Party, 1914–21*, p. 122).

[3] Prager, *op. cit.* pp. 69 ff., where the full text of the Open Letter is given. Bevan, *op. cit.* p. 51.

the veteran journalist and party historian.[1] It was widely circulated as a pamphlet and further signatures were invited. It marked the first opposition on a national scale to the S.P.D.'s war policy.

Almost at the same time a manifesto called 'The Demand of the Hour' was published in the *Leipziger Volkszeitung*. It too was a protest against the S.P.D.'s war policy, though less sharply worded than the Open Letter and containing no reference to class war. Signed by Haase, Kautsky and Bernstein, it was mainly Bernstein's work.[2] As the leading revisionist, he had hitherto been broadly on the party's right wing, but soon after the beginning of the war had crossed to the left in protest against what he felt was a betrayal of socialist ideals.[3] On the evidence available, Bernstein could not accept the government's claim that the war was defensive for Germany. He was one of several—Eisner, the future leader of the Bavarian revolution, was another—who combined reformist leanings at home with international sympathies abroad. 'The Demand of the Hour' referred to a pronouncement by the president of the Prussian upper house, Wedel-Piesdorf, in March 1915, that Germany could have peace quite easily if her aim was purely defensive, but that in view of her sacrifices she expected guarantees against future aggression by her enemies. The manifesto suggested that this represented government policy and urged the S.P.D. to use its influence to bring about a negotiated peace. The reaction of the military censor was to ban the *Leipziger Volkszeitung* for a week and to forbid reproduction of the manifesto elsewhere in the S.P.D. press.[4] Haase's position was now very awkward; he had publicly attacked the policy of a party of which he was co-chairman. He resigned a few months later.

On 26 June the S.P.D. executive replied to these protests in a manifesto entitled *Social Democracy and Peace*, which, by disclaiming any desire for annexations, sought to take the wind out of the sails of its critics. Even this went too far for the censor, who suspended *Vorwaerts* and other socialist newspapers for printing the manifesto on the grounds that war aims should not be discussed at all. The authorities did not, however, impose the same ban on propaganda in favour of annexations.

In August 1915 there was a joint meeting of the parliamentary group and the S.P.D. Council, a body consisting of thirty-two representatives of regional organisations, to discuss the fourth war credits bill. There was general

---

[1] Liebknecht, *Klassenkampf*, p. 94. Mehring was also the author of a biography of Marx.

[2] Prager, *op. cit.* p. 72, where the full text of the manifesto is given. Bevan. *op. cit.* p. 52.

[3] Bernstein had, for example, disapproved of his party's decision to support the Military Tax bill in 1913 on the grounds that what was objectionable in principle could not be justified by financial expediency (Gay, *The Dilemma of Democratic Socialism*, p. 272). On the other hand, in an article dated 25 August 1914, he expressed the hope that, whatever judgement was passed on the origin of the war, Germany would win it, in order to escape the disaster of defeat (*Ausschuss*, 18–19 April 1917).

[4] Prager, *op. cit.* p. 75.

agreement on war aims—no annexations on either side—but the right wing, headed by David, wanted to make the restoration of Belgium depend on guarantees. He modified his position, however, in response to opposition from the left, and in the end the party passed a resolution demanding the restoration of Belgium unconditionally.[1] An amendment proposed by Liebknecht to clarify and strengthen the term 'restoration of Belgium' was rejected, a sign that the party wanted to give the government some freedom of action. The government in turn now persuaded the S.P.D. to withdraw their statement on Belgium so as not to upset the army chiefs. When the war credits bill came before the Reichstag thirty-two socialist parliamentarians, nearly a third of the total, abstained from voting.[2] This was a compromise between disobeying their conscience and defying party discipline. The handling of the Belgian issue shows the party majority yielding to pressure from the Chancellor and the Chancellor unwilling to challenge the supreme command. Bethmann's equivocations once led Haase to describe him as a chest of drawers with a drawer for every answer required.[3] The view taken at the time by socialist leaders such as Scheidemann (and accepted by many subsequent historians) was that Bethmann Hollweg was opposed to annexations at heart but dared not say so openly for fear of offending his nationalist critics. In the light of new evidence adduced by Professor Fischer and others, it seems that this traditional view must now be discarded in favour of the contrary one that Bethmann was privately an annexationist who refused to disclose his real aims in order not to damage his reputation in the eyes of critical socialists and foreigners.[4] How far the S.P.D. leaders were really taken in by the Chancellor's double talk, with its diplomatic references to 'guarantees' in Belgium and Poland, and how far they found it useful as a cover for their own, it is hard to say. But there is no doubt that a considerable degree of confidence, if not of collusion, was established between them and Bethmann Hollweg. Before the Reichstag debate on annexations on 9 December 1915, Scheidemann discussed with him the interpellation he was going to put, and Bethmann read the speech he was going to make.[5] Each seems to have known how far he could go without upsetting the relationship. Confidential talks were also held early in the war between leading socialist revisionists and ministers: David had an interview with Delbrück, secretary of state for the interior and Vice-Chancellor; and Cohen-Reuss[6] saw Wahnschaffe, undersecretary of state and Bethmann's closest collaborator. These meetings showed that an important section of the S.P.D. was willing and

---

[1] *Ibid.* p. 81; Bevan, *op. cit.* pp. 57 ff.　　　[2] Prager, *op. cit.* p. 81.

[3] *Ausschuss*, 7 January 1916. The speaker was Haase.

[4] F. Fischer, *Griff nach der Weltmacht* (Düsseldorf, 1964), p. 113 and *passim*.

[5] Scheidemann, *Zusammenbruch*, pp. 30 ff.; Fischer, *op. cit.* pp. 214 ff.

[6] The name of Max Cohen's constituency, Reuss, was usually added to his surname to distinguish him from namesakes.

even eager to co-operate with the government on terms which the latter could accept. There was indeed talk of a *quid pro quo* in return for socialist support: David mentioned 'national democracy' as the goal, Cohen spoke of franchise reform but indicated that he was willing to accept a solution which fell short of the principle of one man one vote. Cohen thought that the S.P.D. might well follow in the footsteps of the Progressive party and make peace with the monarchy (theoretically the socialists were republicans) and the army. When asked if such a change of policy would not split the S.P.D., Cohen said he was quite prepared for that. Bethmann's opinion was that any *quid pro quo* should be paid to the socialists after, not before the service was rendered.[1] The opportunity, which a more imaginative Chancellor might have seized, of binding the bulk of the socialists to a reformed Hohenzollern state was not taken, partly because Bethmann could rely on majority socialist support without making major concessions, partly because of the conservative pressure to which he was subject.

Meanwhile the war went on. With national passions roused as never before, and more nations joining in, mainly on the Allied side, the question of future frontiers became more involved and intractable. By 1915 the French had made the restoration, or 'de-annexation' of Alsace-Lorraine an official war aim. It was rejected by all Germans except the left wing socialists, who agreed on the holding of a plebiscite to determine the provinces' future. The known territorial ambitions of Russia and Italy (and later of Roumania) were adduced by the majority socialists to prove that the war was defensive for the Central Powers. The retreat of the Russian army in the course of 1915 and its abandonment of Poland opened up alluring prospects in Eastern Europe, where Germany could play the part of a liberator from Tsardom with some plausibility. When the Chancellor assured the Reichstag that never again would the Poles, Letts, Lithuanians and Balts be allowed to return to Russian rule, the socialists could hardly object. The liberation of Poland was an old liberal aim, fully endorsed in their day by Marx and Engels, and now supported by Scheidemann.[2] But the German government had no intention of giving up the Polish provinces in the Hohenzollern and Habsburg empires, or of permitting any independence given to Russian Poland to stand in the way of a separate peace treaty with Russia should this prove possible. Austria too wanted part of Russian Poland for herself. Thus the Polish question caused a fatal split in Germany's eastern policy.

These and other matters were discussed at a meeting of German and Austrian Social Democrats in Vienna in September 1915, at which the Germans were surprised by the Austrians' eagerness to acquire other people's territory. A further meeting of German and Austrian socialists and trade union leaders took place in January 1916 at which general agreement was

---

[1] Fischer, *op. cit.* pp. 430–5.　　　[2] Reichstag, *Verhandlungen*, 6 April 1916.

reached on the creation of a *Mitteleuropa* which involved attachment to the Central Powers of the Balkans and Turkey, an idea propagated by the socially-minded nationalist pastor and publicist, Friedrich Naumann. Some envisaged the adherence to the new constellation of the Scandinavian countries, Holland and Switzerland. Kautsky, however, denounced *Mitteleuropa* as imperialism and containing the seeds of a new war, and he was backed by others who objected to the threat to the independence of the Balkans. The discussion showed how wide divergences in the party had become, and how much support there was in a section of the S.P.D. for the notion of *Mitteleuropa*.[1]

In December 1915 the fifth war credits bill came before the Reichstag. This time twenty socialists, including Haase, voted against it, and a further twenty-two abstained. Thus Liebknecht's example had been followed by a group of his colleagues a year later. The dissidents read a declaration criticising the Chancellor for another of his vaguely annexationist speeches, and urged Germany to take the initiative in proposing terms of peace, for she was in the strongest military position and her frontiers were no longer threatened. The declaration was moderately worded and avoided reference to imperialism and class war.[2] The sequel was a vote by the party executive condemning the Haase group for breach of discipline, and when *Vorwaerts* agreed with Haase it too was censured. Severer action was taken against Liebknecht, who had added to the embarrassment caused by his earlier conduct by a series of interpellations in the Reichstag. He was *de facto* expelled from the S.P.D. parliamentary group, and from now onwards sat in the Reichstag as a '*Wilder*' or rebel socialist.[3] In the Prussian lower house, however, he remained as an official representative of his party; and there in March 1916 he created a sensation by urging those in the trenches and those at home to drop their weapons and turn against their common enemy, capitalist government.[4] On 1 May, Labour Day, he put his doctrine into practice by demonstrating against the war on the Potsdamer Platz in the heart of Berlin. He shouted: 'Down with the government! Down with the war!' and distributed illegal handbills and pamphlets to the assembled crowd. He was arrested on the spot, and as a soldier was court-martialled, the Reichstag refusing to claim immunity for him as a parliamentarian. Rosa Luxemburg, who accompanied him, was for some reason not arrested. Liebknecht was charged not with high treason, which he admitted, but with

[1] Scheidemann, *Zusammenbruch*, p. 29; Stroebel, *The German Revolution and after* (London, 1923), p. 26. Stroebel was an editor of *Vorwaerts* who afterwards joined the Independent socialist party, of which he was a firm right-winger. He became a member of the all-socialist Prussian government during the revolution.
[2] Prager, *op. cit.* pp. 86–8; Ernst Haase, *Hugo Haase, sein Leben und Wirken*, p. 114.
[3] Bevan, *op. cit.* pp. 76–7 and 82.
[4] Liebknecht, *Ausgewaehlte Reden, Briefe und Aufsaetze* (Berlin, 1952), p. 427.

'aiding a hostile power', and sentenced to four years in prison.[1] On the day of his sentence a number of workers went on strike—a gesture of sympathy for a man who was never lacking in courage, rather than of support for his extremist views.

By the time of Liebknecht's demonstration the rift within the S.P.D. had reached a new stage. In March 1916 the sixth war credits bill, forming part of an emergency budget, revived the familiar controversy, and again no agreement was possible. When the debate in the Reichstag began Haase surprised most of his colleagues by announcing his intention to vote against the budget and by going on to make a whole-hearted attack on the government. He criticised its food policy, its tax policy, the censorship. Speaking of the military deadlock, he denied that either side had a margin of strength sufficient to defeat the other. This was the strongest attack on the government since the *Burgfrieden*, and the majority of the S.P.D. were livid. Haase was eventually shouted down by the whole House after a motion calling him to stop had been passed by a majority which included most of the socialists. Ebert afterwards accused Haase of 'outrageous perfidy'.[2]

Such conduct was felt to be unpardonable, and at the next meeting of the S.P.D. executive the minority of eighteen who had voted against the emergency budget were formally deprived of their parliamentary rights and thus muzzled. Under these circumstances, the minority formed a separate or opposition parliamentary group known as the Social Democratic *Arbeitsgemeinschaft*. Haase and Ledebour[3] were co-chairmen and Dittmann was secretary.[4] Thus the break-up of the party, to which events had been moving, slowly before and rapidly during the war, had come at last. The split was really threefold, for fourteen other socialist deputies had abstained from voting; thus thirty-two, almost a third of the total deputies, were in varying degrees of opposition to the party leadership. The civic truce inside German socialism was in ruins.

[1] Frölich, *10 Jahre Krieg und Bürgerkrieg*, pp. 150 ff.; Bevan *op. cit.* pp. 103–4.

[2] Prager, *op. cit.* p. 94; *Prot. S.P.D.* Würzburg (1917), p. 128.

[3] Georg Ledebour, born in 1850 and a member of the Reichstag since 1900, was well known as a left wing militant and parliamentarian. A friend of Bebel's, as a young man he had taken part in the Franco-Prussian war. See also p. 104 below.

[4] Prager. *op. cit.* pp. 95–6; Bevan, *op. cit.* p. 95. Wilhelm Dittmann, born in 1874, was trained as a carpenter before entering socialist politics via journalism. After experience as editor of S.P.D. newspapers Dittmann spent five years (1904–9) as party secretary in Frankfurt. A notable organiser, Dittmann became secretary of the Independent socialist party on its formation in 1917. He was sentenced to a term of imprisonment for his part in the great strike of January 1918 and released in October 1918. One of the three Independent socialist People's Commissars in the revolution, Dittmann, while critical of Ebert, disapproved of his party's swing to the left in 1919–20 and remained with the right wing after the split at Halle. During the Nazi regime he emigrated to Switzerland, returning to Germany in 1951, where he died three years later. He left memoirs (see bibliography) which contain interesting comment on the revolutionary period in Germany and Russia.

ANTI-WAR SOCIALISM AND ZIMMERWALD

Support of the war policy of their respective governments by the socialist parties in almost all belligerent countries (the Serbs, Italians and Russian Bolsheviks were notable exceptions) came as a shattering and almost fatal blow to the Second International. It was a bitter disappointment to those who had believed in the moral power of socialism to keep the peace. What had gone wrong, and who was to blame? French and Belgian socialists could hardly reproach themselves for rallying to the defence of their invaded and ravaged countries, and most British socialists accepted Britain's participation in the war as justified by the breach of Belgian neutrality. For German socialists reconciliation of support for the war with their pledges to the Second International and the ideals of international socialism was more difficult. They knew that their approval of their government's policy was condemned in neutral as well as in allied countries. The German claim to be fighting a defensive war against Russia was belied by the Schlieffen plan, by which seven-eighths of German military strength was deployed in the west. At the headquarters of the Second International, which quickly moved from occupied Brussels to neutral Amsterdam, German socialists were in disgrace: both Vandervelde the chairman, and Huysmans, the secretary, were Belgians and members of the Belgian government in exile. The Germans felt that the cards were clearly stacked against them, and complained bitterly that the International Socialist Bureau was an instrument of the Entente. After being admired for so long as the model socialist party of Europe, it was a novel and galling experience for the S.P.D. to be pilloried and ostracised. They passionately rejected the charge that theirs was the sole guilt for the tragedy that had befallen European socialism.[1]

The International Socialist Bureau was practically paralysed.[2] As a loose federation of autonomous socialist parties, the Second International could act only through those parties. It had no more power to stop the war than to prevent it breaking out. The Bureau kept up correspondence with member parties, but it dared not take sides too openly for fear of disrupting the organisation altogether. Efforts were made to get socialists from both camps to meet, but the French and Belgians refused to sit at the same table as Germans. Socialists in France and Germany no longer had a common language. In France, war fever had turned the extreme war resister Hervé into a militant patriot, while Guesde, another left-winger and orthodox Marxist, had joined the cabinet. In Germany too the effect of the war was to throw existing alignments within the S.P.D. into confusion. Ardent left-wingers like Lensch found Marxist arguments to justify Germany's war policy and

[1] *Ausschuss*, 12 January 1915.
[2] M. Fainsod, *International Socialism and the World War*, p. 44.

became apologists for the government, while right wing socialists like Bernstein and Eisner, trying to uphold the internationalist standard, found themselves carried far to the left. Successive conferences of the Second International, with their idealistic resolutions, their passionate oratory, had all proved to be wasted effort. The dreams of a generation of socialists were trampled in the mud of the trenches as all classes and parties joined in the mutual slaughter.

The most the International Socialist Bureau could do was to arrange discussions between itself and socialists of either side. It was to attend one of these meetings that Ebert and Scheidemann went to The Hague in December 1915.[1] They returned with little hope. A more promising way of breaking through the barrier created by the war seemed to be by meetings of small anti-war groups. The first of such meetings (which were outside the framework of the I.S.B.) was arranged by the well-known German woman socialist Clara Zetkin, who called a gathering of women socialists in March 1915 at Berne to protest against the war. The Belgians were the only notable absentees among the belligerent countries. Then in September 1915 a much larger conference met at Zimmerwald. This was organised by the Swiss and Italian socialist parties, the latter having opposed (unsuccessfully) their country's entry into the war. Twelve nationalities were represented at Zimmerwald, many of the participants having defied the disapproval of their party organisations. From Germany came Ledebour (who had resigned from the S.P.D. executive in the preceding February), two adherents of the Luxemburg–Liebknecht group, and two members of a small left wing group calling themselves the International Socialists of Germany.[2] Neither Haase nor Bernstein had received an invitation as they were considered too lukewarm in their opposition to the war.[3] From France there came only two trade unionists. Russian socialism was strongly represented, Social Revolutionaries, Mensheviks and Bolsheviks being present. The Bolsheviks included Lenin, who was then living in Zürich.

Although the organisers of the conference had been careful to exclude socialists who were known to be 'pro-war', the Zimmerwald conference failed to reach agreement on what should be done. On the extreme left Lenin and his friends demanded uncompromising resistance to the war and denounced those who disagreed as social patriots or social pacifists. This was, however, a minority view. Most of those present refused to abandon the principle, traditional in pre-war socialist policy, that resort to arms was justified for national defence. The outcome was a manifesto which sought to find a middle way by stressing what both groups had in common.[4] It called

---

[1] Scheidemann, *Memoirs*, I, 327.
[2] Frölich, *10 Jahre Krieg und Bürgerkrieg*, pp. 158 ff.   [3] Bevan, *op. cit.* p. 101.
[4] The text of the Zimmerwald Manifesto ('Proletarier Europas!') is given in R. Müller, *op. cit.* pp. 165 ff. See also Fainsod, *op. cit.* p. 50.

for peace without annexations or indemnities (a slogan afterwards taken up by the Petrograd Soviet) and urged a return to the policy of international solidarity and class war. It declared that the socialist parties of the Second International had failed to carry out their solemn obligations and that by helping the war effort of their respective governments they shared in responsibility for its continuation. The International Socialist Bureau was censured for its failure to stop the war. It was only in deference to the wishes of the 'centrists' as the moderate oppositionists were called that a formal break with the International was avoided. The Zimmerwald conference did not however disperse before setting up its own secretariat in Berne under the name of the International Socialist Commission. This was clearly the beginning of a rival or successor organisation to the Second International, which the left regarded as defunct, and later became the nucleus of the Third International.

The S.P.D. naturally disapproved of the Zimmerwald conference and of German participation in it. Like Liebknecht's anti-war speeches, it was inconsistent with the *Burgfrieden*, and the S.P.D. executive issued a circular to young socialists warning them against a young socialist movement sponsored by the Zimmerwald groups.[1] For the moment it seemed that the Zimmerwald movement was of little account. The war went on as before, drawing in more and more countries and becoming more destructive, while the protests of the anti-war socialists were drowned by the patriotic chorus of the belligerents.

Yet the longer the war lasted, the greater the privations it caused, and to the Zimmerwald groups it seemed that the war-weary masses must sooner or later turn against it. Each attempt to strike a decisive blow led to greater sacrifices and new horrors, yet failed to break the enemy. The holocaust at Verdun in the early months of 1916 was followed by that of the Somme, which dragged on from July to November. It was against a background of growing exasperation and despair that the anti-war socialists held their next conference in the Alpine village of Kienthal in the Bernese Oberland. It was attended by forty-three persons, representing parties or groups in Germany, France, Russia, Poland, Italy, Serbia, Portugal and Switzerland. The German contingent consisted of four members of the newly constituted socialist *Arbeitsgemeinschaft*, two Spartacists (the Liebknecht–Luxemburg group) and one member of the extreme left wing socialist organisation at Bremen.[2] There

---

[1] Prager, *op. cit.* p. 83; Frölich, *10 Jahre Krieg und Bürgerkrieg*, p. 158.

[2] Prager, *op. cit.* pp. 104 ff. The *Bremer Linke* group, to which Karl Radek had belonged when he lived in Germany before the war, was closely associated with another extreme left wing group, the International Socialists of Germany (I.S.D.) who had been represented at Zimmerwald. These were the nearest equivalent among the German socialists to the Bolsheviks and voted with the Zimmerwald left, while the Spartacists at first voted with the Zimmerwald centre. See also Meyer, *Spartakus im Kriege*, p. 9. Julian Borchardt of the I.S.D. edited the left wing monthly *Lichtstrahlen*, which appeared between Sept. 1913 and April 1916.

was the same broad division as at Zimmerwald between the centrists, who objected to the war as imperialist but wanted to end it with a 'peace of understanding', and the left, who urged that the whole imperialist system must be overthrown by revolutionary class war. As before, the national groups differed among themselves: the Spartacists found themselves siding with the Russian Bolsheviks against the *Arbeitsgemeinschaft*, whose policy broadly corresponded to that of the Mensheviks. The conference declared that the International Socialist Bureau had lost all importance through its failure to put an end to the war, but an irreconcilable breach was still avoided. In a manifesto using sharper and more militant language than that of Zimmerwald, the Kienthal conference asserted that it was the duty of all socialists to vote against war credits; called on proletarians to fight for peace without conquest; repudiated the Allied slogan that this was a war to end war; and denounced as a crude deception the notion that the war was being fought for the liberation of oppressed peoples or the abolition of militarism.[1] It proclaimed: 'There is only one way of preventing war in future. That is the conquest of power and the abolition of capitalist ownership by the working class. A "lasting peace" will be the fruit of the victory of socialism.' Yet the manifesto represented a compromise between the pacifist centre and the revolutionary left, and its phrasing was not free from ambiguities. Socialists were called on to rise and struggle for peace, but strike action against the war was not openly recommended. Still less did the conference endorse Lenin's slogan of turning the international war into a class war. The masses were urged to exert pressure on governments and parliaments, but revolutionary agitation was not mentioned. It was however symptomatic of the gradual supersession of a 'soft' liberal policy by a 'hard' Bolshevik one that the traditional socialist demands for compulsory arbitration of international disputes and compulsory disarmament were dropped. The war had bred a new cynicism, and moderation was at a discount.

The Zimmerwald and Kienthal conferences were important mainly for their effect in raising the morale and hopes of anti-war socialists. In the belligerent countries, but also in neutral states like Switzerland and Sweden the Zimmerwald movement hastened the split in socialist parties which the war had begun. Apart from that, the only concrete result of the conferences was the establishment of the new International Socialist Commission. Yet the moral effect of French and Germans being able to sit round a table and agree on a common policy was far from negligible at a time when most French and German socialists had been swept off their feet by nationalism. The three French representatives at Kienthal were the first to vote against war credits in the French parliament,[2] and in Germany the socialist opposition

[1] The text of the Kienthal manifesto is in Frölich, *10 Jahre Krieg und Bürgerkrieg*, pp. 238 ff.
[2] Fainsod, *op. cit.* p. 54.

drew comfort from the knowledge that a rising proportion of French socialists, led by Longuet, a grandson of Marx, demanded a return to the policy of the Second International.[1] The left had more support at Kienthal than at Zimmerwald, and counted on becoming still stronger, as the war lengthened. Where the moderates had conspicuously failed, the extremists were determined to succeed.

DEVIATION ON THE RIGHT: NATIONALIST SOCIALISM

The disintegration of European socialist parties brought about by the war had as its main result the formation of anti-war groups which oscillated between pacifist and revolutionary opposition. But another if less significant effect was the emergence of a patriotic and often chauvinist type of socialism. The growth of nationalist feeling inside the S.P.D. before the war has already been noticed as one of the reasons for the party's rightward trend. By 1914 patriotism was becoming respectable for socialists even if socialism was not yet respectable for patriots. This tendency was, of course, greatly accelerated by the war. Many of the new 'national socialists' were converts from the left. One of them, the former editor of the *Leipziger Volkszeitung*, Haenisch, recorded the enormous relief he felt at being able, after August 1914, to join unreservedly in singing the national anthem.[2] Patriotism was a natural instinct, the absence of which in Marxist dogma caused distress to many socialists who were conscious of national as well as of class ties. Some welcomed the collapse of the pre-war international policy as the triumph of reality over illusion.[3] But attempts to reconcile Marxist principles with Pan-German ambitions often had grotesque results. The militants of the right strained party unity in one direction as the rebels of the left did in the other. Yet the nationalists did not present such a problem to the party leaders, partly because they did not endanger the *Burgfrieden*, partly because they did not use embarrassing quotations from the party's past to discredit its present. Nor was the extreme right wing large in numbers. Power within the S.P.D. remained firmly in the hands of the moderate right.

An outstanding representative of the moderate right or new realism was Eduard David, one of the few leaders who was a middle-class intellectual. David was a forceful speaker and writer who advocated adjustment by the S.P.D. to the new situation created by the war and the *Burgfrieden*. He wished the socialists to draw the logical conclusion from the vote of 4 August by coming to terms with the state and abandoning their revolutionary aspira-

---

[1] Zévaès, *Le Socialisme en France depuis 1904* (1934), p. 102 ff. At a meeting of the national council of the French socialist party in April 1916 the Longuet group received 960 votes against 1996 for the 'pro-war' majority. By July 1918 the minority had become the majority.

[2] Prager, *op. cit.* p. 34.

[3] See for example the views of Keil, a right wing socialist from Württemberg, in *Ausschuss*, 27 September 1914.

tions. In a book entitled *Social Democracy and National Defence* David made his own many of the arguments of the nationalists: the war was defensive for Germany, and for the socialists to launch a peace campaign would be a mistake because the Entente would interpret it as a sign of weakness. He was not prepared for Germany to give up Belgium without a guarantee that it would not be used by Great Britain as a base against Germany, and he thought that the peace settlement ought to give Germany economic advantages for her expanding population. David was the author of a pamphlet refuting the Allied charge of war guilt which was used to influence neutrals at the abortive Stockholm socialist peace talks in 1917.

Much more extreme in his nationalism was Paul Lensch, a former left-winger who now violently espoused a policy of expansion hardly distinguishable from that of the Pan-Germans. He differed from them in his use of pseudo-Marxist arguments, saying that the defeat of Germany would retard for decades the mission of the S.P.D. to the international proletariat, whereas a defeat of the British empire would further the cause of progress. Lensch also praised Prussianism as a way to socialism.[1] The new socialist right expressed their views in a periodical called *Die Glocke* which was a counterpart to the left wing *Neue Zeit*.[2] The editor of *Die Glocke* was Haenisch, who advocated *Mitteleuropa* as the world policy of the German working class. According to Haenisch, Germany represented the revolutionary, England the reactionary principle. Another idea put forward in *Die Glocke* was an understanding between Germany and Russia.[3] This was a complete reversal of traditional socialist policy, and quite inconsistent with the S.P.D.'s claim of August 1914 that the war was against Tsarism. Haenisch was in favour of wide annexations by Germany in eastern Europe, with conditional freedom for Belgium. Another indication of the 'reorientation' in the S.P.D. was an attack on parliamentary government as foreign to Germany by Ernst Heil-

---

[1] Lensch wrote five books published during the war: *Die deutsche Sozialdemokratie und der Weltkrieg; Das englische Weltreich; Die Sozialdemokratie in ihrer grossen Krise; Die deutsche Sozialdemokratie: ihr Ende und ihr Glück; Drei Jahre Weltrevolution.* In seeking a synthesis between Prussianism and socialism Lensch was anticipating ideas which Spengler was to make popular, while his contrast between Germany's organic society and the mechanical individualism of the Anglo-Saxon countries was another theme that was to be developed by the Nazis. Lensch's extreme nationalism was the more striking because on 3 August 1914 he had been one of the few socialists in the Reichstag to support Liebknecht in urging the party to reject war credits (Bevan, *op. cit.* p. 39). See also A. Winnig, *Das Reich als Republik* (Berlin, 1928), pp. 105–29, for a discussion of these ideas.

[2] *Die Glocke* was founded in 1915 by Alexander Helphand (Parvus) with financial support from the German government (Fischer, *op. cit.* p. 215). Helphand, Russian by birth and German by adoption, is the subject of an interesting recent biography by Z. A. B. Zeman and W. B. Scharlau, Oxford Univ. Press, 1965.

[3] Yet Helphand, the publisher of *Die Glocke*, was the main advocate of a German-sponsored revolution in Russia, the result of which was to be the disruption of the Russian empire in the interests of Germany.

mann, a leading social democratic journalist.[1] England was rightly seen as Germany's main enemy, and so had to be presented as ideologically most hostile to what Germany stood for. Another organ of right wing socialism, the *Sozialistische Monatshefte*, proclaimed Germany as the natural leader of a continental alliance against the British tyranny of the seas (an argument that was to do service in the second world war). Neither of these periodicals seems, however, to have had much influence on the S.P.D.'s official policy.[2]

Behind the confusion shown in such polemics was a real problem: what did Germany stand for in the battle of ideas?[3] The Allies claimed to be fighting for the rights of small peoples; and though much that they did in the course of the war was inconsistent with these high principles, the world knew that the war had begun with the invasion of two small states, Belgium and Serbia. The west also claimed to be fighting for democracy; German socialists, as the parliamentarian Ludwig Frank once bitterly remarked, were defending the Prussian three-class franchise. Germany was fighting for a larger place in the world, for a share of the earth's resources and territory commensurate with her power and, as the Germans believed, with her deserts. But in the propaganda battle that raged, war aims had to be given an ideological dress, and German imperialism sometimes appeared in socialist clothes.

[1] Bevan, *op. cit.* p. 209. Heilmann was later prominent as a leader of the S.P.D. group in the Prussian parliament. He was murdered in Buchenwald in 1940.

[2] Heidegger, *Die deutsche Sozialdemokratie und der nationale Staat, 1870–1920*, p. 90. But the nationalists, though often bitterly criticised, were not expelled from the S.P.D.

[3] L. Dehio, *Germany and World Politics in the Twentienth Century* (London, 1959), p. 78. Attempts were sometimes made in Germany to draw a parallel between British 'navalism' and German militarism, and to claim that in challenging British naval supremacy Germany was seeking to redress the world balance of power and so acting in the interests of the smaller nations.

CHAPTER 4

GERMAN SOCIALISM IN SCHISM

Either the war will kill the revolution or the revolution will kill the war.
Manifesto of the Zimmerwald Conference

BACKGROUND: GERMANY IN 1916

Since the outbreak of war and the almost simultaneous application of the British blockade the Central Powers had been a beleaguered fortress. Directly or indirectly Germany controlled a solid land mass from Antwerp to Baghdad. Everywhere her armies stood on foreign soil and defied all Allied attempts to break the ring. But Germany's strategic position was not as favourable as it looked on the map; she was therefore never able to exploit her military success diplomatically. Her territorial gains were more than offset by her economic weakness, as well as by her numerical inferiority. The blockade cut her off from the world's markets. Her stocks of food and raw materials were running down partly because of the blockade, partly because of the call-up of agricultural and other workers to the armed forces. She had not been prepared for a long war; indeed the whole object of her initial strategy had been to make such a war unnecessary, and plans to meet a long siege had to be hastily improvised. The organisation and distribution of supplies between 1914 and 1918 was in the circumstances a notable achievement which owed much to the foresight of one of her leading industrialists, Walther Rathenau, who as early as August 1914 started to build up a special government department to control raw materials needed for the war. Germany has been described as the first of the belligerents to accept the challenge of full economic mobilisation. Nevertheless, however skilfully Germany used her resources— and her food rationing system left a good deal to be desired—she could never compete with the Allies, to whom the products of the entire world were available. So far as economic warfare was concerned, time was unquestionably on the side of Germany's enemies. For the Central Powers, a break-through before attrition exhausted them economically offered the only hope of victory. The breakthrough was attempted in three great efforts in successive years: by land in 1916 (Verdun), by sea in 1917 (the U-boat campaign), and again by land in 1918 (Ludendorff's offensive).

Having failed to knock out France in the early weeks of the war, the German supreme command made success in the east their main objective in 1915. In the course of that summer the Russian armies were driven back and Poland was occupied. Only by retreating in depth did the Russians, who were pitifully short of arms and ammunition, escape destruction, leaving behind a trail of casualties and prisoners. Yet despite crippling losses Russia remained in the war, and, as her offensive of 1916 showed, was still a match for the disaffected troops of Austria-Hungary. Meanwhile in the west the Germans sought at Verdun to inflict a mortal wound on the French, who were gravely weakened, but at a similarly high cost to the Germans. The battle of the Somme, which began in July 1916, was almost equally wasteful and inconclusive. Despite an unprecedented concentration of fire power, both battles seemed to reinforce the lessons of earlier, less costly attacks, that defensive methods had become so strong that the war in the west could not be won by frontal assaults, even with prodigious loss of life.

The failure at Verdun led to a change in the German supreme command. In August 1916, just at the moment when Roumania, like Italy one of Germany's lost allies, decided to enter the war against her, Falkenhayn was succeeded as chief of the general staff by Hindenburg, the victor of Tannenberg and a national hero. Ludendorff was brought in as his assistant with the post of quartermaster-general. This duumvirate, in which Ludendorff was the driving force, inspired new confidence in the population at a time when it was badly needed. Politically the change was of great significance; it marked a shift of power from the civilians to the military. The Kaiser, who had ceased to play a prominent part in public affairs since the beginning of the war, was not prepared to contradict or overrule the new supreme command in its disputes with the Chancellor. Nor could the Chancellor count on the support of the political parties against the generals. The result was first the isolation, and later the fall of Bethmann Hollweg. During the last two years of the war Germany was virtually a military dictatorship under Ludendorff, and all important decisions, political as well as military, can be traced to him.

Hopes of victory through the new military leaders contrasted with the increasing war-weariness which prevailed in Germany from 1916 onwards. It was in that year that food shortages became serious. Bread rationing had been introduced early in 1915, and was gradually reduced from 228 grammes a day to 160 grammes in 1918.[1] The scanty supply of flour was eked out by turnips, cabbage stalks and other substitutes. The official meat ration of 1,050 grammes a week was often not available, and a town-dweller would be fortunate to get 100 grammes.[2] Fats were even scarcer, and the amount officially recognised as adequate for a day had to last a fortnight.[3] In 1916 the potato crop failed, and the weekly potato ration fell catastrophically from 10 lb. to

[1] *Reichstag Inquiry*, VI, 437. Other accounts speak of 100 grammes of bread as the daily ration at the end of 1917.

[2] Grzesinski, *Inside Germany*, p. 40. 'Ever since the early days of 1916 an almost unbelievable food shortage had made itself felt throughout the whole of Germany...The people existed almost entirely on *Ersatz*...A person was lucky if he received fifty grams of lard and a hundred grams of meat as his weekly ration.'

[3] *Reichstag Inquiry*, VI, 434.

3 lb.[1] The following winter was the time of greatest scarcity, with less food available than there was to be in 1918. By the end of the war the daily average quantity of food available per head of population had fallen from the pre-war figure of 3,300 calories to 1,100.[2] Other necessities such as coal, textiles and leather were also increasingly hard to obtain. These privations were of course due to the blockade, but they were aggravated by some mismanagement and abuse, such as restriction of the area under the plough, the feeding of grain to livestock and the hoarding of food for the black market. Socialists were prominent in the Reichstag in complaining of such malpractices; the government was accused of favouritism towards the landowners, and of failure to stop speculation in food and to make price control effective.[3] Attention was drawn to widespread undernourishment, especially in towns, where people's capacity for work as well as their morale had been undermined. The shortage of food was also felt in the army.[4]

Political effects of the military deadlock were broadly two. On the right the conclusion was drawn that a further effort must be made to win the war by a knock-out blow; hence a campaign was launched in favour of unrestricted submarine warfare as the one means of forcing Britain to her knees. On the left anti-war feeling became stronger, and the mood of opposition socialists more desperate. The *Burgfrieden*, which had been greeted with such enthusiasm at the beginning of the war, gradually broke down. Intended for a short, victorious war, it could not survive the strain of a prolonged inconclusive struggle. The result was a polarisation of German politics between the annexationists or 'war-prolongers' as they were called by their opponents on the far right and the opponents of war credits on the far left. Neither group was willing to modify its demands to please the Chancellor, whose public attitude remained equivocal. Internally the *Burgfrieden* had worked exclusively against the left, for it had implied the indefinite postponement of constitutional change, including the overdue reform of the Prussian franchise. The virtual abandonment of the political truce made it easier for the left to go their own way. The opposition socialists, who after March 1916 formed a separate group in the Reichstag, regarded the rest of the party as prisoners of the government, and indeed the government, under pressure from the right, did little enough to reward the majority socialists for their support. Moreover with the change in the supreme command the right wing parties could count on the open backing of the powerful Ludendorff. In the controversy that

---

[1] R. Müller, *Vom Kaiserreich zur Republik*, I (1925), 78. By 1918 the potato ration had been restored to 7 lb. a week (Stampfer, *Die ersten 14 Jahre der deutschen Republik*, p. 49).   [2] *Reichstag Inquiry*, V, 137.

[3] Ebert, *Schriften, Aufzeichnungen, Reden* (1926), I, 315 ff. Haase complained of widespread hunger in March 1916 (Hugo Haase, *Reichstagsreden gegen die Kriegspolitik*, Berlin, n.d., p. 21). See also *Reichstag Inquiry*, V, 137.

[4] *Reichstag Inquiry*, IV, 191.

raged between the Chancellor and the Admiralty over the latter's desire for unrestricted submarine warfare against neutrals (it was already in operation against Allied shipping) Ludendorff sided with the admirals, while Bethmann Hollweg feared, with good reason, that it would bring America into the war. The Social Democrats agreed with Bethmann, as did the Progressives and a part of the Centre. But in October 1916 the Centre succeeded in passing a resolution through the Reichstag which stated that in deciding on the sub-marine question the Chancellor should be guided by the supreme command.[1] This meant that if Bethmann continued to oppose Ludendorff on this issue, as he had successfully opposed Tirpitz,[2] he would lose the Reichstag's support. The short-term effect of this move was to undermine Bethmann's position and to lead, despite his reluctant assent to unrestricted submarine warfare in January 1917, to his fall in the following July. In the longer term, however, the Reichstag parties had really struck a blow against themselves, for in isolating and weakening the Chancellor they had only strengthened the military chiefs, as events following Bethmann's dismissal were to show.

Meanwhile the socialists watched the situation with growing concern. They did not believe that unrestricted submarine warfare could be successful, as its supporters claimed, in starving out England in six months, and they fully shared Bethmann's fear that it would make American entry into the war inevit-able. Scheidemann told Zimmermann, the secretary of state for foreign affairs, on 17 January 1917 that the government's decision in favour of sinking neutral ships without warning was a gambler's last throw, and at a meeting of the Reichstag chief committee the S.P.D. spokesman, David, expressed his party's emphatic disagreement.[3] David added the hope that the supporters of the decision would be discreet in their public utterances and not make things more difficult for its opponents so that the moral unity of the German people might not be jeopardised. The majority socialists thus continued to support the government despite their misgivings, partly on patriotic grounds, partly because they dared not contemplate the consequences of a German defeat.

THE BREACH WIDENS

As the last chapter showed, by the spring of 1916 the once proudly united German Social Democratic party had split into two unequal halves: a majority which went on voting for war credits and giving the government's war policy critical support, and a minority which was in opposition. This minority, the parliamentary members of which were the Social Democratic Working Group or *Arbeitsgemeinschaft*, was a heterogeneous body, united in

---

[1] *Ibid.* pp. 67–8.
[2] Grand Admiral von Tirpitz, secretary of state for the navy since 1897, resigned in March 1916 when the government rejected his advice to start ruthless submarine warfare—a decision it rescinded ten months later.　　　　[3] Scheidemann, *Memoirs*, I, 332–5.

its opposition to the war but in little else. It included pacifists and radicals, doctrinaire Marxists and internationally minded reform socialists. On the outside left of the *Arbeitsgemeinschaft*, distinct in policy but not formally separated, was the small revolutionary group headed by Liebknecht and Rosa Luxemburg, known before 1 January 1916 as the 'International Group' and after that date as the Spartacists. Doctrinally the split was really tripartite. The middle group, which consisted of the *Arbeitsgemeinschaft* and their supporters, was engaged in a battle on two fronts: on the right they had to defend themselves against the parent body from which they had broken away, on the left they were in constant feud with the numerically small but intellectually formidable Spartacists.

The starting point for most thinking socialists in deciding their attitude to the war was the question put by Kautsky in an article in *Vorwaerts:* how to reconcile national defence (in which the proletariat was admitted to have an interest) with the solemn anti-war pledges which the German and other socialist parties had made to the Second International.[1] In practice Kautsky considered that the voting of war credits should depend on the military situation. The French socialists, being in an invaded country, were justified in giving support to their government. It followed that if the fortunes of war were reversed and an Allied army succeeded in invading Germany, the pro-credits vote of German socialists would become justified. But this argument failed to meet the majority socialists' objection that unless war credits were approved when the German army was fighting outside its own frontiers, the war could be lost. Nor was it fanciful to imagine a situation in which Germany might be fighting on one front on hostile territory and on another front on her own, in which case how could a socialist know which way to vote? Another objection to basing the socialist attitude to war credits on the military balance at any given moment was that it ignored the highly relevant questions of war guilt and war aims. It was an almost impossible task to draw up a socialist policy on the war which did justice to all these criteria, and in fact the only choice was a choice between evils.

Despite logical weaknesses in their case, minority socialists showed more consistency than their opponents in trying to reconcile their wartime policy with pre-war principles. Their main concern was to salvage as much as they could from the wreck of socialist internationalism. They could not forget their past pledges or write off all the work of the International as futile. Nor were their values and sympathies, like those of pro-government socialists in belligerent countries, entirely upset by the war. And even pragmatically the objective of Kautsky and his friends of a peace without victors and vanquished did not seem wholly unrealisable in 1916. Kautsky compared the military deadlock with the Thirty Years war, which had caused comparable destruc-

[1] Kautsky Archive (A. 64). For Kautsky's views, see also p. 23, n. 3, chapter 1 above.

tion and finally ended without a decisive victory for either side.[1] Minority socialists believed that once the Russian threat (which they had accepted as the justification for going to war in 1914) was removed—as it was by 1916— the war had ceased to be defensive for Germany. They knew that some majority socialists were in favour of annexations, and they distrusted the Chancellor's ambiguity. On these grounds they voted against war credits. In theory there was little to divide them from the majority socialists, who also disclaimed any support for aggression, but who contended that, because the Entente rejected a restoration of the *status quo ante bellum*, only a German victory could guarantee an acceptable peace. It was of course unrealistic to suppose that in the event of a German victory the views of the S.P.D. would have carried much weight with the German government, and the history of the treaty of Brest-Litovsk (which was only half-heartedly opposed by the S.P.D. in the Reichstag) was to show that the supreme command would not be baulked of the fruits of victory by any political party. In short, neither the minority nor the majority socialists were in a position to influence the course of events significantly, especially once Ludendorff was in power.

German socialists hoped that their opposite numbers in Allied countries would influence their respective governments in favour of moderation, and minority socialists pinned their faith on the small groups of pacifists and semi-pacifists such as the British I.L.P. The S.P.D. leaders mocked at such hopes. However much French, Belgian and British socialists might hate the war and criticise their governments' handling of it, few could bring themselves to oppose war credits in parliament.

In practice, the longer the breach between majority and minority socialists lasted, the wider it became, and divergences soon extended to a whole range of subjects, including the day-to-day conduct of the war. When in April 1916 Bernstein, for the *Arbeitsgemeinschaft*, proposed a resolution in the Reichstag against unrestricted submarine warfare, Scheidemann, while disclaiming any intention to support complete ruthlessness, defended the government: 'We must use the submarine weapon, too, in our defence, to save our women and children from being starved to death.'[2] During the same debate Scheidemann upset the minority by remarking in a speech on annexations that it would be unrealistic to exclude the possibility of any changes of frontier. On this and other issues the majority socialists tended to take up an intermediate position between the middle-class parties and the socialist dissidents: a posture which reflected the pressure of events rather than principles. The minority denounced the majority as opportunists.

---

[1] In a letter to Riazanoff, the Russian socialist, in a Russian newspaper published in Paris called *Glos Sotsialdemokrata*. The letter was an answer to criticism of the S.P.D. by Plekhanov, one of the prominent Mensheviks who took a very patriotic line during the war. Kautsky Archive (A. 60).

[2] Bevan, *German Social Democracy during the War*, p. 99.

The majority replied by condemning the *Arbeitsgemeinschaft* for irresponsibility in aligning themselves during Reichstag debates with the extreme right. These tactics were seen when, in the summer of 1916, three bills were introduced by the government: one for the settlement of disabled soldiers on the land with capital supplied by the state, one to amend the trade union law in favour of the unions, and one for the taxation of war profits. All three were supported by the majority socialists and opposed by the minority, who contended that they did not go far enough.[1] But the action of the latter in voting with the conservatives against progressive legislation was condemned by their erstwhile colleagues as perverse and caused more bad blood between them. A writer in the right wing socialist periodical *Die Glocke* wrote at this time: 'The enmity of the different nations—German, French, English, Russian—to each other is child's play compared with the mad fury which at present excites German Social Democrats. If we have not yet turned machine guns on each other it is not for want of will...'[2] The writer was more prophetic than he knew; the time when German socialists would turn machine guns on each other was not far distant.

THE LAST ALL-SOCIALIST CONFERENCE

The internecine conflict in German socialism drove the party leaders to make a last, desperate effort to restore unity through a conference at which both sides would be represented. The meeting, which was held in the Reichstag building in Berlin from 21 to 23 September 1916, was known as the *Reichskonferenz*. Though representation of the party was less complete than at a normal conference or *Parteitag* the Berlin gathering was attended by 302 delegates, 143 ex officio members, the party executive, and a supervisory body called the Control Commission. Of the 445 voting participants, 276 sided with the majority, 169 with the minority.[3] These figures were not an accurate reflection of the strength of the two groups throughout the country, because the system of choosing delegates was such as to favour the majority. Even so, they show that discontent with the war policy of the S.P.D. was widespread, and in fact the opposition was relatively stronger in the electorate than among members of the Reichstag, who now divided into eighty-three for the majority and eighteen for the minority.[4] The last figures are interesting because they show that a number of rebel socialists had now returned to the fold. In the war credits debate of December 1915 some forty-two S.P.D. deputies, nearly two-fifths of the total, either voted against credits or abstained. But when the next war credits vote took place in March 1916, the number who disobeyed the party whip was down to thirty-two, so that the process whereby

---

[1] Bevan, *German Social Democracy during the War*, p. 111.   [2] *Ibid.* p. 121.
[3] *Ibid.* p. 130.   [4] Prager, *Geschichte der U.S.P.D.*, p. 108.

the official party was being abandoned by a steadily growing number of parliamentarians had been arrested and reversed. This was contrary to the expectations of many, such as Bernstein, who confidently looked forward to the time when the minority would become the majority and thus make their policy that of the S.P.D.[1] But these hopes were not fulfilled. Many of the waverers were willing to oppose official policy from within the party but once the *Arbeitsgemeinschaft* was formed they refused to join it and so cut themselves off from the parent body. Moreover, the secession of the rebels reduced their influence within the S.P.D. There remained however a group of socialist parliamentarians who, while staying in the majority party, continued to abstain from voting for war credits, even though they could not bring themselves to vote against them.[2]

The debates in the *Reichskonferenz* ranged over all aspects of politics since the beginning of the war.[3] It was the party's first self-examination since the Jena conference of 1913—more significantly, since the fateful vote of August 1914. The main speakers for the majority were Ebert and Scheidemann, who stoutly defended their record. They claimed that support for war credits had been essential to avert Germany's defeat, which would be more disastrous for the working class than the retention of capitalism. They had used their influence, they declared, to make the government take into account social needs in such matters as profiteering and food rationing, and took credit for

[1] Article in *Vorwaerts*, 24 September 1927.
[2] At a meeting of the S.P.D. Council (*Ausschuss*) in June 1917, a time when the prolongation of the war had produced serious unrest, Fischer, the manager of *Vorwaerts*, and other speakers urged that the only way to make the Chancellor accept their policy of peace without annexations and indemnities was to use their credits vote as a bargaining weapon: they should frankly admit that their aims and Bethmann's were different. Another speaker, Gehl, in support of this view said that the military chiefs were known to have their own war aims, yet Bethmann made out that he and they were in agreement. A further argument for taking a stronger line with the government was that if Germany officially renounced annexations it would be easier to make a separate peace with the Russian socialists. On the other hand, Dr Georg Gradnauer, an influential S.P.D. leader from Saxony and editor of the *Dresdener Volkszeitung*, warned that if they opposed war credits they would overthrow Bethmann Hollweg and might find themselves under a military dictatorship; and David urged that the Russians would not make peace so long as they were encouraged by an anti-credits vote in Germany to believe in the prospect of a German revolution. The result of the discussion was a decision to press the Chancellor for a declaration on war aims; if this turned out to be unsatisfactory, the matter would be referred to the parliamentary party (*Ausschuss*, 26 June 1917). An S.P.D. memorandum calling for the renunciation of annexations and for internal reform was handed to Bethmann Hollweg at the end of June (text in Scheidemann, *Der Zusammenbruch*, p. 161). But despite its forceful language it was no more successful than earlier representations had been: the peace resolution, passed three weeks later, contained an annexations loophole, and Prussian franchise reform remained an unfulfilled promise. An attempt at the party's conference in October 1917 to make continued support for war credits depend on a change of government policy in deed as well as word was heavily defeated (see ch. 5 below).
[3] This summary is based on the report of the conference, published as *Reichskonferenz der Sozialdemokratie Deutschlands*, 1916.

having successfully prevented it from yielding to the Pan-Germans and annexationists with their demands for unrestricted submarine warfare. They stood up for Bethmann Hollweg: however cryptic some of his statements about annexations might be, it would be a fatal mistake to defeat him and thus open the way for another Chancellor who would be a nominee of the generals and big industrialists.

Another way of defending Bethmann Hollweg's policy was to compare it with that of the Allies. If the breach of Belgian neutrality was a crime, so was the breach of Greek neutrality. If the German government was not free from annexationist ambitions, what of the Allied governments, which claimed Alsace-Lorraine for France, Constantinople for Russia and large sections of the Austro-Hungarian empire for Italy and Roumania? Why, the German socialists complained, did the Allied socialists not condemn the aggressive plans of their own governments?

Finally the majority blamed the minority for breaking the long-cherished unity of the party, for holding their own conferences, publishing illegal pamphlets and encouraging strikes. The majority, on the other hand, hoped to reap the reward of their patriotism by winning many middle-class votes. Thus the S.P.D. had tacitly abandoned its revolutionary aims.

The main speaker for the minority was Haase. He too repeated familiar arguments: the vote for war credits made the majority socialists prisoners of the government and was inconsistent with both the party's traditional anti-war policy and its own anti-war demonstrations of July 1914. Haase ridiculed the slogan that the war was a crusade against Tsarism: if Russia was to be liberated, it would be by the efforts of the Russian people, not by German arms—a prophecy that was soon to be fulfilled. For Haase the vote of 4 August 1914 had been a temporary aberration, and in deciding to oppose the war, minority socialism had returned to the right path. He reiterated his group's aim of peace without victory for either side, and denied the genuineness of the German government's desire for peace, for the only terms on which it was prepared to end the war would never be accepted by the Allies. Because Germany was in a more favourable military position, with her troops occupying Belgian and French territory, it was up to her to take the initiative in proposing peace negotiations on a basis of no annexations.

The point of view of the extreme left was also heard at the *Reichskonferenz* where the Spartacists were represented by Käthe Duncker, Liebknecht having followed Rosa Luxemburg to gaol. Käthe Duncker argued that since the war was wholly imperialist in character, the question of which side was more to blame was irrelevant. She declared that the Second International was dead, and that a new International must be set up. As for the charge of splitting the party, unity of principles was more important than unity of organisation. As Rosa Luxemburg wrote on another occasion:

Not unity, but rather clarity on every point. No gentle tolerance—not even in the 'opposition'; rather the sharpest criticism, an accounting down to the last penny. Through merciless disclosure and discussion of differences, to unanimity on principles and tactics, and therewith to capacity for action and to unity. Not at the beginning of the fermentation process which is taking part in the socialist parties and in the 'opposition', [but] only at its end can unity be achieved.[1]

The discussions which followed the speeches showed that these divergences could not be reconciled. Despite a final appeal for agreement by Ebert, the conference had failed. It was the last conference attended by socialists of all shades of opinion, and the unity which eluded it was never to be restored.

Instead, the autumn of 1916 brought a new trial of strength between majority and minority. In October the military authorities suspended *Vorwaerts* for an article criticising as a breach of the *Burgfrieden* the pressure put on the Chancellor by pro-annexationist industrialists. It is probable that this was a pretext and that the real reason for the suspension of the paper was a leading article in the same number which implied that at the beginning of the war the Kaiser had been overborne by an irresponsible clique. *Vorwaerts*, which had left wing editors, had been suspended before; but this time a condition of its reappearance was that there should be a change of staff.[2] It was believed at the time that its manager, a majority socialist member of the Reichstag (Richard Fischer), had actually suggested this purge to the army, and the minority naturally saw it as an act of treachery as well as a blow to left wing influence. Bitterness and suspicion increased. As a Berlin newspaper *Vorwaerts* was justified in expressing left wing views, for there the opposition socialists were the majority; but the critics of *Vorwaerts* contended that as a national newspaper it should reflect socialist opinion more broadly. Finally *Vorwaerts* was allowed to reappear, but with a member of the S.P.D. executive, Hermann Müller, made responsible for the contents. The minority denounced this 'rape of *Vorwaerts*' as an abuse of its powers by the executive and a humiliating surrender to the army and right wing pressure groups. Henceforth *Vorwaerts* was boycotted by the left, and another grievance had been added to the many which now divided the two socialist factions.[3]

There was further fuel for controversy in the Auxiliary Service Law (*Hilfsdienstgesetz*) introduced in November 1916. This was really a measure giving the government power to direct labour; it compelled all male Germans between the ages of 17 and 60 who were not engaged in military service to do work of some kind required by the state. The majority socialists and the trade unions accepted it as justified by the exigencies of war; the minority took the

---

[1] Quoted in Schorske, *German Social Democracy, 1905–17*, p. 307.
[2] Bevan, *op. cit.* p. 138.
[3] *Ibid.* p. 139, and Prager, *op. cit.* p. 118. The S.P.D. did in fact try to persuade the Chancellor to intercede with the army, but the Chancellor had little influence on the army at this stage of the war.

view that it was wrong to confiscate the worker's only possession, his labour power, when nothing had been done to nationalise the possessions of the capitalists.[1] During the Reichstag debate on this bill, reference was made to the Belgian workers who had been deported to work in Germany. It was characteristic of the difference between majority and minority socialists that Haase denounced the deportation as a breach of international law, while Scheidemann was content to appeal to the government to see that the deportees were humanely treated.

Finally, socialist opinion was divided over the German Peace Note of December 1916. The majority approved of it as a genuine attempt to initiate peace negotiations; the minority denounced it for its arrogant tone, its lack of concrete proposals and its threat of intensified warfare in case of rejection. The *Arbeitsgemeinschaft* also criticised the Reichstag parties for acquiescing in the government's refusal to discuss the Peace Note in the Reichstag.[2] Under the constitution the government was not obliged to do so, and indeed foreign affairs had generally been regarded as outside the scope of the Reichstag, fit for debate only by those versed in the arts of government and diplomacy. Thus the *Arbeitsgemeinschaft*'s arguments were based on democratic principles that had not been written into the German constitution. In the debate on the Peace Note the middle parties (Centre, Progressives and majority socialists) formed a bloc—in anticipation of the future Weimar coalition—to defend the government. The minority socialists joined hands with the Conservatives and National Liberals against it, though their aims in doing so were exactly the opposite of those on the right. That socialists who were the most ardent democrats should side with the authoritarians against a coalition which included other democratic socialists was a measure of the changes brought by the war.

DEFIANCE ON THE EXTREME LEFT: SPARTACUS

While the rift between majority and minority socialists had been growing more serious, differences between the moderate and the extreme left had also increased as what Rosa Luxemburg called the fermentation process worked its way through their ranks. It was in that winter of 1915–16 that the Spartacists arrived at a doctrinal position which differentiated them sharply from the rest of the opposition.

Since the beginning of the war the Liebknecht–Luxemburg group, known from January 1916 onwards as Spartacists (after the leader of the Roman slave rebellion), had gone their own way, rejecting the *Burgfrieden* and adopting illegal methods. Their first main activity was to issue a series of Newsletters

---

[1] Haase in a letter to Kurt Eisner dated 4 November 1916, quoted in Ernst Haase, *Hugo Haase, sein Leben und Wirken*, p. 130.
[2] Prager, *op. cit.* p. 123.

primarily intended to inform the dissidents within the S.P.D. of opposition opinions expressed in Reichstag debates (reports of which were censored) and in the parliamentary party.[1] By the end of December 1915 ten such letters had appeared. The group also issued handbills and pamphlets attacking the government for its war policy and the S.P.D. for its support of the government. The first of these, entitled *The world spits blood*, was secretly distributed in January 1915. In April appeared the first (and only) number of a periodical called *Die Internationale* which represented a cross-section of left wing opinion at the time. The main article, written by Rosa Luxemburg, ridiculed the idea that class war must cease to exist in wartime. As the class dictatorship of the bourgeoisie continued in war, so should resistance to it. The socialist capitulation to war in August 1914 proved not that socialism was wrong, but that it should be pursued more unwaveringly and with greater will to translate words into deeds. In another article, written under the pseudonym of Mortimer, Rosa Luxemburg attacked Kautsky for suggesting in a recent book that imperialism was capable of peaceful development because capitalists realised that they did not always profit from war. Luxemburg scornfully rejected the idea that imperialism was compatible with genuine peace, or that any peace made by the imperialist powers could be lasting.

Other articles in *Die Internationale* emphasised the duty of socialists to obey the Stuttgart resolution of the Second International and agitate for peace even after the outbreak of war. Since the party leaders had palpably failed to do so, the rank and file should act without them, and if necessary against them. Ströbel, formerly on the staff of *Vorwaerts*, wrote that the party ought to have voted against war credits in August 1914; and Mehring, as one of the party's leading intellectuals, used the weight of his authority to refute the notion that the policy of 4 August was justified by anything in the writing of Marx, Engels or Lassalle. In reply to those who claimed the authority of Engels for the war credits vote on the strength of his famous article in *Die neue Zeit* in 1892,[2] Mehring explained that Engels had not foreseen the rise of imperialism, which gave modern war a totally different character from the wars of the mid-nineteenth century. The logic of the *Burgfrieden* was the transformation of the S.P.D. into a national liberal workers' party, no longer revolutionary, reconciled with militarism and the monarchy. The whole *Burgfrieden* policy was therefore wrong.

By the time *Die Internationale* appeared Rosa Luxemburg, whom the authorities regarded as a dangerous revolutionary, had been arrested and sent to prison for an offence committed before the war. In prison she wrote (and smuggled out) the long essay on socialism and the war which was the fullest and most passionate statement of her beliefs. It was published in

---

[1] E. Meyer (ed.), *Spartakus Briefe* (1920–26), I, p. vii.
[2] This was the article by Engels referred to in chapter 2, pp. 43–4.

Switzerland for illegal distribution in Germany under the pseudonym of Junius and entitled (in the English version published in New York in 1918) *The Crisis in the Social Democracy*. In it Rosa Luxemburg refuted the contention that the war was defensive for Germany, and she quoted the socialist press of July 1914 to prove that it was caused by Austrian aggression in the Balkans. Further, Germany's naval and colonial policy and her ambitions in Turkey showed that she too was an imperialist power. The claim that the war was a crusade against Tsarism was bogus, and was in any case disproved by the sympathy for the Tsarist government displayed by the German government during the 1905 revolution and since. She attacked the anti-war opposition for lukewarmness as well as the 'pro-war' socialists for jingoism, and quoted against Kautsky a remark he had made in 1907 and with which his attitude in 1915 was clearly inconsistent: 'A war in defence of national freedom in which bourgeoisie and proletariat may unite is nowhere to be expected.' The war, she declared, was one of imperialism on both sides; as she claimed to have demonstrated in her book *The Accumulation of Capital*, it represented an extension to the international and colonial field of irreconcilable conflicts within capitalism:

> The war which began on 4 August was the war which socialist deputies, newspapers and pamphlets had been condemning for many, many years as a monstrous imperialist crime unrelated to the real interests of human culture or the real interests of the peoples, and diametrically opposed to both...Only small countries like Belgium and Serbia are formally waging a war of defence, and even they are only pawns in the game of world politics.[1]

The first casualty of the war had been the working-class movement: 'We are holding an inquest on international socialism.'

Politically, Luxemburg held, there was nothing to choose between the two sides. The Entente's professed aim to liberate the German people from the Kaiser was as false as the German government's claim to liberate the Russian people from the Tsar or the French socialists' claim that militarism and imperialism existed only in Germany. Whichever side won, there would be no real peace, for any settlement would contain the seeds of a new war. Even if Germany won, the German proletariat would suffer from the setback to the cause of proletarian solidarity. As for the allied slogans of self-determination of peoples and the abolition of secret diplomacy, such aims would remain utopian as long as capitalism prevailed: 'For the European proletariat as a class, victory or defeat of either of the two war groups would be equally disastrous...'[2] Only the international revolutionary action of the proletariat could enforce peace, and only its victory could restore

---

[1] Frölich, *Rosa Luxemburg*, p. 246.
[2] Rosa Luxemburg ('Junius'), *The Crisis in the Social Democracy*, p. 121. The American edition names Liebknecht and Mehring as co-authors with Rosa Luxemburg.

Belgium or give democracy to Europe. Rosa Luxemburg saw that a return to the old Europe was impossible and that everything now depended on the willingness of the proletariat to fight against imperialism. But of that there was little sign in 1915.

Somewhat surprisingly, Rosa Luxemburg referred with approval at one point in her book to the idea of a Jacobin-type revolutionary war as propounded by Engels, in which the German socialists would seize power and lead the nation against revolutionary Russia. She pointed out, however, that the policy of the S.P.D. since August 1914 had not been in accordance with Engels' ideas. The concept of a revolutionary defensive war in Germany was not really consistent with her analysis of the war as entirely imperialist, and she seems to have abandoned it fairly soon. There appears to be no trace of it in her later contributions to Spartacist policy.

Her essay ends with a passage notable, as her biographer (Paul Frölich) claims, for its visionary power, and one which vividly conveys the personality of this extraordinary woman and the messianic fervour of her message:

> Imperialist bestiality has been let loose to devastate the fields of Europe and there is one incidental accompaniment for which the 'cultured world' has neither heart nor conscience—the mass slaughter of the European proletariat...It is our hope, our flesh and blood, which is falling in swathes like corn under the sickle. The finest, the most intelligent, the best trained forces of international socialism, the bearers of the heroic tradition of the working-class movement, the advance guard of the world proletariat, the workers of Great Britain, France, Germany and Russia are being slaughtered in masses...That is a greater crime by far than the brutish sack of Louvain or the destruction of Rheims cathedral. It is a deadly blow against the power which holds the whole future of humanity, the only power which can save the values of the past and carry them on into a newer and better human society. Capitalism has revealed its true features; it betrays to the world that it has lost its historical justification, that its continued existence can no longer be reconciled with the progress of mankind....
>
> The madness will cease and the bloody product of hell come to an end only when the workers of Germany and France, of Great Britain and Russia awaken from their frenzy, extend to each other the hand of friendship, and drown the bestial chorus of imperialist hyenas with the thunderous battle cry of the modern working class movement: 'Workers of the world, unite!'[1]

It was a wholly internationalist position that Rosa Luxemburg took up in the document known as *Guiding Principles* (*Leitsaetze*) which was adopted as its programme by the Spartacus group at a meeting on New Year's Day, 1916.[2] The war, she wrote, had destroyed the work of forty years of European socialism. It had eliminated the revolutionary working class as a political factor and left the International in ruins. The most important future task was to build a new International, one in which revolutionary aims would have

---

[1] *Ibid.* pp. 126–7, and Frölich, *Rosa Luxemburg*, p. 249.
[2] Frölich, *10 Jahre Krieg und Bürgerkrieg*, pp. 234 ff.

priority over national ones, and from which nationalist brands of socialism would be excluded. The duty of socialists everywhere was the mental liberation of the proletariat from nationalist (i.e. bourgeois) ideology: 'Today the only defence of all real national freedom is the revolutionary working-class war against imperialism. The fatherland of the proletariat, to which everything else must be subordinated, is the socialist International.[1] Or, as the manifesto of the Zimmerwald conference put it: 'Either the revolution will kill the war or the war will kill the revolution.'

The trenchant logic and militant phraseology of the *Guiding Principles* could not be misunderstood; it was a trumpet call to a new kind of socialism, free from the evasions, compromises and ambiguities which had characterised the era of the Second International, one based on a single-minded waging of the class struggle in all countries. Yet few responded to the call. Despite the power and brilliance with which the Spartacus case was presented, it never succeeded in winning a mass following.[2] Its creed was too abstract. The ordinary German working-class voter could not accept the Spartacist assumption that national defence had ceased to have any meaning or that it would make little difference to him if Germany lost the war. At a time when he and his relations were fighting in the trenches or taking part in the war effort at home, and were exposed to the full force of patriotic propaganda, he could not easily be brought to work for the defeat of his own country. Liebknecht, who was a bourgeois intellectual, was convinced that as the German government was most to blame for the war, and the S.P.D. was the leader of European socialism, it was the S.P.D. which should take the initiative in bringing about a world revolution. Liebknecht was genuinely horrified at his party's betrayal of socialist principles, and he seems to have been prepared to accept German defeat as the price of revolution in much the same way as Lenin was prepared to accept the defeat of Tsarist Russia.[3] Defeat or victory was, in any case, irrelevant if the outcome of the war was to

---

[1] Frölich, *10 Jahre Krieg und Bürgerkrieg*, pp. 234ff.

[2] Liebknecht had a black-and-white view of the world with no intermediate shades. Just as he condemned the S.P.D. for treason to international socialism without regard to any extenuating circumstances, so his revolutionary optimism was unclouded by doubts arising from a realistic appreciation of the opposing forces. At the end of September 1918, for example, he issued (from prison) an appeal to German workers to rise, assuring them that no enemy army would march against a German revolution. Like many of the extreme left in Germany, Liebknecht greatly overestimated the strength of revolutionary feeling in the Entente countries (K. Liebknecht, *Politische Aufzeichnungen aus seinem Nachlass*, Berlin, 1921, p. 145).

[3] Article in the Chemnitz *Volksstimme*, 27 March 1916. Kautsky Archive, H. 32. The *Volksstimme* was a right wing S.P.D. newspaper with which Noske, member of the Reichstag for Chemnitz, was closely associated. The article referred disparagingly to efforts by the extreme left to split the socialist party: the only difference between Lenin and Liebknecht being that Lenin wanted Russia to be defeated first, whereas Liebknecht gave priority to a German defeat, in what was described as a 'competition in lack of patriotism' (*Wettlauf der Vaterlandslosigkeit*). But this naturally hostile view of Liebknecht must be seen in conjunction with his belief that it was the primary duty of each

be a world revolution embracing both winners and losers. Liebknecht over-estimated the chances of revolution in the Entente countries as Lenin over-estimated them in Germany. But signs of revolution in the democratic west (where socialists were in the governments) were difficult to discern, and though Liebknecht was widely respected for his bravery few shared his fanatical convictions.

There was another feature of the new Spartacist programme which was hard to accept: the authoritarian International. If the new socialist International envisaged by Rosa Luxemburg was to carry out its task, it would have to impose its policy on member parties, but how could that be done unless it were given coercive powers and the various parties were run on authoritarian lines? Yet Rosa Luxemburg had always opposed the kind of centralised, disciplined party created by Lenin.[1] The subordination which the new type of International required from its member parties was to be dramatically illustrated in the early years of the Third International by its famous Twenty-One Conditions. Lenin remained an authoritarian socialist in power, as he had been in exile; but Rosa Luxemburg was less realistic in seeking to combine an authoritarian International with democracy and spontaneity inside the party.

Together with the rejection of national socialism by the Spartacists went the rejection of liberal socialism. Already in 1915 Luxemburg had poured scorn on Kautsky for his belief in parliamentary democracy:

Has not Social Democracy always contended that 'full, not just formal democracy, but real and effective democracy' can exist only when social and economic equality has been established, i.e. when a socialist economic order has been introduced, and that, on the other hand, the 'democracy' which prevails in a bourgeois national state is, in the last resort, more or less humbug?[2]

Anti-parliamentarian sentiment is expressed in one of the Spartacus Letters:

It is an inner contradiction that the working class should win its victory on ground that was created by the interests of capitalist society and is preserved by them. Parliamentarianism is a bourgeois growth, from whose fruits the working class gets only the husks...[3]

Such articles showed how far the Spartacists had abandoned belief in the efficacy of parliamentary methods before Lenin's Bolsheviks demonstrated

socialist party to defeat its own (and not someone else's) imperialist government, and his hope of a revolution in the Entente countries. The same article reported the founda-tion in Zürich of a new periodical called *Der Vorbote*, which opposed co-operation between international and 'imperialist' socialists and criticised the Kautsky–Haase–Ledebour group. The significance of the *Vorbote* policy is that it is evidence of an attempt by the extreme left to split German socialism before the Russian revolution. Liebknecht's attitude was summarised in his defence speech at his trial for treason in 1916, quoted in Robert Grimm, *Zimmerwald und Kienthal*, a pamphlet by the Swiss socialist leader published at Berne in 1917, pp. 15–16.

[1] Notably in an article in *Die neue Zeit* in July 1904. See Frölich, *Rosa Luxemburg*, pp. 102 ff.
[2] *Die Internationale* (Düsseldorf, April 1915), p. 73.
[3] Meyer, *op. cit.* II, 55.

the use of workers' and soldiers' councils as instruments of revolution and of party dictatorship. The effect of the Russian example was to strengthen these trends on the socialist left in Germany, and thus to complete what the war had accelerated if not begun—the breakdown of the Erfurt synthesis of reformist and revolutionary socialism.

But the Haase–Ledebour group were far from ready to abandon the Erfurt programme. They claimed to be its only loyal supporters, whether in foreign policy (adherence to the principle of national defence but also to international obligations) or in home policy (attachment to parliamentary methods but no alliance with non-socialists). It was the new left, with its authoritarianism, and the new right with its chauvinism, which deviated from the party tradition.[1] Personal suspicion also played a part; the Spartacists were blamed for having drawn up their policy statement behind the backs of the *Arbeitsgemeinschaft*.[2] This was a discourtesy rather than a point of substance; the gulf between the two was too wide to be bridged by consultation. Liebknecht was particularly severe on the moderate left for not making their opposition to the war absolute. Like Lenin, he attacked the 'social pacifists' more fiercely than the 'social patriots', no doubt because the latter were beyond hope. He scoffed at Haase and Ledebour for voting against war credits on the ground that Germany's frontiers were secure instead of in terms of imperialism and class war. His complaint was that the group's statement in the Reichstag in December 1915 did not mark any advance on that of the party at the beginning of the war; but this did not worry the group because they saw their duty as keeping alive the traditional socialist policy, not introducing a new one.

Liebknecht's description of the *Arbeitsgemeinschaft* and their supporters is worth quoting. They were, he wrote:

a crowd of heterogeneous elements thrown together *ad hoc*, a crowd of such contradictory views on theory and tactics, and such different degrees of energy and firmness, that it would be incapable, to start with, of carrying out as a group a consistent socialist policy, a conglomerate that could do serious damage if it held back and thwarted the most advanced elements in the free use of their initiative.[3]

Criticising the group for weakness, half-heartedness and opportunism, he was right in saying that they did not oppose the war on principle, but he failed to see that national defence could be a principle even for socialists. It was only by abandoning national defence that the Spartacists could advocate revolution, just as the right wing socialists could continue to support the war policy only by giving up the revolutionary part of their creed. Since both majority and minority socialists claimed to oppose annexations, the difference

---

[1] In a printed circular issued by the Haase–Ledebour group dated 25 February 1916 (Kautsky Archive, H. 32).
[2] *Ibid.*
[3] Quoted in R. Müller, *Vom Kaiserreich zur Republik*, I, 175 ff.

between them was a schism; but the Spartacists were heretics. Yet circumstances made the Spartacists and the *Arbeitsgemeinschaft* stay together in uneasy alliance against the forces which oppressed them both.

The seizure of *Vorwaerts* and other encroachments by the majority socialists in the course of 1916 drove the minority to consider measures of protection, and it was mainly with this end in view that a special conference of left wing socialists was held in Berlin in January 1917. It was attended by 157 persons, including nineteen members of the *Arbeitsgemeinschaft* and thirty-five Spartacists.[1] Seventy-two parliamentary constituencies (out of 397) were represented, but only Berlin sent any Spartacist delegates. Haase declared that opposition socialism, not 'government socialism' had the support of the electorate, but he disclaimed any intention to break up the S.P.D. in spite of the *de facto* split which had existed for some time. Hitherto the breach had not had its full effect on party administration, and minority socialists were still paying their contributions to party funds. A Spartacist motion in favour of stopping this payment was rejected. Haase still hoped that his group could remain formally part of the S.P.D. and eventually become the majority, and the tradition of unity and discipline was strong enough to deter the *Arbeitsgemeinschaft* from taking responsibility for the final irrevocable break.[2]

At the end of the conference Kautsky and Eisner spoke about prospects of ending the war, and a manifesto drawn up and read by Kautsky was passed unanimously.[3] It expressed the determination of the socialist opposition to support a peace without victors or vanquished. Such a settlement could be made only through the pressure of the masses on the governments, and a just peace, one based on the self-determination of peoples, disarmament and the settling of international disputes by arbitration, could be only the result of proletarian influence. The manifesto was substantially a reaffirmation of the ideals of the Second International, breathing an optimism which few could share at a time when the helplessness of international socialism was clear for all to see. Even the Spartacists voted for the manifesto, though they must have done so with mental reservations.

Two months later, towards the end of the hungry 'turnip winter', the Russian revolution broke out. It marked the beginning of a new phase in the history of the war, of Europe and of socialism.

---

[1] Prager, *op. cit.* pp. 124 ff. The official account of the January 1917 conference (*Bericht über die Konferenz der Arbeitsgemeinschaft und der Spartakusgruppe*, Berlin, Jan. 1917) is published as an appendix to *Prot. U.S.P.D.* (Gotha, 1917).

[2] Prager, *op. cit.* p. 127. The *Arbeitsgemeinschaft* also objected to the Spartacist proposal to arm the International with new powers, on the ground that advanced socialist parties like that of Germany should not have to take orders from an outside body, which would also reflect the views of less mature parties.

[3] Prager, *op. cit.* p. 127.

CHAPTER 5

THE SOCIALIST RIVALS IN 1917

Democracy is more vindictive than cabinets. The wars of peoples
will be more terrible than those of kings.

WINSTON CHURCHILL in 1901

1917: THE YEAR OF MISSED OPPORTUNITIES

The activities of German socialists in 1917 must be seen against a background
of dramatic events, the most important of which were the Russian revolutions
of March and November. The fall of Tsarism, like the almost simultaneous
entry of America into the war, was a sign that popular forces were going to
count for more than hitherto, especially on the side of the Allies, and both
events sharpened the ideological contrast between the belligerents. The
March revolution in Russia broke the military deadlock which had gripped
Europe for two and a half years and revived hopes of peace, especially on the
left. The new Russian foreign minister, Miliukov, while promising his allies
not to sign a separate peace, was forced by public opinion to issue a declaration in favour of peace based on the self-determination of peoples, the formula urged by the Petrograd Soviet. The western powers believed, wrongly,
that the new Russian regime, freed from the scandals, the incompetence and
the pro-German influences of its predecessor, would prove a more effective
as well as a more desirable ally. They were soon undeceived. The long-
suffering Russian peasant soldiers, to whom the Tsarist government's war
aims of Constantinople and the Straits had never made much appeal, had
had enough. Already by January 1917 there were over a million deserters
from the Russian army, which had ceased to exist as a fighting force. The
disintegration of the army was accelerated by the famous Order No. 1
issued by the Soviet, which called for the formation of soldiers' councils in
all military units and the election of officers by the troops. Inside Russia the
demand for peace at any price and the peasants' hunger for land gave the
Bolsheviks a programme which brought them enough popular support to
make possible their seizure of power in November. After the Bolshevik
coup d'état Russian withdrawal from the war was only a matter of time.

Meanwhile the Petrograd Soviet's appeal to all the belligerent nations for
a peace without annexations and indemnities had given a new lease of life
to the almost defunct Socialist International. Taking their cue from Russia,
socialist leaders in the neutral countries sought to organise a peace conference at Stockholm. Peace talks between neutral socialists and delegations
from Germany and Austria, in which both sections of German socialism

84

took part, were held, but the projected general peace conference of socialist parties never materialised because of Allied boycott. Nor was the Vatican more successful in its peace initiative in the summer of 1917, which failed mainly as a result of Germany's refusal to make an unequivocal promise to restore Belgium. Yet even had Germany been willing to yield on this point, it is difficult to see how a general peace could have been arrived at in view of Allied unwillingness to return to the *status quo ante bellum*. Although the hardships and duration of the war gave rise to immense weariness, they also bred a stubborn determination not to stop short of victory, and the attitude of the warring governments hardened. Advocates of a compromise peace were ignored or shouted down. Moderate politicians were at a discount. At the end of 1916 the easy-going Asquith was replaced by the dynamic Lloyd George, a more pronounced protagonist of a fight to the finish; in July 1917 the arch-annexationist Ludendorff with parliamentary help drove the trimmer Bethmann Hollweg out of office; and in November the pugnacious Clemenceau became French prime minister. It did not follow that, the more democratic the governments became, the more readily they would accept a democratic peace.

A democratic peace was one of the slogans of the Russian revolution, which was an encouragement to radicals and a warning to conservatives everywhere. 'The shock that came from Petrograd', wrote Lloyd George later, 'passed through every workshop and mine and produced a disquiet which made things difficult in recruitment and munitionment.'[1] The advent of democracy in Russia could hardly be a subversive influence in parliamentary states, but even in Britain the I.L.P. and Union of Democratic Control were reported to be inciting workers to strike in order to stop the war. In June 1917 the I.L.P. and British Socialist party organised a convention at Leeds which was intended to 'do for Britain what the Russian Revolution has accomplished in Russia' and passed a resolution calling for the establishment in every town, urban and rural district of local workmen's and soldiers' councils.[2] If such things could happen in Britain, it is not surprising that the example of Russia should cause a stir in Germany, whose autocratic monarchy (though in practice the Kaiser was little more than a figurehead) and three-class franchise in Prussia and other states seemed more than ever anachronistic. 'The democratic ring', wrote Prince Max of Baden, 'seems to be closing tighter and tighter round reactionary Germany.'[3] People asked themselves how much longer reform could be postponed. Under popular pressure the government announced its intention to liberalise the Prussian franchise, and half-hearted steps were taken towards the introduction of a

[1] Lloyd George, *War Memoirs*, p. 1,117.
[2] *Ibid.* p. 1,153.
[3] Prince Max of Baden, *Memoirs* (1928), I, 112.

parliamentary regime.[1] But a small yet stubborn minority prevented franchise reform till the end of the war, and no serious effort was made to subordinate the government to the Reichstag. Fresh hopes of ending the war, inspired by the Russian revolution, lay behind a peace resolution passed by the Reichstag in July 1917. The majority socialists played a leading part in this, as they did in the Stockholm peace talks and in the attempt to influence the German reply to the Papal peace initiative. But despite increased activity on the part of the Reichstag and the adoption of a more flexible attitude to peace and reform by the government, the change in the balance of power in Germany that alone could have produced a decisive change of policy did not occur.

1917 was thus a year of fateful turning points and missed opportunities. By starting unrestricted submarine warfare a few weeks before the fall of the Tsar the German government provoked American intervention at a time when Russia's collapse offered the first real prospect of victory since September 1914. By failing to put into effect internal reforms the government missed taking the only course that could have preserved Germany's basic political structure and averted the revolution of November 1918. By not insisting at the time of the Bethmann Hollweg crisis in July 1917 on appointing a Chancellor of their own choice the parties which commanded a majority in the Reichstag lost a chance of imposing their will on the executive; for had Reichstag and Chancellor joined forces they might even have overcome the resistance of Ludendorff.[2] Instead, by allowing him to depose Bethmann, the majority parties lost the only Chancellor whose policy was broadly in line with their own. In the international field, the failure of the socialist peace initiative was significant mainly in sealing the fate of the provisional government in Russia and thus preparing the way for the Bolshevik seizure of power. Lenin's party was to be the chief beneficiary from the internecine struggle of the European nations, which was to verify Lord Lansdowne's prediction in his letter to the *Daily Telegraph* of 29 November 1917 that the prolongation of the war would spell ruin for the civilised world. No one can say exactly what would have happened had a way been found of ending the war before October 1917, but it is likely that many later catastrophes, including perhaps the second world war, would have been avoided. But the voice of the Lansdownes was not heeded. Instead, the advocates of total victory won the day, and total war ultimately gave rise to totalitarian politics.

[1] Bethmann Hollweg told the Prussian parliament on 14 March 1917: 'Woe to the statesman who does not recognise the signs of the times.' Noske, *Aufstieg und Niedergang der deutschen Sozialdemokratie*, p. 52. The situation required more forceful handling than Bethmann was able to give it.
[2] Epstein, *Matthias Erzberger and the Dilemma of German Democracy* (1959), p. 211.

THE REICHSTAG PEACE RESOLUTION

News of the overthrow of the Tsar's government was welcomed by the majority of the German people. It seemed to open the way to a victorious peace in eastern Europe, and among liberals and socialists there was rejoicing at the fall of a discredited autocracy. Scheidemann, with the German government's approval, sent a congratulatory telegram to the new regime at Petrograd on behalf of the majority socialists.[1] In an article in *Vorwaerts* entitled 'Time for Action' Scheidemann called on the Chancellor to grasp the nettle of Prussian franchise reform and drew the obvious moral: 'The difficulties that may arise, if the government now demands electoral reform for Prussia, are the veriest trifles compared with the difficulties that may arise if a bill to this effect is not brought forward...One has only to mean business and stick to it.'[2] This was seen as a veiled threat of revolution, and angered the moderate parties as well as conservatives; even some socialists were shocked. The Chancellor was in a fix. Any move toward franchise reform would further antagonise the right, where he had powerful enemies who distrusted his 'weak' attitude on annexations and still resented his opposition to unrestricted submarine warfare in 1916 and the consequent enforced resignation of von Tirpitz. On the other hand, Bethmann could not ignore the demand for change, which came from liberals as well as socialists. He proposed to the Kaiser a wide measure of reform. The result was the latter's Easter Message (7 April 1917) which promised direct and secret (but not equal) suffrage in Prussia without naming a date. The left remained unsatisfied. Later (12 July) a royal rescript pledged the government to introduce a bill for equal franchise into the Prussian parliament. It was Bethmann's last triumph but an empty one. Conservative opposition to reform, which had Ludendorff's support, was to defeat all attempts to change the Prussian voting system before the revolution of November 1918 abolished it overnight. In itself, of course, Prussian franchise reform would not have brought Germany nearer parliamentary government, but its attainment meant more to the majority of people. It was class franchise, not the impotence of the Reichstag, that really rankled. There was felt to be something shameful about a voting system which gave a working man who might have won the Iron Cross less political influence than a merchant who might be a war-profiteer. But Prussian conservatives seemed as impervious to the claims of justice as to the purely practical argument that equal franchise would have promoted national unity.[3]

[1] Scheidemann, *Memoirs of a Social Democrat*, I, 359.   [2] *Ibid.* p. 338.
[3] The conservatives' attitude becomes easier to understand when one remembers, first their assumption that Germany was capable of winning the war without appeasing the left by reform of the Prussian constitution, and secondly their fear that such reform, by strengthening socialist influence, would increase the danger of a renunciatory peace. The whole controversy is an interesting example of the interaction of foreign and domestic issues in German politics (Fischer, *Griff nach der Weltmacht*, p. 428).

Stimulated by the new talk of reform, the Reichstag at last became more active. National Liberals, Centre, Progressives and majority socialists agreed to support the demand for constitutional change. The result was the formation of an inter-party constitutional committee of which Scheidemann was chairman. The committee wanted the Chancellor and his assistants the secretaries of state to be made responsible to the Reichstag, and officers' commissions to be signed by the minister of war. But the parties of the right sabotaged the committee's work, and when the minister of war was invited to attend he ignored it.[1] Thus no progress was made. As the Reichstag Committee of Inquiry into the Causes of the German Collapse afterwards observed, whenever the military situation became more favourable, the moderate parties lost interest in constitutional reform.[2] In much the same way they were to lose interest in a conciliatory peace. If the warning example of Russia served as a spur to internal reform, the failure of the much vaunted submarine campaign to bring the promised victory over England within six months was the main stimulus behind the movement that culminated in the Reichstag peace resolution of July 1917. The initiative was taken by Erzberger, who now emerged as the leader of the left wing of the the Centre party, and as one of the ablest though most distrusted politicians. Through his propaganda and intelligence work for the German government in the earlier part of the war Erzberger had acquired a better oversight of Germany's prospects than most of his Reichstag colleagues. At first an ardent annexationist, by the early summer of 1917 he had come round to a more realistic view, confirmed by his talks with the pessimistic Austrian foreign minister, Count Czernin. Having studied the facts about submarine warfare, Erzberger came to the conclusion that in counting on the speedy starving-out of England the German Admiralty had badly miscalculated. Moreover Erzberger believed that a genuine peace move by the German government could take advantage of the growing desire of the Russian people to leave the war, and could thus break the alliance between Russia and the Entente. Looking at the home front, Erzberger saw that a move towards peace and reform was needed to keep the majority socialists voting for war credits and to prevent their disillusioned supporters from defecting to the Independents.[3] Erzberger's judgement is confirmed by a memorandum drawn up by the S.P.D. and presented to the Chancellor at the end of June. The memorandum, which was signed by the executive committees of both the party and the parliamentary party, stressed the worsening morale among the working class caused by hunger and despair and called upon the government to adopt the policy of

---

[1] Scheidemann, *Der Zusammenbruch*, p. 170. In his study of the Reichstag during the war, published as vol. VIII of the *Reichstag Inquiry*, Bredt describes the constitutional committee as having the key to the situation, but making no effective use of it (pp. 172 ff.).

[2] *Reichstag Inquiry*, VII, i, p. 13. Bredt wrote that there was nothing like systematic co-operation between the majority parties in the sense of parliamentary government (*ibid.* VIII, 176).   [3] Epstein, *op. cit.* p. 182.

peace without annexations and indemnities and to press forward with overdue constitutional reforms.[1] In the minds of the socialists, and of Erzberger too, peace and reform went together, and the way to both lay through strengthening the influence of the Reichstag over the government.

Erzberger reported his conclusions, particularly his findings on the submarine situation, to the main committee of the Reichstag on 5 July, where his speech made a considerable impression and led to the formation of a special inter-party committee consisting of the majority socialists, Progressives, Centre and, at first, the National Liberals. This committee drafted the text of a resolution in favour of a negotiated peace. It was mainly the work of David, the S.P.D. spokesman on foreign affairs. Ostensibly it marked the abandonment by the Centre and Progressive parties of a policy of annexations and a return to that of defence proclaimed by the German government on 4 August 1914. The socialists claimed that they had never given up this policy, which they had re-emphasised by including the formula of peace without annexations and indemnities in their programme in April 1917. The resolution passed the Reichstag by 214 votes to 116. It was opposed by conservatives and National Liberals on the right (for whom it went too far in the direction of a 'peace of renunciation') and by the Independent socialists on the left (for whom it did not go far enough in disavowing annexations). The Independents were right: for while the resolution proclaimed the desire of the Reichstag for a peace of understanding and reconciliation, it included the ambiguous words: 'With such a peace compulsory acquisitions of territory and political, economic or financial aggression are incompatible.' Erzberger was later to claim, with the assent of the Progressives and of some majority socialists, that the treaty of Brest-Litovsk was compatible with the peace resolution.

By the time the resolution was passed (19 July) Bethmann Hollweg was no longer Chancellor. His continual equivocations on annexations had lost him the confidence of men of all parties, and now Ludendorff used his influence against him. When Ludendorff told the Kaiser that he or Bethmann must go, Bethmann's fall was inevitable, and the moderate parties made no attempt to save him.[2] His successor, to their dismay, was Dr Georg Michaelis, a worthy civil servant who had been food controller in Prussia, but was, on his own admission, unversed in higher politics, and was obviously unqualified for the supreme office at such a time. His first public act was to accept the peace resolution but to add the words 'As I understand it', which robbed it of any

---

[1] The text of the memorandum is in Scheidemann, *Zusammenbruch*, pp. 161 ff.

[2] Bethmann's dismissal followed a talk between the Crown Prince and David of the S.P.D., in which David let it be known that his party would not object to a new Chancellor, a decision he almost immediately regretted when he saw Bethmann's successor. David took it at its face value an indication conveyed to him by Col. Haeften, Ludendorff's spokesman, that Ludendorff was in favour of a liberal Chancellor. David soon realised that he had been duped. See *Das Tagebuch Eduard Davids*, 11, 13 and 20 July 1917.

significance. Michaelis was an annexationist at heart, and that he never intended to act in the spirit of the resolution is shown by a private letter he wrote to the Crown Prince on 26 July, in which he admitted that while he did not like the resolution, really any kind of peace could be made with it.[1]

The crisis provoked by the peace resolution and the dismissal of Bethmann Hollweg has been described as the turning point in the wartime development of Germany, signalising the 'approaching end of the bureaucratic-authoritarian system and the advance of the Liberal-parliamentary system'.[2] This is to claim too much. Michaelis' gloss on the peace resolution was enough to devalue it, even if its language had been less ambiguous, and the gesture made little impression abroad. Nor did the resolution even mark a successful attempt by the Reichstag parties to impose their policy on the government, for the advent of Michaelis widened the gap between them and the Chancellor. The real victor was Ludendorff, who now had a Chancellor after his own heart and had even taken a hand in drafting the peace resolution.[3] The resolution might have been significant if the Chancellor concerned had meant business, but it is unlikely that Ludendorff would have allowed it to go through had such a Chancellor, or even Bethmann Hollweg, been in office. The refusal of the majority parties to save Bethmann was to prove an error, especially as it was not followed by their insistence on choosing his successor. As David of the S.P.D. later declared, the new order introduced by the change of Chancellor was more apparent than real. Erzberger had hoped that Bülow would be brought back as Chancellor, but the Kaiser had not forgiven Bülow for his behaviour during the *Daily Telegraph* crisis of 1908.

The same evasions and ambiguities which had given Bethmann Hollweg's government a reputation for duplicity at home and abroad reappeared in the exchanges resulting from publication in mid-August of the Papal Peace Note. This followed private conversations between the German government and the Papal nuncio, Pacelli, and proposed a peace based broadly on a return to the *status quo ante bellum*, including the restoration of Belgium, with further modifications such as a revived Polish state. A special Reichstag committee of seven (two from the S.P.D., two from the Centre, and one each from the Progressives, National Liberals and Conservatives) was set up to consider, in consultation with the government, Germany's reply. It was the first time the Reichstag had been given a say in foreign policy. But the new

---

[1] Scheidemann, *Memoirs*, II, 44; *Reichstag Inquiry*, VII, i, pp. 5, 294 ff. The only party which wanted to keep Bethmann Hollweg in office was the Progressives. The S.P.D., Centre and National Liberals thought him too compromised to negotiate a 'peace of understanding'. The two latter parties had approved unrestricted submarine warfare when it was introduced in Feb. 1917. Shortly after becoming Chancellor Michaelis confessed to Scheidemann that hitherto he had merely run alongside the political chariot as an outsider (Scheidemann, *Memoirs*, II, 36).

[2] Epstein, *op. cit.* p. 182.

[3] *Ibid.* p. 205; Scheidemann, *Zusammenbruch*, p. 98.

foreign secretary, von Kuehlmann, did not take the committee into his confidence, and deceived it by failing to give the explicit pledge on Belgium asked for by the Pope and insisted on by Britain and France. Thus the peace talks broke down, and the promise to consult the Reichstag had been ignored.[1]

The episode did not add to the reputation of Michaelis, who had begun his period of office so inauspiciously. A political lightweight, he was regarded as little more than Ludendorff's mouthpiece. Michaelis' inexperience soon led him into trouble. During a debate on a minor mutiny in the navy that occurred in the summer of 1917, he accused the Independent socialists of having instigated it. They indignantly rejected the charge, which Michaelis was unable to substantiate, and on this occasion they received the support of the majority parties.[2] Having lost the confidence of the Reichstag, Michaelis resigned (24 October). The chamber had won a minor victory, but as in the case of Bethmann Hollweg there was no follow through. As the next Chancellor, the Kaiser appointed Count Hertling, the 75-year-old prime minister of Bavaria and a leader of the right wing of the Centre party. Before taking office Hertling had confidential talks with leaders of the Progressive and majority socialist parties, with whom he agreed on a five-point programme, which included his acceptance of the German reply of 19 September to the Papal Peace Note (which had been approved by the committee of seven) and Prussian franchise reform.[3] It was the first time any Chancellor had consulted the parties on appointment, and appeared to establish something approaching parliamentary government. But appearances were deceptive. In fact neither of these promises was effective: the first because the German reply to the Pope did not contain the explicit pledge to restore Belgium which the Reichstag parties were told it would contain; the second, because there was no guarantee that the Chancellor would be able to impose franchise reform on a reluctant Prussian parliament. Hertling himself had never pretended to be in favour of the peace resolution, and his support for franchise reform was noticeably lacking in enthusiasm.[4] Under these circumstances such further gestures in the direction of a parliamentary regime as the appointment of Payer, a Progressive member of the Reichstag, as Vice-Chancellor, and of Friedberg, a National Liberal member of the Reichstag, as deputy prime minister of Prussia, had in reality little significance, especially as both resigned their seats before joining the executive in accordance with the constitution.

---

[1] *Reichstag Inquiry*, VII, i, pp. 9 ff.; Scheidemann, *Memoirs*, II, 67 ff.
[2] *Reichstag Inquiry*, VII, i, p. 11. Ebert made the point that other parties had the same right to propagate their views in the fleet as the Fatherland party founded in 1917 by Tirpitz and other nationalist leaders to promote Pan-German war aims.
[3] Epstein, *op. cit.* pp. 223–8.
[4] *Ibid.*

The politicians showed neither unity nor determination in turning the political situation caused by Bethmann Hollweg's dismissal and Michaelis' ineptitude to their advantage. Some praised the new hybrid system as typically German, and contrasted it favourably with the French or English parliamentary system.[1] The Centre shrank from the notion of getting rid of Michaelis in order not to assume the appearance of overthrowing a minister, and even Haussmann, a Progressive member of the Reichstag, could not conceive the introduction of parliamentary government otherwise than in a form in which 'Hindenburg and Ludendorff would conclude an honourable pact with democracy which would have found expression in a majority ministry'.[2] That the S.P.D. newspaper *Vorwaerts* could incongruously describe the minor constitutional changes as a German counterpart to the Russian revolution, and that Scheidemann could call the Hertling government in the main a parliamentary one prove that the majority socialists too were content to take the shadow for the substance of power.[3] The Reichstag had hardly changed since May 1916 when Dittmann, as an opposition socialist, had appealed to it in vain to use its financial powers to make demands on the government, adding: 'The Reichstag is strong if it wishes to be strong.'[4] In the words of the later Reichstag Committee of Inquiry into the Causes of the German Collapse: 'The fight for parliamentary government is no page of glory in the history of the German Reichstag.'[5] Kautsky had lamented in 1914 that where, as in Germany, a revolution was needed to put the bourgeoisie in power, the bourgeoisie had ceased to believe in democracy.[6] But the S.P.D., by acquiescing in the appointment of Hertling, showed that half-heartedness in pressing for constitutional reform was not confined to the middle-class parties. Thus the opportunity of turning what David called the crypto-parliamentary regime into a genuinely parliamentary one was missed while Germany's military strength was still intact. And not until July 1918 was a bill for equal franchise introduced into the Prussian lower house, only to be rejected. When it finally passed the Prussian upper house in October 1918, it was at the request of Ludendorff, whose conversion to reform followed the collapse of his military hopes. It was then too late for the measure to be debated by the lower house before the whole Chamber was swept away by the November revolution. Similar frustration was experienced by the Constitutional Committee of the Reichstag, which continued to meet in 1918 but without result:

And so in the fourth year of the war [wrote the Reichstag Committee of Inquiry], the German ship of state sailed rudderless across the ocean of hate and enmity

---

[1] Reichstag *Verhandlungen*, 29 November 1917, vol. 311, pp. 3,946–8
[2] *Reichstag Inquiry*, VII, i, p. 17.
[3] Reichstag *Verhandlungen*, 29 November 1917, vol. 311, pp. 3,962 (speech by Haase) and 3,949.
[4] *Reichstag Inquiry*, VII, i, p. 14.   [5] *Ibid.*   [6] *Neue Zeit*, XXXII, ii, p. 934.

amassed by an entire world. Sword in hand, German forces went on fighting for the very existence of the German Reich, and the whole world eyed with astonishment the achievements of the German army and its leaders.[1]

The same absence of firm intelligent political leadership which had caused Germany to plunge into war in 1914 now prevented her from either withdrawing from the war on acceptable terms or from solving her internal constitutional problems. Admittedly to make peace with the Entente in 1917 would have been an almost insuperable task for statesmanship, but with neither Michaelis nor Hertling in sympathy with the deliberately ambiguous peace resolution even the prerequisite of successful peace negotiations was lacking. As for internal reforms, they could have been forced through had the will been present, as the experience of October 1918 was to show. Behind the opposition of Prussian conservatives was the more formidable figure of Ludendorff, who, being formally outside politics and relying on the Kaiser's almost automatic support, was virtually unassailable. Moreover, as a patriotic German who believed in Ludendorff as the architect of a coming German victory, Hertling was unwilling to challenge him on a major issue.

Vorwaerts wrote on 6 September 1917 that Germany was half-way between absolutism and parliamentary government, and must go either forwards or backwards. During the Hertling regime (October 1917 to September 1918) she went slowly backwards as the impulse for reform spent itself and a revival of Germany's military fortunes turned men's thoughts in other directions. Limited though they were, the constitutional innovations had for the time being stilled the demand for fundamental change. Yet the crisis had been postponed, not averted. The Hohenzollern state had a reprieve, but one of which it was to make no use.

THE INDEPENDENT SOCIAL DEMOCRATIC PARTY

While the German government and the majority parties in the Reichstag were wrestling with the problems of the peace resolution and the abortive reform movement, on the extreme left the divergence between the two main socialist groups widened and hardened, and in some of the industrial centres a revolutionary temper began to show itself.

The special conference of opposition socialists in January 1917 was considered by the majority socialists a provocative act, and the S.P.D. executive decided that support of the resolutions passed by that conference was incompatible with membership of the S.P.D. So far the split had in a formal sense been confined to parliamentarians; now it was extended to party members and thus became national in scope. The opposition accepted the challenge, accusing the S.P.D. of having abandoned socialism and become a

---

[1] *Reichstag Inquiry*, VIII, p. 107.

vassal of the government and of the imperialist parties.[1] The organisational consequences were drawn. In branches of the S.P.D. where the opposition was a minority it was declared expelled. Where the opposition was a majority the branch was outlawed and a new branch conforming to S.P.D. policy was formed.[2] The socialist *Arbeitsgemeinschaft* issued a manifesto appealing to its supporters to organise themselves and announcing that a conference of all opposition branches and groups would be held in the near future.[3] This was the origin of the Gotha conference, beginning on Good Friday, 6 April 1917, at which the Independent Social Democratic party acquired a formal existence. Ironically it did so at a place which had witnessed the unification of German socialism forty-two years before.

The Gotha conference was attended by 143 persons, of whom 124 were branch delegates and 15 members of the Reichstag. The main object of the meeting was to agree on some form of opposition; there was at first no general intention to found an entirely separate party.[4] The idea was to set up a standard which would rally all the left and uphold the true doctrine of socialism against a heretical right wing. The old party was considered morally dead; only opposition or genuine socialism could save the honour of German social democracy in the eyes of other nations. The new organisation would be provisional; respect for party unity was still strong enough to make people defy it only with great reluctance. As Kautsky wrote: 'A year of bitterest internal strife, with progressive muzzling of the opposition in the party press, had to pass before the thought of breaking away from the party gripped large sections of it.'[5] As was to be expected, it was the right wing of the *Arbeitsgemeinschaft*, Kautsky himself, Bernstein, Eisner and their friends, who were most opposed to an irrevocable break with the S.P.D. But as the conference went on, opinion swung increasingly in favour of forming a separate party, and this was finally decided on. After some discussion about names the choice fell on one proposed by Haase: the Independent (*Unabhaengige*) Social Democratic party or U.S.P.D. The name did not commit the new party to any definite policy, but indicated a break with the parent body which was seen as hopelessly compromised by its ever closer association with an oppressive government and a distrusted Chancellor. The majority in favour of total separation from the S.P.D. included the Spartacists, who had long pressed for it. They thus helped to decide the destiny of a party in which they never felt at home and which they were later to be instrumental in destroying.

The Gotha conference reaffirmed the tactical alliance with the Spartacists, yet the debates brought out even more clearly than before the differences

---

[1] Prager, *Geschichte der U.S.P.D.* p. 129.
[2] Bevan, *German Social Democracy during the War*, p. 149.
[3] Prager, *op. cit.* pp. 133 ff.
[4] *Ibid.* p. 143. The official report of the conference is in *Prot. U.S.P.D.* (Gotha, 1917).
[5] Kautsky. *Mein Verhaeltnis zur U.S.P.D.* p. 8.

between the two groups over the basic issues of national defence and the role of parliament. The Spartacists again denounced the 'bourgeois pacifism' of the *Arbeitsgemeinschaft* and criticised it for attaching too much importance to parliamentary activity and too little to the revolutionary activity by the masses. Ledebour in reply attacked the defeatism (*Verteidigungsnihilismus*) of the Spartacists, as a Tolstoyan, not a socialist idea, and defended parliament: 'The whole parliamentary system, which has often fallen into discredit, not least through the fault of parliamentarians, including social democratic parliamentarians, is still a necessity. We are democrats. Not only socialists but also democrats...If for any reason we abolished the parliamentary system today, we should have to bring it back tomorrow.'[1] Ledebour was speaking within the framework of the Erfurt programme. But the Spartacists no longer felt bound by it, arguing that the war and the Russian revolution had made it out of date. They criticised the programme's equivocation, by which they meant its double character, reformist and revolutionary. Indeed some of the Spartacists saw little purpose in joining their fortunes to such a nebulous body as the Independent socialist party, but their new leader, Jogiches, believed that his group would gain more than it would lose by doing so. For, as he pointed out in a letter to some colleagues who opposed the tactical alliance with the 'centrists', the Spartacists were attached to the new party on their own terms: retaining their unofficial organisation and policy, and with freedom to criticise. Under theise circumstances, Jogiches continued,

It is not dangerous for us to go with them, but it is dangerous for them to have us, as we shall oppose their policy and no one can stop us...The *Arbeitsgemeinschaft* is going through a process of disintegration, and our very isolation from it in a party of our own would postpone for a long time this disintegration, which will benefit us all and is bound to come.[2]

The Spartacist tactic was thus to use their position under the umbrella of Independent socialism to propagate their gospel and, when the time was ripe, to break up the party. This was all the easier as the new party lacked cohesion: the members were divided among themselves, and no clear-cut policy emerged. Kautsky's distrust of the Spartacists was not generally shared; Haase, optimistic as ever, tended to brush aside fundamental differences, and Eisner naïvely described the Spartacists as 'completely harmless people':[3]

---

[1] *Prot. U.S.P.D.* (Gotha, 1917), p. 52.

[2] *Illustrierte Geschichte der deutschen Revolution* (1929), p. 147. Jogiches was a left wing intellectual socialist who had come to Germany from Lithuania and was a close personal friend of Rosa Luxemburg. After the arrest of Ernst Meyer in August 1916 he became editor of the Spartacus Letters and continued to be the main organiser of the Spartacus group until his own arrest in March 1918. As a leader of the left he attended, probably with some reluctance, the foundation conference of the Communist party at the end of December 1918, was arrested during the January 1919 rising and 'shot while trying to escape' in March.

[3] *Prot. U.S.P.D.* (Gotha, 1917), p. 25.

The results of revolutionary socialism in action, though shortly to be seen in Russia, lay still in the future.

Yet the revolution in Russia created a mood of exultation after the apathy and depression of the 'turnip winter'. In his opening remarks at Gotha, Haase spoke of the dawn of liberty beaming across the Russian frontiers into their conference hall and expressed admiration for their Russian brethren in their struggle for freedom and peace. He wondered if the German Chancellor realised the ferment of discontent in Germany, and wanted to wait with his reforms until the German workers began 'to speak Russian'.[1] There was a general feeling that something must be done to help the Russians, whose cause was theirs, and the optimism engendered by events in Russia was reflected in a manifesto issued by the conference which expressed the hope that the revolution would lead to a Social Democratic peace.[2] Kautsky, scanning the future, said that they were on the threshold of great events: no one could tell exactly what would happen, there might be a hard fight ahead, perhaps defeat; but in the 'social and political confusion' that might precede peace they could reach the 'pinnacle, the dictatorship of the proletariat'.[3] Precisely what Kautsky meant by this phrase he did not say. It had been one of the key ideas in Marxist revolutionary theory, but had not figured in socialist programmes except, significantly, in that of the Russian Social Democratic party. In the same month as the Gotha conference Lenin was reviving the concept of proletarian dictatorship in his April Theses, and the term was soon to have a meaning other than Kautsky imagined or than Marx probably intended. The Independent manifesto made approving reference to the conferences of Zimmerwald and Kienthal, and repeated their demand for a peace without annexations and indemnities, the formula taken up by supporters of the Stockholm peace movement. Apart from this, the manifesto, which was largely Kautsky's work, was in substance a repetition of the one issued after the January conference of opposition socialists. It was a restatement of traditional international socialism at a time of strong challenge from patriotic reformists on the right and from the new Leninist orthodoxy of the left then being forged in the struggle for power in Russia.

Most German socialists had been proud of their party's reputation for organisation and not a few would have taken it as a compliment that in this respect the S.P.D. was compared to the Prussian army. The disruption of the party between 1914 and 1917 inevitably gave rise to a number of organisational problems, and the leaders of the new Independent socialist party found themselves having to create a new structure under difficult wartime conditions. During the pre-war years the left wing had chafed against the growing ascendancy of the party's salaried officials, who tended to be right wing or reformist

---

[1] *Prot. U.S.P.D.* (Gotha, 1917), pp. 8, 39.   [2] *Ibid.* pp. 79 ff.   [3] *Ibid.*

in their views and to exercise, in the eyes of the left, too much power. The founders of the Independent socialist party were determined not to repeat this mistake: 'In the new organisation', declared Dittmann, its secretary, 'officialdom must not dominate.'[1] It was therefore laid down that only one-third of the central committee might consist of salaried officials, and the latter had to be appointed by local branches, not centrally. And with the experience of the seizure of *Vorwaerts* by the S.P.D. fresh in mind, the Independents decided that the executive might not acquire property rights in any business enterprises of the party including especially newspapers and printing presses. For the Spartacists the decentralisation did not go far enough; they called for greater emphasis on mass action such as strikes, and for the use of referenda. The left traditionally contrasted the revolutionary masses with their timid and bureaucratic leaders. This was the belief of Rosa Luxemburg which underlay her reliance on 'spontaneity' as the characteristic of a socialist revolution. 'Only the ruthless unfolding of the power of the mass of the people can perform this miracle', she wrote,[2] the miracle being a popular uprising. The strength of reform socialism among the rank and file, and the enthusiasm of the German proletariat for the S.P.D.'s war policy in 1914 showed that Luxemburg's 'revolutionary romanticism' had little basis in reality. Some Spartacists were aware of the discrepancy: Ernst Meyer had declared at the January conference: 'What is done at any given moment by the masses is not ultimately decisive for us.'[3] But the Spartacists showed no tendency to develop into a disciplined, centralised party such as the Bolsheviks became under Lenin, though, as was evident in the last chapter, only such a party could have put into effect the new kind of international socialism preached by Rosa Luxemburg. In 1915 she had poured scorn on the 'broad and crooked path of compromise' followed by the Haase–Ledebour group in contrast to the straight and narrow path of Spartacist virtue.[4] The Spartacists failed to see that their new orthodoxy implied a rigid organisation. Relying on the—largely mythical—revolutionary mass, they did not develop a tactical means of transforming revolutionary theory into practice; and this was to be a grave source of weakness during the German revolution.

Richard Müller, an opposition trade union leader who was to play a major part in the revolution, wrote of the relation between the Spartacists and the *Arbeitsgemeinschaft*:

---

[1] *Ibid.* p. 18.   [2] Spartacus Letter of 20 September 1916 (*Spartakusbriefe*, II, 4).
[3] *Prot. U.S.P.D.* (Gotha, 1917), p. 95.
[4] Drahn and Leonhard, *Unterirdische Literatur im revolutionären Deutschland während des Weltkrieges* (1920), p. 34. 'The left radicals believed as a matter of faith that the masses, once in motion, would find the proper form of organisation' (Schorske, *German Social Democracy, 1905–17*, p. 249). This was written of the left wing radicals before the war, but is equally true of them during the war. One reason for not announcing their tactics in advance was the wish not to give away secrets to a watchful enemy.

In so far as the Spartacus group fought against the *Arbeitsgemeinschaft* on principle and over real issues the fight was necessary and useful. The *Arbeitsgemeinschaft* viewed all questions indecisively. When it finally acted it did so less from clear insight and its own resolve than from self-defence, and because action was forced on it by its opponents...

And yet there existed a powerful attraction in this motley and confused *Arbeitsgemeinschaft* and later Independent Social Democratic party. It was a good meeting place for all those who for one reason or another were dissatisfied with the policy of the majority socialists. Their illegal handbills and pamphlets, their performance in parliament dealt with the most burning topics of the day in a way which seemed more understandable to the people than the theoretical dissertations of the Spartacist group. It is this which explains their rapid growth, their large numbers, but also their fate...[1]

The U.S.P.D. completed its organisation in the three months that followed the Gotha conference. In sixty-two parliamentary constituencies the Social Democrats opted for the new party, either unanimously or by a majority vote. Among the places making this choice were Berlin, Brunswick, Essen, Frankfurt-on-Main, Halle, Leipzig and the Lower Rhine. In nineteen other constituencies new organisations of the U.S.P.D. were formed, and forty-six smaller local groups also came into existence.[2] At national level the party machinery was modelled on that of the parent S.P.D. with an executive committee representing Berlin and district, an advisory council elected by the rest of the country and a supervisory committee theoretically chosen by the annual congress. The S.P.D. did its best to keep its members from joining the Independents. In the words of a contemporary British observer:

The old party fought hard. They tried to arrest the movement by holding meetings all over the country and starting new branches. But...the Independents continued to make headway. One local branch after another went over to them, or else new local organisations were formed under their auspices side by side with the branch adhering to the old party.[3]

An echo of the controversy was heard at the congress of the metal workers' trade union held at Cologne in June 1917. With a quarter of a million subscribing members, this was the biggest union in Germany. A resolution condemning canvassing for the U.S.P.D. among metal workers was passed by a narrow majority, a sign that in that influential section of the industrial working class the new party had almost as much support as the old one.[4]

How many of the Social Democratic supporters in the country as a whole transferred their allegiance is not known with any certainty. By-elections held during the war are hardly a reliable guide as both martial law and the censorship operated to the disadvantage of the Independents. On 31 March

---

[1] R. Müller, *Vom Kaiserreich zur Republik*, I, 73.
[2] Prager, *op. cit.* p. 154. According to the S.P.D. the number of parliamentary constituencies which opted for the Independents was fifty-seven (*Prot. S.P.D.* Würzburg, 1917, p. 235).
[3] Bevan, *op. cit.* p. 158.
[4] *Ibid.*

1917 the official total of members of the S.P.D. was 243,061. By September of that year it had fallen, according to an Independent estimate, to about 150,000. The Independents claimed at the same date a membership of 120,000, a figure which fell short of the old party's total by only 30,000.[1] Although these statistics probably contain some exaggeration in favour of the new party, they point to a massive swing from S.P.D. to U.S.P.D. in the summer of 1917, as the growing unrest made further converts to the left.[2] On the other hand, it would be a mistake to see in such swing-over as did occur any profound change of conviction. While the leaders debated principles, the followers were swayed mainly by practical considerations. There is no doubt much truth in the comment of a contemporary writer: 'The masses have no knowledge of theoretical disagreements . . . and for that reason are little interested in party controversy as such. . .[which] is carried on almost entirely by the leaders. . .What brings supporters to the Independents is the general embitterment.'[3]

THE FIRST SIX MONTHS OF THE U.S.P.D.

During the first six months of its existence the Independent Social Democratic party had to decide its attitude to the main issues of the day—the strike movement, the Stockholm peace initiative and the Reichstag peace resolution—on all of which it differed from the S.P.D.

The 1917 strikes were a reaction to the hunger, physical exhaustion and sheer despair which were widespread among the civilian population, especially in the great industrial towns. The deterioration of living conditions under pressure of the blockade is attested by many contemporary observers. The Crown Prince wrote in his *Memoirs:*

As early as the beginning of the year 1917. . .war-weariness was already very great. I also saw a great and menacing change in the streets of Berlin. Their characteristic feature had gone; the contented face of the middle-class man had vanished; the honest hard-working bourgeoisie, the clerk and his wife and children, slunk through the streets, hollow-eyed, lantern-jawed, pale-faced and clad in threadbare clothing that had become too wide for their shrunken limbs. Side by side with them jostled the puffed-up profiteer and all the other rogues. . .Nevertheless, nothing was done to remove the evil. . .whoever wished to profiteer profiteered—profiteered in state contracts, in essential victuals, in raw materials. . .[4]

---

[1] Bevan, *op. cit.* p. 232. The S.P.D. view was that the Independents' claim to have 120,000 members was an over-estimate (*Prot. S.P.D.* Würzburg, 1917, p. 245).

[2] *Prot. S.P.D.* (Würzburg, 1917), p. 10. According to Bernstein a major reason for the fact that the majority of socialist voters continued to support the old party was that three-quarters of the socialist press was in S.P.D. hands (Bernstein, *Die deutsche Revolution*, p. 19).

[3] *Die neue Zeit* of 9 November 1917 (XXXVI, 138). Another contributor to the *Neue Zeit* nearly a year later (13 September 1918) wrote that the soldiers were largely indifferent to political controversy and that matters of immediate welfare, such as whether their tobacco was made of beech leaves, meant more to them than Prussian franchise reform.

[4] *The Memoirs of the Crown Prince of Germany* (London, 1922), p. 200.

7-2

Scheidemann describes the situation at the time of the peace resolution:

Workmen were collapsing by hundreds from starvation every day in the factories; postwomen were fainting on the house steps. Hunger, deprivation and sorrowing for the dead; indignation aroused by the Pan-German war proposals; no prospect of an end, and last, but not least, despair verging on revolution.[1]

When the internal state of the country was discussed at a meeting of the S.P.D. council in June 1917 one of the speakers (Löbe) said:

The mood outside is absolutely wretched (*hundsmiserabel*), bad among soldiers, among workers and among the middle class. Everywhere there is no more confidence in Germany's cause and an indescribable war-weariness.[2]

Löbe considered that Germany was on the brink of political catastrophe. There was growing unrest in the south, and in Stettin troops were ready to shoot down demonstrators. Another speaker (Gehl) reported that a month before trouble had broken out in Königsberg: shop windows had been smashed and plundered, with women and children taking part in the riots. According to another council member, Körner, morale had so far deteriorated at the front that the soldiers had to be forced to advance.[3] There was a general feeling in the army that the war could be ended if the German government would accept the Russian formula of peace without annexations and indemnities. Thus the burden of continued war was felt to be unnecessary as well as intolerable. Germany in 1917 was in a pre-revolutionary mood, and socialist witnesses are strikingly confirmed by an observer of a different kind—Hjalmar Schacht—who wrote that revolution was held in check only by the force of the government.[4]

It was a further cut in the bread ration which led to a mass strike in Berlin, Leipzig, Magdeburg, Halle and Brunswick.[5] This was the second strike of its kind during the war, the first having occurred in the summer of 1916 in protest against the court sentence on Liebknecht. Higher food rations were promised by the authorities, who were particularly worried by the effect of the strikes on the supply of munitions. Hindenburg publicly appealed to the munition workers not to strike, and a secret meeting was arranged between General Groener, head of the *Kriegsamt*, a kind of ministry of economic warfare, and Haase, who gave a pledge not to call the workers out on May Day.[6] Although the strikes broke out only a week after the Gotha conference of Independent socialists, the latter had no share in

[1] Scheidemann, *Memoirs*, II, 32.   [2] *Ausschuss*, 26 June 1917.
[3] *Ibid.*
[4] Schacht, *My first 76 years*, p. 148.
[5] R. Müller, *Vom Kaiserreich*, pp. 78 ff. It is estimated that about 300,000 workers took part in the strike.
[6] Dorothea Groener-Geyer, *General Groener, Soldat und Staatsmann* (1955), p. 57. Haase asked Groener not to reveal the secret of their meeting during his (Haase's) lifetime. The risk of compromise was great on both sides, especially Haase's.

organising them and did not even know that they were planned.[1] But once they had started many individual Independents played a leading part in them. The S.P.D. and the trade union leaders refused to have anything to do with the strikes, which Scheidemann described as a most serious danger to peace.[2] Yet peace was the main demand made by the strikers apart from better food and more fuel; they also called for abolition of martial law and of the Auxiliary Service Law, and for free and equal franchise throughout Germany. Socialisation was not among their demands.[3] In Leipzig the strike was held by a workers' council. This was the first time such a council had been formed in Germany, and it showed the influence of the Russian revolution. In August 1917 there was a local strike in Brunswick, a centre of radicalism, which was organised by the Spartacists; but here too the immediate cause was inadequate supplies of food, and the political demands were liberal–democratic, not socialist.[4]

The same undercurrent of discontent which produced the strikes in industry also led to an abortive naval mutiny in the summer of 1917. Morale in the navy was not high, mainly because of boredom induced by prolonged inaction. Specific grievances were bad food and the overbearing attitude of officers towards their men. Above all, the sailors wanted peace. They knew that one of the greatest obstacles was the stubborn insistence on annexations of the Pan-Germans, whose pressure on the government prevented it, they believed, from genuinely seeking peace. There was much resentment against the Patriotic or Fatherland party, founded at this time to publicise the annexationist views of the supreme command, and against the political propaganda spread by officers. The captain of the *Helgoland*, for example, addressing his crew on the first anniversary of the battle of Jutland, said that the aim of Germany's enemies was to destroy the bond between the Kaiser as Supreme War Lord and the army and navy, so that, when the Hohenzollerns had been driven out, a parliamentary regime would be imposed on the Germans. 'Then the shopkeepers, lawyers and journalists will rule here as they do there.' Such speeches, which were not untypical, made the sailors feel that the war was being needlessly prolonged in order to preserve autocracy.[5]

The sailors, or rather the small minority among them who were politically active, naturally turned to the parties of the left for support against the propaganda of the right, and in this way established contact with the Independent socialists. Since both S.P.D. and the Independents supported the

[1] Volkmann, *Der Marxismus und das deutsche Heer im Weltkriege* (1925), p. 142.
[2] *Ibid.* In a letter to his son Georg, dated 1 May 1917, Ebert described the strikes as 'senseless' (Ebert, *Schriften, Aufzeichnungen, Reden*, I, 363).
[3] Volkmann, *Der Marxismus*, p. 144.
[4] R. Müller, *Vom Kaiserreich*, p. 89.
[5] Volkmann, *Der Marxismus*, p. 176; Rosenberg, *Birth of the German Republic*, pp. 182 ff. and 193; Dittmann, *Die Marinejustizmörde von 1917 und die Admiralsrebellion von 1918* (1926), *passim*.

Stockholm peace movement, the sailors saw little or no difference between the two parties, and some of them even contacted the Centre. There were however a few sailors who had had previous connections with left wing socialism, including one who had worked for the *Leipziger Volkszeitung*, and they were furious when in May 1917 a ban on socialist newspapers in the navy was renewed. They went to Berlin to discuss the situation with the U.S.P.D. leaders. The latter promised to send the sailors propaganda material, and advised them to keep in touch with the U.S.P.D. branch in Wilhelmshaven. As a result of this visit to Berlin about four thousand sailors joined the Independent socialist party. Political meetings were held on board ship and on shore. The sailors decided to strike in favour of the Independent peace terms at Stockholm, and in doing so they counted on the approval of the party leaders. They seem also to have believed that similar strike action would be taken in other belligerent armies and navies whose governments rejected the peace initiative. The local U.S.P.D. branches advised the sailors to use passive resistance but not force. Propaganda for the Independent socialists was spread in the fleet, mainly through the food committees (*Menagekommissionen*) which had been elected by the sailors to ensure a fair distribution of rations. Premature acts of insubordination led, however, to the discovery of the organisation and the arrest of the ringleaders. The latter were court-martialled and ten death sentences were passed, only two of which were actually carried out.[1]

When the Michaelis government tried to use the connection between the mutinous sailors and the Independent socialists to discredit the latter in the Reichstag, Haase as leader of the Independents admitted that he and his colleagues had been visited by the sailors and asked for advice and pamphlets, and that canvassing for his party had taken place in the fleet. But he denied treasonable activity, challenged the Chancellor to produce the evidence, and asked why he had not been called as a witness at the sailors' court-martial. As we have seen, Michaelis lacked proof, and, on being out-voted, resigned.[2] The Independents certainly had some moral responsibility for the attempted mutiny, but as a legal party they were entitled to propagate their views, and were only following the example of the Pan-Germans. The whole episode illustrated the difficulty for the U.S.P.D. of opposing the war without recourse to illegal acts. It also foreshadowed the successful naval mutiny that was to form the first act of the German revolution in the following year, just as the industrial strikes with their workers' councils and political demands anticipated the events of 9 November 1918. In the use of strike action, the fratricidal division of socialism, and the Reichstag alliance of S.P.D., Progressives and Centre as a forerunner of the Weimar coalition, the future pattern was taking shape in 1917.

[1] Volkmann, *Der Marxismus*, pp. 178–80.   [2] *Ibid.* p. 181.

Meanwhile both majority and minority socialists had taken part in preliminary peace talks with the Dutch–Scandinavian committee set up in Stockholm by the International Socialist Bureau. A strong S.P.D. delegation headed by Ebert, Scheidemann and David reached Stockholm early in June. It presented, in answer to a lengthy questionnaire on war aims, a memorandum which gave general assent to the formula of no annexations and indemnities, without excluding minor frontier changes by mutual consent; agreed to the restoration of an independent Belgium and Serbia and of (Russian) Poland; and sought to turn the principle of national self-determination against the Allies by proposing its application to Ireland, Egypt, Tripoli, Morocco, India and other dependent territories. Alsace-Lorraine was to remain German, and the Central Powers were neither to gain nor to lose any territory. The subsequent approval of the memorandum by the German government, however, indicates that it was not considered incompatible with some territorial gains, and it was significant that the restoration of Belgium was not defined. The memorandum tried to vindicate the record of the S.P.D. in the eyes of neutrals by stressing its repeated attempts to bring the war to an end and to persuade the Entente socialists to hold peace talks.[1] There was, at first, some likelihood of French and British participation in the proposed general peace conference, but after various delays caused by the governments' refusal to issue passports it became evident that the conference would not take place. Had the western socialists gone to Stockholm, they would have found it much easier to reach agreement with the Independent socialists, whose delegation, headed by Haase, also reached Stockholm in June and presented a memorandum on war aims.[2] This proposed a plebiscite for Alsace-Lorraine; restoration of Belgium, of a Serbia which would include the Slav population of Bosnia and Herzegovina, and of a Poland which would include Prussian and Austrian as well as Russian territory. Thus a break-up of the Habsburg empire was conceded. The Independents claimed that their memorandum lacked the ambiguities in that of the S.P.D., and a contemporary British observer commented on the 'remarkable correspondence' between the Independents' proposals and those which the Allies were willing to accept.[3] In accordance with their practice of opposing war credits, the Independents declared that credits should be refused to any government which did not endorse this programme. In view of the attitude of the Independents, it appears surprising that the Chancellor allowed them to go to Stockholm; the reason was that he did not want to give the impression, by letting only the majority socialists go, that the latter were agents of the government.

The prospect of a general peace conference in which socialists of all shades

[1] Scheidemann, *Memoirs*, II, 6 ff., where the text of the memorandum is given.
[2] The text of the Independent memorandum is given by Prager, *op. cit.* p. 157.
[3] Bevan, *op. cit.* p. 175.

of opinion would take part naturally attracted the radical wing which had sought to promote international action against the war through its conferences at Zimmerwald and Kienthal. The International Socialist Commission which the Zimmerwald movement had set up at Berne saw in the Russian revolution of March a great stimulus to their work, and the secretariat moved from Berne to Stockholm so as to be nearer the main source of revolutionary activity. It was decided to hold a third Zimmerwald conference as a preliminary to the proposed general socialist conference, despite the opposition of the Bolshevik left wing which, under Lenin's direction, was unwilling to sit at the same table as the 'social patriots'. Socialists from France, Britain, Italy and America were forbidden by their governments to attend, and the Russian delegates were divided between the sceptical Bolsheviks and the Mensheviks, who, as a government party, were anxious for the Stockholm peace project to succeed. The German minority socialists were represented by Haase and Ledebour for the U.S.P.D. and by Käthe Duncker for Spartacus. The main result of the conference was the drawing up of a manifesto calling for an international mass struggle for peace, which according to Ledebour meant a general strike in all belligerent countries.[1] The immediate object of the strike was to come to the aid of the Russian socialists, whose revolution was threatened by the German army as well as by counter-revolutionary forces in Russia.[2] By agreeing to an insurrectionary strike in Germany, the Independent socialists had committed themselves to what was legally high treason. This worried Haase, who as a lawyer knew what was involved, and was at heart a man who hated violence. He seems to have feared that he had promised something which he could not, and probably did not even want to perform. He no doubt remembered his secret promise to Groener four months before. As in the case of the mutinous sailors, the party was on the razor's edge between legality and treason, and this agonising dilemma was reflected, according to Angelica Balabanoff who organised the conference for the International Socialist Commission, in his troubled behaviour.[3]

With the collapse of the Stockholm peace project the Second International lost its last chance of staging a come-back and uniting in a common front the 'pacifist' socialist centre as well as the patriotic right. The Stockholm

[1] *Reichstag Inquiry*, v, 24 ff.; *Ledebour Prozess* (1919), p. 23. Ledebour's initiative was characteristic of a man who, despite his advanced age, always showed courage and energy. The third Zimmerwald conference began on 5 September 1917. It showed a majority against taking part in the proposed general socialist conference at Stockholm, a decision which caused the Mensheviks to withdraw but was otherwise of little importance as the larger meeting never materialised. Fainsod, *International Socialism and the World War* p. 160.

[2] Lenin's view at the time was that unless the Bolsheviks succeeded in seizing power in Russia the forces of counter-revolution would triumph. Since the unsuccessful July rising the Bolsheviks had been officially proscribed, and Russia's military vulnerability was emphasised by the German capture of Riga and the implied threat to Petrograd.

[3] Balabanoff, *Erinnerungen und Erlebnisse*, p. 169.

fiasco was thus mainly significant in throwing the moderates, whose hopes of peace had been disappointed once again, into the arms of the extremists, especially in Russia. The Bolshevik seizure of power in November made Lenin the undisputed leader of the Zimmerwald left, and gave his party a physical base and a moral prestige which were to be decisive for the future of revolutionary socialism. At the time, and indeed for long afterwards, it was far from certain that the Bolshevik regime would last, and even the Bolsheviks looked to the revolutionary movement in Germany to ensure their survival. Thus a new and grave responsibility rested on the Independent socialists and Spartacists. Yet that Haase judged the situation in Germany not yet ripe for strike action is shown by his reluctance to agree to the manifesto of the September conference.

Meanwhile the Independents continued to oppose both the government and the majority in the Reichstag. They rejected the peace resolution as ambiguous (which it was) and instead introduced a resolution of their own which called for 'a peace without annexations of any kind whatsoever and without any war indemnity, on the basis of the right of peoples to self-determination. It expects in particular the restoration of Belgium and reparation for the wrong done to her.'[1] This was clear and concrete language, and met the Allied claim on behalf of Belgium in a way which the other parties' peace resolution failed to do. And whereas the other parties spoke in cautious generalities of ministers being appointed who had their confidence, the Independents boldly called for 'complete democratisation of the whole constitution and government of the Reich and of its component states...a democratisation which will culminate in the creation of a socialist republic'.[2] That such demands could be openly made in the Reichstag was a sign of the times.

Haase used the opportunity to launch a general attack on the government, describing the new Chancellor, Michaelis, as the nominee of the supreme command and ridiculing the Reichstag majority for having accepted Michaelis after withdrawing their confidence from Bethmann Hollweg. The fact that the generals did not object to the peace resolution showed, Haase asserted, how worthless it was. Nor was there any guarantee that the promise of Prussian franchise reform would be kept. Finally Haase complained bitterly of the persecution to which Independent socialists were subject: newspapers suppressed, private meetings banned, spying by government officials, harsh prison sentences for rioters. A system of delation had grown up, said Haase, which recalled the worst days of the Roman empire. He warned the Reichstag:

The feeling of the people created by the leaden weight of hunger and martial law is such as to make even the most frivolous and optimistic reflect. You have read of the

[1] Bevan, *op. cit.* p. 187.   [2] *Ibid.*

riots and strikes in Upper and Lower Silesia. Do you think the masses can possibly endure such a state of things for long? Impossible! And when the crash comes, you have no right, at any rate, to be surprised. Every day the working classes come to understand better that if they are to achieve what they have at heart they must act. They will rise up against such conditions as these.[1]

Over a year was to elapse before Haase's warning came true. So long as Germany had a chance of winning the war, the home front held.

REFORMIST SOCIALISM AFTER THE SPLIT

Freed from the incubus of its rebellious left wing the S.P.D. at last felt united enough to hold a full-scale congress, the first for four years. This met at Würzburg in October 1917 and lasted nearly a week. Two hundred and eighty-two delegates including fifty-six Reichstag members attended.[2]

Yet the debates showed how heavily the problem of disunity weighed upon the party and darkened its future prospects. Landsberg, a lawyer of rather right wing views, warned of the consequences if socialists remained divided: 'Comrades, I am horrified to think that the next Reichstag elections will probably present the picture of two Social Democratic parties at daggers drawn. We all realise that those elections will determine the fate of Germany for at least the next fifty years.'[3] The split, said Landsberg, could benefit only their political opponents. It would also spread to the trade unions. Moreover the temper of the Independent socialists was such that they were resorting to sabotage. They had voted with the extreme right against an amendment to the constitution which would bring Germany nearer to parliamentary government. The people, he warned, would not tolerate such sterile tactics, and he stressed that, in spite of all differences, socialist reunification must be the long-term aim. This was also Ebert's view; he hoped that once the war was over, a better atmosphere would make reconciliation possible. Other speakers agreed that if the parties failed to unite, the masses would take matters into their own hands and insist on closing the breach. With only seven dissentient votes, the congress passed a resolution supporting all efforts at restoring socialist unity, though it did not suggest how this should be done other than through the minority returning to the fold by accepting the policy of the majority.[4]

The congress had also to consider relations with the parties to the right of the S.P.D., especially its partners in the newly formed Reichstag bloc. With this development in mind several speakers urged the S.P.D. to make explicit what its policy since August 1914 implied: that it was a reformist party,

---

[1] Bevan, *op. cit.* p. 193.

[2] *Ibid.* p. 240.

[3] *Prot. S.P.D.* (Würzburg, 1917), pp. 300 ff. Landsberg was to be one of the three majority socialist People's Commissars during the revolution.

[4] *Ibid.*

standing for organic evolution not revolutionary break. The logic of this position was willingness to accept office with non-socialist parties, the deviation formerly known as Millerandism. Some socialists at Würzburg, such as Winnig, a right wing trade unionist from Hamburg, wanted the S.P.D. to grasp the opportunity offered by the Reichstag bloc of co-operating with the middle parties in favour of a parliamentary system. The old revolutionary ballast should be thrown overboard:

It was our historical error to believe before the war, at a time of quiet organisational work and rising economic prosperity, in which the lower classes improved their situation by means of tough organisational work, that we should achieve something through a revolutionary ideology. A working class whose progress is guaranteed by organisational and parliamentary work will never let itself be persuaded to risk a revolution.[1]

Winnig went on to repeat a remark of Bernstein which Scheidemann had quoted in the debate, that the British working class had achieved its greatest success not 'in a time of revolutionary phrases' but when it collaborated with the radical wing of the bourgeoisie. It was in similar collaboration with non-socialist radicals that, Winnig suggested, the future of the S.P.D. should lie. The party was now strong enough not to fear losing its soul by co-operating with other parties.

Winnig's contribution to the debate showed a realism which had not been very common in the S.P.D., but it ignored some of the practical difficulties which made the analogy with Britain dangerously misleading: the half-hearted and opportunistic attitude to parliamentary government of the middle-class parties, the implacable hostility of Prussian conservatives, and behind the constitutional façade the dictatorship of Ludendorff. The risk the socialists ran was that in giving up revolutionary aspirations in return for co-operation with liberals they would exchange one shadow for another. They were still dogged by the unsolved problems of 1848.

Yet Scheidemann was optimistic:

During the war a shift of power has occurred to the advantage of the proletariat— a shift on the brink of which we are standing, and through the struggle of the masses, which has been going on amidst hostilities, Social Democracy has won quite a different status from what it had before the war. German democracy—I say it quite frankly—has become a party with a direct prospect of supremacy in the state...Germany after the war will be a parliamentary democratic state.[2]

Scheidemann went on to warn his colleagues against making a fetish of principle (*Prinzipienreiterei*) which had been a bugbear of the left wing doctrinaires, and added: 'We shall be of use only where and when we can show that socialist principles offer practical benefits to the masses.'

Inevitably, the question of war credits was discussed once again. A small

[1] *Ibid.* p. 368.   [2] *Ibid.*

group led by a Reichstag deputy named Hoch who had abstained from voting for them ever since August 1914 declared that the war was being unnecessarily prolonged by the Pan-Germans and that future war credits should be voted only if the government acted as the party wanted: in no other way could they force the government to see reason.[1] There was, however, little support for this view, and a pro-credits resolution was passed by a large majority. Ebert admitted that the Reichstag peace resolution had been a hollow victory. Yet most socialists adhered to the view which had now become traditional, that the vote was for the country not the government, and that nothing should be done which could bring about a German defeat.

The Würzburg congress took place between the Reichstag debate which sealed the fate of Chancellor Michaelis (9 October) and the appointment of Hertling as his successor three weeks later. But Scheidemann's claim that the party deserved credit for its part in the overthrow of Michaelis would be more impressive if the socialists had not acquiesced in the choice of a new Chancellor who, as we have seen, was hostile to both parliamentary government and the peace resolution. The congress was significant mainly because it registered the change that had occurred in the party's outlook during the three years of war. More clearly than ever before the S.P.D. showed that it had turned its back on revolutionary theory as well as practice, and that it was committed to the winning of parliamentary government in collaboration with its partners in the Reichstag bloc. Influenced by the 'war socialism' of rationing and controls, the S.P.D. leaders now conceived of socialisation as a gradual process leading to a mixed economy with a fairly large socialised sector. To this extent the congress represented a triumph for the right, one of whose leaders, Kolb, was at this time busy explaining to the bourgeoisie that the war had for the first time given the S.P.D. a positive attitude to the state. Many liberals agreed that the new S.P.D., shorn of its radicals and pacifists, was fit for partnership with other parties. Moreover the party's consistent voting of war credits and the large proportion of Social Democrats in the army seemed to guarantee its patriotism. Yet distrust on the side of the authorities remained. This was partly because at Würzburg the party leaders, including Ebert, had declared that the S.P.D. would stick to its principles and not abandon the class struggle, and partly because the new tactics were seen as temporary and liable to be changed again if public opinion veered in a revolutionary direction. The German government also feared that international influences would in time regain the upper hand over those of nationalism. This was an unduly suspicious attitude considering how few concessions the authorities had made to the S.P.D.; but it remains true that the party throughout the war pursued a wavering course between two con-

[1] *Prot. S.P.D.* (Würzburg, 1917), p. 339. Hoch's resolution was rejected by 257 votes to 26. See also Bevan *op. cit.* p. 247.

flicting aims. On the one hand it wanted to collaborate with the government and the moderate parties in order to secure reforms which, it believed, could not be indefinitely withheld; on the other hand it had to be radical enough to dissuade its millions of hungry and exhausted supporters from going over to the Independent socialists. In their visits to foreign countries the S.P.D. leaders had to defend Germany's war aims and constitution; at home they had to criticise them.[1] Their task was made harder by the government's failure to translate promises into action.

Meanwhile the S.P.D.'s decision at Würzburg in favour of collaboration with liberals was bitterly criticised by the Independents, who now had new grievances to nurse as well as the old. In July 1917 the S.P.D. had broken another socialist tradition of not 'going to court' by attending a reception for political leaders given by the Kaiser. Scheidemann, who ironically describes the incident in his *Memoirs*, noted that the Kaiser went out of his way to be affable to his socialist guests. The emperor was making a democratic gesture, the socialists were gradually achieving that integration into German society which had so long seemed beyond their reach. For the Independents it was one more example of the betrayal of principles. A more serious practical blow to the Independents was the loss of more newspapers and periodicals, which were seized by the S.P.D. and purged of their Independent staff. Two well-known left wing dailies, the *Bürgerzeitung* of Bremen and the *Volksfreund* of Brunswick, underwent this fate.[2] Then *Die Gleichheit*, a woman's magazine edited by the radical veteran Clara Zetkin, was taken over, and finally the S.P.D. expelled Kautsky from the *Neue Zeit* which he had edited since its foundation in 1883.[3] The left already suffered the handicap of severer censorship, and the loss to its rival of such well-known publications caused strong resentment. The only place where real freedom of speech was still possible was the Reichstag. There in November Haase, for the Independents, denounced the police and military dictatorship, and called for a return to international class war.[4] It is hard to say exactly what Haase meant by this, unless it was the general strike against the war which he had been reluctant to accept at the Stockholm conference of September.

[1] Bevan, *op. cit.* [2] *Ibid.* p. 156.
[3] *Ibid.* p. 154. Clara Zetkin, one of Germany's leading women socialists, had been a teacher in Saxony and married a Russian socialist, whom she outlived. She belonged to the following of Rosa Luxemburg and after 1920 was prominent as a Communist member of the Reichstag, whose 'Alterspräsidentin' she became in 1932. She died in Russia in 1933.
[4] Haase, *Reichstagsreden*, p. 131.

CHAPTER 6

GERMAN SOCIALISM IN THE
LAST YEAR OF THE WAR

Woe to the statesman who does not recognise the signs of the times.
BETHMANN HOLLWEG in 1917

THE TREATY OF BREST-LITOVSK

The period which began at the end of October 1917 with the appointment of Hertling as German Chancellor and ended a year later with the abdication of the Kaiser and the armistice was dominated, after the dictated peace of Brest-Litovsk, by Ludendorff's final attempt to win the war in the west. By July 1918 it was apparent that the offensive had failed, and in August the western powers began a series of counter-attacks which forced the German government to sue for peace early in October, at a time when its three allies were in a state of collapse. Internally the year saw no constitutional progress until, in consequence of military defeat, there occurred the hasty introduction of a parliamentary regime in place of the Bismarckian constitution and the *de facto* dictatorship of Ludendorff. A sign of the growing tension on the home front in the winter of 1917–18 was the mass strike of metal workers in January 1918 in protest against the terms of Brest-Litovsk and the failure of the German government to put into effect the reforms it had promised the year before. The pressures revealed by the strike were to erupt more forcefully ten months later. In the strike movement the Independent socialists played a leading, and the majority socialists a subsidiary part. In the constitutional changes that preceded the downfall of the imperial regime the majority socialists came to the rescue of the state by collaborating with the middle-class parties, while the Independent socialists remained implacably in opposition, their militant left wing being active behind the scenes in preparing for the revolution of November.

The drama of the last year of the war was played out on a larger stage than its predecessors. With America taking an increasing share of the military burden, the war had become more truly global; and the emergence of a Bolshevik government in Russia challenged the west with a more revolutionary ideology than it had ever known. The full impact of Bolshevism in power was not felt immediately, because when Lenin and Trotsky published the Tsar's secret treaties and proceeded to address the peoples over the heads of their governments, they did so in terms calculated to appeal to radical pacifists rather than to the far less numerous revolutionaries. The Bolshevik call for a just and democratic peace and denunciation of the hypocrisies of the old regime created a sensation in America, and evoked a sympathetic response in President Wilson, with whose thinking they largely coincided.[1] The result was the proclamation of the Fourteen Points as a statement of Allied war aims. Both Bolsheviks and Americans believed, it seemed, in open diplomacy, self-determination of peoples and an equitable peace. Yet the Bolsheviks could not long conceal their profound disagreement with liberal democracy, as was shown by their contemptuous dispersal of the Russian constituent assembly in January 1918, and by their appeals for world revolution. The Bolsheviks were convinced that only through the triumph of socialism in western and central Europe—and the only kind they recognised as valid was revolutionary socialism—could their own regime survive. The promotion of subversion everywhere thus became the Bolsheviks' principal aim. These two ideologies—the liberal Wilsonian, and the revolutionary Leninist—disputed for the leadership of a continent at war, giving a wider framework to the activities of German socialists.

The collapse of Russian military strength in 1917, which was confirmed by the failure of Brussilov's offensive in July, opened the Russian empire to the German army. Despite its weak bargaining position the new Bolshevik government was determined to fulfil its pledge to take Russia out of the war, with the agreement of the western allies if possible, without if not. A Russo-German armistice was signed on 15 December, and a week later peace negotiations began at the Polish town of Brest-Litovsk.[2] The German delegation was led by von Kühlmann, the new secretary of state to Hertling, and included as its senior military representative Major-General Hoffmann, commander-in-chief on the eastern front and representative of the supreme command. Disagreements between Kühlmann and Hoffmann, proponents of a 'soft' and 'hard' peace respectively, were usually settled in favour of Hoffmann, who could count on the backing of the Chancellor and the Kaiser. Austria-Hungary was represented by Count Czernin, the foreign minister, whose pessimism about his country's ability to survive another war winter made him a passionate advocate of peace at any price. The Russian delegation was initially headed by Joffe, the later ambassador to Germany, but in the second and succeeding stages of the talks he was superseded by the more dominating personality of Trotsky.

The story of the Brest negotiations is well known and can be briefly summarised. The Russians put forward the formula of peace without

---

[1] Carr, *The Bolshevik Revolution*, III, 13.
[2] The Bolsheviks did not consider themselves bound by the Tsarist government's treaty of 5 September 1914 with France and Britain, whereby all three powers agreed not to conclude a separate peace with Germany. But in their armistice with Germany of December 1917 the Bolsheviks insisted on the inclusion of a clause prohibiting the transfer of German troops from the eastern to the western front except in the case of those already under orders to go (*ibid.* p. 28).

annexations. The Germans said they accepted this, but refused to withdraw their troops from the parts of the Russian empire they occupied—Poland, Lithuania and Courland.[1] The Russians realised with a shock that the Germans were going to use some form of popular consultation in those territories as an excuse for annexation, and on 28 December the talks were broken off and each delegation returned to its capital to receive advice. Negotiations were resumed in a frosty atmosphere on 9 January. After fruitless discussion Hoffmann put an end to argument by saying bluntly that the German army would not abandon the territories it occupied and demanded west Latvia in addition. The Russians, now thoroughly disillusioned, again broke off. When they returned to the conference table on 30 January two delegations from the Ukraine—a nationalist and a Bolshevik—were present. On 8 February the Germans and Austrians signed a separate peace treaty with the nationalist Ukrainians (the *Rada*) whereby the former were to receive a quantity of grain and other foodstuffs. The cutting off of the Ukraine was a heavy blow to the Soviet state and deprived it of the greater part of Russia's industrial resources. On 10 February Trotsky, refusing to sign an ignominious peace but knowing that the Bolsheviks could not continue the war, made his famous 'Neither war nor peace' speech and stamped out of the conference. Kühlmann was prepared to accept this novel formula as signifying a *de facto* settlement, but the generals insisted on a formal treaty in order to safeguard their gains and persuaded the Chancellor and the Kaiser to take their side.[2] To force the Bolsheviks back to the conference table the German troops now resumed their advance into Russia. The Bolshevik leaders went through an agonising reappraisal of policy. When at length, having by a narrow margin followed Lenin's realistic but unpalatable advice to accept the German terms, the Russian delegation returned to the conference for the fourth and final stage of talks they found that the Germans now wanted more: the Russians were to evacuate Livonia and Estonia as well as the Ukraine. On 3 March the Russians signed the treaty feeling that, however humiliating its terms, they were the moral victors. Trotsky left Brest, Prince Max of Baden wrote later, as the martyr of the right of self-determination and the Germans as the bullies of small nations.[3]

Trotsky had used the conference table as a platform from which to rouse the peoples of the warring countries, and particularly of Germany and Austria, against their imperialistic governments and in favour of a democratic peace. The length of the negotiations with their frequent interruptions gave time, which he eagerly welcomed, for the revolutionary movement in Germany to gather its forces in support of the Bolsheviks. How much effect

---

[1] Courland later formed the southern part of Latvia, Livonia its north-eastern part.

[2] Carr, *The Bolshevik Revolution*, III, 38 quoting R. von Kühlmann, *Erinnerungen* (1948), p. 545.   [3] Prince Max of Baden, *Memoirs*, I, 223.

did Trotsky's appeals have?[1] The mass strikes in central Europe in the winter 1917–18 were largely a protest against the failure of the government to make an equitable peace with the Soviets. But the strikes did not seriously affect Germany's military strength, and the strikers' demands showed that while they wanted peace, they were far from being revolutionaries in the Bolshevik sense. Bolshevik propaganda was not without effect on German troops stationed on the eastern front, and especially on prisoners-of-war in Russia, for whose benefit a special magazine, *Die Fackel*, later renamed *Der Völkerfriede*, was issued by the Soviet government. But the influence of indoctrinated soldiers from the east on the German army in the west was to be of no more than marginal importance in undermining morale.[2] Trotsky had expected the population of Germany and Austria-Hungary to rise in revolt after his 'Neither war nor peace' declaration and prevent the resumption of hostilities. Lenin was rather more sceptical about the revolution in central Europe, but like all the Bolsheviks he exaggerated its chances. Not until after defeat were the masses receptive to Bolshevism, and then only a minority.

Meanwhile the Brest negotiations had come under close scrutiny from the German political parties. The proposed peace terms were discussed by the main committee of the Reichstag, several members of which, including Erzberger, had voted for the peace resolution the previous July. Erzberger persuaded himself that the testing of opinion in the territories occupied by the German army amounted to a genuine form of self-determination and not a veiled form of annexation.[3] Scheidemann alone for the S.P.D. protested against the incompatibility of the Brest terms with the peace resolution.[4] The Centre and even the Progressive parties thus abandoned the principles they had affirmed six months before. Hertling described the peace resolution (which he had opposed) as out of date, and the Reichstag agreed with him. When the treaty came up for ratification, Scheidemann repeated that his party could not vote for it because it had been imposed by force: only the genuine application of self-determination to the border peoples could establish friendship between them, Russia and Germany. Speaking with

---

[1] Kamenev, a leading Bolshevik, told the Central Committee of All-Russian Soviets that their words would reach the German people over the heads of the German generals and would strike from the hands of the generals the weapons with which they fooled the people (Carr, *op. cit.* p. 33).

[2] Discontented soldiers from the eastern front, in many cases repatriated prisoners-of-war, were sent, often against their will, as reinforcements to the west, where they were an obvious source of trouble to the military authorities. It is, however, not easy to distinguish this from other attested causes of low morale, such as hatred of officers, bad or inadequate food, the hardships of the home front and the influence of subversive propaganda, whether Allied or German. It was primarily the knowledge that the war was lost which made men unwilling to go on risking their lives; in these circumstances, the wonder is that morale remained as high as it did until the armistice. (Volkmann, *Der Marxismus*, pp. 162–6.)

[3] Epstein, *Erzberger*, p. 234.   [4] *Reichstag Inquiry*, VIII, 236.

the wisdom of foresight, Scheidemann said he hoped that his party would not come to power under circumstances which would compel them to conclude the kind of peace with the Entente which Lenin and Trotsky had had to accept from the Quadruple Alliance. Even Ebert, who was in favour of voting for the treaty, was perturbed by the proposed annexation to Germany of two million Poles through the extension of the frontier to the river Narew, and remarked to Scheidemann: 'Things are developing in such a way that we shan't be able to go along with them [the government] much longer.'[1] The socialists had already accepted the Ukraine treaty (the 'bread peace') on grounds of necessity. Before the Reichstag ratification of the Brest treaty the S.P.D. met and took their own vote: twelve opposed the treaty, twenty-five were in favour and twenty-nine abstained. In the chamber the party's voting was four in favour, with fifty-two abstentions and thirteen absentees.[2] Clearly the party was undecided in its attitude. Members realised that it was a dictated peace, which might well rebound on Germany at a future date: on the other hand, any peace was better than none, and the S.P.D. were loth to defy the supreme command or prejudice Germany's chances of victory. For similar reasons the S.P.D. was to vote for ratification of the treaty of Bucharest with Roumania later in the year.

In contrast to the doubts and hesitations of the majority socialists was the Independent socialists' unequivocal opposition to Brest-Litovsk. There had never been any doubt of their rejection of Ludendorff's plans for eastern Europe. As early as October 1917 Ledebour criticised the policy of annexations in the Baltic: 'In Riga, the largest German centre in the area, only 16 per cent of the population are German. Yet the German military commanders treated Riga as well as the entire region as German, thus laying the foundations for the permanent hostility of their populations to Germany.'[3] Haase also attacked the intention of annexing Lithuanians, Courlanders and Letts under the guise of self-determination, which he said was a mockery. The peoples of Russia had freed themselves and needed no liberation by Germany. Referring to the secret treaties between the Tsarist government and the Entente now published by the Bolsheviks, Haase said this was proof of what his party had always maintained—that the war was being fought for imperialistic ends. He can hardly have expected that the imperial German government would respond to his appeal to publish its own secret treaties. He concluded with a call for a general peace.[4]

When, after the break in the Brest talks in February 1918, the German government issued a new ultimatum to the Bolsheviks, Haase told the Reichstag that it would go down to history as a document of an exorbitant policy

[1] Scheidemann, *Memoirs*, II, 157.
[2] Heidegger, *Die deutsche Sozialdemokratie und der nationale Staat, 1870–1920*, p. 159.
[3] Berlau, *German Social Democracy, 1914–21*, p. 150.
[4] Haase, *Reichstagsreden gegen die Kriegspolitik*, pp. 117 ff.

of force and annexation.[1] He went on to denounce the farce of self-determination in the occupied territories, the breach with the Reichstag peace resolution and the harshness of the terms imposed on the Russians. German soldiers in the Ukraine were being made hangmen of the Russian revolution, and the treaty with the *Rada* was useless because the latter was a puppet government. The hope of permanently detaching the Ukraine from Russia was illusory.

Haase also urged the German government not to intervene in Finland (where civil war between reds and whites had begun) and criticised the decision to annex more Polish territory. His warning was prophetic:

So much can already be said with certainty, however much in the dark the future lies, that the way in which we are ending the war in the East will turn—and I especially emphasise this—to the harm of our own people.[2]

After quoting from the Swiss, Dutch and Danish press to show that neutral opinion condemned the treaty Haase continued:

Nowhere in the world after the experience of Brest-Litovsk will Germany's word be believed any more...The declared task of our policy was to break down distrust against Germany and regain confidence. The result of our eastern policy is, on the contrary, the increase of hate and fear. And it will lead to the prolongation of the war. As for the enemies against whom we are still fighting, their determination will be strengthened in order to prevent the policy of force from triumphing throughout the world, and all those who approve the means of continuing the war must share the responsibility for its prolongation.[3]

The real purpose of Brest-Litovsk, Haase asserted, was to throttle the Russian revolution, but in this it would not succeed. The treaty refuted those who, like Scheidemann, argued that the annexationists were unimportant. But few were willing to heed this Cassandra, and the Brest treaty was ratified by the Reichstag on 22 March, the day after the start of Ludendorff's offensive in the west.

The same opportunism which marked S.P.D. policy towards that treaty was noticeable in its attitude to other aspects of the war. *Vorwaerts* in November 1917, after the Italian defeat on the Isonzo, suggested that Germany's military success was the only obstacle to peace, but in January 1918 Scheidemann denied that Germany could win the war. In April, however, under the influence of Ludendorff's first victories in the west, *Vorwaerts* wrote of a complete and imminent German victory. A recent German historian has commented: 'Anyone who carefully reads through *Vorwaerts* and tries to imagine the effect of the articles addressed to the members of the party day by day cannot be surprised if he comes to the familiar conclusion that there was unsureness and a certain aimlessness in the whole party.'[4]

[1] *Ibid.* p. 133.   [2] *Ibid.* p. 140.   [3] *Ibid.* p. 161.
[4] Heidegger, *op. cit.* p. 186.

THE STRIKE OF JANUARY 1918

Indignation at the German government's failure to make a speedy peace with Soviet Russia on the basis of no annexations was the main though not the only motive behind the wave of strikes which occurred in central Europe in the winter of 1917–18. They began in Vienna and Budapest, where the tottering Habsburg empire was enduring a fourth war winter which many people had not expected it to survive. In Vienna food supplies were so reduced that the government had to send an urgent appeal to the Germans for grain in order to avert catastrophe. Germany's hopes of relieving its own acute shortage depended on how much food its army was able to extract from the farms of the Ukraine, where production had fallen during the war. The amount of grain yielded by the Ukraine turned out to be disappointingly small, and most of this had to go to Austria. Food scarcity was among the causes of the strikes.

The leadership behind the German strikes came from a well organised group of left wing shop-stewards in the metal industry known as the revolutionary *Obleute*.[1] These shop-stewards, instigated by Richard Müller (who was to play an important part in the German revolution) had broken away from the policy of collaborating with the government which the metal workers' union, like other German trade unions, had more or less willingly followed since the beginning of the war. The shop-stewards thus formed a militant opposition to the official trade unions in much the same way as earlier in the war the *Arbeitsgemeinschaft* had done to the S.P.D. By March 1916 the metal workers' union had already split into two groups with the opposition in the majority, but Adolf Cohen, a pro-government man, managed to remain union president. Both the Independent socialists and the Spartacists tried to draw the dissident shop-stewards under their wing, but without success, for the stewards did not want the industrial split to take on a political character.[2] The government kept a sharp eye on the shop-stewards and in April 1917, just before the strike in that month began, Müller was called up for military service though he was in fact unfit. Cohen succeeded in keeping the strike non-political.[3] But in the winter of 1917–18 war weariness, privation and resentment at the government's tactics at Brest-Litovsk combined to shift the balance among the metal workers in favour of the extremists.

In the middle of January 1918 the leaders of the shop-stewards, including Müller who had now returned to civilian life, met the executive committee of the Independent socialist party to discuss a political mass strike. The Sparta-

[1] For the origin and growth of the *Obleute* see R. Müller's own history of the German Revolution, *Vom Kaiserreich zur Republik*, I, pp. 55 ff., 78 ff.
[2] *Ibid.* p. 66.
[3] *Ibid.* p. 82.

cists were not invited because the stewards feared their propensity to adopt putsch tactics.[1] The meeting was divided: one section was enthusiastically in favour of striking, another was opposed. The third and largest section, led by Haase, considered the strike justified as a means of forcing the government to make peace, but recognised that the Independent socialist party could not call a strike without risking its existence. (The party had narrowly escaped being outlawed as a result of its connection with the naval mutiny a few months before.) Finally, however, a manifesto was agreed on which called on all workers in Germany to go on strike and this was distributed as a handbill. The strike was carefully organised. On Monday 28 January some 400,000 workers in Berlin downed tools. The strikers' main object was peace; they also demanded workers' representation in peace negotiations, better food, the abolition of martial law and a democratic regime in Germany with equal franchise in Prussia. They appealed to the proletariat of all belligerent countries to join them and so put an end to the war.[2]

A strike committee was formed consisting of eleven representatives of the shop-stewards and three Independent socialists. The S.P.D. were invited to send three delegates; it agreed to do so but refused to endorse all the demands. A meeting of strike leaders attended by Ebert, Scheidemann and Braun of the S.P.D. was broken up by the police, much to their embarrassment.[3] Next day another 100,000 men joined the strike. The committee appointed a commission to negotiate with the government, for this was a political strike, not directed against the employers. The government agreed to meet the commission's political representatives but not the others, a distinction the commission refused to recognise. The government also forbade further meetings of the strike leaders. Meanwhile clashes between strikers and police led to casualties, damage and arrests. The strike had now reached the point at which it must either back its demands by force or accept the government's terms for negotiations.[4] The government made a concession by consenting to negotiate with the strike commission provided official delegates of the trade unions took part. The strike leaders now had to choose between continuing talks on this basis, the course recommended by Haase and the S.P.D.; going on with the strike in defiance of the authorities, as desired by the Spartacists; and calling off the strike without having achieved any result. The shop-stewards chose the third course, and the strike ended after a week. Its continuation in Berlin would have been an isolated effort, as by this time most of the supporting strikes that had broken out in the main provincial centres had been called off.[5]

---

[1] *Ibid.* p. 102.
[2] *Ibid.* p. 103. Scheidemann wrote that things had recently got worse: the censorship was stricter, workers' meetings were forbidden. There was also some discontent at the Chancellor's answer to Wilson's Fourteen Points. (*Zusammenbruch*, pp. 67–8.)
[3] R. Müller, *Vom Kaiserreich*, p. 104. [4] *Ibid.* p. 107. [5] *Ibid.* pp. 107–11.

The strike had failed in its purpose of forcing the government to change its policies; but it was hailed as an achievement by the left, for it had been an impressive demonstration of solidarity, and both the spirit and organisation of the participants remained unbroken.[1] Among those arrested was Dittmann, who (like Ebert) had spoken at a strikers' meeting in a Berlin park and was sentenced to five years' detention. Haase described the strike in the Reichstag (which characteristically did not meet while it was on, despite S.P.D. wishes) as one of the greatest events in German working-class history.[2] Affecting about a million workers and their families, it was the last widespread manifestation of popular discontent before the November revolution. Many of the January strike leaders were drafted into the army or navy, where they spread revolutionary ideas—which bore fruit in days to come. Nevertheless, the German revolution would never have taken place but for military defeat, and very little of the revolutionary spirit was to be observed among civilians or soldiers during the next few months, when Ludendorff's initially successful offensive revived hopes of victory.

In the key role played by revolutionary shop-stewards, in the contrast between illegal acts and moderate demands, and in the equivocal attitude of the majority socialists, the January mass strike foreshadowed the greater upheaval of November. The S.P.D. were in a quandary. This was the first time the party had taken part in a strike during the war, and they did so now in order to control it. On the one hand they loyally supported the war effort; on the other hand they could hardly ignore the popular demand for policies which were almost identical with their own, nor could they afford to leave the field to their more radical rivals. The resolution passed by the S.P.D. executive committee on 30 January was a delicate compromise. It asserted the necessity for the strike and denied that it endangered national defence, but declared that it must not get out of hand.[3] Writing in *Vorwaerts* shortly after the strike was called off, Braun sought to restore the somewhat tarnished image of his party in the eyes of right wing critics by promising that they would have nothing to do with methods of violence, which were Bolshevik and repugnant to the S.P.D.[4] Thus the majority socialists seemed to have walked the tight-rope successfully.

The main organisational link between the January strike and the November revolution was the shop-stewards' committee which, after Müller's second recall to the army, came under the chairmanship of one of the most militant of the younger shop stewards, Emil Barth. Barth addressed the committee in

---

[1] Dittmann describes the incident in ch. 13 of his memoirs (*Lebenserinnerungen*).
[2] Haase, *Reichstagsreden*, p. 150. Kautsky issued a handbill listing the achievements of the strike. But Mehring took a more sceptical view. Never, he wrote, had an undefeated military state renounced its conquests. See his *Kriegsartikel* (1918), p. 78.
[3] R. Müller, *Vom Kaiserreich*, p. 208.
[4] Heidegger, *op. cit.* p. 184.

a speech full of revolutionary rhetoric in which he indicated its future task: 'The objective is proletarian peace, i.e. a peace imposed by the proletariat, that is socialism, that is the dictatorship of the proletariat.'[1] Barth, who had a lively imagination, saw himself as the chief of staff of the coming revolution, and set about collecting arms and money. He knew that a rising would have no chance as long as the German army was undefeated, but he seems to have expected its defeat. He later claimed that he began training the first 'shock troops' in the summer of 1918. Barth was to receive help from the Russian embassy after its reopening in April. He maintained close ties with Ledebour and Däumig among Independent socialist leaders. Relations between shop-stewards and Spartacists remained cool, Barth and his friends distrusting the latter as too inclined to sporadic and premature risings.

It was another Independent socialist who, reviewing the January strike and the Brest-Litovsk ultimatum against the background of Bolshevik revolution in Russia and continuing war in the west, issued a warning to those who considered Germany immune from the revolutionary virus:

The revolution, which has begun in Russia, will spread to Germany. And if the princes and statesmen do not know how to end the war on the lines of a peace of understanding which will reconcile the peoples, then the peoples themselves will end the war. I hail the day when this shall come to pass. I hail the day when peoples will take their destinies into their own hands against the princes and statesmen, against militarism, above all against German militarism.[2]

THE 'REVOLUTION FROM ABOVE'

Serious though the metal workers' strike was as a mark of public discontent and as a challenge to the government's authority, it did not interfere with the army commanders' plans for the spring offensive. Ludendorff had decided to make this supreme effort, the last of which Germany would be capable, before American reinforcements could give the Allies numerical superiority. A number of prominent civilians, including Prince Max of Baden, whom some had wished to see made Chancellor instead of Hertling, viewed Luden-dorff's plans with dismay. They advocated the alternative policy of continued defence accompanied by a genuine effort to end the war by negotiation while Germany was still, as it seemed, militarily impregnable and capable, should negotiations fail, of striking a powerful blow. As the Kaiser's cousin and

[1] Barth, *Aus der Werkstatt der deutschen Revolution* (1919), p. 24. Barth was one of the most controversial figures in the revolutionary period. The most radical member of the Council of People's Commissars during the revolution, Barth was one of the small group of left wing Independents who never became a Communist. He had served several prison sentences and his personal reputation was unsavoury, but he showed considerable shrewdness and courage in politics. His account of the revolution is known to be unreliable but contains important first-hand evidence.

[2] Oskar Cohn in the Reichstag (*Verhandlungen*, 22 February 1918, vol. 311, pp. 4,081 ff.).

with a reputation for humanitarianism gained through his work as head of the German Red Cross, Max had the ear of the government, and he appealed to the Chancellor to make Ludendorff stay his hand.[1] Hertling refused, though his state secretary, Kühlmann, had no faith in the promised victory. Nor was Payer, the Progressive politician who had been made Vice-Chancellor the previous autumn and was supposed to represent the left, prepared to interfere with the general's plans. Finally a memorandum, representing the views of Prince Max and signed by, among others, Friedrich Naumann the 'national socialist', and two trade union leaders, Legien and Stegerwald, and urging that before the offensive was launched Germany should make an unambiguous promise to restore Belgium, was presented to Ludendorff himself.[2] Its sponsors believed that if such an offer was made and rejected, it would at least throw on the Allies responsibility for prolonging the war, unite the German people behind the government, and strengthen the peace movement in Allied countries. On 19 February, a few days after this appeal had been sent to Ludendorff, Prince Max went to see him at Bad Kreuznach, and asked him bluntly what would happen if the offensive failed. 'In that case', was the reply, 'Germany must just go under.'[3] Ludendorff's whole behaviour during his period of power showed that a negotiated peace had no place in his calculations; he believed only in victory or defeat. He had no valid answer to Prince Max's argument that it would be better to negotiate from strength than to risk the loss of the last reserves. Max described Ludendorff's attitude as that of a fatalist. But there were few people in Germany who did not believe the army capable of the task assigned to it by its commanders. The political parties did not interfere with Ludendorff's gamble, which was to cost Germany 600,000 casualties. Only the Independent socialists remained adamant in their opposition, refusing to vary their war aims according to the chances of victory.

At first Ludendorff's offensive went well. The British were driven back to a depth of fifty miles, torn apart from the French, and the fifth army was smashed. But the breach was not complete, and the Allies held grimly on and unified their command under Foch, who flung in French reserves to plug the gap. In April Ludendorff delivered his second blow, on the river Lys in Flanders; again the Germans broke through but lacked the strength to exploit their success. In May came the third thrust against the French on the Chemin des Dames, but this too proved strategically fruitless. The great offensive had spent its force and failed to gain its objective. Every week that passed saw a lowering of the German reserves and an increase in Allied strength, thanks to the American troops who rose from 300,000 in March to

---

[1] Prince Max of Baden, *Memoirs*, I, 252.

[2] *Ibid.* p. 254. Ex-Chancellor Bethmann Hollweg also implored Hertling to make a 'clear statement' on Belgium before the offensive was launched, but without success.

[3] *Ibid.* p. 258.

over a million by 1 July. A more prudent and less obstinate general than Ludendorff would have decided to ask for peace terms while the German army was still in possession of its new gains and not yet hopelessly outnumbered. It was to rouse the country to face facts that Kühlmann made a speech in the Reichstag on 24 June in which he declared that the war could not be won by military action and that a negotiated peace must be sought. The background to this speech, which was really a call to return to the peace resolution policy, was a memorandum by Colonel von Haeften, head of the military department of the German foreign office, recommending such a course. The memorandum had been seen and even approved by Ludendorff, who, however, now denounced Kühlmann for trying to undermine his authority and insisted to the Kaiser on his dismissal.[1] Although the Kaiser privately agreed with his foreign minister, he gave way as so often before to the supreme command. Nor did the Chancellor defend his colleague, though he too had been warned at the beginning of June by Crown Prince Rupprecht of Bavaria, who commanded an army group on the western front, that Germany could no longer win the war and that peace talks must begin.[2] The Reichstag parties accepted 'Ludendorff's show of force, and the Vice-Chancellor also made no protest. The S.P.D. showed some signs of impatience when on 3 July Scheidemann announced that, for the first time, his party would refuse to vote war credits, but Ebert brought them back to their old course in a speech arguing that, however much they objected to the Pan-Germans (whose victim Kühlmann had been) the terms of peace offered by the Allies were still more objectionable.[3]

Ludendorff's victory over Kühlmann was his last, for his political power depended on his military prestige, which was now in decline. A German thrust over the Marne in mid-July, which renewed the threat to Paris, led to unexpected disaster when Foch successfully counter-attacked. This reverse marked, as perceptive observers noted at the time, the turn of the tide: the German army could no longer enforce its will on the enemy. Yet not until after a British break-through with tanks near Albert on 8 August inflicted a sharp defeat would Ludendorff abandon his offensive plans. But by now even a successful defence was beyond Germany's powers. There were signs of cracking morale: troops gave themselves up, and for the first time incoming reinforcements were mockingly hailed as strike-breakers. On 14 August the Kaiser held a Crown Council to 'strike the balance'. Hindenburg, Ludendorff and the Chancellor were present. The generals, especially Ludendorff, still refused to admit the whole truth, but enough was said to have convinced a more alert Chancellor than Hertling that the war was lost. The Council

---

[1] *Ibid.* p. 308.
[2] *Reichstag Inquiry*, VIII, 280.
[3] *Ibid* p. 177; Ebert, *Schriften, Aufzeichnungen, Reden*, II, 62.

decided that the government should negotiate for peace through a neutral power 'at the right moment'. In fact that moment had passed. Yet more valuable time was lost. On 25 August the supreme command was asked by the government, deferential as usual, to agree to a peace proposal which included the unconditional restoration of Belgium, but this was still more than Ludendorff would accept.[1] The Allies, however, now realised the plight of Germany and of her allies, whose power of resistance had been undermined by the failure of Germany's offensive. On all fronts the situation changed rapidly in favour of the Entente. By the middle of September the German army had lost all its conquests since March and was back on the Siegfried line, its main line of defence. Austria was suing for an armistice. By the end of the month Bulgaria had collapsed and the Siegfried line had been breached.

Meanwhile, despite attempts by the supreme command to minimise the seriousness of the military situation, morale both at the front and at home had been dealt a staggering blow by the realisation that the war was lost. The shock was all the greater because hitherto the censorship had suppressed unpalatable facts, and it was particularly marked on the political right, where belief in Germany's invincibility had been unquestioned. People's nerves snapped. The physical and moral strain, the iron discipline accepted for over four years in the hope of ultimate victory, had now become intolerable. In the army confidence had gone and the number of deserters grew. Sheer exhaustion caused by continuous fighting and lack of reserves added to the burden; but most of the troops continued to resist tenaciously, even if they were sustained only by the courage of despair. Inside Germany there was a run on the banks, talk of collapse on the home front and mutterings of revolution.[2] The Hertling government, its credit exhausted, was wholly incapable of dealing with the situation. Ludendorff told the Chancellor that the government must ask for an armistice in 24 hours: the army could not wait. The sudden ultimatum horrified the Kaiser and Hertling and stunned the party leaders, though some of the socialists, like Scheidemann, seem to have been prepared for it. Even more surprising was Ludendorff's other *volte face*, when he told the Chancellor that the government must be reorganised on a broader basis, by which he meant the introduction of a parliamentary regime. A new Chancellor had to be found in a hurry. The Kaiser announced to his subjects his wish that 'men who are supported by the confidence of the people shall participate to a larger extent in the rights and duties of government'.

---

[1] *Reichstag Inquiry*, VIII, 308.

[2] G. Mayer, *Erinnerungen* (1949), p. 301. In his memoirs Ludendorff admits that the war should have been ended after 8 August. Scheidemann told the main committee of the Reichstag at the end of September: 'In a week workers' and soldiers' councils may be sitting in this hall' (Max, *Memoirs*, I, 362).

The new Chancellor was Prince Max of Baden. As heir to the most progressive German state, president of the Baden upper house, a liberally minded public figure and an expounder of 'ethical imperialism' Max was not without some qualifications for the office, but he was hardly the ideal man to head Germany's first parliamentary government, especially in the very radical mood of October 1918. He symbolised the transition to democracy, not its full attainment. The new government contained men of the Centre, Progressives and (for the first time) Social Democratic parties—the Reichstag bloc of July 1917. But it also retained ministers who were not in the Reichstag, such as Solf, secretary of state for foreign affairs, and Scheüch, minister of war. It did not include the conservatives, despite their readiness to serve even under the changed conditions, for Prince Max knew that their unpopularity both at home and abroad was a liability, and that the socialists would not join a government that included them.[1] Socialist participation was, indeed, far from a foregone conclusion. When the question was first mooted in the S.P.D. there was a good deal of opposition. Some, like Scheidemann, were against coming to the rescue of a 'bankrupt concern' and assuming responsibility for the consequences of policies they had disapproved; they also resented the choice of a prince as Chancellor. Others, including Ebert, urged that to join the government was their patriotic duty.[2] Just before the meeting of the parliamentary socialist party Ebert had been present at a meeting of leaders of all political parties at which a spokesman of the supreme command had for the first time given them the truth about Germany's military defeat. The effect on Ebert had been crushing. Speaking with deep emotion, he won over the support of the majority of his colleagues. The reasons for his attitude were later summarised in a speech in the Reichstag that deserves quotation:

Certainly it would have been more comfortable for us to stand aside and wash our hands in innocence. But in the German people's hour of destiny such a policy could never be justified before history, before the nation and before the German working class. We joined the government because what is at stake today is the whole nation, its future, its existence or non-existence...We know what we have risked by taking this step. But if we succeed by our decision in shortening the horror of war by only a few days, and thereby save the lives of tens of thousands, that would be justification and satisfaction enough...[3]

Yet it was Scheidemann, and Bauer, a trade union leader, who joined the government: Scheidemann as minister without portfolio, Bauer in charge of the newly formed labour ministry. The S.P.D. insisted on six conditions,

---

[1] Max, *Memoirs*, II, 14. Max did not include in his government the National Liberals, whose leaders, such as Stresemann, had been loud in support of annexations.

[2] Scheidemann, *Memoirs*, II, 159. In joining the government the majority socialists were more interested in bringing the war to an end than in starting on a programme of reform.

[3] Ebert, *op. cit.* II, pp. 90–1 (speech of 22 October 1918).

some of which had already been overtaken by events: return to the policy of the peace resolution of 1917; restoration of Belgium with reparations; democratic government in the territories occupied by Germany under the treaties of Brest-Litovsk and Bucharest; modification of martial law and the censorship; the government to be made responsible to the Reichstag; equal franchise in all German states.[1]

The introduction of parliamentary government involved radical alteration of the constitution, and the necessary legislation, retrospective in effect, was hastily prepared for enactment by the compliant Reichstag. In the national emergency technical and legal obstacles, which in the past had seemed almost insurmountable, were quickly disposed of. The main difference was that the Reichstag replaced the federal council or *Bundesrat* as the source of authority, the latter becoming a kind of upper chamber. It was laid down that the Chancellor must have the confidence of the Reichstag, that the Reichstag must approve all declarations of war and conclusions of peace, and that the appointment of officers must be approved by the minister of war, or the Chancellor in the case of the higher ranks. Thus William II became a parliamentary monarch, Ludendorff ceased to be a dictator, and for the first time in Prussian history the army was made subordinate to parliamentary authority.[2]

Had these changes preceded military defeat, and had they come through popular pressure instead of the will of Ludendorff, they could have made the desired impression at home and abroad which in the event they completely failed to do.[3] Clearly the new government still bore, as has been noticed, many marks of compromise: its head was not an elected parliamentarian, the balance of parties in the cabinet did not reflect their strength in the Reichstag, Prussia still lacked equal franchise, martial law and censorship continued in force, men associated with the policies of Brest-Litovsk and annexations were still in office. Prince Max, though a man of excellent intentions, lacked both the political experience and the physical toughness needed at this critical juncture. He was forced to lean heavily on the advice of officials and

---

[1] Scheidemann, *Memoirs*, II, 158.

[2] *Reichstag Inquiry*, VIII, 198 ff. Prince Max found it significant that the S.P.D. did not demand parliamentary government after the French pattern (*Memoirs*, I, 359).

[3] In a leader of 4 October headed 'The German Crisis' *The Times* opined that the change of government would make no real difference as Germany's real rulers would still be the military clique and the Kaiser. Max was not a democrat, Payer (who remained Vice-Chancellor) was a nationalist who had supported Brest-Litovsk, and there was little sign of moral regeneration or purpose of reform. The new government was 'political scene-shifting and nothing more'. Napoleon too, *The Times* acidly recalled, had been a liberal in his Hundred Days. Lloyd George later referred to the introduction of parliamentary government in Germany as a 'dummy façade': 'The hands might be sketchily gloved in a democratic pelt, but the voice was the voice of Ludendorff' (*War Memoirs*, p. 1,959). The impending dismissal of Ludendorff was to show that things had altered more than *The Times* believed; but it is significant that as late as 12 September 1918 Payer had made a public speech against the Fourteen Points (Max, *Memoirs*, II, 22).

friends (especially of Kurt Hahn) and this irked some of his cabinet colleagues.[1] As an armistice negotiator and parliamentary leader Max was badly compromised by his past support for annexations and antipathy for democracy, revealed when a Swiss newspaper published a private letter he had written the previous January. Scheidemann regarded this letter as so damaging that he wanted to resign and had to be persuaded by Ebert to remain so as not to create further difficulties.[2] Not the least of the ironies of the situation was that the Reichstag owed its new powers to a dictator who had consistently treated it as his tool. Ludendorff had several motives. No doubt he was anxious to shuffle off responsibility for the lost war on to civilian shoulders. He also knew of President Wilson's declarations that America could have no confidence in a Germany ruled by autocrats and militarists, the implication being that a parliamentary Germany could expect more lenient terms of peace.

Ludendorff had a third motive: popular government, he hoped, would unify the country, raise morale and enable last-ditch resistance to be organised more effectively.[3] Logically it could be argued that he should have introduced democracy earlier so as to reap its benefits while victory was still possible. It is hard to say how far the government's failure to enforce Prussian franchise reform alienated opinion; it probably had little influence on the soldiers at the front, who were more concerned with immediate needs and with the shortage of food and tobacco. But that it was a sore point among the civilian population is shown by the frequent references to it in Reichstag debates, in socialist speeches and in the strike movement. There can be little doubt that the inclusion of liberal and socialist leaders in a reconstructed government—an equivalent of the French *union sacrée*—would have helped the German war effort. Stresemann urged such a course on Ludendorff in 1917, apparently receiving a sympathetic answer.[4] But Ludendorff knew that his extreme advocacy of annexations was unacceptable to most of the socialists, and with his overbearing nature he could hardly have shared power with a strong popular government. The ineffective Hertling suited him much better. The one senior general who was far-sighted enough to read the signs of the times was Groener, a genuinely 'social general', who favoured franchise reform and wanted the S.P.D. to join the government in 1917. But having incurred the disapproval of Ludendorff, he was posted that summer to the eastern front. When he returned a year later the war was lost.

---

[1] Kurt Hahn was later to achieve greater fame as the founder and headmaster of Salem School in Baden and, after 1933, of Gordonstoun in Scotland.

[2] Scheidemann, *Memoirs*, II, 173 ff.

[3] *Reichstag Inquiry*, VIII, 199; Rosenberg, *Birth of the German Republic* (1931), pp. 141–2.

[4] Heidegger, *op. cit.* p. 120. Stresemann had spoken in the Reichstag in favour of parliamentary government on 29 March 1917. *Reichstag Inquiry*, VII, i, p. 11. As for morale in the army, 'a menu from an officers' club might excite more bitterness than an order to attack which cost thousands of lives and achieved nothing' (Theodor Wolff, *Through two Decades* (1936), p. 121).

When Prince Max accepted the Chancellorship at the beginning of October he knew he would have to ask for an armistice, but he had expected to have time to prepare the ground. Instead, he was told to approach Wilson immediately, for the army, Hindenburg warned, could not wait twenty-four hours. This urgency fatally weakened the Chancellor's bargaining position, but there was no alternative; the Kaiser supported the generals. Max's First Note to Wilson despatched via Switzerland, had therefore to be drafted within a few hours of his taking office. It asked for the immediate conclusion of an armistice on the basis of the President's Fourteen Points in his Message to Congress of 8 January 1918 with subsequent additions. Max told the Reichstag that Germany wanted a peace compatible with her honour, but as the exchange of Notes across the Atlantic proceeded prospects of a lenient armistice receded. The demand in Wilson's First Note (8 October) for German evacuation of occupied France and Belgium meant that she would be deprived of her chief bargaining assets. But Max dared not refuse. Wilson's Second Note (14 October) was noticeably harsher in tone. It demanded guarantees of Allied military superiority, an end of the submarine campaign (the *Leinster* had just been torpedoed in the Irish Sea) and denounced 'arbitrary power' in Germany. Wilson's Third Note (23 October) practically required the abdication of the Kaiser and indicated that otherwise the armistice would be imposed not negotiated. The Germans now realised that the terms would be humilating as well as severe.

The Kaiser's future had for some time been the subject of lively speculation in the German press, and even in conservative and monarchist circles there was a growing feeling that he must sacrifice himself for the sake of the nation. By 15 October Prince Max doubted if even the dynasty could survive, but as the Kaiser's first minister, loyal subject and cousin he was determined to do his best to save it. In this task he saw the Social Democrats, ironically, as his allies.[1] The Kaiser's change of role from autocrat to parliamentary monarch had come too late to retrieve his reputation. For Wilson and the Allies he was still the embodiment of Prussian militarism, the man who had plunged Europe into war, instigated the Belgian atrocities and the ruthless submarine campaign, the ogre of a thousand caricatures. His self-effacing role since August 1914 was hardly noticed. Nevertheless, William II could probably still have saved his dynasty if he had abdicated in time; by postponing a decision he destroyed any chances of a Hohenzollern successor and also failed to propitiate Wilson and the Allies.

Prince Max was in a dilemma. If the Kaiser did not go, his government was doomed. Owing to what Max Weber called his 'dynastic sentimentality',

---

[1] Max, *Memoirs*, II, 85-6. 'Thank God I have in the Social Democrats allies on whose loyalty towards me I can entirely rely. With their help I hope to save the Kaiser. Such is the irony of fate.' Payer told Max: 'The keenest on overthrowing the Emperor are the respectable citizens' (Scheidemann, *Memoirs*, II, 215).

and handicapped by severe influenza, Max failed to act with the ruthlessness the situation demanded, as he afterwards admitted. He took every opportunity of inducing the Kaiser to abdicate by sending him reports of public criticism and by pressing his views on the Kaiser's closest advisers, while still insisting that abdication must be a voluntary act. These methods were useless; the Kaiser was deaf. On 29 October the Chancellor at last made up his mind to go to the Kaiser himself when the astonishing news arrived that William was leaving for army headquarters at Spa in Belgium that evening. Max rang up William and entreated him as his cousin to stay, but in vain; the Kaiser was adamant, alleging that his presence at Spa was urgently needed. Perhaps if Max had threatened to resign the Kaiser would have remained, and a more determined Chancellor would not have hesitated to do so. William had ceased to play the unfamiliar part of a constitutional monarch. He knew that among his generals he would be safer and shielded from hostile public opinion; what he did not know was that even in the army loyalty to him had almost reached breaking point. The Chancellor was left in Berlin to face the storm alone.

The same evening (29 October) Max received a private letter from Scheidemann calling on him to 'advise' the Kaiser to abdicate in order to mitigate the terms of the armistice. This, Scheidemann wrote, was the conviction of the majority of the German people. Still playing for time, Max persuaded Scheidemann to withdraw the letter so as to give him one more opportunity of 'arranging' the abdication.[1] An appeal from Max to William next day received a brusque answer. When, at the Chancellor's instigation, the Prussian minister of the interior, Drews, made a special journey to Spa to plead with the Kaiser on 1 November, he was accused of insolence and effrontery. If he abdicated, said William indignantly, none of his sons would take his place, all the dynasties in Germany would fall, the army would lose its chief and Germany be given over to chaos. According to the Kaiser's own account of this highly unorthodox interview, he still assumed that the demand for his abdication came from a revolutionary minority, not from the majority of his subjects, nor does he appear to have considered the possible effect of abdication on the armistice terms. Germany was already on the brink of chaos, for the first signs of naval mutiny at Kiel had in fact appeared. On 7 November the Social Democrats told the Chancellor in a formal ultimatum that unless the Kaiser abdicated the following day they would leave the government.[2] Max knew he could not survive without them, but he also knew that if the majority socialists did not go with the tide they would lose their followers to the Independents. The revolution was now in full flood in many parts of Germany. Still no word of abdication came from Spa.

[1] Max, *Memoirs*, II, 233.
[2] *Ibid.* p. 279.

The Kaiser's obduracy was driving the country into the very 'Bolshevism' which he feared.

While the future of the Hohenzollerns hung by a thread, the lesser Ludendorff crisis also reached its climax. By the middle of October Ludendorff, having recovered from his panic mood of late September, took a calmer and less pessimistic view of Germany's military prospects. On 17 October he told the Chancellor privately that the government ought to take a tougher line in its negotiations with Wilson because it would not matter if they were broken off; Germany would be able to get better terms next year. But this attempt to undo the consequences of his ultimatum three weeks before was unsuccessful. Ludendorff's military judgement was no longer regarded as infallible, and the war cabinet agreed that, as one minister expressed it, the supreme command, having vainly tried to use diplomacy to avert military catastrophe, was now advocating military catastrophe rather than the acceptance of an unpalatable armistice.[1] When Ludendorff demanded more reinforcements from the home front Scheidemann denied that such recruits as were available could bolster army morale. And when Ludendorff complained of civilian morale Scheidemann replied:

That is a question of potatoes. We have no more meat. Potatoes cannot be delivered because we are short of 4,000 trucks a day. Fat is absolutely unobtainable. The want is so great that to me it is just a riddle what North and East Berlin live on... The workmen are more and more inclined to say: Better a horrible end than an endless horror.[2]

The population was too exhausted to respond to the *levée en masse* which Rathenau and others advocated as a way of rallying the nation's last energies. The popular mood was strongly in favour of accepting almost any terms in order to end the war. On 28 October the patriotic S.P.D. newspaper *Vorwaerts* abandoned the cause of national defence, and Käthe Kollwitz, the socialist artist, expressed the mood of many people when she declared: 'Seed corn must not be milled. Enough of death, not one more man must fall.' It was in this atmosphere that Prince Max had to negotiate with an antagonist who had no illusions about the internal state of Germany.

The final breach between Max and Ludendorff came after the receipt of Wilson's Third Note. Ludendorff had reacted sharply to Wilson's Second Note which, by demanding military guarantees against any resumption of the war by Germany, nullified Ludendorff's plan of using the armistice as a breathing space to regroup the army for further resistance on the German

---

[1] Max, *Memoirs*, II, 139. In a memorandum on Ludendorff and the armistice negotiations Max wrote that while it was appropriate for an individual to choose to die honourably, a responsible statesman must recognise that the people as a whole had a right to prefer an unheroic life to a glorious death (*War Cabinet*, 17 October 1918).

[2] *Ibid.* p. 114.

frontier. This amounted in fact to unconditional surrender since it undermined what remained of Germany's bargaining position. Ludendorff decided that the Third Note, which added insult to injury, must be rejected, and issued an order to the army to that effect. But this was too much for Prince Max, who made up his mind to get rid of the truculent general, a step for which Ludendorff conveniently prepared the way by threatening to resign if his advice was rejected. On 26 October Ludendorff received his formal dismissal from the Kaiser in a stormy interview. Hindenburg, who was less compromised, stayed. Ludendorff's dismissal has been described as the first great test of the new system of government.[1] But its significance was overshadowed by other events, and to the world at large the Kaiser remained the chief stumbling block. 'If the Kaiser goes', said Noske, 'we'll get a decent peace.'[2] The Times wrote on 28 October that Ludendorff's dismissal was designed to persuade people that a new era had begun in Germany; this was clearly not The Times' own opinion. But the significance of Ludendorff's departure was underlined by the almost simultaneous announcement that Karl Liebknecht had been released from prison and welcomed back to Berlin by his supporters.

THE EVE OF THE NOVEMBER REVOLUTION

If the revolution from above came too late to save the Kaiser it also came too late to avert the revolution from below—that spontaneous, popular upheaval in which exasperation, war-weariness and genuine revolutionary enthusiasm all played a part. In such organisational preparation as existed the Independent socialists were prominent, especially in the 'revolutionary committee' of Barth and his militant shop-stewards, which became more active as the day of reckoning approached. More important was the general moral or psychological influence of the party on public opinion, especially in the last weeks before the armistice, when the old order's metamorphosis seemed due to a failure of nerve rather than a change of heart. As for the majority socialists, now a government party, they followed the public mood instead of forming it. As late as 3 October Vorwaerts warned against a premature armistice and not until 20 October did it admit defeat. Right up to the end of the war the S.P.D. leaders stressed the folly of disorders at home, which would make it harder for Germany to get an acceptable peace.[3] When news of the naval

---

[1] Rosenberg, op. cit. p. 252. Max wrote: 'It was my loss of confidence in Ludendorff that was really decisive' (Memoirs, II, 195). In this Third Note Wilson 'intimated that the armistice terms would involve a complete surrender by the Central Powers' (Lloyd George, War Memoirs, p. 1,967).

[2] Max, Memoirs, II, 192.

[3] An S.P.D. manifesto published in Vorwaerts on 18 October attacked advocates of 'Bolshevik chaos' and civil war. As late as 13 October Vorwaerts had been in favour of

mutiny at Kiel was published in *Vorwaerts* on 5 November (some days after the disturbances had started) it was described as regrettable. Although the S.P.D. had not obtained all their demands from Prince Max's government, they were loyal to it as long as they dared be, and they had little to gain from its overthrow.

One source of revolutionary influence was the Russian embassy in Berlin which reopened in April 1918 after the ratification of the Brest-Litovsk treaty, flying a red flag inscribed with the revolutionary slogan 'Workers of all countries, unite!' The ambassador, Joffé, who had been the chief Russian delegate at Brest in the first round of negotiations, regarded himself as the emissary of the Bolshevik party rather than as a conventional diplomat, and refused to present his credentials to the Kaiser, the head of a state which it was his purpose to undermine. The leaders of the Independent socialists, including Haase, were invited to his first official reception, and again on May Day, when Haase toasted the Soviet government. Joffé later described his embassy as the staff headquarters for a German revolution.[1] He provided the radical politicians with secret information from official German sources, with quantities of anti-Kaiser literature imported from Russia or printed in Germany, with arms and with money. Almost every evening after dark, Independent socialist leaders slipped into the embassy building in Unter den Linden to consult Joffé, as an experienced conspirator, on questions of tactics. The Independent socialist Reichstag member Oskar Cohn became the embassy's legal adviser. Haase received money for the printing of pamphlets, though he later denied it, and Barth both arms and money for the purchase of arms. On the eve of his enforced departure from Germany early in November 1918 Joffé, handed a large sum of money to Cohn, part of which (RM 50,000) was to be spent on propaganda.[2] During the Russian revolution of 1905 the S.P.D. had sent financial help to the Russian socialists; now the Russians could repay the debt. What was novel in Joffé's case was the gift of funds from a party which was also a government to a foreign political party. That it was also in breach of the Brest treaty did not worry the Bolsheviks, who regarded the treaty as something to be evaded where possible. For Lenin and his party it appeared vital to do all in their power to stimulate the revolution in Germany on which, they were convinced, their own future depended. It is nevertheless unlikely that the course of the German revolu-

Germany's carrying on the war even after the evacuation of France and Belgium, but on 18 October its leader urged that Germany should haul down her flag without bringing it home victorious—a comment later used by the nationalists to impugn the party's patriotism.

[1] Carr, *op. cit.* p. 76. Since he arrived in Berlin on 20 April, it is possible that Joffé's May Day reception was in fact his first.

[2] *Reichstag Inquiry*, v, 31 ff., 202 ff. Among the pamphlets imported from Russia was Lenin's April Theses.

tion would have been greatly different had Joffé's help and advice not been forthcoming, and Joffé afterwards admitted that his co-operation with the German socialists accomplished little or nothing of permanent value.[1] Joffé's disclosure early in December 1918 that Independent socialists had received money and arms from him was to be as embarrassing to Haase as it was grist to the mill of his political enemies.[2]

Indeed in their attitude to the Soviet regime Independent socialists were already deeply divided. By the summer of 1918 the impact of Leninism on the party can be seen, though it cannot be measured with any accuracy. A revealing debate was conducted in the columns of the left wing *Leipziger Volkszeitung* between Kautsky, who grew increasingly critical of the Bolsheviks, and Mehring, who defended them. In the first of three articles, written almost immediately after the Bolshevik seizure of power, Kautsky was inclined to suspend judgement. His second article, written in January 1918, condemned Bolshevism for its hostility to democracy; Lenin had just used bayonets to disperse the constituent assembly. Kautsky developed his criticism in a third article which appeared in March;[3] and expanded his views in a book published in August 1918 as *The Dictatorship of the Proletariat*. As an orthodox Marxist Kautsky agreed with the Mensheviks that Russia, with her small proletariat and undeveloped industry, was unripe for a socialist revolution; he was equally horrified by Lenin's distribution of land to the peasants and the consequent strengthening of proprietorship. In Kautsky's view the Bolshevik dictatorship, which was over, not of, the proletariat, was the measure of Russia's unreadiness for a socialist regime—an example to be avoided.

Mehring, on the other hand, who was a Spartacist, urged that the Bolsheviks should not be judged too soon; even the English and French revolutions, under much less difficult circumstances, had taken forty years or so to work themselves out. Mehring acknowledged the Soviets as the historically necessary form of proletarian dictatorship, successor to the Paris Commune

---

[1] Carr, *op. cit.* p. 77. Joffé's admission was made to Louis Fischer. But for Joffé's first reaction see p. 173, n. 2, below. According to Louis Fischer (*Life of Lenin*, London, 1965, p. 314) Joffé also told Fischer: 'We probably shortened the war by a month and saved lives.' But the time-table of the German revolution was determined more by the outcome of the war than by anything the Soviet embassy could do.

[2] *Reichstag Inquiry*, v, 203, where the text of Joffé's broadcast to Copenhagen of 15 December 1918 is given, together with comments by Oskar Cohn and others. Haase disputed the accuracy of Joffé's account so far as the transfer of Russian money to the U.S.P.D. was concerned. The matter caused an angry scene between Haase and Solf in cabinet on 9 December 1918, see ch. 8, p. 173, below.

[3] The three articles are in the Kautsky Archive at Amsterdam. Kautsky's criticism of the Bolsheviks was resented by many in his party who, however, later agreed with him (Kautsky, *Mein Verhaeltnis zur U.S.P.D.* p. 9). Kautsky, who had previously favoured the exercise of pressure from outside parliament as an additional expression of the popular will, now argued that parliament must be paramount even if it had a reactionary majority. He rejected the Bolshevik claim to represent the proletariat.

which had excited Marx's admiration. Only the Bolsheviks, wrote Mehring, could guarantee the conclusion of a democratic peace, free from all imperialism, British as well as German. In a letter to the Bolshevik newspaper *Pravda*, published on 13 June 1918, Mehring echoed Liebknecht's criticism of the Independent socialists as hesitant and half-hearted, and he regretted that the Spartacists had attached themselves to the U.S.P.D.[1] Some Independents resented Mehring's attack, but in their judgement of Soviet Russia more agreed with the majority than with Kautsky.[2] When in September 1918 the party held a conference, the majority appears to have been enthusiastic for Bolshevik methods, and the minority had difficulty in preventing the inclusion in the programme of a demand for dictatorship of the proletariat.[3] This amounted to a rejection of the Erfurt programme with its parliamentary emphasis and a return to Marxism in its original form.

Light is thrown on the state of mind of the two socialist parties in the late summer of 1918 by their reaction to a proposal made to each of them by the Berlin metal workers, who sought their co-operation for a big demonstration which was to have the same general purpose as the January strikes—peace abroad and democratisation at home. Both parties expressed willingness to take part, but the S.P.D. stipulated that all parliamentary means must be tried first and that written propaganda should not be used. The Independents' conditions were that only parties or groups which had opposed war credits and any form of co-operation with non-socialist parties should be included: this was a clear attempt to exclude the S.P.D. Thus nothing came of the metal workers' project.[4] The distrust and bitterness between the two parties, particularly on the side of the Independents, remained, and the events of the next few weeks were to do nothing to reduce them.

The difference between the two parties emerged again at the conference of political leaders on 2 October at which a spokesman of the supreme command broke news of Germany's military plight. Whereas Ebert, the patriot, became 'white as a corpse' and could not utter a word, Haase after the meeting rushed up to his colleague Ledebour, who was waiting outside the room, with the words 'Now we've got them'.[5] It was a foregone conclusion that the Independent socialists condemned the S.P.D.'s decision to join the

---

[1] Hanke (ed.), *Sechzig Jahre Leipziger Volkszeitung* (1954), pp. 93–5. Mehring had by now come to the conclusion that the Spartacist decision to join the U.S.P.D. in April 1917 had been a mistake. Kautsky, unpublished essay on Mehring in Kautsky Archive (A. 78a).

[2] Rosa Luxemburg, who followed events in Russia with passionate concern from prison (she had been rearrested and interned since July 1916), was, despite her general admiration for the Bolsheviks as revolutionaries, critical of their methods, particularly the use of violence to suppress opposition, as well as of their 'petty bourgeois' tactics exemplified by the distribution of land to the peasants. But few Spartacists shared her misgivings about methods (E. Meyer (ed.), *Spartakus im Kriege*, p. 17). See also p. 277 below.

[3] Stuemke, *Die deutsche Revolution* (1923), p. 92. Stroebel, *The German Revolution*, p. 198.

[4] Bernstein, *Die deutsche Revolution*, p. 27.

[5] Max, *Memoirs*, II, 12.

coalition government under Prince Max. Haase believed that the coalition would soon discredit itself and that events were moving rapidly in favour of his party. On 5 October the U.S.P.D. issued a manifesto[1] declaring that the policy of the S.P.D. as well as of the government had now collapsed, and denouncing the S.P.D. for allowing itself to be used as a prop by the bourgeois order in its extremity. The manifesto criticised as inadequate the conditions on which the majority socialists had accepted office: they should have insisted on abolition (not merely modification) of martial law and censorship; abolition of the Auxiliary Service Law; an amnesty for political prisoners; proportional representation; women's suffrage; a fully parliamentary regime; and the evacuation by Germany of all territory conquered from Russia. It added that nothing short of a socialist republic would satisfy the Independents. The party saw in the crumbling of German military power and in the hastily improvised change of government the grim fulfilment of their warnings and the vindication of their consistently advocated policy. They alone had nothing to recant or regret: 'Only the U.S.P.D. need abandon nothing of its peace programme. The memorandum it drew up at Stockholm in July 1917, which the censors suppressed at the time and which was attacked by the other parties, including the S.P.D., will now come into its own.'[2]

The Independents hoped for a peace based on Wilson's Fourteen Points, though Haase warned them in a speech on 23 October that a Wilsonian peace would not bring justice to the workers, and he feared that a peace conference might be only the prelude to a joint attack on Russia by the capitalist powers, including Germany.[3]

The Reichstag met for its last session under the monarchy from 22 to 26 October. Its main business was legislation to alter the constitution. It was characteristic of the supine role of the Reichstag even under the new regime that despite the national emergency it did not meet between 5 and 22 October, or again after 26 October. Hence it was in no position to influence events, still less control them; and it entirely failed to win the popular confidence that would have ensured its survival during the forthcoming upheaval. Prince Max, in a speech in which he was careful not to include anything that could cause a rupture of the armistice negotiations, commended the reforms, and said that the aim of the government was the coming of age of the German people. He tried to show that parliamentary government was not just something wished on Germany by her enemies or adopted as an expedient, but was genuinely desired by the people. He admitted that it was the lack of the people's will to rule itself that had kept paternal government alive so long, but went on:

---

[1] Text in Prager, *op. cit.* pp. 172 ff. For Haase's attitude see Ernst Haase, *Hugo Haase* p. 165 ff.

[2] Prager, *op. cit.* p. 173.   [3] Haase, *Reichstagsreden*, p. 202.

Since July 1917 the determination to secure political responsibility has been budding —now at the end of September it has burst into flower, and all things are made new...[The new system] came into being as the result of a decisive phase of growth in the character of the German people, a phase rendered inevitable by its exertions, its heroic deeds and sacrifices in this war.[1]

There was naturally no mention of Ludendorff's part in bringing about this desirable consummation. The speech was written with an eye to foreign reactions as much as for domestic consumption.

Ebert, who spoke for the S.P.D., was also emphatic that German democracy, despite the regrettable circumstances of its birth, sprang from the German people's own initiative and was deeply rooted in popular consciousness. The reforms now proposed, Ebert complained, did not go far enough; the sailors imprisoned for mutinying in 1917 should be released. He expressed relief at the passing of the old system with its bureaucracy, its 'narrow police spirit, sabre-rattling and Junker arrogance', which had brought on Germany the distrust of the world. As a socialist he naturally wanted to reshape the economy, but political reforms must come first. Referring to the proposed *levée en masse*, Ebert said his party opposed a 'desperate struggle', and that the government, the first in which socialists had taken part, should be a government of peace. Behind these remarks may be discerned the wish not to lose supporters to the Independents by advocating an unpopular course, but Ebert warned the Allies:

We may lose our possessions—but no one can take from us our creative power. Whatever happens: we shall remain in the middle of Europe as a populous, efficient, honour-loving nation. If the other nations want to be our friends in future, it will be a gain for us and for them; if they want to be our enemies, by treating us as the scum of humanity and their bond-slaves, we shall tell them: Look out, every slavery comes to an end some time.[2]

Ebert had given up the war as irretrievably lost and was obviously prepared for a harsh peace.

Haase made the main speech for the Independent socialists. He reminded the other parties that they could have had peace on reasonable terms in 1915 or 1917; now they must pay the price for their shortsightedness. He complained that the censorship was still in force, books and newspapers still banned, left wing politicians still muzzled, political prisoners still interned. Germany, he said, could not recover without going socialist; in contrast to Russia, socialism in Germany need not cause great convulsions. Hailing the world revolution which he saw breaking over Europe, Haase prophesied that just as militarism had collapsed, so would capitalism, though this was hardly consistent with his admission that 'Entente capitalism' had grown in strength, and with it the British and French empires. Germany must become

---

[1] Max, *Memoirs*, II, 178. [2] Ebert, *op. cit.*, II, 92.

a republic.[1] Ledebour spoke in the same strain, adding that the financial ruin brought by the war would make the proletariat in all countries demand socialisation. Cohn emphasised the guilt of the Hohenzollern monarchy for the war and appealed to the workers of the Entente countries to join those of Germany in spreading the revolution.[2]

Meanwhile the pressure for the Kaiser's abdication had disturbed the supreme command, for whom abandonment of the August War Lord would be an act of personal dishonour and disastrous for army discipline and morale. Groener, Ludendorff's successor as quartermaster-general, tried to dissuade the S.P.D. from insisting on abdication. On 6 November he met Ebert, David and other socialist and trade union leaders in Berlin. They explained that while they were ready to work with a parliamentary monarchy headed by one of the Kaiser's sons, William himself must go if there was not to be a popular revolt. Theoretically the socialists were republicans, but Scheidemann had told the war cabinet on 24 October that his party did not insist on the abolition of the monarchy, which he hoped would not be necessary. Groener, who had just given the Chancellor a very gloomy report on the front, refused to accept the socialists' advice, though he afterwards regretted not having done so. Haeften, head of the military section of the foreign office, who was present, told Groener: 'This means revolution. These leaders no longer have the masses in hand.'[3] But the interview was not without significance; both sides parted with mutual respect. Groener had already shown his ability to find a common language with the socialist politicians. At the *Kriegsamt*, the department of economic warfare of which he had been in charge in 1916–17, he had maintained good relations with the trade unions, and the seeds sown were to come to fruition in the 'special relationship' which he was soon to establish with Ebert.

It was only after the Groener interview that the majority socialists decided on their ultimatum to Prince Max. By staying in a government which was rapidly losing support the S.P.D. was jeopardising its future; already there had been talk in the Berlin factories of a Haase–Ledebour government. Prince Max describes the scene when Ebert and Scheidemann brought their ultimatum:

The two leaders arrived...In the words of explanation they gave was nothing of the menace and defiance which from the contents of the ultimatum might have been

[1] Haase, *Reichstagsreden*, pp. 184–204.
[2] Prager, *op. cit.* pp. 168–9.
[3] Max, *Memoirs*, II, 304; Groener, *Lebenserinnerungen*, pp. 450–1. During the war Groener had been in favour of a government of national concentration. 'The war', he wrote, 'is the greatest democratic wave that has ever passed over this planet. Whoever opposes it will be dashed to pieces; the point is how to ride it...' Groener himself called for immediate reform of the three-class franchise, and urged drastic measures against the 'cancer' of war profiteering (Groener-Geyer, *General Groener*, pp. 58–70, 77–80).

expected. They had been simply overwhelmed by the way in which power was slipping from their hands.

'The Kaiser must abdicate at once or we shall have the revolution'—this was the substance of the short explanation they gave.[1]

Prince Max knew the pressure the socialist leaders were under, but that very morning (7 November) Ebert had privately assured him that he hated the social revolution like sin and would do all in his power not to embarrass him.[2] Now, however, begged by the Chancellor to withdraw the ultimatum so as to give him one final chance of securing the Kaiser's abdication, Ebert refused, saying to Simons, Max's secretary:

This evening there are twenty-six meetings taking place in all the big public halls. This evening we must announce the ultimatum from every platform or the whole lot will desert to the Independents.

Max continues:

Ebert was a changed man. Simons encountered an unexpected determination; Ebert seemed all at once to be reaching out his hand to grasp the leadership of the state. This impression was so strong that it led Simons to ask: 'Then I suppose you want to be Imperial Chancellor?' Ebert replied: 'That has not yet been decided.'[3]

For Prince Max this was the end of the road, for he could not stay in office without the majority socialists. He survived for two more days, long enough to see the armistice safe if not signed, hardly long enough to see the Kaiser go.

While the reformist wing of German socialism was doing its best to assuage popular discontent and save the monarchy, its radical wing was plotting how to bring revolution about. Barth's shop-stewards' committee met on 2 November. Of the Independent leaders Haase, Ledebour, Dittmann and Däumig were present, as was Liebknecht, like Dittmann newly amnestied. The naval mutiny had now begun, and this was a good reason for the radicals in Berlin to act without delay. Barth himself spoke in favour of organising the rising, for which he had long been preparing, on the following Monday (4 November). Ledebour and Däumig supported him. Haase and Dittmann urged that they should wait until the armistice was signed, and Haase suggested that in any case their chances of success were slight. The shop-stewards were also divided as to the date. When the vote, in which only shop-stewards were allowed to take part, was counted there was a narrow majority (twenty-one to nineteen) in favour of organising the strike which would start the revolution on 11 November, a week later than Barth wanted.[4]

---

[1] Max, *Memoirs*, II, 318.

[2] *Ibid.* p. 312. Up to the last moment Ebert believed that a general upheaval could be avoided if peace was signed and political concessions made (Scheidemann, *Zusammenbruch*, p. 206).

[3] Max, *Memoirs*, II, 318.

[4] Barth, *op. cit.* p. 47. With this decision, wrote the embittered Barth, evolution throttled revolution.

The difference between Haase and Barth over the choice of date pointed to a basic difference in approach. Like most German socialists of his time, Haase believed that revolutions are produced by circumstances; this was a somewhat over-simplified deduction from Marxist determinism, reinforced by Haase's natural caution and sobriety. Barth, on the other hand, had become convinced that revolutions are made, a view which suited his natural impulsiveness and ebullience. The result of the 2 November meeting was a heavy blow to Barth, who now realised that Haase had no plans for the morning after the seizure of power. In Barth's own words:

I urged Däumig to speak seriously to Haase and Ledebour, so that we could meet at last to discuss in detail what ought to happen on the day after the revolution, to agree on the main lines and to give it organisational shape as far as possible. I had been pressing for meetings of this kind for the past four months. At first Däumig had shown unwillingness, but then he had enthusiastically supported me for the last three months. But always in vain. Haase simply explained that things could not be fixed in advance. It was fear of his own courage, fear that in case of failure he could be proved to have played an active part [in the revolution]. The meeting never took place. Everything was well prepared, almost better than one could expect in the prevailing circumstances, up till the day of the revolution; then parliamentary cretinism triumphed, then not revolution but trickery was trumps...[1]

In this characteristic passage Barth overestimated his own importance in the revolutionary movement, and his criticism of Haase for lacking moral courage is hardly justified. What Haase lacked was a revolutionary temperament. He was also, from Barth's point of view, inhibited by his democratic or parliamentary convictions. He formed a striking contrast to Liebknecht, whose addiction to quasi-revolutionary street demonstrations was too much even for Barth, who derided them as 'revolutionary gymnastics'.

Liebknecht's views were reflected in a programme drawn up by the Spartacists and the Bremen radicals who met secretly at Gotha on 7 October to decide on a policy for the new situation created by the impending collapse of the old regime. The programme, which was frankly inspired by Bolshevik precedent, demanded the transfer of power to workers' and soldiers' councils and the nationalisation of all land and property. It had no use for parliament: 'The struggle for real democratisation is not concerned with parliament, franchise or parliamentary ministers and other swindle; it has to do with the real basis of all enemies of the people: ownership of land and capital, power over the armed forces, and over justice.'[2] The Independent socialists were blamed for making 'futile speeches' in the Reichstag at a time when only mass actions outside parliament were important. The action of workers' and soldiers' councils should be reinforced by demonstrations, strikes, sabotage,

---

[1] *Ibid.* p. 35.
[2] Frölich, *10 Jahre Krieg und Bürgerkrieg*, pp. 249 ff., Volkmann, *Der Marxismus und das deutsche Heer im Weltkriege*, pp. 208 ff.

desertion from the forces and mutiny. Spartacists should not shirk temporary defeat, imprisonment or death, for such initial setbacks would but raise the revolutionary temper of the masses and spur them to ultimate victory. Spartacist pamphlets distributed in September and October 1918 called for the forcible overthrow of the government and establishment of a republic. A pamphlet dated 7 November and signed by Liebknecht and Ernst Meyer, editor of the Spartacus Letters, demanded a council dictatorship. Leaders of the S.P.D. were compared to Lafayette, who tried to ingratiate himself with the revolutionaries while serving the old regime.[1] In fact, all over Germany workers' and soldiers' councils were being formed, but with aims which rarely coincided with those of the Spartacists.

Thus on the eve of the revolution the left was deeply divided. The S.P.D. had the hardest task: as a government party to resist popular pressure, as a popular party to lead it. The reformist leaders wanted a reshuffle of the government to give them a share commensurate with their strength in the Reichstag, and the end of martial law and the censorship; but they desired neither the fall of the monarchy nor a popular uprising. A manifesto issued by the S.P.D. on 17 October warned against 'Bolshevik chaos' or civil war, and *Vorwaerts* came out openly for the Kaiser's abdication only after non-socialist papers had already done so. Repugnance of the majority socialists for Russian methods was shown by their hostility to the activities of the Soviet embassy. At Scheidemann's suggestion, a packing case belonging to the embassy was deliberately dropped by a porter at one of the Berlin stations and discharged a large quantity of revolutionary propaganda. On the strength of this discovery, which showed the Russians as technically in breach of the Brest treaty, Joffé was ordered to leave Germany.[2] On the day he reached the Russian frontier (9 November) the German revolution triumphed in Berlin, but it was to prove a bitter disappointment to the Bolsheviks.

The Independent socialists did not have to play the same double role as the S.P.D., but they were far from united. On the left they were involved in the plans of Barth and his shop-stewards for proletarian dictatorship; on the right, in the mind of Kautsky and even of Haase, they were still committed to parliamentary tactics. Hitherto opposition to the government's war policy and annexations had held the party together; now, confronted with the problems of how to seize power and what to do when they had got it, they stumbled on new differences. Alone of the left wing groups the Spartacists had a clear-cut programme, but they lacked the numbers which would have enabled them to carry it out. And while the radical leaders in Berlin were still deliberating, the provinces and the sailors acted.

Richard Müller, the revolutionary shop-steward, describes how on the

---

[1] Meyer (ed.), *Spartakusbriefe*, II, 192–7.
[2] Scheidemann, *Memoirs*, II, 210 ff.

evening of 8 November, when most of Germany was under the red flag, he watched the entry into Berlin of heavily armed troops intended to protect the government against the revolution.

The warlike procession of the old rulers and the plans of the Social Democratic leaders occupied me till the next morning. I had been at the head of the revolutionary movement since the beginning of the war. Never, even during the worst reverses, had I doubted the victory of the proletariat. But now that the hour of decision was approaching, a feeling of anguish came over me, of great anxiety for my class comrades, for the proletariat. No infallible leader shows the proletariat the path it will have to tread. 'Historical experience is its only teacher, its stony road of self-liberation is paved not only with infinite suffering but also with endless mistakes.'[1]

The experience of the next three months was to prove Müller's forebodings justified.

[1] R. Müller, op. cit. pp. 142–3.

CHAPTER 7

THE NOVEMBER REVOLUTION

> The most important question of every revolution is the question of
> state power.   LENIN

THE NAVAL MUTINY

On 28 October 1918 the German fleet received orders from the Admiralty
to put to sea. The professed object was to cut Britain off from the Continent
and relieve the hard-pressed German forces on the western front. Given the
numerical superiority of the British fleet such a defiant challenge could have
only one result. Moreover at that stage even a German naval victory could
not have affected the outcome of the war; in its replies to Wilson's Second and
Third Notes the German government had implicitly admitted defeat. The
order to a fleet which, apart from the episode of the battle of Jutland, had
been confined to harbour throughout the war, came as a shock to the sailors,
who knew that armistice negotiations had been going on for three weeks
and that the war might end in a matter of days. The sailors' desire for peace
had been shown in the abortive mutiny of 1917, and some of them had
continued to keep in touch with the Independent socialists. At the time of the
January 1918 strike, attempts to form a sailors' council in Kiel led to arrests and
court-martials.[1] In the tense atmosphere that prevailed at the end of October
the admirals' order was seen as a suicidal gesture, which would involve the
death of thousands of men for an officer's conception of honour they did not
share. It had an explosive effect. The crews of battleships at Kiel and Wilhelmshaven disobeyed the command to raise anchor, and let their fires go out.
They were ready to defend the German coast but not to go to sea.[2] On
30 October the Admiralty reissued its order, which was again ignored.
Finally it was withdrawn, and the sailors had won a moral victory. The
admirals had been technically within their rights in planning the move, but
politically and psychologically it was a blunder.

The mutinous sailors were arrested and locked up, but the movement
spread from the ships to the shore. On 3 November a sailors' meeting in Kiel
demanded the release of their arrested colleagues and demonstrated in the
streets. Speeches were made in favour of a republic, and when an officers'

---

[1] Popp and Artelt, *Ursprung und Entwicklung der November-Revolution* (Kiel, 1918),
pp. 6 ff. Both the authors of this pamphlet were sailors who took part in the events they
described.

[2] Bernstein, *Die deutsche Revolution*, p. 15. Other main sources used in this section are
Volkmann, *Der Marxismus und das deutsche Heer im Weltkriege* and *Revolution über
Deutschland*, and Noske, *Von Kiel bis Kapp*.

patrol opened fire on the demonstrators eight were killed and twenty-nine wounded. Troops despatched against the rebels on the following day went over to them. The sailors succeeded in freeing their arrested comrades, hoisted the red flag and proceeded to elect sailors' councils. The authorities sent for reinforcements but made only a half-hearted attempt to overcome the mutineers, hoping to bring them to reason by negotiations. An appeal to the sailors was issued by the government, assuring them that their lives would not be sacrificed and promising an investigation of their grievances. The appeal, which was signed by the Chancellor (Prince Max of Baden), the secretary to the navy (von Mann) and Scheidemann, added: 'We are not putting an end to the war between the nations in order to start a civil war.' In response to a telegram from the governor of Kiel, Admiral Souchon, two members of the Reichstag, Haussmann, a Progressive who was now a minister, and Noske, the socialist who was known for his interest in naval matters, were sent to Kiel by the government to try to bring the situation under control.[1]

Noske was warmly welcomed by the sailors when he and Haussmann arrived in Kiel on 4 November. Many of the sailors' leaders were members or supporters of the Independent socialist party, and they telegraphed to Haase to come himself or send one of his colleagues (Ledebour or Cohn). The message was delayed, apparently for political reasons,[2] and by the time it reached Haase, Noske and Haussmann had already left Berlin. When Haase himself arrived at Kiel, order had been restored. The sailors' demands were far from extreme: abdication of the Hohenzollerns, abolition of martial law, equal suffrage for men and women throughout Germany, and the liberation of political prisoners including sailors convicted of mutiny in 1917. The sailors also wanted less overbearing treatment by their officers and the right to use less deference in addressing them.[3] Noske accepted the demands with modifications (on the abdication issue he could only promise to hasten a decision), and was thereupon elected co-chairman of the Kiel sailors' council. An Independent socialist sailor then moved that Noske be elected governor of Kiel in succession to Souchon. This motion was approved unanimously.[4]

The animosities between right and left wing socialists which made co-operation between them difficult in Berlin were not reproduced at Kiel, where the sailors were little interested in questions of doctrine and policy, and where the Independents were hardly more radical than the majority socialists.[5] The spontaneity of the mutiny is attested by the fact that to Haase as leader of the Independent socialist party it came as a complete surprise. 'We had heard nothing of unrest in the fleet', he wrote in a letter to his wife on 4 November.[6]

[1] Volkmann, *Der Marxismus*, pp. 217 ff., Noske, *Von Kiel bis Kapp*, pp. 8 ff.
[2] Popp and Artelt, *op. cit.* p. 22.   [3] *Ibid.* pp. 10–16.
[4] Noske, *Von Kiel bis Kapp*, pp. 17, 25.
[5] *Ibid.* p. 27.
[6] Ernst Haase, *Hugo Haase*, p. 171.

And when Haase reached Kiel he found no reason to disagree with what Noske was doing.[1] But the inter-socialist harmony which characterised the outbreak at Kiel was possible only because it was not really a political revolution. The sailors were basically concerned only to save their lives and end the war.

Seen from Berlin, the sailors' revolt was unwelcome, though for opposite reasons, to both right and left wing socialists. As members of the government against which the sailors had risen, the S.P.D. leaders were naturally embarrassed; and although for the moment Noske had achieved some success at Kiel, they feared that the subversion would spread beyond their control. As for the revolutionary shop-stewards, their regret was that the outbreak occurred before they were ready to direct it, and Barth described it as highly damaging to the revolutionary cause.[2] Under the impact of defeat the old regime, despite the bid for popularity of the October reforms, had lost authority more rapidly than anyone on either right or left had foreseen.

THE REVOLUTION IN THE STATES AND CITIES

Noske had managed to 'roll back', as Prince Max put it, the revolutionary wave in Kiel: the authority of the Admiralty had not been restored, but so long as Noske was governor of Kiel no extremism would gain the upper hand there. What even Noske could not do was to prevent the triumphant sailors from carrying the infection along the coast and into the interior of Germany, where it soon acquired a more radical character. By the evening of 6 November Cuxhaven, Bremen and the great port of Hamburg were in the hands of workers' and soldiers' councils. In Hamburg, in contrast to Kiel, the rising had a political aim—socialism—from the very beginning, and the Independent socialists gave the lead by calling a general strike. They also seized the offices of the *Hamburger Echo* and issued through them a *Rote Fahne* as the organ of a provisional workers' and soldiers' council.[3] The first number was strongly Spartacist in tone, proclaiming the German revolution as the beginning of world revolution. This annoyed the majority socialists, and a struggle began between them and the Spartacists. On 8 November the workers' and soldiers' council announced that it was the sole authority in Hamburg, all others being deposed. Three days later a properly elected workers' and soldiers' council replaced the provisional one. The S.P.D. demanded that the existing organs of government (senate and city council or *Bürgerschaft*) be allowed to continue after new elections based on universal suffrage instead of

---

[1] Noske, *Von Kiel bis Kapp*, p. 27; Popp and Artelt, *op. cit.* p. 27. See also H. Müller, *Die November Revolution* (1928), pp. 27 ff.

[2] Barth, *Aus der Werkstatt der deutschen Revolution*, p. 52.

[3] For the revolution in Hamburg see *Illustrierte Geschichte der deutschen Revolution*, pp. 190 ff.; R. Müller, *Vom Kaiserreich zur Republik*, I, 135; H. Müller, *op. cit.* p. 35.

the existing limited franchise.[1] The Independents sided with the Spartacists in opposing this suggestion and wanted Hamburg, hitherto a city state, to be merged in the Reich: centralisation had been standard socialist policy in Germany since Marx's day. A week later both senate and *Bürgerschaft* were reinstated in some of their functions, subject to the supervision of the workers' and soldiers' council. But this compromise did not work. Authority could not be divided. The rivalry between the new proletarian organs of power and the old bourgeois ones, the former representing a mild form of proletarian dictatorship, the latter formal democracy, was to recur in varying forms all over Germany during the next few weeks.

Although the revolt in Hamburg was not, as in Kiel, a mutiny, it too had a markedly anti-militarist character, as indeed the revolution had everywhere. A revealing account of a journey from Berlin to Hamburg on 6 November is given by Hermann Müller, the S.P.D. leader. Before the train reached Hamburg it was stopped by a band of sailors who searched it, forcing any officers they found to give up their swords and cutting off their epaulettes, symbols of authority, with bayonets. The officers made no attempt at resistance, nor did any of the onlookers protest. 'Whoever witnessed this scene', wrote Müller, 'knew that Prussian militarism had come to its dying hour.'[2] Two months later he would not have been so sure. But in early November scenes like this were daily occurrences. In behaving in this way the sailors and soldiers were acting on their own initiative, not following the programme of any party. As Dittmann, the Independent socialist secretary, afterwards wrote, no one in their ranks would have believed that the revolution would start in the fleet. They took it for granted that the workers in the big cities and industrial districts would be the first to hoist the flag of rebellion.[3] What Dittmann called the spontaneous and eruptive elements had emerged as more important than the planning of the radical theorists.

Not least of the surprises was the sudden success of the revolution in Bavaria, whose population was predominantly Catholic and conservative.[4] That Munich was the seat of a revolutionary government by 8 November was largely due to the initiative of the Independent socialist leader Kurt Eisner. A well-known critic, essayist and ex-editor of *Vorwaerts*, a former revisionist whom the war had driven far to the left, Eisner was a man of idealism and intellectual force (and vanity) who was carried away by ideas he was unable to put into effect. His short career at the head of Bavarian politics was to show that his flair for revolutionary leadership was not matched by a sureness of judgement or administrative ability. That such a man, a Berlin

---

[1] R. Müller, *Vom Kaiserreich zur Republik*, II, 77.   [2] H. Müller, *op. cit.* pp. 27 ff.
[3] Dittmann, *Lebenserinnerungen*, ch. 14.
[4] For the revolution in Bavaria, see F. Schade, *Kurt Eisner und die bayrische Sozial-demokratie* (Hanover, 1961), *passim*; Bernstein, *op. cit.*, pp. 52–7; M. J. Bonn, *Wandering Scholar* (1949), pp. 194–224; and relevant sections of *Illustrierte Geschichte*.

Jew and the leader of a small extremist party should be able with little effort to depose the Wittelsbach dynasty which had ruled Bavaria for nearly a thousand years was one of the least predictable episodes in the German revolution, and Eisner himself was surprised by the ease with which it was accomplished. It is to be explained only by the strongly pacifist mood which prevailed early in November. The Bavarian peasants had suffered severely from the food requisitioning of the Berlin government as well as from the other sacrifices of the war. When on 2 November defeated Austria signed an armistice, the Bavarians feared that the Allied armies would cross the Tyrol and invade their country from the south.[1] Anti-Prussian feeling combined with an overwhelming desire to end the war produced a state of mind receptive to Eisner's unique mixture of quixotic radicalism and Bavarian particularism.

Eisner, who had been imprisoned for playing a leading part in the January 1918 strike, was amnestied on 14 October, and immediately plunged into the activities of the Independent socialist party. His great rival was Auer, right wing leader of the Bavarian S.P.D. and a much more typical figure of Bavarian socialism. Auer's aim was to carry out a peaceful transformation on lines similar to those being followed by Prince Max at national level: the authoritarian state would become a people's state by legal methods. The King, Ludwig III, was quite prepared to play his part, and early in November declared that a new government would be formed of ministers proposed by the Bavarian Diet and including two Social Democrats. In Eisner's view such measures were no longer adequate. He demanded the abolition of the monarchy, and wanted all German states to become socialist republics with Liebknecht as Chancellor. Some Independent speakers called for the formation of workers' and soldiers' councils on the Russian model. The arrival in Munich of a thousand sailors from the Adriatic added to the revolutionary mood.

The decisive event in the Bavarian revolution was a demonstration by a crowd of 50,000 on the Theresienwiese on 7 November which was organised by both socialist parties and the trade unions. The meeting demanded the immediate abdication of the Kaiser, the complete democratisation of Germany and the removal of reactionaries from the civil service. One of the soldiers present raised a red flag and called on the crowd to unite behind Eisner, who, joined by an S.P.D. leader, led a procession which occupied the barracks and public buildings and released prisoners from the gaols. The garrison, as elsewhere in similar circumstances, made common cause with the revolutionaries. By nightfall Eisner, who was in effective control of Munich, proclaimed

---

[1] Volkmann, *Der Marxismus*, p. 230. Borkenau wrote (*The Communist International*, 1938, p. 135) that the Bavarian peasants, who expressed their enmity against war and monarchy in particularly violent forms, were a few months later in the vanguard of counter-revolution.

1*a*   Eduard Bernstein

1*b*   Karl Kautsky

2 *a*   Chancellor Bethmann Hollweg   2 *b*   General Wilhelm Groener

3 a   Friedrich Ebert

3 b   Hindenburg and Ludendorff in front of G.H.Q.,
the Hotel Britannique, Spa, 1918

4 *a* Hugo Haase

4 *b* Karl Liebknecht

5 Rosa Luxemburg

6*a*   Rudolf Hilferding

6*b*   Women giving refreshments to
revolutionary sailors

6*c*   The leaders of the Berlin soldiers' council in the Reichstag

7a Ebert welcoming the returning German army, Berlin, December 1918

7b Ledebour speaking from the terrace of the royal palace, Berlin, winter 1918/19

8 Scheidemann proclaiming the republic from the Reichstag, 9 November 1918

9 *a*   The Council of People's Commissars (from left to right: Barth, Landsberg, Ebert, Haase, Dittmann, Scheidemann)

9 *b*   Spartacists demonstrating against counter-revolution, 7 December 1918

10*a*   The royal stables after being hit by a shell

10*b*   Machine guns in one of the state rooms of the royal palace

11a An armed lorry of the workers' and soldiers' council at the Brandenburg Gate during the revolution

11b Infantry with machine gun, Munich, 1919

12 *a*   Kurt Eisner with his wife and a ministerial colleague in Munich

12 *b*   Counter-revolutionary Freikorps in Munich, 1919

34 Prost Noske! Die junge Revolution ist tot!

13 'Here's to Noske! The young revolution is dead.' Caricature of the Freikorps
by Georg Grosz, April 1919

14a　Spartacist guards during the Berlin rising, January 1919

14b　A scene in front of the royal palace

15*a* A Freikorps formation marching past Noske, summer 1919

15*b* Independent Socialists and Communists protesting in front of the Reichstag
against the Works Council bill, 13 January 1920

16a The Pariser Platz, Berlin, during the Kapp Putsch, March 1920

16b Kapp Putsch: distribution of handbills

the Bavarian republic.[1] A provisional council of workers, peasants and soldiers was set up, and local authorities and the police were told to obey its orders. Next day (8 November) a provisional national council was formed as a kind of revolutionary parliament. It consisted of representatives of the proletarian council together with liberal and socialist members of the Diet, and was intended to replace the Diet until a constituent national assembly for Bavaria could be convened. The Wittelsbachs having been formally deposed, Eisner became president of the new republic. Other Bavarian towns followed Munich's example, and in Upper Bavaria peasants' councils were formed, almost the only examples of their kind in Germany.

In the neighbouring state of Württemberg the revolution began as a strike by workers in the Daimler and other factories near Stuttgart who, led by Independent socialists, demanded radical changes in the government. In Friedrichschafen the workers of the Zeppelin factory made up their own council. On 7 November the Württemberg government was reorganised so as to include Social Democrats; two days later Independents were added. The new government announced that these changes had occurred with the approval of the workers' and soldiers' councils. Non-socialist ministers with specialist qualifications were allowed to remain, despite Spartacist protests. As elsewhere, the upper house was abolished, and new elections to the Diet, based on universal suffrage, were promised. The king had to abdicate although, like most South German monarchs, he was neither markedly illiberal nor unpopular, nor had he identified himself with the Ludendorff party during the war. The Independent socialists actually joined the other parties in thanking the king for his services to the people of Württemberg. The majority socialists showed little enthusiasm for these changes, but took part in them to prevent their Independent rivals from gaining control.[2] Yet the alliance between the two was short-lived; no genuine understanding proved possible. In Baden, on the other hand, the most liberal state in Germany, the working alliance which had grown up before the war between socialists and the moderate middle-class parties survived the revolution. The new Baden government was a broad coalition stretching from the National Liberals to the Independent socialists.

Frankfurt-on-Main was one of the towns where the revolution was triggered off by a party of sailors. They were soon joined by a crowd of soldiers who, after being addressed by Independent socialist leaders, organised the election of soldiers' councils, one of which met in a leading hotel. The mayor of Frankfurt was given the choice of resigning or recognising

---

[1] Bernstein, *Die deutsche Revolution*, pp. 52 ff. 'The majority socialists with their leader Auer were still hesitating and warning on 8 November; but when nearly all government offices and officials put their services at Eisner's disposal, they joined the coalition government' (Stroebel, *The German Revolution*, p. 58).

[2] Bernstein, *Die deutsche Revolution*, pp. 54 ff.

145

the new authority; he and the city council chose the latter course. The university followed suit. Two prominent liberals, the deputy mayor and the editor of the liberal *Frankfurter Zeitung*, applied unsuccessfully to become members of the workers' council. In reply to the criticism that rule by the councils was class dictatorship, Dissmann, one of the leading Independents in Frankfurt, spoke sarcastically of the love of democracy now evinced by men of the old regime after they had refused for sixty years to give the people of Prussia equal voting rights.[1]

In Kassel the course of events was similar. Majority socialists, Independent socialists and trade unionists joined in forming a workers' council which was recognised by the civic authorities and the police after the mayor had resigned. The entire garrison, including the commander, went over to the new order. As in Frankfurt, the middle classes mostly held aloof, though here too a few liberals unsuccessfully tried to join the workers' council. A leading socialist trade unionist wrote of this time: 'In Kassel, as in other parts of Germany, the revolution followed its bloodless and comparatively orderly course. Without hatred and vengeance, without beatings and murder, without concentration camps and inhuman methods, the revolutionary forces consolidated themselves and began to shape a new country.'[2] This was hardly how it was to look in retrospect. The consolidation never really took place. Their deceptively easy victory over the old regime gave the revolutionary forces a feeling of over-confidence; and their mildness, instead of propitiating their enemies, often simply permitted the latter's survival. Lack of resistance to the claims of the new councils was almost universal. In Hanover an attempt by the authorities to use troops against the rebels failed when the soldiers joined the crowd and handed over their weapons.[3] In Cologne the garrison of 45,000 changed sides almost without a shot and hoisted the red flag.[4] In Bremen an all-socialist council superseded the senate, but differences between the two socialist parties soon came to the surface.[5]

Nowhere was the rivalry between the two keener than in Saxony, where socialism had strong roots, especially in the industrial districts. The Saxon revolution began on 8 November when a procession of workers and soldiers led by Independent socialists in Leipzig, where the latter were relatively strong, forced the military authorities to capitulate and occupied the main

[1] For the revolution in Frankfurt, see Toni Sender's book, *The Autobiography of a German Rebel* (1940), pp. 94–104, and a pamphlet by Jacob Altmaier, *Frankfurter Revolutionstage* (1919). Robert Dissmann, a leader of the engineers' trade union, is to be distinguished from his near-namesake and fellow Independent socialist, Wilhelm Dittmann.
[2] Grzesinski, *Inside Germany*, p. 47.
[3] For the revolution in Hanover, see Karl Anlauf's pamphlet *Die Revolution in Niedersachsen* (1919).
[4] Volkmann, *Der Marxismus*, p. 228.
[5] *Illustrierte Geschichte*, pp. 334 ff.

buildings.[1] A workers' council and a soldiers' council then chose a small executive committee from both bodies. In Dresden, the capital of Saxony, where the majority socialists were more numerous, each socialist party elected its own joint workers' and soldiers' council. The two councils then joined forces and declared the royal family deposed, the upper house of parliament abolished and the lower dissolved pending new elections based on equal universal suffrage. In the interests of order the ministers did not resign at once, and for the same reason the officials were told to stay in office. On 14 November, however, representatives of the workers' and soldiers' councils of Dresden, Leipzig and Chemnitz issued a manifesto asserting that the capitalist system had collapsed, and that power had been seized by the revolutionary proletariat. It promised a far-reaching programme of socialisation, including the 'taking over of production by the proletariat', abolition of unearned income, arming of the people to safeguard the gains of the revolution, abolition of all existing courts of law and the merging of the Saxon state in a new unified German socialist republic. This document, which was the work of the Independent socialists with Spartacist help, showed that Saxony was nearer to a genuine Communist revolution than any other German state. A new cabinet of six People's Commissars was set up, three from each socialist party, with the key posts going to the Independents. It was, however, due to S.P.D. influence that a statement of policy by the new government was distinctly more moderate in tone. The result of the election of a new workers' and soldiers' council in Dresden, which gave the majority socialists forty-seven seats and the Independents three, also had a sobering effect on the latter, who resigned from the state council. The experiment of an all-socialist coalition in Saxony had lasted less than a week.

Enough about the course of revolution in the different states and cities has been said to show that it displayed, despite local variations, certain common features and trends. The example of Prussia, which will shortly be considered, fits into the same pattern. The revolution began as a naval mutiny or workers' strike; old rulers were deposed and new left wing governments were formed which consisted of or depended on the workers' and soldiers' councils that were in power at all levels; the army and police melted away or fraternised with the rebels while the officers were insulted or ignored. In Bavaria, Silesia and the Rhineland separatist movements appeared which threatened the unity of the Reich. Two aspects of the revolution stood out as of particular importance: the relationship of the rival socialist parties, and the connected problem of the role of the councils.

As has been seen, the leaders of the majority socialists made no preparations for the November rising because they did not want it. They were more

---

[1] For the revolution in Saxony see Bernstein, *Die deutsche Revolution*, pp. 57 ff., *Illustrierte Geschichte*, and Lorenz's pamphlet, *Fünf Jahre U.S.P.D. in Dresden*, pp. 48 ff.

10-2

concerned to preserve Germany from chaos and internal strife in the last days of a disastrous war than to take advantage of their opponents' plight to press for radical policies. But once an upsurge from below was inevitable the S.P.D. could not stand aside; as during the strike of January 1918, they had to intervene to prevent leadership in the factories from falling to the Independents. When early in November the Independents invited them to join in demonstrations and electing workers' councils, majority socialists did not refuse. To many of the rank and file in both parties there seemed no reason to perpetuate the socialist split now that with the end of the war the old disputes about annexations had become meaningless. Eisner declared in Munich that the war between the socialist brethren was over. His optimism was premature; in a sense it was only just beginning. The response of the two rivals to the revolution was quite different. The S.P.D. regarded it as a temporary deviation from the path of parliamentary democracy on which Germany had entered through the October reforms, while the Independents saw it as a heaven-sent opportunity of establishing a socialist order more quickly than would otherwise have been possible. These differences crystallised in the parties' attitudes to the workers' and soldiers' councils.

The nation-wide emergence of these councils as the *de facto* rulers of Germany was the main surprise of the revolution. Significantly, in their manifesto of 5 October the Independent socialists had made no mention of councils; the party's later championing of councils was an adjustment to a situation they welcomed but had not foreseen. The councils were a rapidly improvised elementary form of self-government which expressed the popular will at a time when the government had lost the nation's confidence. The constitutional reforms came too late to impress the man in the street, just as they came too late to convince sceptical foreign observers. Local government was still in the hands of the upper classes, the generals were still administering martial law and the censorship, a prince not a Reichstag politician was Chancellor. The Reichstag, though the main beneficiary of the reforms, had trailed behind events, not directed them. The councils occupied the vacuum which the Reichstag conspicuously failed to fill. The sailors' councils started as a continuation of the food committees set up in the navy during the war. The workers' councils stemmed from the strike committees formed in factories during the strikes of 1917 and 1918. The Russian soviets were an important influence, and the use of terms borrowed from Soviet Russia such as People's Commissars and Executive Council was obviously significant. Like the Russian soviets in April 1917, the German councils reflected all shades of radical opinion, but the moderates preponderated, especially among the soldiers. In some well-to-do districts, like the Charlottenburg suburb of Berlin, the councils were middle class in character. Most of the conncils turned out to be more revolutionary in form than in content. Few of their members saw them as permanent institutions or as a substitute for parliament. With certain exceptions they interfered little in the civil service and the economy. Even in radical Saxony the old officials stayed at their posts to keep order and guarantee food supplies. In Munich Eisner announced that the banks would not be confiscated, and there was little disruption of business life.[1] In Kassel the governing council was chiefly preoccupied with demobilisation and introducing the eight-hour day.[2] The ordinary routine of life went on; plundering and attacks on private property were rare, and in the early stages of the revolution acts of violence were exceptional. The greatest hostility was shown to officers, symbols of privilege and militarism, but though officers were humiliated they were rarely injured. When in December 1918 the supreme command retired to Kassel, Hindenburg and Groener found that the local revolutionary council behaved 'very reasonably'.[3]

9 NOVEMBER IN BERLIN

While all over Germany dynasties were falling and hastily elected councils of workers and soldiers were asserting their authority, the government of Prince Max of Baden passed through its final agonising phase. Still formally bound to the Kaiser at Spa, it had become dangerously isolated from the rest of the country. Max's twin aims of saving the monarchy and signing the armistice had become one, for Germany could not sign unless she had a government, and the government was doomed now that the socialists were on the point of resigning. The day after the S.P.D. ultimatum the Chancellor drew the only consequence and offered his resignation to the Kaiser, but adding that he regarded it as his duty to remain in charge of affairs for the time being in view of the armistice negotiations.[4] The German armistice commission, led by Erzberger, who was a minister in Max's cabinet, had arrived at Compiègne on 6 November. Even the socialists wanted Max to stay in office until the armistice was signed, and on 8 November they agreed to postpone the expiry of their ultimatum until nine o'clock on 9 November in order to give the harassed Chancellor a few more hours in which to exert pressure on the Kaiser.[5] In his reply William wrote that he reserved his decision on Max's 'request for leave to resign' until after the conclusion of the armistice. He was still not convinced that to let the majority socialists' leave the government was to abandon Germany to the revolution, news of the spread of which arrived every hour. By the evening of 8 November even

[1] Bernstein, *Die deutsche Revolution*, p. 56.
[2] Grzesinski, *op. cit.* p. 52.
[3] Groener, *Lebenserinnerungen*, p. 471. Hindenburg and Groener were welcomed by the mayor of Kassel, who prevented any molestation by extremists. But a previous attempt by the generals to settle at Homburg had failed owing to opposition from the local workers' and soldiers' council.
Prince Max of Baden, *Memoirs*, II, 326.   [5] *Ibid.* p. 346.

the non-socialist members of the cabinet had made up their minds to resign. About 8 o'clock Max telephoned the Kaiser, appealing to him not to postpone the decision. The abdication, urged Max, could still decisively affect the peace negotiations (it was certainly too late to influence the armistice terms) and take the wind out of the Entente jingoes' sails. 'The troops are not to be relied on...We are steering straight for civil war...'[1] Max wanted to be able to announce the abdication in time for publication in next morning's newspapers, for the S.P.D. national executive had at last told the workers that otherwise they could go on strike. But William's answer was still a refusal. Not until his generals told him next morning that the army would no longer follow him did he decide to go, and even then he was thinking in terms of a partial and conditional abdication at a time when the pursuit of such constitutional phantoms could not be taken seriously by his exasperated subjects.

Meanwhile Prince Max was preoccupied with the question of his successor. His resignation would, he knew, open the way to an all-socialist government, including the Independents whom he identified with the revolution. He had confidence in Ebert, his chosen successor, but less in other S.P.D. leaders such as Scheidemann, who was easily swayed by popular sentiment. Max decided that the only way of resisting subversion was by calling a national assembly to work out a new constitution: 'To combat the revolution we must conjure up the democratic idea.'[2] He had reason to believe that the majority socialists would accept such a policy, which also had the advantage of facilitating the union of Austria, now bereft of her empire, with Germany. But could a constituent assembly be called at a time when the democratic idea was being forcefully if crudely embodied in workers' and soldiers' councils? Whatever his doubts, Prince Max knew that he had no choice but to put his trust in the S.P.D. It would be Ebert's task to repeat on a national scale the feat of his colleague Noske in Kiel.[3]

There was a dramatic scene in the Chancellery that morning (9 November). The secretary of state (Hintze) rang up from Spa at 9.15 to say that the supreme command had resolved to tell the Kaiser that in the event of civil war he would not be able to reckon on the support of the armed forces. The call was taken by Wahnschaffe, an undersecretary of state in the Chancellery; when he remarked that this news left no alternative to abdication, he was not contradicted. Wahnschaffe rang up Ebert, gave him the news and appealed to him to hold up the planned demonstrations:

Ebert answered: 'Too late! The ball has been set rolling. One factory has already come out on the streets.'

Wahnschaffe replied: 'They can be brought to reason again.'

Ebert: 'We will see what can be done.'

I shall never forget [Max continued] the agony of this senseless inexplicable wait

---

[1] Prince Max of Baden, *Memoirs*, II, 341.   [2] *Ibid.* p. 310.   [3] *Ibid.* p. 317.

that followed. The party that was plotting revolution [the Independents] was bound to win once the masses got on the move...

About ten o'clock the message reached us that many thousands of unarmed workers were marching in procession upon the centre of the city. They carried placards with the inscription 'Brothers, no shooting!' The column was headed by women and children.[1]

Other similar reports followed. Even more alarming was the news received directly afterwards that troops on which the government was relying to uphold its authority had gone over to the insurgents. All these reports were telephoned through to Spa in the hope that at last the Kaiser would see the futility of putting off the abdication which by now everyone expected hourly. After eleven o'clock word was received that the Kaiser had resolved on abdication and that Spa needed half an hour to find the right form of words. Max decided that unless the abdication was announced within half an hour or so the Kaiser would simply be deposed by the mob. He had now made up his mind to make Ebert Chancellor:

I said to myself that the Revolution was on the point of winning, that it could not be beaten down, but might perhaps be stifled out. Now is the time to come out with the abdication, with Ebert's Chancellorship, with the appeal to the people to determine its own constitution in a Constituent National Assembly. If Ebert is presented to me as tribune of the people by the mob, we shall have the Republic; if Liebknecht is, we shall have Bolshevism as well. But should Ebert be appointed Imperial Chancellor by the Kaiser at the moment of abdication, then there would still be a slender hope for the monarchy left. Perhaps we should then succeed in diverting the revolutionary energy into the lawful channels of an election campaign.[2]

Prince Max did not wait for any further news from Spa before issuing, shortly before noon, the following statement to the Wolff Telegraphic Agency:

The Kaiser and King has resolved to *renounce the throne*. The Chancellor remains in office until the questions connected with the abdication of the Kaiser, the renunciation by the Crown Prince of the German Empire and of Prussia, and the setting up of the Regency have been regulated. He intends to propose to the Regent the appointment of Herr Ebert to the Chancellorship and the bringing in of a bill to enact that election writs be issued immediately for a *German Constituent National Assembly*.[3]

Hardly had this communiqué been published than Max was visited by a deputation from the Social Democratic party, led by Ebert, which formally asked for the Chancellorship. Ebert added:

In this matter we have the entire support of the Independent Social Democrats as well as of our own party. The troops also have been won over to our side. The Independents are not yet clear whether they will join the new government or not; if they should decide to do so, we shall welcome them and demand their inclusion. We have nothing against the inclusion of representatives of the bourgeois parties; only the government must be one in which we have a decisive majority.[4]

[1] *Ibid.* p. 349.   [2] *Ibid.* p. 351.   [3] *Ibid.* p. 353.   [4] *Ibid.* p. 354.

Asked by Max about the S.P.D. attitude to the proposed constituent assembly, Ebert said that they could agree to it in principle. He also undertook to carry on the government in accordance with the constitution. But when Max said: 'We must now solve the question of the Regency', Ebert's reply, which was echoed by his party delegates in chorus, was: 'It is too late for that.' The absence of a Regent meant that Ebert's appointment as Chancellor was not legal, because under the constitution an outgoing Chancellor had no power to appoint his successor.[1] The point was of academic interest only, because with the disappearance of the Kaiser, and the monarchy, the constitution automatically lapsed.

Nevertheless the significance of Ebert's appointment was that *de facto* it represented constitutional continuity instead of revolutionary change. As Max wrote, Ebert was anxious not to break the organic connection with the past. His first proclamations show, both in form and content, his concern to emphasise the quasi-legality of his assumption of office and to re-establish law and order. 'The new government has taken over the conduct of affairs to save the German people from civil war and famine and to see that their right to self-determination is respected. It can only fulfil this task if all authorities and officials in town and country lend a helping hand...'[2] It was also significant that the new government described itself as a people's government, without any mention of socialism, and that Ebert was willing to include non-socialists in his cabinet.[3]

Meanwhile it had at last been reported from Spa that the Kaiser would abdicate as emperor but not as king of Prussia. This tardy half-measure, a constitutional absurdity, was a final manifestation of the stubborn and uncomprehending reluctance with which William II bowed to the inevitable. It came as the climax of a series of conferences at Spa in the course of which, after consulting some thirty-nine senior officers on the attitude of the army, Hindenburg and Groener had to tell the Kaiser bluntly that if he insisted on reconquering Germany at the head of his troops, they would no longer follow him. Not only was Germany now in the hands of the revolutionaries; the army in the west was faced by the threat to its supplies and communications from the rebels who held the Rhine bridgeheads, the railways and telegraphs. 'The army', explained Groener, 'will re-enter Germany as an organised force under the orders of its generals, but not under those of Your Majesty. The army is no longer with Your Majesty.'[4] Inside Germany the

---

[1] Prince Max could appoint Ebert Chancellor only on the legal fiction that he (Max) was Regent (Rosenberg, *Birth of the German Republic*, p. 271). By the time Ebert received the Chancellorship from Max the S.P.D. were—technically—no longer in the government. Scheidemann's letter of resignation was presented to Prince Max on the morning of 9 November (Max, *op. cit.* p. 352; Scheidemann, *Memoirs*, II, 297).

[2] Ebert, *Schriften, Aufzeichungen, Reden*, II, 93.

[3] War Cabinet Minutes, 10 November 1918.

[4] Groener, *op. cit.* p. 460.

Kaiser's message came too late to influence events. Under pressure of the workers and soldiers Scheidemann, addressing a large and excited crowd from a balcony of the Reichstag, proclaimed the republic. He was somewhat taken aback to be rebuked almost immediately by his colleague Ebert, who, 'purple with anger', told him bluntly: 'You have no right to proclaim the republic. What becomes of Germany—whether she becomes a republic or something else—a constituent assembly must decide.' Scheidemann did not know that even now Ebert hoped to preserve the monarchy in some form; his speech was a spontaneous reaction to the popular mood, not an attempt to force Ebert's hand. It was also intended to forestall the expected proclamation of a soviet republic by Liebknecht, of which Scheidemann had been warned. Indeed Scheidemann spoke none too soon, for only two hours later (about four o'clock) Liebknecht, cheered by an enthusiastic crowd, hoisted the red flag on the royal palace and declared Germany a free socialist republic. The rule of capitalism, which had turned Europe into a graveyard, said Liebknecht, was shattered, and he appealed to his audience to join him in completing the world revolution, begun in Russia and now continued in Germany.[1] The same afternoon Ebert was asking Prince Max to stay on as Regent, on the assumption that the monarchical constitution would remain.[2] Max refused; had he accepted, an awkward situation would have been created. Such were the two extreme points reached by what had once been the united Social Democratic party.

It was, nevertheless, the wish of the S.P.D., whose executive committee and parliamentary party met at the Reichstag on the morning of 9 November, to co-operate with the Independents, as Ebert had told Prince Max.[3] It was not easy to find a basis for agreement. Mutual dislike and distrust were strong. One practical difficulty was that Haase, the Independent leader, had not yet returned from Kiel. The absence of a leader at such a crisis would have been serious for any party, but it was doubly so in the case of one as divided as the Independents. On the question of co-operation with the S.P.D. opinions varied widely. Ledebour was vehemently opposed. He objected to the majority socialists for trying to 'smuggle themselves into the revolution'.[4] Scheidemann had resigned from the government only that morning, and until the day before the S.P.D. as a government party shared responsibility for

---

[1] R. Müller, *Vom Kaiserreich zur Republik*, II, 12–13.

[2] Max told Ebert: 'I know you are on the point of concluding an agreement with the Independents, and I cannot work with the Independents' (Max, *op. cit.* p. 362). Ebert's implied desire to save the monarchy illustrates not only his more right wing attitude, compared with Scheidemann, but also an attachment to strictly constitutional procedure, even during a revolution, which was on the whole typical of the S.P.D.

[3] According to Payer, who was present when Ebert received the three Independent socialist representatives at the Chancellery on 9 November, the tone of their conversation was brusque: Ebert was haughty and the Independents rather subdued. Friedrich Payer, *Von Bethmann Hollweg bis Ebert* (1923), p. 165.

[4] *Der Ledebour Prozess* (1919), p. 33.

suppressing Independent meetings and arresting their members. The U.S.P.D. could not so easily accept as colleagues a party whose opposition to the revolution was well known, and which had joined in the general strike only when no other course seemed possible. (*Vorwaerts* of 9 November contained a call for strike action in its midday, but not in its early morning edition.[1] This was in accordance with the S.P.D.'s decision of the day before to give the Kaiser till 9 a.m. on the 9th to announce his abdication. To the Independents it was additional evidence of the reluctance with which the S.P.D. took part in the popular movement.) Liebknecht, who represented the extreme left wing of the U.S.P.D., fully shared Ledebour's distrust. He argued that they should take up Ebert's offer only on condition that all legislative, executive and judicial power was placed in the hands of the workers' and soldiers' councils.[2] He was willing for the Independents to stay in office for three days only, in order to enable the government to sign the armistice. This was a direct challenge to Ebert, whose acceptance of Prince Max's suggestion to call a constituent assembly ruled out the dictatorship of the proletariat desired by Liebknecht. Right wing members of the U.S.P.D. were, however, by no means averse to a constituent assembly. After much debate the party finally agreed that they would join the S.P.D. on six conditions.[3] These included both Liebknecht's demand for government by councils, and the exclusion of all non-socialists from the new government. Neither was accepted by the S.P.D., which pointed out that a class dictatorship was contrary to their democratic principles. In the ensuing discussion Liebknecht was overruled and finally the Independents agreed to take part in an all-socialist government on terms which represented an uneasy compromise. The Independents did not drop their demand for council government but put it in a modified form: 'Political power lies in the hands of the workers' and soldiers' councils, which are forthwith to be called to a plenary meeting from the whole Reich.' On their part the S.P.D. conceded that their negotiations with the Independents would become topical only after 'the consolidation of the circumstances created by the revolution.'[4]

On this ambiguous formula the new government was based. It consisted of six 'People's Commissars', three from each socialist party. The S.P.D. members were Ebert (chairman), Scheidemann and Landsberg; from the U.S.P.D. came Haase (co-chairman), Dittmann and Barth.[5] Barth, representing the revolutionary shop-stewards, replaced Liebknecht who refused to compromise. Barth prided himself on being as radical as Liebknecht, but believed that it would be disastrous for the left to leave the field to the S.P.D.

---

[1] Stroebel, *op. cit.* p. 59; Bernstein, *Die deutsche Revolution*, pp. 19–31; H. Müller, *op cit.* p. 50.

[2] Scheidemann, *Memoirs*, II, 318.

[3] *Ibid.* p. 319.   [4] *Ibid.*

[5] Bernstein, *Die deutsche Revolution*, p. 45; Haase, *op. cit.* p. 63.

He himself would have preferred an all-Independent government, but clearly such a government would have lacked public support. The over-riding question whether Germany was to be governed by workers' and soldiers' councils or by a national parliament had been shelved, not solved. This was to be the main bone of contention between socialists during the ensuing period.

Meanwhile the revolution—'the greatest of all revolutions', according to the *Berliner Tageblatt* of 10 November—had triumphed in the streets of Berlin. From the middle of the morning onwards (when work ceased in the factories) tens of thousands of workers marched through the grey November streets in endless columns from the industrial suburbs to the heart of the city, the great squares before the Reichstag and the royal palace. Alongside them converging from all directions trooped processions of soldiers, many with their uniform jackets turned inside out and hanging loosely on their shoulders as a symbol of protest. Red flags were carried and red armbands worn; some of the demonstrators bore placards inscribed: 'Freedom! Peace! Bread! Brothers, do not shoot!' Most soldiers and some civilians were armed. Lorries and army cars rumbled by, packed with soldiers and decorated with red flags, their occupants exchanging cheers with the crowds in the street. The crowds swarmed into the public buildings, including those two strongholds of vanished power, the royal palace and the police headquarters. Although the government order to the troops not to shoot did not reach them till the afternoon, there was hardly any resistance to the insurgents; as in other German cities, police and soldiers simply fraternised with the crowd.[1]

Richard Müller, the leader of the shop-stewards, describes the scene:

The characteristic feature of this rising lay in the elemental force with which it broke out, in its wide range, and in its uniform, almost methodical activity in all parts of the enormous area of Greater Berlin. The rising did not develop from partial actions into one big action, it began as a single entity and evolved according to plan, like the great campaigns of the mass armies of the world war. It was as though the millions of workers and soldiers had been guided from a single spot. But there was no direction of that kind.[2]

[1] This brief account of 9 November in Berlin is based on a number of sources, of which the following are among the more important: *Illustrierte Geschichte der deutschen Revolution;* Buchner, *Revolutionsdokumente* (1921); T. Wolff, *Through Two Decades;* the works already cited of Scheidemann, R. Müller, Bernstein and H. Müller; and *Vorwaerts*. Among the regiments which went over to the revolution were the Naumburg Rifles (*Naumburger Jaeger*) at the Alexander Barracks, who had been considered especially reliable. At that barracks in 1901 William II had made one of his most notorious speeches telling the soldiers that in case of disturbances they must be ready to shoot at their own families to defend the emperor. The position of General von Linsingen, commanding the Brandenburg district of which Berlin formed a part, was rather obscure; he had resigned on 8 November but was apparently still at his post the following day, when he warned the minister of war that whatever orders were given to his troops they would not use their weapons against the revolution. Max, *op. cit.* p. 355.

[2] R. Müller, *Vom Kaiserreich zur Republik*, II, 16.

Neither the Social Democrats, who as late as the evening of 8 November had tried to stop the rising, nor the Independent socialists played the decisive part. Nor did the group of revolutionary shop-stewards headed by Barth, who, as we have seen, had decided to make their *coup* on 11 November and were overtaken by events. Barth had produced a handbill calling on the workers to strike and his men marched in the vanguard, but this cannot have made much difference to the numbers who came out.[1] The day before the government had tried to foil Barth's plans, of which it had heard, possibly through Ebert, by arresting Däumig, the Independent Reichstag member on Barth's committee.[2] Barth, who mistakenly believed that Liebknecht too had been arrested, gave the signal to his followers to rise, but their action was merged or submerged in the general revolutionary tide that was to carry Barth into the new government.

Some reports of 9 November mention signs of rejoicing at the fall of an unlamented regime, but to most people it was a bitter victory which the haggard working population of Berlin celebrated at the end of a lost war and in face of a future as sombre as the November weather. The German people had triumphed all along the line, proclaimed Scheidemann from the Reichstag, reminding them that the 'people's state' for which they had struggled so long was now an accomplished fact.[3] But the burdens of the present weighed too heavily to be offset by enthusiasm about the democratic future. The republican era had made an inauspicious start.

THE SOCIALISTS IN OFFICE

The agreement reached after some haggling between the two socialist parties had to be ratified by the workers' and soldiers' councils of Berlin, which were to meet on 10 November in a large hall known as the Circus Busch. Much therefore depended on the composition of that body. Both parties made feverish preparations to get their own supporters elected. Late on the evening of 9 November the Spartacists and their sympathisers in the U.S.P.D. met in the Reichstag building and planned the exclusion of the S.P.D. from the new government to be approved next day. To defeat this plan, the S.P.D. worked hard the same night to secure the election of delegates who were in favour of the constituent assembly, which the left had denounced.[4] Next morning it was the turn of the workers in the factories and the soldiers in the barracks to elect their representatives. Socialist differences were also reflected in the press. *Vorwaerts* appealed for reconciliation and unity between socialists of both parties, while the newly established Spartacist *Rote Fahne* urged true socialists to boycott a government which contained the S.P.D. The

---

[1] Barth, *op. cit.* p. 53.   [2] Max, *op. cit.* p. 279; Barth, *op. cit.* p. 30.
[3] Scheidemann, *Memoirs*, II, 263.
[4] *Prot. S.P.D.* (Weimar, 1919), pp. 12–13.

Spartacists even urged people not to vote for any Independent socialist who favoured collaboration.

The Circus Busch meeting was attended by about 3,000.[1] Barth and Richard Müller, the two leaders of the revolutionary shop-stewards, were elected chairman and secretary respectively of the workers' side of the assembly; a Lieutenant Walz and a soldier named Molkenbuhr were chosen for the corresponding offices by the soldiers. Speeches made by Ebert and by Haase (who had now returned from Kiel), urging unity, were warmly applauded, especially by the soldiers, to whom policy differences between socialists meant little. Liebknecht, who attacked Ebert as an enemy of the revolution, was given quite a cold reception, notably by the soldiers. When Barth proposed the election of an executive committee from which he wished to exclude the S.P.D., Ebert was quick to reply that while he did not see the necessity of such a committee, if there was to be one, it should include both parties in equal numbers. After a stormy scene an executive committee was chosen which contained fourteen workers and fourteen soldiers, half of each group being S.P.D. and half U.S.P.D. or shop-stewards. The meeting also approved the new cabinet of People's Commissars. A motion introduced by a left wing Independent, Däumig, declared that Germany was a socialist republic, and that political power lay with the workers' and soldiers' councils.[2] It affirmed that speedy socialisation was possible without causing serious disturbance to the country, expressed its admiration for the Russian revolutionaries and pride in following their example, and urged the resumption of diplomatic relations with the Soviet government. The Executive Council, as the newly elected committee was called, regarded itself as the German equivalent of the Executive Council of the Petrograd Soviet and claimed to be the supreme authority in the Reich, though it represented only the workers and soldiers of Greater Berlin.

The left had failed to win a tactical success at the Circus Busch because of lack of support from the rank and file. Yet the meeting had passed against negligible opposition a resolution which committed it to a left wing policy, and significantly omitted any reference to a constituent assembly. On the other hand, most of the worker delegates and a still larger majority of soldiers clearly opposed the left's attempt to debar the majority socialists from the Executive Council and to monopolise the revolution. In the excitement of the meeting the inconsistency between Däumig's resolution and the other decisions seems to have escaped notice. Most of the soldiers were, in any case, too uninitiated politically to grasp the implications of the resolution and were an easy prey to a persuasive orator. Ebert probably thought it best to let the radicals expend their energy in revolutionary speeches, in the belief that the

[1] Bernstein, *Die deutsche Revolution*, pp. 36 ff.
[2] The text of the proclamation is in R. Müller, *Vom Kaiserreich zur Republik*, II, 234–5.

tide would soon turn. For the moment, however, the main significance of the meeting was to show the world that the new all-socialist government of Germany had received its credentials from the democracy of the factory and barrack room. The break with the past was evident.

Thus by the evening of 10 November Ebert was ruling in a double capacity, after being for about twenty-four hours (9–10 November) Chancellor on his own. To the army, the civil servants, the middle classes generally he was the chosen quasi-legal successor to Prince Max, pledged to preserve law and order and to continue parliamentary government where Max had left off. Privy Councillor Simons, one of Max's trusted advisers, wrote: 'It is quite unthinkable that the old officers and officials would have offered their services to the new government had the Prince not given it some shred of legitimacy.'[1] To the Independents and Spartacists he was co-chairman of a revolutionary cabinet answerable to a workers' and soldiers' council and pledged to a more or less revolutionary programme. This double commitment involved a double policy. The incompatibility of these conflicting obligations was soon to be shown.

The main question was whether Germany was to be governed by workers' councils or by a parliament based on universal suffrage. The Independent socialists in a manifesto of 12 November seemed to range themselves with the former, for it contained an approving reference to councils but none to a constituent assembly.[2] Yet council government implied disfranchisement of the middle and upper classes, and was thus irreconcilable with the universal suffrage which all Social Democrats traditionally supported. Proletarian dictatorship had never been part of the S.P.D. programme. On the other hand, to proceed at once to the election of a constituent assembly would be to lose the revolutionary *élan* of the councils, which alone could transform German society and establish socialism. The solution of the problem seemed to lie in postponing the date of the constituent assembly until after a period of rule by the councils, and this proposal was put forward by the U.S.P.D in another manifesto. In this way they hoped to make a start in socialising the economy and to ensure their victory over the old regime without abandoning the democratic principle.

This situation represented a compromise between left-wingers like Däumig who did not want to have a constituent assembly at all, and right-wingers like Hilferding who regarded it as indispensable and urgent. A middle of the road view was expressed by the new Independent daily newspaper, *Freiheit*, which began publication on 15 November. In an early article *Freiheit* warned the left that proletarian dictatorship despite the stamp of approval given it

[1] Max, *op. cit.* II, 362 n. Simons later became president of the German Federal Supreme Court.
[2] Prager, *Geschichte der U.S.P.D.* pp. 184 ff.

by Lenin, would lead to civil war if the attempt were made to introduce it as a permanent form of government; such a policy would also split the workers, and would make peace with the Entente more difficult.[1] Haase, in a speech on 25 November, confirmed this view with a difference of emphasis by saying that government by workers' and soldiers' councils was necessary for a transitional period; formal democracy should be re-established only after the gains of the revolution had been consolidated—the vaguely reassuring formula used by his party on 10 November.[2]

The S.P.D. on the other hand did not waver in their belief that the future form of government in Germany should be decided by a constituent assembly. Ebert never had any doubt about it. On 12 November the cabinet had issued a proclamation to the German people which referred in general terms to a national assembly as a future event, about which further details would be announced. The only objection came from Barth, who, however, did not press it to the point of resignation.[3] The opposition of Haase and Dittmann to a constituent assembly was somewhat half-hearted. Moreover on 15 November the Independents agreed with their S.P.D. colleagues that the press should be told semi-officially that the government was working for the speediest possible calling of a constituent assembly.[4] But behind the issue of councils versus parliament lay a fundamental difference about the nature of the revolution. As early as 11 November Ebert told a Dutch newsagency that the revolution was over. For the Independents on the other hand, the taking of power was only the prelude to a radical transformation of German society: by that criterion the revolution had hardly begun, despite the grossly exaggerated claims in their manifesto of 12 November that the revolutionary people had 'made short shrift of the old rulers, the generals and bureaucrats ...broken the power of the officers in the army, the domination of the Junker caste in the government, the domination of the capitalist clique in public life, and taken control of the government'.[5] The Independent socialists soon realised that far less had in fact been achieved. Beneath the shifting surface of events the old institutions of the empire survived: the bureaucracy, the army command, the big industrialists, even the Junkers. The workers' and soldiers' councils were superimposed on the old system, but did not destroy it; and after a period of uneasy co-existence between the two, the councils were to disappear having accomplished little of their purpose. Meanwhile the split between the two socialist parties, so far from having ended with the armistice, had widened at a time when their co-operation was most essential.

[1] *Freiheit*, 18 November 1918.   [2] Haase, *op. cit.* p. 64.
[3] Barth, *op. cit.* p. 67. Barth signed the proclamation.
[4] *Cabinet*, 15 November 1918.   [5] Prager, *op. cit.* p. 184.

THE SOCIALIST GOVERNMENT AND
THE GENERALS

It is doubtful whether any co-operation between the two socialist parties would have been possible had the Independents known more about the secret conversations between Ebert and Groener, the first of which took place on the evening of 10 November. Earlier that day Hindenburg, on Groener's advice, had sent a message to all army groups telling them how to behave in the new situation created by the fall of the monarchy and the socialist assumption of power.[1] Hindenburg, the message explained, was now commander-in-chief in succession to the Kaiser. Since the growth of soldiers' councils in the field army could no longer be prevented, officers should accept them but try to bring them under control. Officers were to retain their power of command and their badges of rank. The last and most important part of the message was that the supreme command had decided to co-operate with Ebert, the new Chancellor and leader of the moderate Social Democratic party 'in order to prevent the spread of terroristic Bolshevism in Germany'. The message made no reference to the Council of People's Commissars, which formally came into existence the same day. But even after this information had become common knowledge Hindenburg and Groener significantly continued to address Ebert as Chancellor, though from 10 November onwards his power rested on the councils. It was fortunate for Groener that Ebert was responsible for military matters within the cabinet, and Ebert's double function—as chairman and as Commissar for the army— was one of which he was to make full use.

It was not enough for the generals to assure those under their command that the officer's authority remained; they also had to make sure that this was the policy of the new government, so that the field army would not be exposed to the demoralisation which had undermined the home army. Groener accordingly asked Ebert if the government would uphold the officer's authority and military discipline. The government's reply, dated 12 November, confirmed the retention by the officers of their power of command and the maintenance of discipline, and explained that the first duty of the soldiers' councils was to prevent disorder and mutiny.[2] Some historians have seen in this decision the turning point of the German revolution and the capitulation of the socialists to the generals.[3] The decision was crucial, but it was inevitable.

[1] Volkmann, *Der Marxismus*, p. 315.
[2] Schüddekopf, *Das Heer und die Republik* (Hanover and Frankfurt, 1955), p. 20.
[3] Caro and Oehme, for example, in their book *Schleichers Aufstieg* (Berlin, 1932), commented: 'The democratic republic had lost its battle of the Marne on the fourth day of the revolution.' Quoted in Schüddekopf, *op. cit.* p. 17. Another German historian (Leber) quoted by Schüddekopf mocked at the 'pacifist revolutionaries' as a contradiction in terms (*ibid.* p. 33 n.).

Even the Independent members of the cabinet voted for it, including Barth who at first objected.[1] The cabinet knew that if the officers in the field army lost their power of command the resultant breakdown of organisation and discipline would make impossible the orderly withdrawal of the three-million-strong army across the German frontier within the fifteen days allowed by the armistice. Any German soldiers left behind would automatically become prisoners-of-war. It was with these considerations in mind that Ebert's Independent colleagues accepted a concession to the generals which ran counter to their wishes and to the claim in their party manifesto of 12 November asserting that power in the army lay with soldiers' councils.[2] Liebknecht denounced the decision as a mortal blow and declared that the success of the revolution was more important than the orderly evacuation of the army.[3] That few of the soldiers in the field army would have agreed with Liebknecht is evident from the attitude of the soldiers' council at G.H.Q. when Groener explained to them the organisational complexities involved. The councils in the field army indeed showed little desire to go beyond the welfare function assigned to them.

How much further did Ebert go in his conversation with Groener on 10 November? In return for the pledge of army support he promised that the government would fight Bolshevism. But what was Bolshevism, and did Groener and Ebert understand the same thing by it?[4] For Ebert it meant Liebknecht and his policy of council dictatorship on soviet lines. For Groener it probably meant the claims of the Executive Council to be the sovereign power in Germany. Ebert shared Groener's mistrust of the Executive Council and general distaste for council government; but he had as his colleagues in the cabinet the Independent socialists who supported, at least temporarily, the Council regime. It is unlikely, despite Groener's later testimony, that Ebert promised Groener that he would try to oust the Independents from the government.[5] Yet Ebert's pact with Groener was

---

[1] Barth, *op. cit.* p. 65. Dittmann's reasons for not opposing the generals' wishes are given in ch. 15 of his memoirs.

[2] Dittmann, *op. cit.*

[3] Liebknecht, *Ausgewählte Reden, Briefe und Aufsätze*, p. 489.

[4] The initiative in the Groener–Ebert talks came from Groener. Friedrich Naumann, who had long been in favour of a *rapprochement* between the nationalists and the socialists and happened to be at G.H.Q. on 10 November took a message from Groener to Ebert, but while Naumann was still making his way to Berlin—in those circumstances a journey of uncertain duration—Groener decided to ring up Ebert and talk to him direct (Groener, *op. cit.* p. 467). An account of the first Ebert–Groener conversation is in Volkmann, *Revolution über Deutschland* (1930), p. 67. Hindenburg later approved Groener's action.

[5] Groener's account of his understanding or pact with Ebert was given during the 'stab in the back' trial of October 1925 in which Groener was a witness. In weighing his evidence, allowance must be made for the fact that Groener was concerned to clear his own name and that of Ebert (who had died a few months before) of libel by their nationalist critics. (Groener-Geyer, *General Groener*, pp. 190–201.)

hardly compatible with his pledge to the U.S.P.D. that the gains of the revolution would be consolidated before Germany returned to parliamentary government.

On 16 November the field army received a further directive from its chiefs informing them that it was returning to a country in which power was shared between the civil servants of the old regime and the workers' and soldiers' councils of the new. The latter were not efficient, and wherever possible troops should co-operate with the former; where this was not possible, soldiers' councils should act on their own responsibility. The directive explained that these councils had been sanctioned by the supreme command as an 'inoculation' against the extremists, and that a pact had been made between the army command and the new government under Ebert's leadership. The government needed a power factor, and the army would fill that role.[1]

Socialist distrust of the army was kept alive, however, by incidents that occurred during its return through Germany, such as the hauling down of the red flag from public buildings and anti-revolutionary speeches by officers. It was not long before the generals felt a renewal of the confidence they had momentarily lost through the shock of defeat and the Kaiser's abdication. On 8 December Hindenburg wrote a letter to Ebert putting forward political demands such as withdrawal of the recognition of soldiers' councils and the convening of a constituent assembly to end the council regime.[2] Ebert was in a difficult position: he needed the help of the army more than ever after the events of 6 December described in the next chapter, in view of the growing threat of the Spartacists against his government. Ebert asked the generals to send ten divisions to Berlin.[3] When news of this request reached the Executive Council their suspicions were aroused and they insisted that the troops should arrive unarmed.[4] This, of course, was contrary to the intentions of both Ebert and of the supreme command, and when the troops marched through the Brandenburg Gate it was with arms carried, bands playing and the monarchist red white and black flag flying.[5] There Ebert addressed them, thanking them for their services to the country and welcoming them to the socialist republic which would shortly be 'consolidated' by a constituent assembly. It was on this occasion that he told the soldiers that they returned undefeated—an unwise remark as well as an untrue one because it helped to feed the legend of the stab in the back already being circulated by the incorrigibles of the right. The immediate result of the despatch of troops to Berlin was, however, not what Ebert and Groener hoped for: the soldiers

---

[1] Volkmann, *Der Marxismus und das deutsche Heer im Weltkriege*, pp. 317 ff.
[2] Schüddekopf, *op. cit.* pp. 34 ff.
[3] *Ibid.* p. 29.
[4] Barth, *op. cit.* p. 84; Groener, *op. cit.* p. 473.
[5] Ebert, *op. cit.* II, 127.

quickly succumbed to the revolutionary atmosphere of the capital or went home to spend Christmas with their families.[1]

Although the full implications of the Ebert–Groener pact could not be guessed by Ebert's colleagues, the Independents were uneasy about it, and Haase's son afterwards wrote of his father at this time that he 'very soon suspected that Ebert was intriguing behind the backs of the other People's Commissars and was in very close contact with the army. But he could not realise to what extent that was in fact the case.'[2] Dittmann later denounced Ebert's policy as one of sabotage and claims to have noticed at the time the effect of Ebert's nocturnal talks with Groener in his attitude at the cabinet next morning. Ebert's relationship with the supreme command has been described as 'bordering on treason towards his own party',[3] an impression certainly strengthened by Groener's testimony during the 'stab in the back' trial at Munich in 1925. The cabinet minutes do not show that Ebert found it difficult to work with Haase and Dittmann; indeed the line of division often ran between Barth and the rest rather than between the two parties. Ebert was disingenuous in concealing what he told Groener from his colleagues, and he was probably wrong in taking Groener too far into his confidence. On the other hand, he had never made a secret of his disapproval of government by workers' and soldiers' councils, and he no doubt sincerely believed that his balancing act was in the national interest. Neither Ebert nor the Independents, nor Groener, foresaw the Spartacist rising which, more than anything else, was to encourage the revival of German militarism.

The problem before Ebert and his colleagues, that of the relationship between a socialist government and the army, was one to which little attention had been paid in socialist thinking. As Marxists the German socialists had always conceived the revolution in economic terms, never as a mutiny by sailors and soldiers, in which the officer, not the employer, would be the target of popular indignation. Before the war Liebknecht had campaigned against militarism, but in general left wing socialists saw militarism as a by-product of imperialism, to be eradicated only by the overthrow of capitalism. Liebknecht recognised that in the German revolution the soldiers were anti-officer rather than anti-capitalist; as he wrote in the *Rote Fahne* of 19 November: 'The bulk of the soldiers are revolutionary against militarism, against war and the open representatives of imperialism: in relation to socialism they are still divided, hesitant and immature.'[4] There was of course a class element in this revolt against officers: the dislike of the conscripted

---

[1] Dittmann, *op. cit.* Of the ten divisions only some 1,800–2,000 men were still in the army by 23 December.
[2] Haase, *op. cit.* p. 63.
[3] Volkmann, *Revolution über Deutschland*, p. 54.
[4] Liebknecht, *op. cit.* p. 469.

man in the street for the representatives of a professional caste, whose 20,000 members had held a unique position in pre-war Germany, and who during the war often continued to act in an overbearing way. The November revolution was for most of its supporters a movement for democracy even more than for socialism, and hatred of Prussian militarism was shared by many who were far from being extremists. But the rapid disintegration of the imperial army in November and December 1918 seemed to such people to have solved the militarist problem.

CHAPTER 8

THE EXPERIMENT IN
REVOLUTIONARY GOVERNMENT

Pacifist revolutionaries—what a contradiction!   TROTSKY
For us, socialism without democracy is unthinkable.
         KAUTSKY in 1918

THE PEOPLE'S COMMISSARS AT WORK

The tasks which faced the group of inexperienced and divided men who formed the first government of Republican Germany were daunting enough to have taxed the abilities of a much more expert and united body. Apart from Scheidemann's membership of Prince Max's short-lived government, none of the People's Commissars had held public office before, and they were very much aware of their own limitations and of the immensity of the problems confronting them. First they were responsible for carrying out the extremely onerous terms of an armistice signed within hours of their taking office. The army in the west, consisting of about 183 divisions, had to be withdrawn, with such equipment as it could carry and was not obliged to hand over to the Allies, to the German frontier within fifteen days; and within a further fifteen days to a line east of the Rhine. This was a formidable undertaking, for which Groener's administrative talent and transport experience were invaluable. These troops, with those to be brought back from other fronts, had to be demobilised and absorbed into civilian employment. Industry, which was short of capital and raw materials and almost entirely geared to war production, had to be converted to peacetime uses. As the Allied blockade remained in force, special measures had to be taken to import essential food and other supplies. The political unity of Germany, which was only a generation old, had to be safeguarded against the various centrifugal forces which threatened it pending the adoption of a new constitution. Until then, too, a way had to be found of reconciling differences between Social Democrats and Independents on the vexed question of the role of workers' and soldiers' councils. Closely connected with this question was the policy to be followed in regard to Soviet Russia, whose hostility to the S.P.D. and support of Liebknecht had been hardened by the recent expulsion of the Soviet ambassador in Berlin. The new government had also to take into account the restored state of Poland, with its claims to Posen (Poznań), West Prussia and part of Upper Silesia. Underlying the debates of the People's Commissars on all these subjects was the fundamental divergence between the Social Democrats, who wanted to control and contain the revolution, and the Independents, who wanted to accelerate and expand it. The picture was complicated by the emergence within the U.S.P.D. of a right and left wing, so that three different policies were being simultaneously pursued by the various leaders of the governmental and quasi-governmental bodies.

One of the first acts of the new government was to issue (on 12 November) a proclamation to the German people which put an end to the restrictions imposed during the war by abolishing martial law and the censorship, established freedom of the written and spoken word, amnestied all remaining political prisoners, rescinded the wartime direction of labour (*Hilfsdienstgesetz*), and restored the pre-war laws for the protection of labour. The proclamation decreed that all future elections should be by secret ballot, with votes for both sexes over the age of twenty, and that this franchise would apply to the election of a constituent assembly, about which a further announcement would be made. It also laid down an eight-hour day (a measure for which the trade unions had been pressing for thirty years) and provided for unemployment relief. As a whole this proclamation represented one of the few gains of the German revolution which was not swept away in the reaction which followed; and Dittmann described it as the revolution's Magna Carta.[1] It did something to satisfy the strong desire for immediate social and economic reform among the rank and file of both socialist parties.[2]

[1] R. Müller, *Vom Kaiserreich zur Republik*, II, 47.
[2] Dittmann, *Lebenserinnerungen*, ch. 15. Meanwhile another development had also helped to blunt the edge of the more radical economic demands—an agreement between employers and trade unions. During the war the unions, which, with their emphasis on practical reforms, had always sided with the revisionist wing of the S.P.D. against the revolutionaries, had established a relationship with the government not unlike that between the government and the majority socialists. In return for concessions, such as recognition of the unions' status and new wage scales in state factories, the unions gave loyal support on the whole to the government's war policy, and their leaders co-operated with Groener in the work of the *Kriegsamt*, and in carrying out the conscription of labour law. In the course of the war far-sighted industrialists such as Rathenau realised that a new age was beginning in which the employers would have to adopt a less paternal attitude to their men, and that the unions would have to be accepted and their co-operation sought. The unions drew up a list of demands early in 1918, but their opportunity came when signs of approaching defeat multiplied in the early autumn. At the beginning of October (when the trade union leader Bauer entered the new government as minister of labour) the Ruhr employers, foreseeing revolution with its threat of socialisation, met in Düsseldorf and decided to negotiate with the unions, whom they viewed as future allies in place of an unreliable middle class. The negotiations lasted several weeks and led to an agreement which was signed on 15 November and endorsed by the socialist cabinet. It dealt with such matters as demobilisation procedure, the eight-hour day, unemployment pay, official recognition of the General Trade Unions to the exclusion of the 'yellow' unions, and the representation of workers at all levels of industry to negotiate with employers on wage claims and other matters. On 23 November a government decree made agreed wage rates and arbitration in case of dispute legally binding. These gains gave the unions a great deal of what they wanted, while the industrialists believed they had saved themselves from socialisation. The left wing Independents and Spartacists denounced the

A more controversial matter on which an urgent decision was needed was the completion of the new government. The People's Commissars were a small super-cabinet; below them were the secretaries of state and other ministers who continued in office as heads of departments. The S.P.D. view was that existing ministers, none of whom were socialists, should stay on, because many of these posts required technical qualifications which socialists did not possess. It was also felt desirable that responsibility for carrying out the onerous and unpopular armistice terms should not rest exclusively on socialist shoulders.[1] The Independents, however, feared that non-socialist ministers might sabotage the revolution; hence their insistence before taking office that any 'bourgeois specialists' appointed or left in office should rank only as technical assistants.[2] On these terms Solf, the foreign secretary, and Scheüch, the secretary for war, were allowed to remain; and two liberals, Schiffer and Preuss, were made ministers of finance and home affairs respectively. To allay the fears of the left, two assistants (*Beigeordnete*), one from each socialist party, were attached to each Reich ministry in a supervisory capacity.[3] The cabinet minutes show that Schiffer for one used his influence to persuade the government not to embark on a policy of hasty socialisation, so that the suspicions of the left proved not without foundation. On the other hand, as far as Ebert was concerned such influence was not of great importance as it coincided with his own thinking.

In their proclamation of 12 November the People's Commissars also announced that they were beginning to implement the socialist programme, but added a caveat that they would maintain orderly production and protect property. Barth tried to persuade his colleagues to include in the proclamation a pledge to socialise mining and other industries but they refused to commit themselves.[4] On 18 November the cabinet discussed the industries which could be considered ripe for socialisation, and decided to refer the whole question to a special commission. This commission was set up with a total of nine, four of whom were well-known members of the two socialist parties, and five professors of economics, mostly of left wing sympathies. Kautsky, who had written a book on socialisation, was made chairman. Among the other socialist members was Hilferding, who had written a Marxist study of imperialism (*Das Finanzkapital*, 1910) and was now editor of the Independent daily *Freiheit*.[5]

agreement of 15 November as a betrayal of the revolution. See R. Müller, *Vom Kaiserreich zur Republik*, II, 106–113, and *Freiheit* of 18 November 1918 and 26 February 1919.

[1] Barth, *Aus der Werkstatt der deutschen Revolution*, p. 64.
[2] Scheidemann, *Memoirs*, II, 270.
[3] R. Müller, *Vom Kaiserreich zur Republik*, p. 47.
[4] Barth, *op. cit.* p. 68; *Cabinet*, 21 November.
[5] Born in Vienna in 1877, Rudolf Hilferding qualified as a doctor of medicine before joining the socialist movement and throwing in his lot with the S.P.D. He became one of the party's leading experts on financial and economic questions, and was on the staff

The socialisation commission began its meetings on 5 December. By that time some of the difficulties involved in a policy of immediate socialisation had become apparent and doubts about its wisdom had accumulated. Following Marx, German socialists conceived of socialism as something that would come about when the productive capacity of industry was ready to burst its capitalist husk. But in November 1918 German industry presented just the opposite picture: not capitalist forms of production or under-consumption, but shortage of capital and raw materials were the restricting factors. Eisner, speaking as socialist prime minister of Bavaria, told the Bavarian people as early as 15 November that one could hardly socialise where there was barely anything to be socialised, and the same point was made by many other socialist leaders, including some Independents. That was certainly Kautsky's view.[1] One of the few dissentient voices was that of Liebknecht, who argued that state control of the economy during the war had shown that socialism could work under conditions of scarcity.[2] But Scheidemann urged in cabinet that too much talk of socialism would frighten the employers and make it harder to provide jobs for the millions awaiting demobilisation, while Bauer, the S.P.D. minister of labour, warned that premature socialisation would produce 'Russian conditions'.[3] Haase did not disagree. The threat of socialism made employers unwilling to place orders for their factories, and their nervousness was heightened by incidents in Berlin in which workers seized factories on their own initiative and tried to set up a form of 'workers' control'. To help the economy over the critical transition between war and peace, the government placed a number of contracts, but at the cost of weakening the mark, already only two-fifths of its pre-war value.

of *Vorwaerts* at the beginning of the war. Like many of his journalist colleagues, he supported the opposition to the S.P.D.'s war policy, and played a part in the U.S.P.D. He was especially active in the Independent socialist conferences of Leipzig (1919) and Halle (1920), where he resisted the pro-Communist orientation of the party's left wing. A member of the Reichstag from 1924 to 1933 for the S.P.D. (which he rejoined after the split of the U.S.P.D.), Hilferding was twice Reich finance minister in coalition governments during the Weimar period. In 1933 he fled to France, where he was arrested by the Gestapo in 1940. He committed suicide in a Paris prison in 1941.

[1] H. Müller, *Die November Revolution*, p. 198. Having set up the socialisation commission, the S.P.D. leaders were content to await its report, while the left wing Independents continued to demand immediate measures of socialisation, and under their pressure Ebert asked the commission to draw up plans for nationalising the coalmines. The commission issued an interim report on 7 January which proved to be a cautious and judicious document, giving little comfort to the 'whole-hoggers': while upholding the principle of socialisation, it stressed the dangers of disrupting production and the need to study the industries concerned before acting. By this date the government was preoccupied with the rising in Berlin and other towns and with preparations for the election of the constituent assembly. The failure of the socialist parties to win the majority of seats made it harder, as the Independents had foreseen, to carry out a radical policy; but Ebert was almost certainly right in his belief that a full-scale socialist programme not backed by a parliamentary majority would have been rejected by the country. See also p. 226 below.

[2] Liebknecht, *Ausgewaehlte Reden, Briefe und Aufsätze*, p. 514.

[3] *Cabinet*, 21 November.

One of the arguments used by the opponents of socialism was that any firms or industries socialised might be treated by the Allies as Reich property and thus earmarked for reparations; and it was suggested that the coalmines of Upper Silesia would be less likely to be handed over to the Poles if they remained in private hands.[1] Similar objections were urged to state interference in the ownership of land. But the main reason why the big estates east of the river Elbe were not divided among the peasants was fear that the resulting dislocation would deter farmers from planting next year's harvest and aggravate the food shortage.[2] Thus the war and the defeat, which alone made the German revolution possible, raised serious practical obstacles to the realisation of a revolutionary programme.

The Spartacists sought to embarrass the government not only by demanding immediate socialisation but by pressing for a shorter working day (six hours instead of eight) and inciting to strikes. This was very galling to Barth as the most left wing member of the cabinet; he warned the workers' councils in Berlin that it was wrong to use the revolution simply as a lever for pushing up wages, and denounced the Spartacists for irresponsibility in trying to wreck the economy.[3] Ebert had to call for restraint. He told a big public meeting on 1 December that socialism meant orderly planning of the economy for the whole community: 'Socialism excludes everything arbitrary, it is order on the highest level; disorder, personal caprice and violence are the mortal enemies of socialism.'[4] He went on to quote Lenin's praise of discipline and order, ignoring Lenin's emphasis, as in *The State and Revolution*, on destroying the old before building the new. That Ebert had no desire for radical change is clear not only from such speeches as this, and from his earlier assurance to Prince Max ('I hate the social revolution like sin'); but above all from his repeated desire to get Germany back on the road of parliamentary democracy through the earliest possible election of a constituent assembly.

Socialisation and the question of a constituent assembly were the two most important issues discussed at a conference of the prime ministers of all German states held at Berlin on 25 November.[5] This was one of the two crucial all-German gatherings held during the revolutionary period, the other being the congress of workers' and soldiers' councils three weeks later. The conference was addressed by the ministers of food, demobilisation, labour and finance, whose warning of the unfavourable consequences of hasty and ill advised socialisation on the precarious German economy with its weak currency made a considerable impression. A resolution in favour of leaving the banks and savings banks alone in order to safeguard food-supplies and

[1] Dittmann, *Lebenserinnerungen*, ch. 15.   [2] *Ibid.*
[3] Barth, *op. cit.* pp. 79, 127.   [4] Ebert, *op. cit.* II, 123.
[5] Bernstein, *Die deutsche Revolution*, pp. 67 ff.; H. Müller, *op. cit.* pp. 152 ff.

imports was passed unanimously. The finance minister, Schiffer, foreshadowed a programme of radical taxation but emphasised that such a measure needed the authority which only a constituent assembly could give. And so when another resolution in favour of such an assembly was put it was passed with only two dissentients (Brunswick and Gotha). Some of the Independents, like Eisner, wanted the assembly delayed, but it was finally agreed that the date should be left to the forthcoming congress of workers' and soldiers' councils. It was a triumph for Ebert that twenty-three out of twenty-five prime ministers, including several Independent socialists, should support him in desiring a return to a parliamentary regime. Another result of the conference which gave him satisfaction was that this agreement on a common policy represented a check to the separatist trends that in different parts of the country threatened to break up the unity formed by Bismarck, which some at least of the Allies were thinking of destroying.

It was at this conference that Eisner demanded the dismissal of Solf, the foreign secretary, and Erzberger, the leader of the armistice commission, on the grounds that they were compromised with the old regime.[1] Although Eisner did not get much support, Solf was dismissed soon afterwards. Eisner also criticised Scheidemann and David—who was an undersecretary at the foreign office—which did not add to his popularity among the majority socialists. The purging of the foreign office was part of Eisner's general policy of repudiating the past and showing the world that the new Germany was different from the old. Eisner proceeded to make public certain documents from the Bavarian foreign ministry which purported to prove Germany's war guilt—in which Eisner himself believed; and he urged that the Reich government should do likewise. In this way, he was convinced, German opinion would be enlightened, the Allies persuaded of Germany's sincerity, and the way cleared for the reconciliation of peoples. Eisner was really more concerned with the ethical and pacifist aspects of the revolution than with the Marxist and economic. His idealism was as genuine as President Wilson's, but like Wilson, Eisner failed to evoke an adequate response from his fellow-countrymen. Indeed in the eyes of German nationalists Eisner's proclamation of German war guilt was just gratuitously damaging to the German case and likely to produce a hardening of the terms of peace.

Meanwhile, despite the decision by the conference of 25 November in favour of a constituent assembly, the left wing of the Independent socialists continued to oppose it, and Richard Müller, the Independent chairman of the Executive Council, rhetorically declared that the assembly would meet only over his dead body.[2] When the question was again discussed in cabinet on

---

[1] H. Müller, *op. cit.* p. 152; R. Müller, *op. cit.*, pp. 133–5.
[2] *Ibid.* pp. 84–5. From this time onwards his nickname was 'Müller the corpse'.

29 November, the three Independents urged that for the time being no election date should be fixed, using the argument that it would be wrong to hold the elections before the 800,000 prisoners in Allied hands returned to Germany. This seemed plausible, but the real reason for the delay insisted on was to provide more time in which to bring about such changes in German society as would guarantee the revolutionary settlement. After much wrangling it was decided by five of the People's Commissars (Barth abstaining) that the date of election should be 16 February, but that this should be subject to ratification by the forthcoming congress of workers' and soldiers' councils.[1] The Independents still optimistically hoped that by the time the assembly met it would be faced with a number of accomplished facts.

Richard Müller's opposition to the constituent assembly was typical of the attitude of the Executive Council, which throughout this period remained a thorn in the side of the People's Commissars. In the rivalry between these two bodies doctrinal differences within socialism assumed an institutional form. The Council saw itself as the supreme authority in Germany since it had the right to appoint and dismiss the People's Commissars. It claimed and exercised the right to appoint the government of Prussia, where, as in the Reich, Social Democrats and Independents sat in equal numbers. The Council also demanded a general right of supervision over the Reich ministries, thus clashing with the Commissars, who regarded this as interference in their sphere.[2] The Executive Council put another spoke in the wheel of the cabinet and greatly embarrassed Ebert by countermanding the cabinet's telegram to Hindenburg confirming the officers' power of command. (Groener in his *Memoirs* refers to the Executive Council as a kind of second government.) When the new Prussian government ordered that senior government officials (*Regierungspräsidente* and *Landräte*) should stay in office, the Executive Council came back with a tart counter-order telling the officials concerned that their tenure of office would be subject to supervision by the local peasants' or workers' council, and that any who performed their duties in the spirit of the old regime or showed counter-revolutionary tendencies would be dismissed.[3] Nor were foreign affairs exempt from the Council's interference. It appealed, forlornly, to the proletariat of the Allied countries and America to make their governments soften the armistice terms and to follow the German example by carrying out their own revolutions.[4] The Executive Council came nearer to success when the Independent Däumig moved a resolution in favour of setting up a 'proletarian democracy', by which he meant the enlargement of the Executive Council to represent the whole of Germany instead of just Berlin (but not, of course, the non-proletarian

[1] *Ibid.* p. 53; Bernstein, *op. cit.* p. 79.
[2] R. Müller, *op. cit.* p. 146; Bernstein, *op. cit.* p. 51.
[3] R. Müller, *op. cit.* p. 54.   [4] *Ibid.* p. 55.

classes) and the abandonment of plans for the constituent assembly. This resolution received some support from S.P.D. and soldier members of the Council and was rejected by the narrow margin of two votes.[1] Had it been passed a showdown with the People's Commissars could not have been avoided, for Ebert would not have given way. Angrily, he declared that the cabinet would not be puppets of the Executive Council.

Some limitation of the powers of the Executive Council had become an urgent necessity, and on 23 November it was agreed that the Council should exercise supervision of the government only until the meeting of the congress of councils, which would represent Germany and not, like the Executive Council, mainly Berlin.[2] Ebert was gradually successful in pressing his view that the Executive Council, despite its name, should not intervene in executive matters, which were the responsibility of the People's Commissars. Yet the Council retained, by the agreement of 23 November, a vague general mandate to safeguard the 'achievements of the revolution'. Theoretically it and the cabinet should have pursued the same policy because both were composed of representatives of the two socialist parties in equal numbers. In practice S.P.D. views tended to prevail in the cabinet and Independent views in the Council, with right wing Independents unsuccessfully trying to steer a middle course. The Council damaged its case by making exaggerated claims. It acquired a reputation for incompetence as well as for meddling in matters outside its scope, and in the provinces was criticised for seeking to impose a Berlin dictatorship on the rest of Germany.[3] One example of its attempt to assert authority in a way which brought discredit on itself was the arrest on 7 December of two prominent Ruhr industrialists, Stinnes and Thyssen, on a charge of conspiring with other industrialists to induce the Allies to occupy the Ruhr, the implication being that they would have preferred foreign occupation to socialism. The charges could not be substantiated, and after a protest to the Executive Council from the cabinet the two men were released.[4] The Council earned a name for financial waste as well as administrative inefficiency. Nor was criticism confined to the right. Rosa Luxemburg made a scornful comparison between the Council and the Soviet body after which it was named:

The Executive Council of the United Russian Soviets is—whatever one may say against it—admittedly something different from the Berlin Executive Council. The former is the head and brain of an important revolutionary-proletarian organisation, the latter the fifth wheel on the cart of a crypto-capitalist government clique, the former is the inexhaustible source of proletarian power, the latter is like an emptied flask hanging at one's side on a hot summer day, the former is the living body of the revolution and the latter its coffin.[5]

---

[1] R. Müller, *op. cit.* p. 82.   [2] *Ibid.* p. 147.   [3] *Ibid.* p. 106.
[4] *Ibid.* p. 206; *Cabinet*, 11 December.
[5] R. Müller, *op. cit.* p. 160.

Her exasperation was shared, though for different reasons, by Ebert, who told his cabinet colleagues on 13 December that the S.P.D. would leave the government unless the Executive Council ceased to encourage local workers' and soldiers' councils to interfere in government matters.[1] Three days later however, the congress of workers' and soldiers' councils solved the problem by relegating the Executive Council to the status of a purely Berlin body.

In foreign policy disagreements between the two socialist parties were usually, though not always, less pronounced. Haase was the People's Commissar responsible for foreign affairs, with Solf as his minister. Solf, who had occupied that position since Hertling's Chancellorship, was unsympathetic to the revolution, and the Independents had already decided that he must go before Eisner's bitter attack on Solf at the congress of prime ministers on 25 November. One of the most urgent and controversial problems was Germany's relation to Soviet Russia. The Soviets naturally resented the expulsion of their ambassador, Joffé, after the incident of the dropped propaganda boxes early in November, but since then a new government had come to power in Berlin, including the Independent socialists with whom Joffé had been on terms of cordiality; and the Russians expected some return for the moral and material help they had given the revolutionary groups in Germany.[2] As early as 22 October Lenin had told the All-Russian Soviet that the German revolution had begun. In the middle of November he declared: 'The Scheidemann gang will not remain at the helm very long; it does not represent the broad masses of the people.'[3] (This was not the first or last time that Lenin was to misjudge the situation in Germany.) The workers' and soldiers' councils at the Circus Busch on 10 November passed a resolution, drafted by Haase, in favour of resuming diplomatic relations with the Soviets, and proposed to invite Russian delegates to the forthcoming councils' congress. Yet when the question of inviting Joffé back was discussed in the German cabinet, Haase urged delaying tactics and was supported by the strongly anti-Bolshevik Kautsky, whose advice was sought as one of the new controllers of the foreign office.[4] There was resentment in Berlin at a Russian broadcast of 11 November urging the German people to seize power by force and establish a council regime under Liebknecht. The People's Commissars replied rejecting Russian interference in German internal affairs, and demanding that, before diplomatic relations were re-established,

---

[1] *Cabinet*, 13 December. It was on this occasion that Ebert, impatient with the obstructiveness of the Executive Council, and having heard a report from Preuss that the councils might interfere with the election of the constituent assembly, exclaimed: 'Things can't go on like this! We are making fools of ourselves before history and the whole world.'

[2] After 9 November Joffé wired to Haase: 'I congratulate myself and I rejoice on having personally, in accord with the Independent ministers, contributed to the victory of the German Revolution' (Fainsod, *International Socialism and the World War*, p. 179). But the mood in Russia soon changed, as the broadcast of 11 November showed.

[3] *Ibid.*   [4] *Cabinet*, 18 November.

the Soviets should recognise the Ebert–Haase government and clarify the circumstances under which the German consulates in Petrograd and Moscow had recently been closed.[1] The Germans believed that any *rapprochement* with Soviet Russia would excite the distrust of the Allies, on whom they depended entirely for imports of food and raw materials, and from whom they hoped for a relaxation of the armistice terms.[2] That German misgivings were not without foundation is clear from a Russian proposal that one of the Bolsheviks (probably Radek) should be allowed to conduct revolutionary propaganda among British and French prisoners-of-war in Germany. But the mixture of caution and suspicion which characterised the attitude of most of the cabinet towards Soviet Russia was not shared by the more radical Executive Council, which remained anxious for cordial relations with Moscow. The cabinet also asked the Soviet government to 'declare its attitude' to the broadcasts, but invited it to send a representative to the general congress of workers' and soldiers' councils. The door was left open for Joffé's eventual return; Kautsky added that he would have to promise not to conduct propaganda among the Allied occupation troops in western Germany. Haase warned his colleagues that German socialists should not let themselves take part in an anti-Bolshevik crusade.

Fresh embarrassment was caused early in December when Joffé, in a further broadcast from Russia, gave details of the money and arms which he had supplied to the revolutionary socialists in Germany. When the matter was discussed in cabinet on 9 and 18 December, Haase denied having received any money from the Russians and said that though the latter had distributed pamphlets they had done so through the Spartacists, not the U.S.P.D. Solf, who was present, remained unconvinced, and refused to shake hands with Haase. Barth admitted having accepted for his revolutionary shop-stewards arms and money from foreign pacifists, 'German idealists' and another unspecified source, which was generally understood to be Russia. But Barth denied that any Russian money had been given to him, and Haase disclaimed knowledge of Barth's having received Russian arms or buying arms with Russian money.[3] Joffé's broadcast was widely publicised and was used by the right to discredit the government and reinforce the stab in the back legend. The *Deutsche Tageszeitung* of 11 December headed its leading article: 'German Revolution, Russian Money.' Against the sole opposition of Barth, the cabinet decided to withdraw the invitation to a Russian delegate to the congress of councils; even Barth's patience gave out when in another broad-

---

[1] *Cabinet*, 18 November; Barth, *op. cit.* p. 86.
[2] Ebert showed the cabinet a note from the German ambassador at The Hague declaring that any return of the Soviet ambassador to Berlin would be viewed by the Allies as confirmation of the Russo-German offensive alliance advocated in Radek's notorious broadcast, and would cause an immediate termination of the armistice (Barth, *op. cit.* p. 68).
[3] *Cabinet*, 9 and 18 December.

cast Radek, the Bolshevik leader who had lived in Germany before the war and was to play a key part in Russo-German relations in the next few years, appealed for a common struggle between Germany and Russia against Entente capitalism. 'This stupid phrase', commented Barth, 'was a great blunder and the greatest possible damage to the world revolution.'[1] The German masses felt themselves too much at the mercy of the Entente, and too exhausted by the war and the blockade, to contemplate reviving hostilities with Russian help. Scheidemann, strongly anti-Bolshevik as he was, admitted that on this issue there was little difference between the S.P.D. and the Independents. The Russian attitude was understandable; they saw in the victorious German revolution (confidently predicted by Lenin in a letter to the Spartacists written on 18 October) the salvation of their own hard pressed regime and expected that, just as Kerensky had been superseded by Lenin, so Ebert would be by Liebknecht.[2]

Another urgent and difficult problem was Germany's attitude to the Poles, their new, uncomfortable eastern neighbour. Poland, whose frontiers were to be decided at Versailles, occupied a key position across the lines of communication of the German armies still deployed in the former Russian empire. Numbering half a million, these were strung out in an arc stretching from the

---

[1] Barth, *op. cit.* p. 68. Soviet disillusion with the Independent socialists was deepened when Haase refused the Russian offer of two trainloads of grain (or flour as stated in the official history of the German Communist party), while an offer of food by the American secretary of state Lansing on 13 November was gratefully accepted. Proof has now come to light of what was formerly only suspected—that Ebert made unscrupulous use of the prevailing and genuine fear of Bolshevism by exaggerating the unfavourable reaction of the Americans and the Allies to any Russo-German *rapprochement* (see p. 266, n. 1 below, and Kolb, *Die Arbeiterräte in der deutschen Innenpolitik, 1918–19* (1962), pp. 184 ff.). This attitude, confirmed by the refusal to admit a Soviet delegation to the congress of workers' and soldiers' councils in December 1918, caused resentment in Russia, which was especially directed at the Independents' acquiescence in the anti-Soviet policy of Ebert and Scheidemann. The Russian view is summed up in the words of a Soviet historian (M. Tanin) that their fraternal hand extended to Germany was left hanging in mid-air (see L. Kochan, *The Struggle for Germany* (1964), p. 12). But a Soviet broadcast to Germany of 11 November called on the workers', soldiers' and sailors' councils to rise against the new government and form a government headed by Liebknecht, and to reject the proposed constituent assembly. This was seen by the Ebert–Haase cabinet as an unwarrantable interference in Germany's internal affairs and as making normal relations with Russia impossible. In short, the Soviet terms for friendship were unacceptable for any German government that was not Spartacist. Radek's speech at the foundation conference of the German Communist party (see ch. 9 below) gives the wider context: Radek offered co-operation between the two countries on conditions which no prudent German government could have accepted and which showed how far the Bolsheviks were from grasping the mood and problems of post-war Germany (see also Bernstein, *op. cit.* p. 187, and Scheidemann, *Der Zusammenbruch*, p. 225). That the Independents in the government broadly agreed with their S.P.D. colleagues over Russia (except that the former were much more concerned to avoid any hostile action towards the Soviet regime) is no doubt partly due to the influence of the right wing Independent Kautsky in the Foreign Office. But even Barth is said to have declared that a resumption of relations with Soviet Russia would be a *casus belli* for the Entente.

[2] *Zur Geschichte der Kommunistischen Partei Deutschlands* (1954), p. 43.

Baltic to the Caucasus. Barth suggested that special all-socialist commissions be formed to arrange for the orderly withdrawal of the German troops through the states of eastern Europe, and he urged that by establishing friendly relations with the Poles, Germany would make sure of supplies of food and coal as well as fulfil a moral obligation.[1] Such a policy, however, was made impossible by the German refusal to cede to the Poles the former Polish territories of West Prussia and Posen. By an impromptu agreement on 11 November between the German soldiers' councils, which had been formed in Warsaw and other towns, and the Polish authorities, headed by Pilsudski, the future ruler of Poland, the German troops were guaranteed a safe return to their country provided they gave up their arms at the last station before entering Germany. The German supreme command was distressed to learn of this agreement, which it considered shameful.[2] The People's Commissars debated the possibility of forming a defence force, originally intended to safeguard food supplies from the east, but now needed, Ebert said, to protect Upper Silesia from Polish armed bands and political propaganda. Haase and Barth disagreed. Such a force, they pointed out, would annoy the Poles and so endanger the safe return of the troops; it would also be a source of counter-revolution.[3] By now the supreme command had taken the law into their own hands and issued a secret order to Eastern Command (*Oberost*) that evacuation of the disputed territories should be only partial, and authorising the formation of volunteer units for use at key points in those territories.[4] When news of this despatch reached the cabinet, Barth was furious. He demanded that Groener be dismissed and charged with insubordination and high treason. His colleagues were content to require an explanation from Groener. Ebert pooh-poohed talk of counter-revolution, saying such expressions would get them nowhere.[5] There is irony in an entry in Ebert's diary for 19 November, in which he noted that a guarantee that the new eastern defence force (*Heimatschutz Ost*) would not be counter-revolutionary was given by Erzberger and Kapp—the same Kapp who was to stage a counter-revolutionary putsch sixteen months later.[6]

The Polish situation came up again in cabinet on 24 and 26 December. A spokesman of the foreign office reported a Polish ultimatum: in exchange for the safe return of German troops in or beyond Poland, the German government should sell the Poles 10,000 rifles and 500 machine guns for use against

---

[1] Barth, *op. cit.* p. 69.

[2] Volkmann, *Revolution über Deutschland* (1930), p. 108; Benoist-Méchin, *Histoire de l'armée allemande* (1936), I, 257. The German army in the east, which contained a large number of Poles and Alsace-Lorrainers, had been more influenced than the army in the west by the Russian revolution, and when the German revolution broke out soldiers' councils were rapidly elected and deprived the officers of effective power (Volkmann, *op. cit.* pp. 262 ff.).

[3] *Cabinet*, 19 and 21 November.   [4] Barth, *op. cit.* p. 75.

[5] *Cabinet*, 21 November.   [6] Ebert, *op. cit.* II, p. 105.

the Bolsheviks. The S.P.D. members of the cabinet agreed to this demand; the Independents objected. Haase feared that by supplying arms to the Poles they would further embroil themselves with the Soviets who feared Polish encroachments. Erzberger, who was present on 26 December as leader of the armistice commission, sided with Haase, saying that the proposed sale of arms would be a breach of the armistice. Next day a foreign office official told the cabinet that an armed clash between Poles and Germans had taken place in Posen, which Paderewski had entered the day before, and recommended that war be declared on Poland. Landsberg, who was anti-Polish, strongly supported him, and, according to Barth's account, only the determined opposition of the Independents prevented war breaking out. They accused their S.P.D. colleagues of inconsistency in wanting to sell arms to the Poles one day and proposing to fight them the next. A state of undeclared war persisted on the German–Polish frontier, with the Germans holding their own but unable to reconquer Posen.[1]

The denunciation of the treaty of Brest-Litovsk by the Allies also raised the question of the future of German troops in the Baltic. Winnig, the S.P.D. trade unionist who had been conspicuous on the right wing of his party, was by now Reich Commissioner in the Baltic, and he engaged in negotiations with the British for common action against the Soviets. This was the period of Allied intervention in Russia, which began as an attempt to keep her in the war and developed into a half-hearted anti-Bolshevik crusade. By the armistice terms German troops had to withdraw from Russia but were to stay in the border territories for the time being as a bulwark against the westward advance of Bolshevism. The Germans had planned to bring the Baltic states wholly under their influence, for the ties between Germany and the Baltic barons of German descent and language were rooted in a long history. There was accordingly great reluctance in Berlin to abandon the *Baltikum*, and spokesmen of the government and army claimed that since neither the Latvians nor the Lithuanians were allowed to have their own armies, Germany was morally bound to defend them against the Reds. The Independent socialists, however, again opposed this policy as imperialist. The cabinet failed to agree; but the U.S.P.D. vote at least prevented any anti-Soviet action.[2]

THE CONGRESS OF WORKERS' AND SOLDIERS' COUNCILS: CLIMAX OF THE REVOLUTION

The clashes in policy and outlook between the two socialist parties which marked the experiment in revolutionary government that began on 10 November did not augur well for the success of the all-German congress of workers' and soldiers' councils that was to decide the fate of the German

---

[1] Barth, *op. cit.* p. 110; *Cabinet*, 26 December.   [2] Barth, *op. cit.* p. 110.

revolution. The congress, for which the Executive Council and the Independent socialists had pressed, had been agreed to by the cabinet on 23 November, and was to meet in Berlin in the middle of December. While preparations for it were still going on, several events occurred which increased the suspicion in which Ebert was held by the left, and threatened to break up the precarious coalition.

On the afternoon of 6 December a group of soldiers, some from the Berlin garrison and some who had recently returned from the front, occupied the building of the Prussian parliament, in which the Executive Council held its meetings, and a sergeant, accompanied by about thirty very young soldiers, declared the Council arrested in the name of the Reich government. He refused to say on whose authority he was acting, and the Executive Council protested energetically. The tragi-comic situation was saved by Barth, who suddenly appeared and ordered the soldiers to leave immediately. The Executive Council had the ringleaders arrested. On being interrogated, the latter admitted that they had been hired to arrest the Council. The same evening another group of soldiers, headed by a sergeant named Spiro, went to the Chancellery, where they demanded to see Ebert and announced their intention of making him president of Germany. Ebert, who was received with cheers, made a tactfully evasive reply; he could not, he said, commit himself without consulting his colleagues. Spiro criticised the Executive Council for its interference in government and wanted the constituent assembly to meet on 20 December. Ebert explained that the date when the assembly would meet was now a matter for the forthcoming congress of workers' and soldiers' councils. Thereupon the soldiers withdrew.[1]

More serious and more tragic in its consequences was a third incident that occurred on the same date. A large crowd of Spartacists, many of whom were deserters, gathered in the working-class suburb of Wedding in North Berlin to protest against the government's plan to convene a constituent assembly, and to demand a left wing dictatorship. When word reached the crowd that the Executive Council had been arrested and Ebert 'made' president, a demonstration march was formed which headed for the centre of Berlin. The government was on the alert and instructions were given to the soldiers, by Wels, the town commandant, that the procession was not to be allowed through but that force was to be used only if the Spartacists resisted. The soldiers tried with little success to break the demonstrators up into small groups. In the resulting tumult a shot was fired, allegedly by someone in the crowd, whereupon the troops replied with a burst of machine-gun fire that killed sixteen Spartacists and wounded another twelve.[2]

These three incidents were seen as related parts of a counter-revolutionary

[1] R. Müller, *Vom Kaiserreich zur Republik*, pp. 165 ff.; Scheidemann, *Der Zusammenbruch*, pp. 281 ff.   [2] R. Müller, *op. cit.* pp. 165–9.

plot and aroused a storm of indignation on the left. When on the following day the cabinet held a joint session with the Executive Council Wels was criticised for having given orders to fire on a supposedly unarmed crowd, and Ebert was accused of connivance at the attempt to establish himself as a dictator. There was no conclusive evidence against Wels, as the truth about who first gave the order to shoot could never be established; but it came to light that Ebert's secretaries had been informed of the soldiers' plans on 5 December, and the left wing Independent socialists refused to believe that they had failed to pass on the warning to Ebert. Again the evidence was inconclusive, since the document in which the secretaries recorded the information mysteriously vanished. Clearly, however, Ebert appeared in a very unfavourable light, and his resignation was demanded.[1] The government were forced to set up a special commission to investigate the whole matter. Meanwhile it was established that the soldiers had been instigated by high officials in the foreign office, two of whom promptly disappeared to escape arrest, and by others in the war office. They had received money from suspect sources, and were acting as the tools of enemies of the revolution, sinister wire-pullers with whom Ebert was said to be in league.[2]

From now onwards it was war to the knife between Ebert and Liebknecht, and the latter seemed by his threatening speeches and armed demonstrations to be preparing for civil war. The position of the Independents in the government became more difficult. Their suspicions of Ebert had grown, and they were sensitive to the Spartacist criticism that they were in alliance with the counter-revolution; on the other hand, they distrusted Liebknecht's putschist tactics, and they were loath to abandon the destinies of the revolution to Ebert and his party. So they remained in office, but with growing uneasiness. To the majority socialists the challenge from Liebknecht seemed the only real threat, and Landsberg spoke for his colleagues when he told the cabinet that the danger of counter-revolution was slight.[3] He saw that Spartacus meant civil war; he could hardly foresee that militarism would ultimately mean fascism.

The effect of the 6 December on opinion among the Independent socialists was seen at a meeting of the party's Berlin branch on the eve of the congress of workers' and soldiers' councils. This was the first of such meetings since the revolution. Haase had to defend himself against critics who urged that the Independents should have resigned from the government. He admitted

---

[1] *Cabinet*, 7 December.

[2] R. Müller, *op. cit.* p. 169; *Cabinet*, 7 and 11 December.

[3] *Cabinet*, 28 December 1918. Landsberg had two arguments: the reaction of the supreme command to the Lamp'l Points had been a threat of resignation, not a march on Berlin; and the soldiers had shown by their behaviour on 24 December that they were not willing to be used as a tool of counter-revolution. Scheidemann also believed that compared with the threat from the Spartacists the danger from the right was 'child's play'. H. Königswald, *Revolution, 1918* (1933), p. 182. For the Lamp'l Points see p. 182 below.

that he would have preferred the constituent assembly to meet at a later date, but said that if the congress, as he feared, refused to postpone it, the U.S.P.D. should do its best to be strongly represented in it. When Rosa Luxemburg demanded that the party boycott the election of the constituent assembly, Haase brusquely answered that rather than allow Spartacus to disrupt the party from the inside it would be better for them to part company. When it came to the vote, Haase received 486 votes out of 680, proof that the anti-parliamentarian policy of the Spartacists was rejected by the great majority even in such a radical stronghold as Berlin.[1] It would have been better for his party had Haase carried out his threat against Spartacus.[2] Such an act would have required the touch of ruthlessness which all political leaders need, especially in a revolutionary period, but which Haase conspicuously lacked. The uneasy partnership with Spartacus was to last only a fortnight longer. Haase's victory at this meeting was to be the last of the right wing over the left, whose demand for dictatorship by the councils was growing more insistent as its distrust of the S.P.D. increased.

Yet the composition of the congress of workers' and soldiers' councils, which met in Berlin on 16 December and lasted five days, showed that the great majority were on the side of parliamentary government.[3] Each civilian delegate represented about 200,000, each soldier delegate about 100,000. Of the 488 elected delegates, 289 or about 60 per cent were S.P.D., 90 or about 20 per cent U.S.P.D., 25 or 5 per cent belonged to the newly formed Democratic party or small radical groups, and 74 or about 15 per cent (27 soldiers and 47 workers) had no party affiliation.[4] About ten of the Independent contingent were Spartacists, but neither Liebknecht nor Rosa Luxemburg was elected, and a resolution authorising their admission on a non-voting basis was rejected. These figures show what a relatively minute following the two Spartacist leaders had.

The main decision before the congress was, of course, the date of election of the constituent assembly: that the assembly should meet was hardly in doubt. Richard Müller, chairman of the Berlin Executive Council, called on the delegates to lay the foundations of a socialist republic, by which he meant one governed by workers' and soldiers' councils; Ebert appealed for the rule of law, by which he meant parliamentary democracy. Müller, defending the record of the Executive Council against critics of both right and left, attacked the People's Commissars for following a policy favourable to the counter-revolution and he accused Ebert of collusion with the right wing putschists of 6 December. Müller complained of the provocative conduct of the army,

[1] Haase, *Hugo Haase*, pp. 66–7; Bernstein, *Die deutsche Revolution*, p. 78.
[2] Rosenberg, *History of the German Republic* (1936), p. 30.
[3] This summary is based on the stenographic report of the congress, here referred to as *Congress*.　　　　　　　　　　　　　[4] *Congress*, p. 6; R. Müller, *op. cit.* p. 203.

whose officers had threatened workers' and soldiers' councils and made monarchist speeches, while posters had appeared in the streets inciting to the murder of Liebknecht. Moreover, the old, reactionary officials had remained in office.[1] Ebert was defended by Dittmann, representing the Independents' right wing as Müller represented their revolutionary left.

One of the outstanding contributions to the debate on the constituent assembly was made by Cohen, a right wing Social Democrat and member of the Reichstag. Cohen warned the gathering not to let Germany follow the Russian example of abolishing parliament: such a course would discredit socialism, put an end to democracy and make civil war inevitable. He pointed out that the German middle class was much stronger than the Russian, that its co-operation was essential to maintain production, and that the Entente would not recognise a council republic. The future of workers' councils lay in the economic, not the political field. Finally, Cohen proposed that the elections for the National Assembly should be on 19 January instead of 16 February, as previously suggested.[2] Cohen was answered by Däumig, who, with Ledebour, had become an ardent advocate of the council system. Parliament, he explained, had been the appropriate representative institution for bourgeois democracy, but for proletarian democracy workers' councils were the right form. In Germany, unlike Russia, the proletariat was the majority, and its dictatorship would be that of the majority. The proposed constituent assembly would be little better than a revived Reichstag, and it would not contain a socialist majority. By voting for it, the congress of councils would be signing its own death warrant. The revolution must go on, but this would be impossible if the constituent assembly met.[3]

When the vote was taken, Cohen's resolution was passed by 400 to 50, Däumig's defeated by 344 to 98. Such was the measure of support for parliamentary democracy by the revolutionary parliament. Däumig was right in seeing in this decision the suicide of the German revolution; but Cohen was also right in predicting civil war as the alternative. There was, nevertheless, something paradoxical in this renunciation of power by those who had so lately seized it. The councils' congress must have known that the probable balance of parties in the new parliament would make it harder to carry out those economic and military reforms which most of its members had at heart. A compromise gesture by Haase, who argued that the workers' councils could retain some political functions in a parliamentary state, was an ineffectual attempt to reconcile the opposing sections of his deeply divided party.[4]

That the masses, however much they might repudiate proletarian dictator-

[1] *Congress*, pp. 7 ff.
[2] *Ibid.* pp. 105 ff. This is the same Cohen, usually known as Cohen-Reuss, as the one mentioned on p. 55 above.   [3] *Ibid.* pp. 113 ff.   [4] *Ibid.* p. 127.

ship, were enthusiastic for socialisation of the economy and democratisation of the army was shown by the other debates. There was a dramatic scene on the second day, when a soldiers' deputation, organised by Ledebour, interrupted the debate with a series of demands which led to such tumult that the congress had to be adjourned. Next day, in a calmer atmosphere the soldiers' demands were presented and debated. They were introduced by Lamp'l, a Social Democrat who was chairman of the Hamburg soldiers' council; hence they were known as the Hamburg or Lamp'l Points. They were, in brief, that the People's Commissars, not the supreme command, should be the highest authority in the army; that all badges of rank should be abolished as symbols of servitude; that soldiers' councils should be responsible for military discipline; that officers should be elected by their men and that a national militia should replace the standing army.[1] These demands were passed by the congress without opposition, though they caused embarrassment to Ebert because he knew that Hindenburg and Groener would never accept them. The S.P.D. ministers did not, however, openly oppose them, in order not to antagonise the congress.[2] But a further congress decision that the Points should be treated as a general directive and that instructions on their implementation should be issued by the People's Commissars under the supervision of the Executive Council gave Ebert a loophole of which he was to take advantage.

The last day was given up to a debate on socialisation. The main speaker was Hilferding, the Independent socialist economist and journalist who was a member of the socialisation commission.[3] He explained the difficulties of socialising at a time when the economy was completely run down, but added that the problems were not insoluble; they would simply need more time. Hilferding pleaded for patience and for fewer strikes. He recalled the ideals of socialism, which was much more than a movement for higher wages. But the desire for immediate socialisation of the industries ripe for it (except for mining they were not specified) was strong enough to make the congress pass a resolution to that effect against the opposition only of the small minority of non-socialists.[4]

The congress made two things very clear. One was that the great majority of the working class and of the soldiers wanted to live in a parliamentary state; the other was that in reforming the army and socialising the economy they wanted to carry the revolution a good deal further. They ignored the warning of the experts on the right that socialism could only be achieved gradually. They also ignored the warning of those on the left who contended that socialism and demilitarisation were impossible except through a dictatorship of workers' and soldiers' councils.

---

[1] *Congress*, pp. 61 ff. [2] *Ibid.* p. 212; Dittmann, *op. cit.* ch. 15.
[3] *Congress*, pp. 156 ff. [4] *Ibid.* p. 172.

One other decision of the congress was to have a significant effect on the future course of the German revolution. It had been agreed that a new Central Council, representing the whole of Germany, should be set up as a supervisory organ to the cabinet in succession to the Executive Council, which was still predominantly representative of Berlin. But the question what powers should be assigned to the Central Council reopened the whole controversial issue of councils versus People's Commissars. The left wanted the new council to have exclusive responsibility for legislation; the moderates, including the S.P.D. and Haase, would not give them more than power of consultation. The left wing of the Independents refused to support Haase and the S.P.D.; and as the congress rejected their conception of a more powerful Central Council (a kind of second government in fact) they decided to boycott it altogether. The result was the election of a Central Council containing 27 majority socialists and soldiers, but not a single Independent.[1] From the point of view of the U.S.P.D. this boycott was a great blunder, for it meant that the Independents in the cabinet were henceforth isolated, and could not expect any backing from the Central Council. It would have been both more logical and more realistic for the Independents either to have taken part in both bodies or to have resigned from the government altogether. For this mistake they were to pay dearly. The revolt of the doctrinaire left wing against their leaders was a symptom of the crisis through which the party was passing. Indeed it almost split in two: little now divided the left wing from the Spartacists, and the right wing could have come to terms with the S.P.D., as Kautsky, for one, desired. As he afterwards observed:

Our party presented a grotesque appearance, as perhaps no other party has done in the history of the world. Its right wing was in the government, and its left wing worked for the downfall of that very government.... What kept it together was no longer a common programme, a common tactic, but only a common hatred of the majority socialists which had been inherited from wartime.[2]

Haase, a good parliamentarian, was fatally irresolute in action, and Dittmann, though a good organiser, could not supply the leadership the party lacked. Nor had the party assimilated the revolutionary shop-stewards, whose leaning to direct action made them likely allies of the Spartacists. The Independent party had always had more than its fair share of idealists, doctrinaires and cranks, less than its modicum of practical revolutionary organisers. A group as disunited as the U.S.P.D. leaders in December 1918 was not really fit to hold office; and in any case the pressure of events was soon to end the uneasy experiment in coalition government.

---

[1] Dittmann, *op. cit.* ch. 15; Bernstein, *op. cit.* p. 95.

[2] Kautsky, *Mein Verhältnis zur U.S.P.D.* p. 10. Rosenberg (*op. cit.* pp. 32 ff.) believed that Haase and the right wing Independents should have jettisoned their intransigent left wing after the congress of councils and joined forces with the left wing of the S.P.D. so as to create a strong parliamentary but radical socialist party.

THE PROBLEM OF ARMED FORCE IN THE GERMAN REVOLUTION

The adoption by an overwhelming majority at the congress of workers' and soldiers' councils of the Hamburg Points imposed a new strain on the Ebert–Groener pact. The Points, if put into effect, would have destroyed the authority of the officers including, of course, that of the generals over what remained of the field army, and would have completed the 'demilitarisation' of Germany which the sailors' mutiny and the revolt of the home army had begun. If Ebert's position had been precarious on 10 November, when he had the first of his nightly telephone conversations with Groener, it was not much better in the middle of December. The constituent assembly was now a certainty, and the end of government by councils—what Groener called Bolshevism—was in sight; but this very prospect was rousing the Spartacists and their allies to new efforts to overthrow the government, and the danger of a left wing putsch had grown. Ebert still relied on the army, as he had relied on it five weeks before. Yet in so far as it remained under the influence of its officers it was hardly a suitable instrument for a supposedly revolutionary government. This raises the question why the Social Democrats had not used their opportunity while in power to create an effective armed force of their own.

The answer is that three main obstacles made such a step difficult. In the first place, as heirs to the humanitarianism of the nineteenth century German socialists, like their colleagues in western Europe, were deeply influenced by pacifist ideals and opposed to the use of force, which they regarded, as the elder Liebknecht used to say, as essentially reactionary. Secondly, there was in German socialism, as was noted in the first chapter, a strong tendency to accept a crude and mechanical interpretation of Marxism according to which the revolution would occur through the almost automatic operation of impersonal forces: capitalism would collapse as a result of its inherent contradictions, and an opportunity for the seizure of power would follow—it need not be 'made'. These moral and economic or pseudo-economic arguments against the use of force were reinforced by a lack of realism in socialist thinking which was the consequence of the party's long exclusion from power and responsibility. The third difficulty was a practical one. Those socialists in the German army who might have formed the nucleus of a reliable republican force were unwilling to remain in uniform any longer to defend the Ebert or any other government against either reactionaries or Spartacists: their one aim was speedy demobilisation.

It is true that Ebert and his colleagues had made efforts to form units of armed men who would support the republican regime. As early as 15 November he had discussed the formation of a *Republikanische Soldatenwehr* with the new commandant of Berlin, Wels; and a *Sicherheitswehr*[1] was set up under the new chief of Berlin police, Eichhorn.[2] But Wels, as a majority socialist, was on bad terms with Eichhorn who was an Independent, and their forces not infrequently clashed. Wels's unit was suspect in the eyes of the left because it was financed from private sources, while Eichhorn was distrusted on the right because he had recently been head of the telegraph department of the Soviet embassy.[3] In theory Wels was in charge of 5,000 revolutionary sailors, the People's Naval Division, who had come to Berlin from Kiel ostensibly to protect the socialist government. In fact the sailors sided with the Independents and soon became a thorn in Ebert's side. Then on 6 December the People's Commissars decided to form a national militia or *Volkswehr* which was to consist of 11,000 men and to be responsible for guarding the government and food supplies.[4] The troop was to be made up of volunteers, and officers were to be elected by their men. Little progress appears to have been made in establishing this force, the military value of which would in any case have been doubtful. All these formations lacked the will to fight, were undisciplined and often at loggerheads with each other. For this reason the government seemed to be at the mercy of Liebknecht's men, who after 6 December assumed a new militancy, marching armed through the streets of Berlin and threatening the People's Commissars. Many of Liebknecht's followers were former deserters, financed by funds left behind by Joffé and using arms abandoned or sold off cheap by returning soldiers.

On the left, protagonists of a Red Guard were not lacking, and one of them, Däumig, raised the matter in the Executive Council. He was overruled, however, by the soldiers, who declared themselves capable of defending the revolutionary government and said that any such guard would be superfluous and a sign of lack of confidence in themselves.[5] Ebert was against a Red Guard for obvious reasons; it would have antagonised the supreme command and the middle classes, his opposition to it also won him popularity with the soldiers. Däumig had to accept defeat, but on 15 December he had the chance of becoming minister of war in succession to Scheüch, who resigned.[6] Despite the support of the Independent People's Commissars, Däumig refused; radical as he was, he had no desire to play the part of a German Trotsky. Like many other German socialists, Däumig was more at home as an opposition agitator than in office; it was, Dittmann wrote later, as if he feared responsibility. But such chances did not recur.

It was in an atmosphere of growing violence that Ebert received the two

---

[1] In English, the Republican Guard and Security Guard respectively.
[2] *Cabinet*, 15 November; R. Müller, *op. cit.* p. 143.
[3] R. Müller, *op. cit.* p. 144; Anton Fischer, *Die Revolutions-Kommandatur in Berlin*, p. 10.
[4] *Cabinet*, 3, 6 and 12 December 1918.
[5] R. Müller, *op. cit.* p. 137; Schüddekopf, *Das Heer und die Republik*, p. 34.
[6] Dittmann, *op. cit.* ch. 15. Scheüch's successor was Colonel, afterwards General, Walter Reinhardt, who was, however, not appointed until 31 December.

conflicting and incompatible demands: Hindenburg's letter of 8 December calling for a reduction in the powers of soldiers' councils and the abolition of council government;[1] and the soldiers' demand for an extension of council powers embodied in the Hamburg Points. As was inevitable, the generals reacted sharply to the latter, which they regarded as a breach of the pact with Ebert. Hindenburg sent a message to all army commands telling them that he refused to recognise the Points and that so far-reaching a change could be made only by a fully representative assembly. He and Groener would do all in their power to oppose the decision of the congress, and in the meantime the existing regulations were to continue in force. Groener later wrote: 'I made it clear to Ebert in the strongest terms that the leadership of the army stood or fell on this question. Ebert asked me to go to Berlin; I agreed, in order not to leave untried the last chance of supporting the Ebert government.'[2] On 20 December Groener, in full uniform and accompanied by a Major von Schleicher,[3] attended a joint meeting of the People's Commissars and Central Council. In a private talk beforehand with Ebert and Landsberg, the two members of the cabinet whom he could rely on against the radicals, Groener reminded them that without the army the government would not survive.[4] Ebert steered the subsequent meeting, which was a stormy one, with masterly skill.[5] This was the crisis that could ruin his plans, and he was determined to avoid a break. Groener used every argument in his armoury in a dignified but passionate protest against the Hamburg Points. He was fighting for the survival of the general staff and, as he believed, for Germany's future. He admitted that reform of the army was overdue, but urged that this was no time for experiment, when Germany was surrounded by implacable enemies, including the two new states of Poland and Czechoslovakia. Even the armistice terms could not be carried out if officers lost their power of command. The necessity of discipline was now being recognised, he continued, even in Soviet Russia, where the trend of electing officers by their men was being reversed. If, despite all these objections the Points were put into effect, he and the field marshal would resign, and the army would fall to pieces.

Dittmann now joined in, warning the government that if they gave way on this issue they would be committing suicide. He made the valid point that relaxation of discipline in the field army would no longer involve the risk of losing men as prisoners-of-war to the Allies, for the army was now back behind the Rhine. But, objected Groener, enforcement of the Hamburg

---

[1] Schüddekopf, *op. cit.* pp. 34–6. See also p. 162 above.
[2] Groener, *Lebenserinnerungen*, p. 475.
[3] He was later, briefly, German Chancellor and was shot by Hitler in 1934.
[4] *Ibid.*
[5] *Cabinet*, 20 December. The cabinet minutes contain a fairly full account of this crucial meeting between the military chiefs and their socialist critics. Groener in his brief comments on the confrontation remarks that Barth alone demanded his dismissal, and would have carried out his threat had he been able.

Points would make impossible the orderly withdrawal of the army in Poland and Russia. Barth, who arrived late, angered because he had not been told about the meeting, supported Dittmann, and asked scornfully why the supreme command attached so much importance to externals such as badges of rank and swords.[1] What were mere externals to Herr Barth, Groener replied with warmth, were full of meaning to an officer and were in fact essential for discipline. The Points were dishonouring for the Officers' Corps.

There was deadlock: neither side was willing to give way, and some of the majority socialists, including Lamp'l, the sponsor of the Hamburg Points, sided with the Independents. Finally Ebert relieved the tension by proposing that the Points, which had been drawn up rather hastily, should not apply to the field army, and he added that their application to the home army should anyhow await the issue of implementation regulations. Groener was soothed, the conciliatory Haase agreed, and Barth was left protesting. The Independents' chances of overcoming Groener's opposition would have been greater had they been represented on the Central Council. The disastrous consequences of the party's boycott of that Council were beginning to show themselves. By temporising Ebert had in fact come down on the side of the generals, for every day that passed brought nearer the election of the constituent assembly.

By this time the content of Hindenburg's secret telegram to the army rejecting the Hamburg Points had become known to the Independent socialists in the cabinet. They saw in it fresh proof of the generals' presumptuousness, and Barth demanded their dismissal and arrest.[2] He urged Ebert to start putting the Hamburg Points and the socialisation programme into effect at once. Ebert assured Barth that Hindenburg had been told of the government's disapproval of his telegram. Still he defended the generals as best he could. He was more worried at the growing and immediate threat from the Spartacists.[3] When he mentioned that the government might have to leave Berlin, Haase objected that this could not be done without the consent of the Executive Council. Barth burst out, accusing Ebert and the majority socialists of deliberately seeking a conflict with the left and sabotaging the revolution. Clearly for him the pressure of the crowd was necessary to make the government carry out the revolutionary programme to which it was committed by the congress of councils. At this moment, however, there occurred another crisis of the coalition cabinet which was first to raise and finally to destroy Barth's hopes.

---

[1] Barth, *op. cit.* p. 93.　　　　　　[2] *Ibid.* pp. 95–6.

[3] When the question of protecting the government from the insurrectionary left was discussed on 28 December, Ebert told the cabinet that difficulties had been found in forming the militia or *Volkswehr*. Haase agreed on the need for protection but suggested that the right course would be to arm the proletariat. To this Landsberg replied: 'You couldn't do much with that'. *Cabinet*, 28 December.

CHAPTER 9

THE 'SECOND REVOLUTION'

We
Who wanted to prepare the ground for friendliness
Could not ourselves be friendly.   BERTOLT BRECHT

THE SAILORS' REVOLT

The decision in favour of parliamentary government by the congress of workers' and soldiers' councils came as a welcome support to Ebert and the right wing Independent socialists, and sowed confusion in the ranks of their opponents, whose slogan of all power to the councils had broken in their hand. The extreme left now realised that if there was to be any revolutionary progress before the constituent assembly met, they had no time to lose. The growing militancy of the Spartacists, described later in this chapter, reflected this mood. It put the all-socialist government, in which the Independents stayed with growing misgivings, in an increasingly precarious position, as was shown by the next and final crisis in its short but tumultuous life. It was, however, from the revolutionary sailors, not from the Spartacists, that the new challenge came.

For some time about a thousand sailors belonging to the People's Naval Division had been quartered in the royal palace and adjacent stables, where they performed no useful service (they had long since ceased to 'protect' the government, which they embarrassed by plundering the valuable works of art in the palace).[1] The sailors were suspicious because they knew that the government wanted to reduce their numbers, and they had a further grievance in that their wages were in arrears. The government promised to pay them in full provided they evacuated the palace. The sailors agreed, but insisted on handing the keys to People's Commissar Barth instead of to the town commandant Wels, whom they accused of responsibility for the bloodshed in Wedding on 6 December. So on the afternoon of 23 December Barth found his office invaded by about twenty excited sailors who handed him the palace keys and demanded their pay of 80,000 marks. Barth, not being authorised to accept the keys, rang up Wels, who refused to allow Barth to take them except

---

[1] This brief summary of the sailors' revolt is based on several sources, the most important of which are Barth, *Aus der Werkstatt der deutschen Revolution;* Bernstein, *Die deutsche Revolution; Der Ledebour Prozess;* R. Müller, *Vom Kaiserreich zur Republik,* vol. II; A. Fischer, *Die Revolutionskommandantur in Berlin;* Dittmann's *Lebenserinnerungen; Vorwaerts* of 28 December, and the cabinet minutes of that day. The versions given by Ebert on the one hand, and by Barth and Ledebour on the other, clash at several points, and it must be assumed that the contradictions and obscurities will never be completely cleared up.

on the authority of Ebert, who could not be found. Ebert was in fact having lunch with Landsberg at the Chancellery. The sailors did not make a very serious effort to find him. To show their annoyance the sailors persuaded their colleagues, who were guarding the Chancellery in the Wilhelmstrasse, to seal off the building and thus make the government their prisoners. The telephone lines were also cut, except for the secret line from Ebert to army headquarters of which the sailors did not know. Barth, however, probably because he did not share the unpopularity of his colleagues, was allowed to receive an incoming call from the soldiers' council at Potsdam with information that army units were being sent from Potsdam to Berlin to suppress the Spartacists. Barth hurried to Ebert to ask if this was true; Ebert denied any knowledge of it. By this time the sailors had raised their 'blockade' of the Chancellery but had invaded the commandant's office. Shooting broke out when troops of the Republican Guard rushed to the scene to protect Wels; and the sailors, who suffered several casualties, were enraged and seized Wels as a hostage. He was taken to the palace and roughly treated. Just before his arrest, however, he had managed to telephone General Lequis to ask for help. Ebert, hearing of Wels's plight, appealed in vain to the sailors for his release.

At about 8.30 that evening, according to Barth's account, his suspicions were revived by news that a number of troops with cannon and machine guns had arrived in the Tiergarten, the park in central Berlin. He again challenged Ebert, who denied having ordered up any army units, whereupon Barth went to see for himself. On asking an officer who had sent them there, Barth received the reply that the troops had come on government orders. With Ebert's concurrence he managed to persuade the troops to accept a suggestion that they and the sailors, who had in the meantime reoccupied the Wilhelmstrasse contiguous to the Tiergarten, should both withdraw for the night and settle matters in the morning.

The next moves came in the middle of the night. Some time after 1 a.m. Ebert received a telephone call from the palace in reply to repeated inquiries about Wels to say that he was not in immediate danger but that if he were released then anything might happen to him.[1] The meaning of the message appears to have been that it was in Wels's own interest to remain a prisoner

---

[1] According to Anton Fischer, Wels's successor as commandant of Berlin, Ledebour had arranged with the sailors at 4 a.m. that Wels should be released. Wels, who was exhausted and perhaps incredulous, asked to be kept in the palace until dawn (Fischer, *op. cit.* p. 26). Ledebour testified afterwards that he was rung up in the night by the sailors and asked to mediate. He had talks with both the sailors and the army during the night and next morning in which a government nominee from the Central Council and Richard Müller, chairman of the Executive Council, took part (*Ledebour Prozess*, pp. 40 ff.). According to Ledebour, there was readiness on both sides to negotiate, and, since the mediation efforts were still going on, there was no justification for the government's unexpected use of force at 8 a.m. on 24 December. The army was, however, acting on instructions given to it during the night.

until the morning. Whether Ebert himself understood it in that sense is not clear; at any rate, he rang up Scheüch, minister of war, and asked him to arrange for the rescue of Wels by the army. Scheüch passed the order on to General Lequis of the Garde-Kavallerie-Schützen Division. According to Groener, he too rang up Ebert and reproved him for lack of firmness towards the sailors. What had begun as a foolish prank had now become a serious threat to the government, and gave point to a renewed proposal by Ebert, supported by Landsberg, that they should leave Berlin for a place where they would not be exposed to the attacks of the revolutionary mob. The government no longer felt safe in its own capital.[1]

The results of Ebert's summons to Scheüch in the middle of the night were soon apparent. At eight in the morning Barth was horrified to hear the boom of guns in the centre of Berlin. Hurrying to the scene he found that the army had arrived in force and was shelling the palace. The bombardment had begun after the sailors had failed to reply to a curt ten-minute ultimatum put to them by a young officer. Barth telephoned Ebert, who was not in his office, and then went to the Chancellery where he met Haase. The two of them then went to see Ebert, who by now had arrived. Ebert who, according to Barth, showed some embarrassment, denied that he had given orders to the army to use artillery against the sailors. He immediately called up Scheüch and asked him to order the troops to cease fire. By this time a large crowd which had gathered near the palace openly sided with the sailors, who now received unexpected support from Eichhorn's Security Guard. The troops, fraternising with the crowd, were soon in no mood to continue the action. A truce was arranged whereby the sailors were allowed to leave the palace, receive their arrears of pay and become formally incorporated in the Republican Guard. Wels himself was liberated but was too badly shaken to continue as town commandant. The affair cost the lives of about thirty people, mostly sailors. It was also agreed that the Lequis troops should leave Berlin. This was a moral victory for the sailors, who were technically rebels and regarded themselves as martyrs. The army, on the other hand, had proved ineffective. Major von Harbou, chief of staff of the Lequis force, telegraphed to the supreme command advising its dissolution on the grounds that the soldiers were not reliable.[2] Groener's weapon too had broken in his hand; and the government's position was more precarious than ever. This was the fact most obvious to the war-weary people of Berlin as they prepared for the first peacetime Christmas in a city marked by the scars of civil war.

[1] Barth, *op. cit.* p. 97. Scheüch stayed in office until the end of December.
[2] R. Müller, *op. cit.* p. 200. The *Berliner Tageblatt* wrote that the government had capitulated. In his telegram to the supreme command on the afternoon of 24 December, Harbou warned them that the outcome of the day's clash would be catastrophic for the government (Schüddekopf, *Das Herr und die Republik*, p. 43).

But the physical scars were not the only ones. The affairs gave the death blow to the socialist coalition which had barely survived the crisis of 6 December. The Independents were furious with Ebert and accused him of bad faith. He had lied, they said, in denying that the troops which Barth saw in the Tiergarten on 23 December had come there by his orders, and in disclaiming that he had told the army to shell the palace or authorised an unlimited use of arms. They found it inexcusable that Ebert without their assent should have ordered Scheüch to use force to release Wels, and that to save the life of one man (who was perhaps not even in serious danger) many people had been killed and wounded. There was a stormy scene at the next cabinet meeting, Ebert maintaining that it had not occurred to him to consult his Independent colleagues and denying that he had given the army a blank cheque.[1] The Independents were not convinced, especially as *Vorwaerts* of 27 December carried a statement signed by Ebert, Scheidemann and Landsberg in which they admitted that they had given an order on the night in question to use force against the sailors. Dittmann drew the conclusion that the release of Wels had been a pretext for an attack on the sailors (who in Landsberg's eyes must be treated like any other rebels), and he noted discrepancies in statements made by Ebert on different dates. Dittmann's suspicions were confirmed by Scheüch, who told him that Ebert's instructions on 23 December had been to drive the sailors out of the palace by all available means, not just to liberate Wels. Dittmann complained that the Independent socialists in the cabinet had been lied to for three days, duped by men with whom they were supposed to conduct the business of government: confidence had been utterly broken, co-operation inside the cabinet had become impossible.[2] Dittmann's strictures on Ebert were the more significant because like Haase he had honestly tried to make a success of the coalition government. Coming after a series of disagreements on policy and after the suspicions aroused by Ebert's behaviour on 6 December and by his

---

[1] *Cabinet*, 28 December 1918. According to another version Ebert said he had tried but failed to reach his U.S.P.D. colleagues on the telephone.

[2] Dittmann, *op. cit.* ch. 16. Despite the indignation felt by Dittmann and his colleagues at the events of 23–24 December, in view of the violent disagreement between them and the S.P.D. leaders on matters of greater importance than the sailors' revolt, such as the Lamp'l Points and policy towards Poland, it is misleading of Dittmann to suggest that confidence had been smashed at one blow. As the cabinet minutes and other evidence show, there had not been very much confidence at the beginning of the coalition, and what there was was eroded in stages, marked chiefly by the crises of 6 December (attempted putsch and armed clash) and 20 December (Groener's threat to resign). Ernst Haase is nearer the truth when he speaks of the Independents' resignation as the culmination of a lengthy process (E. Haase, *Hugo Haase*, p. 69). Behind the differences of the two socialist parties *vis-à-vis* the sailors lay their very different attitudes to the army chiefs; as Dittmann recognised (see p. 193 n. 1 below), the real bone of contention was militarism. Scheüch, the dismissed minister of war, suggested to the Independents that Ebert, in denying that he had ordered more than the liberation of Wels, has been trying not only to place the political odium for the action on other shoulders, but also to escape the ridicule of choosing such an inappropriate method of saving his colleague (Dittman, *op. cit.* ch. 16).

relations with Groener, Ebert's handling of the sailors' revolt was the last straw.

Haase and his colleagues decided to make the affair a test case. They had joined the government to safeguard the gains of the revolution; but the government was favouring militarism. They drew up a list of questions for presentation to the Central Council: if the replies were unsatisfactory, they would resign. Did the Central Council approve the order to use force on the night of 23–24 December against the sailors, and the ten-minute ultimatum on the morning of the 24th? Did it believe that the Hamburg Points should be carried out in full and immediately, or did it approve the supreme command's secret telegram repudiating the Points? Would it favour the transfer of the government to a place outside Berlin; did it approve non-demobilisation of soldiers born in 1898 (i.e. the youngest conscripts, whose retention in the army the left viewed with suspicion); was it in favour of a volunteer militia instead of a standing army, and of immediate socialisation?[1]

These questions were not easy for the Central Council to answer. On the one hand, some of its members had actively supported the Hamburg Points and the demand for immediate socialisation at the congress of councils. On the other, as majority socialists they had to stand by Ebert. On the first question they hedged, to the second and fourth they answered no, to the third yes. On numbers 5, 6 and 7 they said that they could not reply without consulting the cabinet (which meant Ebert and his two majority socialist colleagues), and to number 8 they replied that they wanted to hear the views of the socialisation commission, whose interim report was imminent. In its turn the Central Council addressed two questions to the Independents: Would they protect public and private property from attack, and would they shield the government from acts of violence from any quarter?[2]

The Independent People's Commissars found these answers unsatisfactory, and decided to resign, giving this as the reason for not answering the questions put to them. In fact the answers of the Central Council were as conciliatory as they could be in the circumstances: the Council accepted criticism of the army and indirectly of Ebert in questions 2 and 4, and it did not dissent from the policies of 'demilitarisation' and immediate socialisation for which the U.S.P.D. stood. Had the Independents not short-sightedly boycotted the Central Council at the time of its election they would certainly have received more support from it, and in that case Ebert would probably have had to resign. He had blundered, but the Independents had put themselves in a position in which they could not take advantage of his blunder. Bernstein (at this time a member of both socialist parties) doubted whether differences between the Independents and the Central Council were serious enough to

---

[1] Bernstein, *Die deutsche Revolution*, p. 123, where the text of the questions is given; *Cabinet*, 28 December 1918. [2] *Ibid.*

justify the former's[1] resignation. The real cause of the break up of the coalition, as Dittmann later pointed out, was the S.P.D.'s refusal to dissolve the old army altogether and replace it with a popular militia.[1] Yet suspicion of militarism as represented by the supreme command was far from being confined to the Independents; it was shared, as support for the Hamburg Points showed, by many majority socialists. Had Haase and his colleagues stayed in office they would have gained the backing of some of these in the Central Council; by resigning they left the field to Ebert and his friends. Their resignation also removed the hesitations of those on the left who would not rise against the government only so long as the Independents were part of it. Thus the sailors' revolt brought Germany one stage nearer civil war.

The departure of the Independents left three vacancies in the cabinet. The newcomers, both S.P.D. men, were Wissell, who took charge of economic affairs, and Noske, who became responsible for defence. The third place was offered to a prominent Silesian socialist, Paul Löbe (later to be president of the Reichstag), who was too preoccupied with the political problems of Silesia to accept, and it remained unfilled. There was again a homogeneous cabinet, which significantly ceased to use the name of People's Commissars.[2] Noske, who had gained in reputation by his handling of the Kiel sailors and did not shirk responsibility, was to be Ebert's right hand man in the impending struggle with the left. He soon acquired the confidence of the generals, which of course deepened the suspicions of the radicals. On the left the resignation of Haase and his colleagues came too late to appease the party's extremists like Ledebour and Däumig, who preferred co-operation with the Spartacists. The latter had already burnt their boats with the Independents. The shop-stewards too were restive and nearly left the party. Haase tried to defend himself by pointing out that it was the fault of the left wing that they had no representation on the Central Council; if all co-operation with majority socialists was wrong, he asked, why was it right for Independents to sit in the Executive Council?[3] Yet valid as these arguments were, they failed to regain for Haase the confidence of his recalcitrant critics.

THE FOUNDATION CONFERENCE OF THE K.P.D.

The resignation of the Independent People's Commissars brought the struggle of socialists against socialists to a new pitch of intensity. It was followed almost immediately by the long-expected break between Independents and Spartacists as the latter, encouraged by Haase's breach with Ebert, prepared to step up their challenge to the Ebert regime.

From the beginning of the revolution the Spartacists had been in opposition

---

[1] *Ibid.* Dittmann told the cabinet on 28 December that militarism was the greatest threat to the revolution.
[2] *Cabinet*, 30 December 1918.　　　　[3] *Freiheit*, 1 January 1919.

to Ebert, and attacks on the Ebert–Haase government became steadily more virulent in the *Rote Fahne*, of which Rosa Luxemburg was editor. On 23 November, for example, it wrote that the victory of the revolution would come when not only William II, Hindenburg and Ludendorff but also Ebert and Scheidemann lay prostrate. On 24 November it thundered that the day and hour belonged to the dictatorship of the proletariat, and that whoever opposed the stormy waves of the revolution would himself lie on the ground with shattered limbs. The events of 6 December confirmed the Spartacists in their belief that Ebert was counter-revolutionary; and since the Independents were his accomplices, they were tarred with the same brush. Having no use for the constituent assembly, the Spartacists put their faith in the congress of workers' and soldiers' councils, whose rejection of the Spartacist programme came as a bitter disappointment. Hence they denounced the congress too as counter-revolutionary and its members as 'Ebert's mamelukes'.[1] The Spartacists were left without a means (except force) of putting their policy into effect. Nevertheless they continued to press for the armed proletarian dictatorship demanded in a manifesto issued by the group in the middle of December:

The bourgeoisie is arming for defence, and the working class will have to choose between enslavement by the bourgeoisie and its own rule over the bourgeoisie. The constituent assembly being prepared for by the present government would become an organ of the counter-revolutionaries for the throttling of the workers' revolution. Every means must be used to prevent its coming into existence.[2]

As Bernstein later commented, this was a threat to hold down by force all non-Spartacists, a defiance of the vote of the congress of councils and an incitement to civil war. The admission that the bourgeoisie was arming for *defence* was also significant. On 22 December *Vorwaerts* replied for the S.P.D.:

We want the free democratic order of the republic. Liebknecht is inciting to civil war with lies and then complains of the victims of his own unscrupulous activity. He is not to be brought to reason. But we put our hopes in the reason, good sense and sense of justice of the workers.[3]

The Spartacists' threats could only increase Ebert's dependence on the generals, and make him more receptive to their arguments that Spartacus must be suppressed by force. Yet as the events of 24 December had shown, the government did not possess a force capable of maintaining its authority. What were the Spartacists going to do? In an article of 28 December *Rote Fahne* boldly claimed that the revolution would not tolerate half measures, yet had to admit that the masses were behind Ebert. The Spartacist leaders had already decided to cut the tenuous links which still bound them to the Independent party. On 22 December they had accused the U.S.P.D. central

---

[1] *Rote Fahne*, 20 December 1918. [2] Bernstein, *op. cit.* p. 101.
[3] *Ibid.* p. 100.

committee of encouraging counter-revolution and demanded an immediate party conference to clarify policy.[1] It is unlikely that the demand was meant to be taken seriously: the time, within a month of the election of the constituent assembly, was hardly suitable for such a conference even had the socialist leaders not been heavily engaged in government, and the Spartacists knew that Haase's party would never endorse their manifesto of 14 December. Instead, on receiving a negative answer from Haase, the Spartacists went ahead with plans for a conference of their own, to which members of the Bremen left wing socialist group were also invited. One hundred and fourteen people took part, including eighty-three delegates from different parts of Germany.[2]

The conference, which met in Berlin on 30 December and lasted three days, was intended to rally those forces which wanted a revolution on the Soviet model before the convening of the constituent assembly created less favourable conditions. Liebknecht, who made one of the principal speeches, said that the time had come to break with the Independent socialists, whom he attacked for weakness during the war, for holding a too mechanical conception of revolution, and for co-operation in government with the renegade Ebert.[3] The conference went on to pass with a large majority a resolution constituting themselves the German Communist party (Spartacus League), and the manifesto of 14 December was now adopted as the new party's official programme.

This programme was the main subject of an address by Rosa Luxemburg which was the outstanding feature of the conference. With power and eloquence she set the new party in its historical perspective. As she had never ceased to proclaim since the beginning of the war, the age of reformist socialism, of exclusive reliance on parliamentary methods and of liberal illusions, was over: 'Today we are living in a moment in which we can say: We are with Marx, under his banner...We are standing on the same ground as Marx and Engels in 1848 and from which in principle they never swerved...'[4] In 1848, she went on, the masses had been amorphous and unorganised: now they were organised in a party and exercised power through workers' and soldiers' councils. In fact, however, the workers were organised in three mutually antagonistic parties, not in one, and the largest was far from being revolutionary. The new Communist party had only a few thousand supporters in the whole of Germany.[5] Even in towns where

---

[1] *Rote Fahne*, 24 December 1918.
[2] The minutes of the conference are in the official *Bericht über den Gründungsparteitag der Kommunistischen Partei Deutschlands (Spartakusbund) vom 30 Dezember 1918–1 Januar 1919)*, henceforth referred to as *Bericht*.
[3] *Bericht*, pp. 4–6.   [4] *Ibid.* pp. 24–5.
[5] The number of Spartacus Letters distributed was between 5,000 and 6,000, according to Ernst Meyer, their later editor (*Reichstag Inquiry*, v, 215). 'The Spartacus League

left wing socialism was strong 95 per cent of the workers stayed with the Independents and did not secede to the K.P.D. Yet the party incongruously incorporated into its programme the concluding words of the Spartacist manifesto of mid-December, drawn up before the rejection of Spartacus by the congress of councils, that 'the victory of the Spartacist League is identical with the victory of the mass millions of the socialist proletariat'.

Rosa Luxemburg was aware how little her party was in fact representative of the German working class. Yet despite disappointment over the workers' councils she declared that they must be the future power in the state: they had played a key part in the Bolshevik revolution, and were obviously preferable to a bourgeois parliament. The hope lay in making the German workers' councils truly revolutionary. Since they were not yet that, she admitted: 'It would be a criminal error to seize power now. The German working class is not ready for such an act...The workers should fight, fight inside the factories and in the streets against Ebert and Scheidemann, but they should not aim at the overthrow of the Ebert government...'[1] Rosa Luxemburg repeated, however, the pledge in the December manifesto that the party would never take power unless it was supported by the clear, unambiguous will of the great majority of the German proletariat. This repudiation of minority dictatorship was underlined by another passage in the party programme, also typical of Rosa Luxemburg, disclaiming the use of terror.[2] In effect, as Ruth Fischer later wrote, the Communist programme was equivalent to a critical toleration of the Ebert government combined with militant propaganda against the army and for socialism.[3] But as events were shortly to show, the use of quasi-revolutionary tactics was to precipitate a showdown with the government for which the Communists were ill-prepared.

Rosa Luxemburg realised, in fact, that the congress of councils, by voting

remained a comparatively small and uninfluential group as long as the war lasted, even when opposition to the war had become almost universal within the German working class', Evelyn Anderson, *Hammer or Anvil: the Story of the German Working Class Movement* (1945), p. 31. An indication of the lack of support for the Spartacists after the war is that of the 490 or so delegates to the first congress of workers' and soldiers' councils only ten were Spartacists, and even this small group did not include Liebknecht or Luxemburg. At the foundation conference of the German Communist party Meyer admitted the Spartacists' 'numerical weakness' (*Bericht*, p. 3).

[1] Quoted in R. Fischer, *Stalin and German Communism*, p. 74. I have been unable to find this statement in the report of the K.P.D. conference as coming from Rosa Luxemburg or anyone else, and in view of Ruth Fischer's known unreliability as a historian it may be regarded as suspect. In her main address to the conference, on the party programme (*Bericht*, pp. 18–42), Rosa Luxemburg nowhere expresses so sharp a warning against the immediate seizure of power in the sense of ousting the government. On the other hand, the views attributed to Luxemburg by Fischer are consistent with the former's warning that the seizure of power might be long drawn out, with the state being undermined from below by strikes and workers' councils rather than captured from above.

[2] In conversation with Radek, Rosa Luxemburg criticised Dzerzhinsky and the Cheka, whereas Liebknecht like Radek defended the use of terror (Fischer, *Life of Lenin*, p. 318).

[3] *Ibid.* p. 75.

for the constituent assembly, had upset the whole revolutionary time-table. Since the masses were less radical than had been assumed, if the new party was not to abandon all pretence of democracy it would have to wait until disillusion with capitalism brought the demobilised soldiers now streaming back to the factories to a revolutionary frame of mind. In this new appraisal of revolutionary prospects, success, though ultimately certain, would be neither quick nor easy. The 9 November had marked the beginning of the political phase of the revolution; now the economic phase, with which socialism was really concerned, was about to begin. Rosa Luxemburg was obviously worried by the dilemma represented by the choice between seizing power offered by the revolution without mass support, and wasting the chance through waiting for the masses to develop a revolutionary consciousness. It might be some time, she admitted, before the proletariat was ready to complete the socialist revolution, but what did it matter so long as they lived to see it?[1] The full irony of these words was to become clear a fortnight later, when both Luxemburg and Liebknecht were to be brutally murdered. Yet history might have taken a different course had the party, so largely the creation of Rosa Luxemburg, taken to heart this speech, probably the last she ever made, and its conclusion that the conquest of power might be a long, piecemeal process, with the state being undermined by a combination of mass strikes and action by workers' councils. The balance sheet which she drew up recognised as the party's main liability its failure to wean the masses away from Ebert and Haase: its main assets were the government's military weakness, shown by the soldiers' refusal to fight the Spartacists; the revolutionary temper evident in the prevailing wave of strikes; and the possibility of broadening the revolutionary movement—which, she declared, had hitherto been exclusively urban—by mobilising the landless peasants and rural proletariat. Rosa Luxemburg saw that the struggle for power was about to enter a fiercer stage, in which their opponents might have recourse to desperate measures: Ebert–Scheidemann might give place to a more right wing government, or there might even be a military dictatorship under Groener or Hindenburg. She did not foresee the gravity of the threat presented by the Freikorps, and her constant branding of Ebert and even Haase as 'counter-revolutionary' led her to overlook the menace of the real counter-revolutionaries.

The most urgent tactical question was whether the party should boycott the election of the constituent assembly, a course that was consistent with its declared hostility to that body. Yet Rosa Luxemburg, Liebknecht and Jogiches —the last-named had been mainly responsible for maintaining the organisation of the Group during the last two years of the war, when nearly all the leaders were in gaol[2]—used their eloquence to persuade the conference to

---

[1] *Bericht*, p. 42.   [2] Rosa Luxemburg had been released from gaol on 9 November.

reject a boycott, and pointed out that even as a sounding board for propaganda a parliamentary assembly had its uses. 'Comrades,' Rosa Luxemburg warned the left wing incorrigibles, 'you are taking your radicalism too easily.'[1] Yet the conference decided against taking part in the elections by sixty-two votes to twenty-three, a result which confirmed Jogiches in his belief that the new party had been formed too soon. As Roland-Holst was to observe in her book on Rosa Luxemburg, the German Communists at that time were neither maturely Marxist nor an *élite* group in Lenin's sense, but a collection of youthful enthusiasts.[2] Yet it is hardly surprising that the neophytes, remembering Lenin's contemptuous dismissal of the Russian constituent assembly and Luxemburg's shrill demands in the recent past for the immediate seizure of power, could not easily follow her in this temporary tactical retreat. On the other hand, it was largely the refusal of the revolutionary shop-stewards to join in a boycott of the constituent assembly that prevented their entry into the Communist party. Liebknecht was in fact engaged in negotiations with the shop-stewards for fusion of the two groups while the Spartacist conference was in progress. But the talks broke down when the Spartacists rejected some of the conditions put forward on by the shop-stewards.[3] Apart from the question of the elections, the latter insisted on the Spartacists' abandoning their propensity to indulge in putsches. Ironically, it was the shop-stewards who were to drag the Spartacists into the January rising a few days later.

One colourful figure at the conference was Karl Radek, the Bolshevik leader who had originally been invited as a Soviet delegate to the congress of workers' and soldiers' councils but had been prevented from attending by the German government in its displeasure at the hostile Soviet broadcasts. Radek managed to cross the frontier in disguise, and arrived in Berlin on 19 December. He brought the conference fraternal greetings from the Soviet Republic, where, he said, news of the German revolution had been received with joy.[4] His main object was to convince his German comrades that a socialist Germany would have much to gain, and in the long run nothing to

---

[1] *Bericht*, p. 11.

[2] Roland-Holst, *Rosa Luxemburg, ihr Leben und Wirken*, pp. 190–4. For the views of Jogiches, see *Illustrierte Geschichte der deutschen Revolution*, p. 267.

[3] *Bericht*, pp. 44, 46 ff.; Stroebel, *The German Revolution and after*, p. 108.

[4] Radek, who had returned to Russia with Lenin in April 1917, had been active in propagating Bolshevik views abroad both before and after the Bolshevik seizure of power, and on the strength of his knowledge of Germany and pre-war work for the S.P.D. in Bremen was regarded as an expert on German politics. His address to the foundation congress of the K.P.D. is referred to very briefly in the *Bericht* and published separately as *Die russische und deutsche Revolution und die Weltlage* (Berlin, 1919). There is interesting information about Radek in the year he spent in Germany after December 1918 in an article, 'Radek in Berlin', by O. E. Schüddekopf in *Archiv für Sozialgeschichte*, vol. II (Hanover, 1962), pp. 87–166, which also includes Radek's own account of his experiences in Germany, first published in Russia in 1926.

lose, from an alliance with Bolshevik Russia.[1] The German workers, he declared, should seize the factories, and form a red army. In answer to the objection that such action would lead to Allied intervention, Radek argued that the German workers would put up an effective defence since they would be protecting their own possessions, and that the French soldiers would be so impressed by proletarian government in Germany that they would go home and start a revolution in their own country.[2] As for the danger of an economic blockade by the Allies, Radek suggested that a Communist Germany could rely on Russia's resources of raw materials, and he referred to the recent offer of food which the German government had rejected. Such a policy in the circumstances could hardly have been less realistic, and even Radek did not propose its immediate application, though he expected the world revolution to spread to France and Italy. The conference returned fraternal greetings to the Bolshevik party, but carefully refrained from making any commitments that could damage Germany's relations with the west.

Despite the pledge in the Communist programme not to seize power as a minority, acts of violence by the party's less disciplined hotheads were increasing. On Christmas Day an excited crowd, infuriated by the shelling of the sailors in the royal palace the day before, and harangued by Liebknecht and Ledebour, occupied the offices of *Vorwaerts*, the socialist daily newspaper which had been 'stolen' from the Independents during the war. This was a way of letting off steam, defying the Ebert government and paying off old scores, but it was hardly effective as a step towards the conquest of Berlin. It showed, or seemed to show, that the crowd expected the leaders to act. The Spartacists were finally induced to release the *Vorwaerts* building by the shop-stewards acting as mediators after the newspaper's staff had been forced to publish a front page article denouncing the Ebert government. *Vorwaerts* then denounced the Spartacists for endangering the achievements of the revolution and incitement to civil war, and accused them of wanting destruction, anarchy and terror.[3] In reply, the Spartacists pilloried the majority socialists as hand in glove with the nationalists and anti-Bolshevik organisations, which put up placards in the streets inciting to the murder of Liebknecht and putting a price on his head. Thus enmity between the two socialist factions had grown to a passionate hatred.

[1] Radek is reported to have told the K.P.D. conference: 'Die erste Pflicht der deutschen Sozialistischen Republik wäre es, sich aufs engste an die Sozialistische Schwesterrepublik anzuschliessen.' Quoted from Karl Radek, *Die deutsche Revolution* (Moscow, 1918), in Fainsod, *International Socialism and the World War*, p. 180.

[2] Radek remembered the pro-revolutionary reaction of some of the Allied soldiers who had come to Russia during the civil war, notably the French troops then in and around Odessa. The Soviet Commissar for foreign affairs, Chicherin, said in a broadcast on 15 February 1919, that only in case of a further German revolution and a consequent invasion by the West would Soviet troops come to the aid of the German proletariat (Schüddekopf, *op. cit.*).

[3] Bernstein, *op. cit.* pp. 119–121.

The Independent socialists in the Prussian government followed the example of their colleagues in the German government by resigning a few days later. By 3 January only one prominent Independent was still in office: Eichhorn, the chief of police in Berlin, who held a key position in the approaching struggle for power. The all-S.P.D. Prussian government now decided to dismiss Eichhorn, who was known to sympathise with the Spartacists and who had helped the rebellious sailors on 24 December. Under these circumstances the dismissal of Eichhorn was reasonable, but that the left would resist such a move was also predictable. He was charged with anti-government activities and also with embezzlement of police funds. Eichhorn refused to go, on the grounds that only the body which had appointed him, the Berlin Executive Council, had the power to dismiss him, and he demanded the right to answer the personal charges, which remained unproven.[1] The executive committee of the Independent socialists of Berlin and the shop-stewards' committee met and decided to give Eichhorn full support. The central committee of the new Communist party at first hesitated to join their colleagues in making this a test case because they realised that they were not ready for the showdown with the Ebert government which such action would provoke. But at this point the crowd swayed its leaders. On Sunday, 5 January, a pro-Eichhorn demonstration in which 700,000 people are said to have taken part filled the central squares and streets of Berlin, the largest political gathering ever seen there.[2] It was addressed by the shop-stewards' leaders, Däumig and Ledebour, and also by Liebknecht. During the day a group of militants occupied the offices of *Vorwaerts* (for the second time) and other newspapers. That evening the leaders met again and decided, in view of the revolutionary temper of the crowd, to strike a decisive blow against the government. Dorrenbach, one of the sailors' leaders, reported that the sailors and the Berlin garrison were ready to take part in a *coup*, and another speaker promised the help of some troops at Spandau near Berlin. Reinforcements from Frankfurt-on-Oder were also counted on. Despite objections from Däumig and Richard Müller, who urged that neither the political nor the military preparations were complete, a large majority of those present, mostly shop-stewards, voted in favour of a rising. A revolutionary committee of fifty-three was set up with three presidents: Ledebour, Liebknecht and a shop-steward named Scholze. Neither Ledebour nor Liebknecht had been authorised by their parties to take part in the venture, and Rosa Luxemburg is known to have opposed it.[3] Radek, according to his own

---

[1] R. Müller, *Der Bürgerkrieg in Deutschland*, pp. 26 ff.   [2] *Ibid.* p. 30.

[3] *Ibid.* p. 34. For Radek's attitude to the Spartacist rising, see Schüddekopf's article cited on p. 198, n. 4, above. Radek was surprised at the stridence of *Rote Fahne*, realised the immaturity of the new Communist party and the weakness of its links with the masses,

testimony, was against it, and it was, of course, inconsistent with the Communist party's decision, made a few days before, not to seek power by force. The initiative came mainly from the shop-stewards, who were piqued by accusations of half-heartedness and were determined to show that they were not behind the Spartacists in action. The shop-stewards were now indulging in the very 'putschism' for which they had criticised the Spartacists. The leaders felt bound to go on with the action in order not to let down the masses. The revolutionary committee issued a manifesto proclaiming a general strike and the overthrow of the Ebert–Scheidemann government in favour of itself.[1] This was to be the 'second revolution' for which the left had been waiting.

From the beginning everything went wrong for the rebels. The promised help from Spandau and Frankfurt did not arrive, the sailors declared their neutrality, and only a few hundred of the demonstrators actually joined in the fighting.[2] A number of public buildings were occupied, but these gains were not exploited because there was no general strategic plan. One incident was revealing of the insouciance with which the rising was conducted. A sailor called Lemmgen received orders to occupy the ministry of war. On arriving there with a group of men he was asked by the under-secretary of state to show his credentials. Lemmgen produced a piece of paper saying that the Ebert–Scheidemann government had been deposed, but the under-secretary politely pointed out that it was unsigned and asked him to return with the necessary signature. On his way back to revolutionary headquarters Lemmgen changed his mind, went home and reported sick for a week.[3] On the other hand, neither

and warned against a premature rising in the Bremen *Kommunist*. On 9 January, after the rising had begun, Radek wrote to the central committee of the K.P.D. warning them to break off the strike (which in his view should have had a purely defensive character, a protest against the dismissal of Eichhorn) and not risk an armed clash. But by then it was too late. Jogiches and (at first) Rosa Luxemburg shared Radek's doubts about the wisdom of the rising, and Radek had even agreed with Jogiches at the end of December that the Spartacists should for the time being remain in the Independent party. Radek repeated his criticism in a pamphlet. In the hunt for Spartacist leaders that followed the failure of the rising a warrant was issued for Radek's arrest, but he managed to hide for nearly a month and was eventually arrested on 12 February (Schüddekopf, *op. cit.*, and *Illustrierte Geschichte*, p. 284).

[1] R. Müller, *op. cit.* p. 38 and *Ledebour Prozess*, p. 55. The text of the declaration (see also p. ii) was as follows:

'Comrades! Workers!

The Ebert–Scheidemann government has made itself impossible. It is declared deposed by the undersigned Revolutionary Committee of the representatives of the revolutionary socialist workers and soldiers (Independent Social Democratic party and Communist party).

The undersigned Revolutionary Committee has taken over the business of government for the time being.   Comrades! Workers!

Join the action taken by the Revolutionary Committee.'

[2] R. Müller, *op. cit.* pp. 35, 49, 58. The masses, wrote Müller, were prepared to go on strike, but not to take up arms.

[3] Volkmann, *Revolution über Deutschland* (1930), p. 181.

the garrison nor the Republican Guard was solid for the government, which had only a few hundred troops at its disposal. Noske has described the mood of depression in which the People's Commissars met on 6 January, in hiding because the Chancellery was surrounded by a hostile crowd, unable to decide on a course of action.[1] At a joint meeting between the cabinet and the Central Council the new minister of war, Colonel Reinhardt, urged that a commander-in-chief be appointed for Berlin. When the objection was made that the workers would not like to have a general over them, someone suggested Noske. With a characteristic 'All right! Someone's got to be the bloodhound, I won't shirk the responsibility[2], Noske accepted the invidious task that was to make him the saviour of Germany in the eyes of the right, the hangman of the revolution in the eyes of the left.[2] He immediately set about organising a force capable of restoring order in Berlin. His headquarters in a girls' school in the quiet middle-class suburb of Dahlem became a hive of activity. In central Berlin where Spartacist armed bands roamed the streets there was continual alarm and the sound of firing. A number of majority socialists and trade unionists joined a republican volunteer force which had its headquarters in the Reichstag building. But Noske was pinning his hopes on the Freikorps which were being formed in different parts of Germany by officers of the demobilising imperial army.

The idea of forming volunteer corps as an *élite* force, militarily capable and politically dependable, had been put forward some time before with the double purpose of protecting Germany's vulnerable eastern frontier against Russians and Poles, and combating the Spartacists inside Germany. The supreme command issued an appeal for volunteers at the end of November, and some progress had been made. One of the first Freikorps to be formed was the *Landesjaeger* of General Maercker at Zossen near Berlin, which was inspected by Ebert and Noske on 4 January and consisted of 4,000 men, fully equipped and well disciplined.[3] The appointment of Noske as commander-in-chief of Berlin encouraged the generals to increase the number of Freikorps because the government was at last showing firm leadership. A

---

[1] From 9 a.m. a vast crowd responding to the general strike filled the centre of Berlin from the Tiergarten in the west to the Alexanderplatz in the east, waiting to be told what to do by their leaders who spent the whole day deliberating. Finally as the dusk fell and the fog returned the crowd dispersed, cold, hungry and bitterly disappointed. The atmosphere is caught in a sardonic description of the day which appeared a year later in the *Rote Fahne* (Bernstein, *Die deutsche Revolution*, p. 141).

[2] Noske, *Von Kiel bis Kapp*, pp. 67 ff. Noske compared the government's position to that of a mouse in a trap. On the same day Ebert summoned his party colleague Hermann Müller and told him that the survival of the government during the next five or six days—the time needed by Noske to organise military help—was far from certain. Müller was to make all necessary preparations so that in case the worst happened a new socialist-bourgeois government could be set up in Magdeburg, Dessau or Weimar (Volkmann, *Revolution über Deutschland*, p. 180).

[3] Schüddekopf, *op. cit.* pp. 43 ff.; Wheeler-Bennett, *The Nemesis of Power*, p. 36.

high percentage of the volunteers were officers and n.c.o.s; hardly any workers or socialists applied. The Freikorps contained genuine patriots, but also many soldiers of fortune, uprooted by the war and unable to find their way back into a civilian world which since the revolution had become alien and repugnant. Some were embittered idealists or desperate characters from whose ranks were to emerge the future murderers of prominent republicans.

While the rebels held the keypoints of Berlin and Noske was gathering his forces on the outskirts the Independent socialist party (whose Berlin branch had acted on their own responsibility in supporting the rebellion) tried to break the deadlock by mediation. Both the government and the revolutionary committee agreed, and two sets of mediators were nominated, one to negotiate with each side.[1] Negotiations failed, however, when the rebels refused to evacuate the *Vorwaerts* building, which they insisted on keeping as an act of revenge for past injustice.[2] A further attempt at mediation by workers in two large factories in Berlin also broke down. *Rote Fahne* of 9 January reiterated its determination to overthrow the government and re-elect the workers' and soldiers' councils. In a manifesto issued the day before the government had taken up the challenge:

Fellow citizens! Spartacus is now fighting for absolute power. The government, which within ten days wants to bring about the free decision of the people on its own destiny, is to be overthrown by force. The people are not to be allowed to speak. Their voice is to be suppressed. You have seen the results. Where Spartacus rules all personal freedom and safety are abolished. The press is suppressed, the traffic is brought to a standstill. Parts of Berlin are the scene of bloody battles. Others are already without food and light. Food offices are being stormed and food supplies for the soldiers and civilian population are being stopped...[3]

The manifesto promised that the government was taking steps to end the 'reign of terror' and that the hour of reckoning was approaching.

The government's first success against the rebels was the recapture of the *Vorwaerts* building on the night of 10–11 January. The first atrocities of the revolution now occurred, when a number of prisoners were shot by the Freikorps and others brutally mishandled.[4] A search was made for the rebel leaders, whose committee had ceased to function after 9 January. Ledebour

---

[1] Bernstein, *op. cit.* pp. 140 ff. The central committee of the U.S.P.D. was not at all pleased at the action taken by its Berlin branch. See also R. Müller, *op. cit.* p. 48.

[2] Ledebour, who was chairman of the mediation committee of seven set up by the rebels, believed that the government used the talks as an excuse to gain time until it was ready to strike. Ledebour himself was arrested on the night of 10–11 January after the talks had failed. Dittmann, who was chairman of the government's mediation committee of seven, was also convinced that, under the influence of Noske, the government was not sincere in wanting agreement after 8 January (see Minna Ledebour *et al.*, *Georg Ledebour, Mensch und Kaempfer*, p. 110 and Dittmann, *op. cit.* ch. 16).

[3] Bernstein, *op. cit.* p. 151.

[4] *Ibid.* pp. 158–61. The whole section is headed: Maltreatment and shooting of prisoners.

was arrested; his trial for high treason took place a few months later. Liebknecht and Rosa Luxemburg were in hiding, and the *Rote Fahne* office had to be evacuated. On 11 January Noske led a demonstrative march of 3,000 troops into central Berlin, and the systematic reconquest of the city followed. Two days later the two hunted Spartacist leaders, who had refused to leave Berlin, were caught in the house of a sympathiser in Wilmersdorf and taken to the Eden hotel, headquarters of the Garde-Kavallerie-Schützen Division, one of the Freikorps. Their capture was not reported to the government. When Liebknecht arrived at the hotel he was struck over the head with a rifle butt. Profusely bleeding, he was questioned by a Captain Pabst, again struck, and put into a car which was supposed to be heading for Moabit prison. On the way the car was stopped, and Liebknecht was dragged out semi-conscious and shot. The corpse was handed to the nearest mortuary as that of an unknown man found dead in the Tiergarten. Rosa Luxemburg, who arrived at the Eden hotel a few minutes later, met a similar fate. Her skull smashed with a blow from a rifle butt, the frail, crippled woman was lifted, half-dead, into a waiting car in which she was shot in the head shortly after leaving the hotel. The body was loaded and flung into the nearby Landwehr canal, from which it was not recovered until the following May.[1]

News of the cowardly and brutal double murder shocked many who had little sympathy with the aims of Rosa Luxemburg and Liebknecht, and the pair became martyrs of the revolution, the heart of a myth which gave Liebknecht a more potent influence after death than he had had in life. Many workers swore to avenge the crime although, as Bernstein points out, condemnation of the Spartacists for their ill-conceived attempt to overthrow the government and prevent the election of a constituent assembly was by no means confined to the middle and upper classes. But left wing indignation rose when it became known that the official announcement by the Garde-Kavallerie-Schützen Division that Liebknecht had been shot while trying to escape and Luxemburg lynched by a crowd (the streets were in fact deserted at the time) and shot by an unknown person was untrue. The government ordered an official inquiry to establish the facts but refused a demand from socialists of both major parties to appoint a commission consisting wholly or largely of socialists to hold the trial. Instead, the trial was a court-martial conducted by officers with the intended participation of four socialists, two from the Central Council and two from the Berlin Executive Council. The trial did not take place until May, by which time it was plain that justice was not going to be done. One of the accused officers had been helped to escape by foreign ministry officials, and evidence had been suppressed. Three of the socialists concerned accordingly refused to serve, and the findings of the trial were suspect in the eyes of many people. The four officers accused of murder

---

[1] Bernstein, *op. cit.* pp. 165 ff.; R. Müller, *op. cit.* p. 82; *Ledebour Prozess*, pp. 68 ff.

were acquitted, and the trooper who had struck the two victims with his rifle butt was given two years imprisonment for attempted manslaughter. The government was rightly blamed for allowing the military court to whitewash the perpetrators, some of whom later held high office in Nazi Germany.[1]

Through the death of Rosa Luxemburg the young Communist party lost the one leader who might have guided it between the Scylla of political impotence and the Charybdis of a Leninism totally unsuited to German conditions. It was ironic that Luxemburg died in a rising of which she disapproved and which her party decided to join only at the last moment. Yet she was also a victim of her aggressive zeal as well as of illusions based on wishful thinking. Despite the note of caution in her address to the foundation meeting of the Communist party, her articles in *Rote Fahne* since 10 November had constantly incited the masses to action against the Ebert government, and even after the congress of councils had voted by a large majority for parliamentary government she had gone on demanding all power for the workers' and soldiers' councils. As Bernstein saw, the proletariat for which she gave her life was an abstract ideal which had little in common with the real one.[2] (Liebknecht too in his last contribution to *Rote Fahne* characteristically combined idealism and personal courage with fatal self-deception.)[3] That Rosa Luxemburg miscalculated the revolutionary capacity of her followers is evident from the half-hearted support they gave once the rising had begun, though *Rote Fahne* did its best to boost morale. On 9 January it boasted that the government was half beaten, next day it poured scorn on those who were trying to mediate, demanding not parity with the much more numerous majority socialists but their submission to Spartacist force. On 11 January it confessed that the bid for power had failed.

The January rising, which came both too early and too late, was the greatest mistake made by the extreme left, and one for which they and others had to pay dearly. For the counter-revolution it provoked not only destroyed their leaders (in March the invaluable Leo Jogiches was arrested and shot 'while trying to escape') but threatened the republic. In her last articles in

---

[1] Bernstein, *op. cit.* pp. 165–71; R. Müller, *op. cit.* p. 82; Horkenbach, *Das deutsche Reich von 1918 bis heute* (1930), p. 70.

[2] Bernstein, *op. cit.* p. 171.

[3] Apart from his undeniable courage, Liebknecht was not much admired even in left wing circles, where he was regarded as an egoist and a dilettante (Bernstein, p. 170). Examples of his misjudgement are his absurd belief that when the S.P.D. joined the government at the beginning of October 1918 they were doing so in order to enjoy the fleshpots of power and the 'Paradise of the Wilhelmstrasse', when in fact they were sacrificing popularity and assuming very harsh responsibilities, and his conviction that the Allies would not continue the war against a revolutionary Germany despite the obvious lack of revolutionary feeling in England and France at that juncture (Liebknecht, *Politische Aufzeichnungen aus seinem Nachlass, 1917–18* (Berlin, 1921). pp. 143–5). On the other hand, Liebknecht showed prescience when he admitted to Radek at the end of December 1918 that the road before them was a long one (Liebknecht, *Klassenkampf gegen den Krieg* p. 108).

Rote Fahne Rosa Luxemburg sought to analyse the reasons for the failure of the rising and to draw conclusions. There had been a lack of organisation and unpreparedness, divided counsels among the leaders, lukewarmness in the ranks of the proletariat, immaturity on the part of the soldiers; and the decision to strike had been taken too soon. Once the rising had begun a sense of loyalty prevented Rosa Luxemburg from accepting mediation as the best way out of an impossible situation; the romantic in her triumphed over the realist. She consoled her supporters with the reflection, hardly justified by historical precedent, that all revolutions had begun in defeat. That the German Communist party had not yet learnt the folly of putschism was evident from the further abortive rising in Berlin in March 1919 and from other revolts in the early history of the Weimar Republic. Richard Müller, one of the shop-stewards who had vainly opposed it, wrote that the January Putsch cut off the head and broke the back of the revolutionary movement, but neither in Berlin nor in Moscow were the necessary conclusions drawn.

The question of responsibility for the January rising has been much debated. Independent and Communist writers have accused the Ebert government of deliberately using the dismissal of Eichhorn to provoke the left, and interpret the affair as a counter-revolutionary plot.[1] This explanation is hard to reconcile with the facts. Despite the reassurance given to Ebert and Noske by their inspection of the Freikorps at Zossen on 4 January, they knew that at that date and on the days immediately following the government was too weak to face a trial of strength. It is generally agreed that had the left had more determined leadership and organisation they could have seized the whole of Berlin on 5 or 6 January.[2] Nor could Ebert and Noske foresee that neither the revolutionary sailors nor Eichhorn's forces would give the rebels effective help. But the main reason why the government did not want a showdown with the Spartacists was that its whole policy was orientated towards the election of a constituent assembly which was then only a fortnight away, and the last thing Ebert wanted to do (as an S.P.D. manifesto issued at the same time shows) was to create disturbances that might put it in jeopardy. The initiative for the rising came from the left, which felt, as Trotsky noted, that with every day that passed since 9 November they were losing control of a situation which they had at first appeared to dominate. The rising was a desperate effort to recover the lost revolutionary momentum. Noske, once the battle was joined, fought with a blunt and brutal energy which roused the fury of the left as much as the admiration of the right, and the Freikorps were not

---

[1] For example Frölich in *Rosa Luxemburg*, p. 316. Among the rebels were some *agents provocateurs* planted by the government, but it is unlikely that they played the decisive part attributed to them by Frölich and others. Nor is it easy to account for the Communist risings in Bremen, Brunswick and elsewhere if the initiative came from the government.

[2] Frölich admits (*ibid.* p. 322) that even if the rebels had been able to seize power they would have been too weak to hold it.

sorry to have the opportunity of killing Spartacists. But Stroebel, the Independent socialist who was a participant in these events as well as their historian, passed a realistic judgement: 'The left wing Independents and the Spartacists, as well as the right wing socialists, were bent upon ruthlessly appropriating political power. They welcomed the brutal trial of strength as much as the right wing socialists. And they succumbed because, as strategists, they allowed themselves to be pushed into a decisive struggle under the most unfavourable circumstances.'[1] The only truly peaceful participants in the situation were the right wing Independents such as Kautsky, whose attempts to mediate were thwarted mainly by Spartacist intransigence.

One result of the subjugation of Berlin by the Freikorps was the gradual elimination of the republican forces, which had played an ineffective part, except for the volunteer regiments, recruited almost entirely from socialists by the editor of *Vorwaerts*, Erich Kuttner, and others. Noske regarded the regular republican troops, such as those under the town commandant, as of doubtful military value because they lacked discipline and were politically unreliable, and he came to depend almost entirely on the Freikorps, who, in occupying Berlin, abruptly changed the political atmosphere.[2] On 13 January Kautsky complained that as a result of Spartacus the danger of counter-revolution was becoming real, and three days later Haase wrote that the white terror could only be compared to the Tsarist regime.[3] Attempts to 'democratise' the Freikorps by introducing working-class recruits failed.[4] The unwillingness of socialists to accept military responsibilities, exemplified in the refusal of Däumig to become minister of war in succession to Scheüch at the end of December, had left a vacuum to be filled by their enemies.[5] It was soon evident that in the Freikorps the republic had created a Frankenstein's monster.

[1] Stroebel, *The German Revolution and after*, p. 123. During the abortive merger talks between the Spartacists and the revolutionary shop-stewards at the time of the foundation conference of the Communist party, Richard Müller, on behalf of the shop-stewards, begged Liebknecht to give up his putschist tactics. Liebknecht's sharp reply was: 'You seem to be an envoy of *Vorwaerts*' (Roland-Holst, *Rosa Luxemburg*, p. 200). According to Clara Zetkin, Liebknecht was tortured by the thought that if he did not rise against the government the sailors might think he was letting them down (*ibid.* p. 205).

[2] Writers on the German revolution disagree on the part played by republican forces, including the middle-class *Einwohnerwehr*, in defeating the Spartacists. Dittmann and Anton Fischer claim that they had a big share, and an outside but well-informed observer, Wolff, the editor of the *Berliner Tageblatt*, agreed with them. Noske on the other hand argues that the republican troops were of little use, and that it was the Freikorps who effectively reconquered Berlin. But Kuttner's *Regiment Reichstag* lost over a hundred dead in one week's fighting (Bernstein, *op. cit.* p. 157).

[3] Noske, *Von Kiel bis Kapp*, p. 115; Haase, *Hugo Haase*, p. 175.

[4] Noske, *op. cit.* p. 121. *Vorwaerts* carried full-page recruiting advertisements for the Freikorps.

[5] M. J. Bonn (*Wandering Scholar*, p. 217) describes the socialists as sharing 'the most conspicuous quality of German radical youth—fear of responsibility'.

FURTHER REVOLT AND SUPPRESSION

Four days after the murder of the two Communist leaders the German people voted into power the 421 men and women who were to form the constituent assembly. Of the electorate of thirty-five million, which now for the first time included women, over thirty million went to the polls. The result was a substantial majority for the parties supporting the new republic. One hundred and eighty-five seats were won by the two socialist parties, eighty-nine by the Centre, seventy-four by the Democrats (the renamed Progressives), twenty-two by the People's party and forty-two by the Nationalist People's party, as the National Liberals and Conservatives had now respectively styled themselves to be in keeping with the times. These two parties remained, however, monarchist and formed the right wing opposition to the three republican parties (majority socialists, Democrats and Centre) which together made up over two-thirds of the assembly. This majority was a revival of the coalition that had passed the Reichstag peace resolution, but with the difference that the majority socialists were now the dominating partners. They had, however, failed to win the absolute majority on which many of them had counted, and which might have been theirs had the election been held two months earlier, before the enthusiasm of the revolution was exhausted. Nor could they rely on support from the Independents; indeed during the election campaign the two socialist parties had attacked each other more fiercely than their non-socialist opponents. With twenty-two seats the Independents had done less well than seemed likely in view of the backing they had gained during the war; now in January 1919 only in two big towns (Düsseldorf and Leipzig) did they outnumber their S.P.D. rivals. The sharp reaction of many rank and file workers and soldiers against Noske's policy and Freikorps excesses was to lead to a revival of the Independents, which however, came too late to influence the results of the general election.

On 6 February the assembly met at Weimar. The choice of Weimar was partly symbolic, for the new regime wished to identify itself with Germany's past cultural glories rather than with the power politics of Berlin or Potsdam, but also had a practical motive—to escape from the left wing turbulence of the capital. Even at Weimar the assembly needed military protection. The People's Commissars and the Central Council surrendered their powers to the assembly, which elected Ebert president of the republic and established a temporary constitution.[1] Ebert then nominated a new government consisting of seven majority socialists, three Democrats and three Centrists with Scheide-

---

[1] The Central Council remained in being for some time longer, but after the National Assembly met it fell between two stools: to the supporters of parliamentary government it was suspect as a rival body, to the protagonists of council government it was too closely identified with the S.P.D.

mann as prime minister. At first the majority socialists tried to include the Independents but the latter brusquely refused; after the murder of Liebknecht and Luxemburg by Noske's troops they were in no mood to share government again with the S.P.D. even had the latter not been forced to include at least one non-socialist party in order to have a majority.[1] The S.P.D. could have secured that majority with the Democrats alone and thus been free from the clerical influence on policy which was to be expected of the Centre, but the Democrats were keen on the inclusion of the Centre, and so the coalition was formed. The majority socialists were not sorry that it was a broad one, for the government thereby gained in standing at home and abroad, and responsibility for unpopular decisions was shared. The most serious concession the socialists had to make to their coalition partners was to abandon any idea of wholesale socialisation, but most of the S.P.D. leaders were decidedly cautious in this respect, and the Democrats were prepared to see at least the coalmines nationalised. Despite some inevitable give and take, the S.P.D. were in a very strong position, having the presidency, the key ministerial posts (the premiership and the ministries of economics, labour, defence, justice, and food in addition to a minister without portfolio) as well as the premiership of Prussia. Brockdorff-Rantzau, a non-party man and former ambassador to Denmark, remained as foreign minister, the post to which he had been appointed by the People's Commissars.

With the coming into force of a provisional constitution the revolutionary government set up on 10 November formally ended. The new regime, in a country depleted, improverished, strike-bound and awaiting an uncertain peace, began in a mood of grim sobriety. The new assembly, it was observed, was very like the old Reichstag, and Germany had returned after a brief experiment in proletarian rule to the parliamentary regime initiated the previous October. But this was precisely what infuriated the many thousands on the left who had built their hopes on the workers' and soldiers' councils as a new and better form of democracy, and the lack of a socialist majority confirmed the fears of those who had warned that the National Assembly would prevent the completion of the revolution. What chance was there now of the Hamburg Points being put into effect in the army against officer opposition, or of large-scale public ownership in defiance of the wishes of the big industrialists? The paradox of the decision of the congress of workers' and soldiers' councils, in voting for a parliamentary regime while insisting on immediate socialisation and the Hamburg Points, was now clearly seen. In failing to realise that the attainment of these aims depended on the retention of government by councils, the German revolution had, in Däumig's words, committed suicide. Now all those who passionately desired sweeping changes rallied round the councils as their only hope. The councils had been the one

---

[1] H. Müller, *Die November Revolution*, p. 283.

institutional novelty of the revolution, and there were many socialists, not only among the Independents, who wanted the workers' councils in the new social democracy of Germany to continue to play a part in the making of policy. The weeks and months that followed the first meeting of the National Assembly were marked by a tenacious and at times desperate rearguard action by the councils and their supporters. The return to parliamentary government brought not the end of violence but its recurrence, and the new government's writ was ineffective in most parts of the country. The late winter and early spring of 1919 saw a succession of Communist risings analogous to that of January in Berlin, and a wave of political strikes which were suppressed in turn by General Maercker and other Freikorps commanders occupying one town after another and declaring martial law.

One of the first places to defy the government was the self-governing city of Bremen, the home of the militant left wing group to which Karl Radek had belonged, and which had now joined the Communist party.[1] The all-socialist government set up in Berlin in November had broken down by January, with the left wing Independents siding with the Communists against the Social Democrats. On 10 January, encouraged by the Spartacus revolt in Berlin, the Bremen Communists seized power, distributed arms to their supporters, suppressed the bourgeois press and proclaimed a dictatorship of the proletariat. Three days later, when news of the Spartacists' failure in Berlin became known, the dictatorship was revoked and elections to the constituent assembly were allowed to proceed in an orderly manner. The government then demanded that the workers' and soldiers' council, which the left had purged, be reconstituted in accordance with the strength of the parties shown in the votes cast in Bremen for the National Assembly. The workers were also to be disarmed. To enforce these demands against local opposition government troops occupied Bremen and set up a new government consisting entirely of majority socialists. The soldiers' council in Hamburg had threatened armed intervention if Noske occupied Bremen, but he ignored the threat and Hamburg opposition proved half-hearted. In Bremen, as elsewhere, the Communists and their allies were in the minority: in the general election the Independents had received 30,000 votes compared with nearly 70,000 for the S.P.D. and 65,000 for the middle-class parties. Municipal elections in Bremen in March showed that the Communists and Independents together received fewer votes than the S.P.D. and many fewer that the non-socialist parties. Only a section of the Bremen proletariat supported the dictatorship fleetingly established in its name. In another state of north-west Germany, Brunswick, where radicalism was also strong,

---

[1] For the rising in Bremen, see *Illustrierte Geschichte der deutschen Revolution*, pp. 334 ff.; R. Müller, *op. cit.* pp. 116 ff.; Noske, *op. cit.* pp. 79 ff.

a similar sequence of events led through a minority-based Communist dictatorship to occupation by Noske's troops.[1]

In the Ruhr the anti-government movement was more broadly based, and the main issue was socialisation, a policy to which the majority as well as the Independent socialists were committed. It was generally agreed that of all the industries which might be ripe for socialism the coalmines were the first choice, and the miners could hardly wait. Even before the election of the National Assembly a meeting of workers' and soldiers' councils in the Ruhr resolved to bring the mines under control and set up a commission of nine to run them as national property.[2] Each of the three socialist parties was represented by three delegates. The trade unions were favourably disposed. In Essen the mines were occupied by the local workers' and soldiers' council. A socialist delegation went from the Ruhr to Weimar to urge the government to act. The result was the introduction in the National Assembly early in March of two bills: one empowering the government to nationalise any industry in general terms, with compensation to the owners, the other transferring management of the coal industry to a national commission consisting of mine-owners, workers and consumers. In April a similar commission was set up for the potash industry.

Meanwhile the majority socialists had fallen out with the extremists over an incident at Münster in Westphalia, where the soldiers' council was broken up by the local army commander, General von Watter, after it had refused to recognise a government order on 19 January confirming the officers' power of command. In the middle of February a workers' and soldiers' council in Essen threatened a general strike in the Ruhr and armed opposition to the Freikorps if the Münster soldiers' council was not reinstated and Watter punished. So far the majority socialists had gone along with their left wing colleagues in the commission of nine in supporting the Münster demands, but now they resigned. Bitter recriminations occurred between the right and left wing socialists and on one occasion an S.P.D. meeting was broken up by the Independents using machine guns. In the meantime clashes took place between the armed workers led by Communists and the Freikorps. A truce was then arranged and the workers let themselves be disarmed. The Freikorps occupied the towns. For a time things were quiet, but in April there was another general strike in the Ruhr, followed by a fresh incursion of troops and the declaration of martial law. The majority socialist trade unionist Carl Severing (later to be minister of the interior in Prussia and in the Reich) was appointed Reich Commissioner for the Ruhr. The government granted a seven-hour shift and increased rations to the miners, for coal was vital to the German economy, and by the end of April the strike was over.

---

[1] For the rising in Brunswick, see Horkenbach, *op. cit.* p. 66; Noske, *op. cit.* pp. 127–29.
[2] For the strike movement in the Ruhr, see R. Müller, *op. cit.* pp. 117 ff.

Next to the Ruhr Saxony contained the greatest industrial concentration in Germany, and there too pressure was strong for nationalisation and for some form of workers' control in the factories.[1] The government promised that nationalisation would be speeded up and that works' councils would form an integral part of the new constitution—a promise which was kept, though not to the extent demanded by the extreme left. In the course of the strike movement power was concentrated in the hands of a small group of Communists and Independents who defied both the local state parliament and the constituent assembly. On 12 April the Saxon minister of war, a majority socialist called Neuring, was lynched by infuriated demonstrators at Dresden and thrown into the Elbe; when he tried to swim out, he was shot dead. The Saxon government appealed to the German government for help and Noske's Freikorps duly marched in to restore order. The council of five which had ruled Saxony in the name of the proletariat quickly disappeared.

If revolutionary government failed to maintain itself in radical Saxony it could hardly hope to succeed in conservative Bavaria; yet Munich was to see the most extreme experiment in minority dictatorship. Eisner, despite his limitations a man of creative ideas and a more original personality than the average party boss whom the revolution had brought to power, sought to introduce a new form of radical democracy.[2] A gifted orator, and an idealist in the tradition of Shelley rather than Marx, Eisner strove to inaugurate the kingdom of light, beauty and reason. Few people in Bavaria shared his vision; abroad, his attempts to convince the Allies that they could trust the new regime made no impression on the cynical Clemenceau. Like most of his Independent colleagues in Berlin, Eisner accepted the necessity for a constituent assembly, but he wished to keep the workers' councils so as to provide a proletarian balance to the bourgeois democracy of parliament and to combine the two in some form of dual control. Yet this notion became unrealistic after the election of a new Bavarian parliament in January gave 64 per cent of the votes to the middle-class parties, 33 per cent to the majority socialists and only 2·5 per cent to the Independents. This vote of no confidence in Eisner led to a demand from the right wing parties for his resignation. The S.P.D. too considered him obviously discredited and wanted a coalition of themselves with the Bavarian People's party. Eisner unwisely clung to office, and early in February went to Berne to take part in the first post-war meeting of the Socialist International, where he tried to influence the Allied socialists to mitigate the terms of peace. On his return to Munich in mid-February, Eisner addressed a congress of workers' and soldiers' councils of Bavaria and again put forward proposals for combining councils with

[1] R. Müller, *op. cit.* pp. 142 ff.; Noske, *op. cit.* p. 191.
[2] For Eisner and Bavarian socialism see Schade, *Kurt Eisner und die bayrische Sozialdemokratie, passim*; R. Müller, *op. cit.* pp. 191 ff.; Stroebel, *op. cit.* pp. 154 ff.

parliamentary government. Given the very different political composition of the two bodies in Bavaria it is hard to see how such co-operation could have worked apart from the intrinsic difficulty of shared responsibility.

On 21 February Eisner was murdered by a nationalist student while on his way to the opening session of the new Bavarian parliament, where he was to announce his resignation. When news of the murder reached the horrified chamber one of Eisner's supporters shot and wounded Erhard Auer, Eisner's S.P.D. rival, who was suspected of complicity in the crime. After more shooting, in the course of which one of the leaders of the Bavarian People's party lost his life, the parliament dispersed in panic. Consternation at the assassination of Eisner caused a wave of indignation against the right. Martial law and a general strike were declared, suspects were arrested, and a new all-socialist government headed by an S.P.D. teacher named Hoffmann was appointed by the central workers' and soldiers' council. Under the influence of Bela Kun's soviet dictatorship in Hungary, proclaimed on 20 March, and in order to forestall the reassembly of the Bavarian parliament, a left wing group in Munich organised a *coup d'état* and put themselves in power as a soviet dictatorship (6 April). The new regime had little popular support, but it was accepted by many majority socialists as well as by the Independents, though not by the small group of Communists.[1] Hoffmann fled to Bamberg, a Catholic centre in north Bavaria, so that Bavaria now had two rival socialist governments. The new cabinet in Munich, which included Landauer, a talented literary historian of anarchist sympathies, and the young pacifist writer Toller, reflected the Bohemian and intellectual life of Schwabing, the artists' quarter of Munich, rather than the working people of Bavaria. It was, however, soon discredited after the new 'foreign minister', Dr Lipp, sent crazy telegrams to Berlin and Moscow which introduced a note of farce into a macabre situation. The war minister Schneppenhorst defected to Bamberg. On 13 April the Munich garrison revolted and the Landauer government fell. A group of tough young Communists, mostly of Russian-Jewish origin, took advantage of the confusion to set themselves up as a second soviet dictatorship. This time the government began to arm the workers, banned the bourgeois press, seized the banks and commandeered food from the peasants. The latter, however, resisted, and Munich was soon short of bread and milk. An attempt by Reichswehr troops to recapture Munich was repulsed in a skirmish at Dachau in which the young Toller unexpectedly distinguished himself; but elsewhere anti-Communist forces, including the Bavarian Freikorps, were massing under Colonel von Epp, and preparing to co-operate with the troops assembled in the north by Noske. On 1 May Noske's Reichswehr entered Munich and reconquered the city. The red terror was followed by a white. During the fighting many brutalities were

---

[1] R. Müller, *op. cit.* pp. 192 ff.; Flechtheim, *Die K.P.D. in der Weimarer Republik*, p. 53.

committed, including the shooting in cold blood of twenty-one Catholic apprentices who were thought to be Communists. Leviné, the leader of the second dictatorship, was arrested, tried and executed for treason; Landauer was shot after arrest; and hundreds of Communist soldiers were court-martialled. Munich became what it was to remain throughout the Weimar regime, a hotbed of anti-Communism. It was the opinion of Ruth Fischer, then a leading member of the German Communist party, that without the civil war Munich would never have become the birthplace of the Hitler movement. Richard Müller passed a harsh verdict on Bavaria's soviet governments: 'The declaration of the soviet republic (on 6 April) was nothing but miserable and unscrupulous play acting at revolution by political pushers and coffee house scribblers, who became intoxicated by their own words and could not find their bearings in the confusion of revolutionary events.'[1]

Bavaria was the last of the states to be reconquered by the Berlin government. In the meantime, however, Berlin had been the scene of renewed street fighting. Trouble started early in March with the declaration of a general strike by the Executive Council, which contained a small number of Democrats as well as representatives of all three socialist parties. The aims of the strike were recognition by the government of the role of workers' and soldiers' councils; implementation of the Hamburg Points; the formation of a workers' defence force; dissolution of the Freikorps; and resumption of diplomatic relations with the Soviet Union.[2] The Democrats refused to endorse these aims, and the Communists characteristically decided to have a separate strike of their own. That majority socialists should endorse these demands was a measure of their discontent with the government. Some members of the all-S.P.D. Central Council had expressed serious misgivings about the Freikorps, condemned their brutalities and deplored the government's dependence on them.[3] The dismissal of Hindenburg and Groener had also been called for. As in December there was strong pressure in the S.P.D. for speedy socialisation and 'democratisation' of the army. But the difference between the majority socialists who joined the general strike in March 1919 and the Communists was that the former did not want to overthrow the government in which their party had the predominant voice, whereas the Communists had precisely that aim. Hence when the Independents with Communist backing decided to extend the strike to water, gas and electricity the S.P.D. withdrew. Rioting had, however, already begun. Police stations were stormed and shops plundered. Noske declared martial law. The Freikorps attacked public buildings held by the rebels, mostly in the

---

[1] R. Müller, *op. cit.* p. 194.
[2] *Ibid.* p. 154.
[3] Minutes of the Central Council (*Zentralrat*) for 9 and 10 January 1919.

working-class east end, but also engaged in fighting with the few republican forces that remained. False rumours of the mass shootings of prisoners by the rebels exacerbated hatred on the other side. On 9 March Noske issued an order that anyone found fighting against the government with a weapon in his hand would be shot on the spot.[1] It was a drastic and much criticised measure, but it proved effective. By the time order had been restored, however, at least 1,200 people had lost their lives, many of whom were innocent victims. Among the proved atrocities was the shooting of twenty-nine sailors of the People's Naval Division by a Lieutenant Marloh, which Noske admitted to have been horrible and irresponsible. What made the matter more reprehensible was that at his trial nine months later Marloh was acquitted. This verdict, seen in conjunction with the incongruously mild sentence passed on the killers of Liebknecht and Rosa Luxemburg, suggested that republican justice was always willing to find extenuating circumstances in cases of political murder committed by the right.

Some socialist writers have denied that the street fighting in Berlin was due to the general strike, and ascribed it to government provocation. Yet an inflammatory article in the Communist *Rote Fahne* of 3 March demanding the abolition of the constituent assembly and the transfer of power to the councils, and denouncing Ebert, Scheidemann and Noske as traitors and murderers, spoke a language that could not be misunderstood. Despite their defeat in January, and the subsequent conclusion that 'Spartacus Week' had been a mistake, the party was once again indulging in a challenge to the government for which the conditions of success were lacking. Ebert was still seen as the Kerensky of Germany, and shortly afterwards Sverdlov, president of the Supreme Soviet in Russia, had written to the German Communist party comparing Spartacus Week with the Petrograd July Days and assuring them that it was one of those reverses which would bring final victory nearer.[2] In Moscow hopes of world revolution still ran high; the Third International was founded in March, and the temporary success of Communists in Hungary, Bavaria and north Italy added to the euphoria. In Germany disillusion with the republican government was driving many of the workers from majority to Independent socialism. Moscow's backing gave the tiny Communist party a significance they would otherwise have lacked, but also made them suspect as the instrument of a foreign power.

The notion of councils as organs of political power was discredited by their use in Bremen, Brunswick and Bavaria for the dictatorship of a minority, and once the constituent assembly had established itself at Weimar the

---

[1] R. Müller, *op. cit.* pp. 174 ff.; Noske, *op. cit.* p. 109, and *Aufstieg und Niedergang der deutschen Sozialdemokratie*, pp. 93–7.

[2] *Rote Fahne*, 11 February 1919. R. Müller described Noske and his friends as traitors to the revolution; and because of their needless provocation of the Freikorps, the Communists as the asses of the revolution.

disappearance of political councils was only a question of time.[1] Protagonists of the council system succeeded in organising a second congress of workers' and soldiers' councils in Berlin in April 1919, but apart from claiming a say in foreign policy the meeting did not adopt a radical programme, largely because the greater part of its delegates were majority socialists.[2] Only in the economic sphere did councils survive; they were given a status and function in the Weimar constitution, as will be seen in the next chapter. This was the main institutional legacy of the revolution to the Weimar Republic, but little use was made of it in practice.[3]

As for the soldiers' councils, there was no future for them in the provisional Reichswehr, the creation of which was approved by the constituent assembly on 25 February. Already on 19 January Noske's decree confirming the officers' power of command in the army had settled a dispute which had been raging since the beginning of the revolution and effectively marked the end of the policy embodied in the Hamburg Points.[4] It was followed by indignant protests from soldiers' councils in different parts of Germany: the soldiers' council in Hanover passed a resolution against the attempt to reintroduce 'slavery', and only energetic action by Noske prevented the establishment of a permanent soldiers' council in the ministry of war.[5] In some places soldiers' councils tried to stop recruitment to the Freikorps. But demobilisation was continually reducing the number of councils and the soldiers were fighting a losing battle. Meanwhile Noske recruited enough Freikorps not only to occupy the rebellious towns and states but also to replace the council-dominated and militarily ineffective army units on the disputed eastern frontier.

The continuation and intensification of the strike movement with its political demands and use of force despite the convening of the constituent assembly testifies to the strength of revolutionary feeling in Germany, which also explains the growth of political radicalism in the year leading up to the Kapp Putsch. Behind the political grievances were genuine economic hardships: prices had risen more than wages, food was scarce and expensive.[6]

---

[1] Among the reasons for the failure of the councils to establish themselves as organs of political power was the hostile attitude of the trade unions. Legien, the free Trade Union leader, said on 2 February 1919: 'The council system is no organisation at all and at any rate not an efficient one' (H. J. Varain, *Freie Gewerkschaften, Demokratie und Staat*, 1956, p. 1946). The unions were naturally jealous of the councils, though they recognised that as economic bodies the councils had a part to play, and sought to gain control of them. The trade unions also condemned the wild cat strikes in which many workers' councils were involved.

[2] R. Müller, *op. cit.* p. 209; Horkenbach, *op. cit.* p. 65.

[3] Horkenbach, *op. cit.* p. 380; Stampfer, *Die ersten vierzehn Jahre der deutschen Republik*, p. 142.　　　　　[4] R. Müller, *op. cit.* pp. 104 ff.; Noske, *Von Kiel bis Kapp*, p. 96.

[5] Noske, *op. cit.* p. 97.

[6] By 1918 German real wages had fallen by 25 % since 1914. Food rations in the period 1 July–28 December 1918 were below one-sixth of the average pre-war consumption of meat, fish, eggs, lard, cheese and cereals. J. Kuczynski, *A short History of Labour Conditions in Germany, 1800 to the Present Day* (1945), p. 218–19.

In the year 1919 there were nearly 5,000 strikes, with the loss of forty-eight million working days.[1] (The 1920 figures were to be even higher.) Under these circumstances output continued to lag.[2] Had the strikes in the early months of 1919 in the Ruhr, central Germany and Berlin occurred simultaneously, the government would have found it difficult to survive. But the left lacked co-ordination. Another source of weakness was that the majority socialists, while willing to take part in the strike movement, would not go over into open rebellion. While the left was crippled by division, the Freikorps were able to acquire such a dominating position largely because of the passivity of the middle class. General Maercker, the 'conqueror of cities' wrote early in 1919:

Almost every time we entered a town I had to ask myself the question: Would our intervention have been necessary if everyone had been at his post? Where was the German bourgeoisie? Where were the pro-government workers? Where were our students, our ex-officers, n.c.o.s and soldiers?...I have acquired in the five months of my activity in central Germany little respect for the constructive ability (*Gestaltungskraft*) of the German bourgeoisie, but a high opinion of the organised workers...The workers, well organised, disciplined and ready to make sacrifices, are faced almost everywhere by a bourgeoisie which is completely unorganised, split up into four or five mutually hostile parties, little inclined to make any sacrifices. While the anti-government workers dispose of a large number of determined leaders...in twenty towns of central Germany I have found hardly one really outstanding leader of the pro-government population.[3]

[1] *Illustrierte Geschichte*, p. 422.
[2] After the signing of the peace treaty, when the Allied blockade was formally lifted, Germany imported American foodstuffs in considerable quantities, and other imports rose; but she had lost all her foreign assets during the war, and in August 1919 German exports were only one-sixth of the pre-war level. Stampfer, *op. cit.* p. 129.
[3] Schüddekopf, *op. cit.* p. 48. Groener wrote to his wife on 17 November 1918: 'But where is the courage of the middle classes?', Groener, *Lebenserinnerungen*, p. 471.

CHAPTER 10

THE TRANSFORMATION OF INDEPENDENT SOCIALISM

> The naked truth is: we are heading for dictatorship, proletarian or
> Praetorian.   RATHENAU in 1919

THE U.S.P.D. TURN TO PROLETARIAN DICTATORSHIP

On 1 January 1919 the Independent socialist newspaper *Freiheit* confidently predicted that the New Year would see the completion of the German revolution and that a return to the past was impossible. A fortnight later the Berlin rising had been crushed and the party's optimism had vanished. Nor was it revived by its lack of success in the election of the National Assembly. With twenty-two seats the U.S.P.D. trailed far behind the S.P.D.'s 165 seats. *Freiheit* now complained of a rebirth of militarism and of a white terror exercised by the counter-revolutionary Freikorps.[1] Haase censured the behaviour of the troops, who arrested socialists and searched their homes without a warrant.[2] That such things could happen under a socialist government was particularly galling. Yet they were the consequence of an action for which the party's Berlin branch and the revolutionary shop-stewards which formed its extreme left were largely responsible. The danger now, as farsighted observers noted, was that the Freikorps, called in to protect the democratic republic against its enemies on the left, might themselves become a threat to the republic.[3] The new mood of bitter disillusion was expressed in a manifesto issued by the U.S.P.D. on 8 February which accused the government of being the prisoner of militarism, the overthrow of which had been the main object of the revolution, and of allowing 'degenerate soldiers' to murder Liebknecht and Rosa Luxemburg.[4] The government was blamed for disregarding the demands for radical army reform (the Lamp'l Points) and socialisation put forward by the congress of councils. It was also rebuked, though with much less justification, for having rejected negotiations and compromise during the Berlin rising. But the Independents were apt to be undiscriminating in their denunciation of at the majority socialist leaders, and their indignation was heightened by the murder of Eisner on 21 February.

Against this background of Freikorps violence on the one hand, and the

[1] *Freiheit* of 15 and 16 January 1919.
[2] Haase, *Hugo Haase*, p. 173. Ledebour, who had been arrested during the January rising, was tried for high treason in May 1919 and acquitted after a brilliant defence largely conducted by himself.
[3] G. Mayer, *Erinnerungen* (1949), p. 326. Mayer himself was wrongfully arrested.
[4] Prager, *Geschichte der U.S.P.D.* p. 189.

insurrectionary strike movement briefly described in the last chapter on the other, opinion inside the Independent socialist party moved between two lines of thought. The right, represented by Kautsky and Hilferding, reiterated the need for working-class unity despite the misdeeds of the S.P.D. government. A united socialist party, wrote Hilferding in a retrospective article in *Freiheit* on 9 February, could have created a democratic army and got rid of the old militarism, established a new, democratic civil service, won a majority in the National Assembly and made a start in socialising the economy. Hilferding overlooked some of the practical difficulties: there was little sign that the workers would have been willing to join even a democratic army, or that, at a time of dislocation and shortages, the population would have been ready to exchange the highly trained professional civil service for an untrained one. Where Hilferding was significantly right was in his belief that many majority socialists were unhappy about the course being taken by their leaders and would have been glad to join forces with the right wing Independents in opposition to reviving militarism. This is shown by the minutes of the all-majority socialist Central Council which contain many criticisms of the Freikorps and Noske and demands for the dismissal of Hindenburg and Groener. 'It seems to me disconcerting (*bedenklich*)', said one speaker, 'that the socialist government must...rely for its support on an army that is basically reactionary.'[1] Another, whose name was Wäger, commented:

The blame for this situation lies with the Independents and their mistaken policy. But the greatest blame lies with our party comrades who are sitting in the government...I do not believe that the people [the Freikorps] who are fighting beside us will become our masters. But history will record the fact that the German socialists were able to remain at the head of affairs only through the help of these people.[2]

Cohen-Reuss, known for his right wing views, described a visit to army headquarters and heard how they recruited volunteers:

I must say I felt a chill down my spine. There are a lot of officers there who will have nothing to do with socialism and are looking forward to beating people up again. I must say what may happen horrifies me. These people have learnt nothing at all. I have a terrible fear that we're simply fighting with militarists of another persuasion; this became quite obvious to me as I spoke to these people.[3]

Another member of the Central Council, Kohl, spoke of a conversation in the Chancellery the day before, when a secretary said of the shooting outside: 'A lot of blood has got to flow in Berlin, then things will change.'[4] Kohl bitterly referred to the officers' pleasure in bloodshed as the trump card on which the government were relying. Under these circumstances those Independents who favoured co-operation with the majority socialists could

---

[1] *Zentralrat*, 9 January 1919. The speaker was Grzesinski, who was later in turn under-secretary of state for war and minister of the interior in Prussia.
[2] *Zentralrat*, 9 January.
[3] *Ibid.*   [4] *Ibid.*

appeal to vital common interests. And indeed throughout the revolution, especially outside Berlin, most of the rank and file had paid little attention to inter-socialist differences. A contributor to *Freiheit* wrote: 'The slogan of the day, wherever one goes, in workshops, meetings, labour exchanges, anywhere where workers meet, is the unification of the proletariat.'[1]

But this trend had to compete with another in the ranks of the Independents. In the eyes of the left as represented by Däumig, who was the chief link between the parliamentary party and the revolutionary shop-stewards, the majority socialist leaders had ceased to be socialists in any meaningful sense (Ebert had long abandoned the use of class-war language) and had become junior partners of the militarists.[2] The suppression of the workers' and soldiers' councils was also a grievance. Däumig, who had deplored and vainly opposed the congress of councils' decision in favour of the National Assembly as a fatal mistake pressed for the councils to remain in being as the only means of keeping the revolutionary spirit alive in an institutional form. In a series of articles in *Der Arbeiterrat*, the weekly periodical of which he was editor, Däumig exalted councils as superseding political parties (which wasted time in disputes) and trade unions (which belonged to the past). Councils should become responsible for the functions of government at all levels from the state to the parish. Though probably only a minority of Independents shared this extreme view, many wished, like Eisner, to combine councils and parliament in a dual system. Despite the fiasco of council dictatorships in Munich and elsewhere, growing disillusion with the parliamentary democracy of Weimar made the attractions of government by workers' councils more obvious to the left wing radicals.

Not only in Germany, but in Europe as a whole, the choice between parliamentary democracy and council dictatorship was now recognised as the cardinal question for socialists, as was shown by its place on the agenda at the congress of parties of the Second International, held at Berne in February 1919. This was the first time since the war that German socialists had met their Allied opposite numbers. For the U.S.P.D. Eisner made an important speech in which he refused to abandon the democratic position. Haase, however, maintained that the issue was one of tactics;[4] he failed to realise how far means determined ends. If he was right, the difference between the Independents and the Communists was of minor importance. When Haase spoke approvingly of proletarian dictatorship, as he was to do at the forthcoming party congress, he meant a short-term dictatorship, lasting only long enough to forestall the danger of counter-revolution. He knew that in

---

[1] 12 February 1919.
[2] An example of their rejection of half-measures was the Independents' vote against the socialisation bill of March 1919.
[3] R. Müller, *Der Bürgerkrieg in Deutschland*, p. 209.
[4] *Zentralrat*, 15 January.

the Germany of 1919 even a socialist government with a parliamentary majority would have found it difficult, perhaps impossible, to enforce a radical policy against the opposition of generals and higher civil servants, not to mention industrialists and landowners. But he was less ready to admit that any attempt to set up proletarian dictatorship would have led to civil war, as Cohen had warned the December congress. Since the congress itself had opted for a parliamentary regime, Haase was prepared to accept its verdict pending the conversion of the proletariat to a pro-councils policy. But his left wing colleagues were less patient and pressed for the priority of workers' councils to be recognised in the party programme.

This was the main issue before an extraordinary congress of the U.S.P.D. held in Berlin at the beginning of March. It coincided with the second Berlin rising and the street fighting added to the nervous tension in which the debates were held. Hitherto the party had abstained from making any alteration in the Erfurt programme of 1891 of which the Independents claimed, with considerable justification, to be the true heirs and to which the S.P.D. still officially adhered. The new congress spent a good deal of time analysing the party's role in the German revolution and discussing what had gone wrong. Everyone was depressed by the failure of the socialists to win a majority in the National Assembly, by the murder of socialist leaders, the domination of the Freikorps, the delay in the socialisation programme.[1] But there was some encouragement in the greater support which the party was now receiving. Membership was 300,000 in January and by March was known to be higher. Branches had sprung up in parts of the country where Independent socialism had hardly been known, and the party was beginning to make up for its wartime handicaps—inadequate organisation, the censorship, lack of newspapers. The local election results of January and February had shown gains, and the party's greater popularity was interpreted as a sign that people wanted a more radical policy, and would go to the Communists if they did not get it from the Independents. This became an important consideration in the minds of the left wing of the party from now until its split a year and a half later.

Surveying the revolution at the Berlin congress, Haase defended his decisions to share power with the majority socialists on 9 November, and not to resign before 29 December.[2] The soldiers and most of the workers had insisted on a socialist coalition; and it would have been a mistake to let the majority socialists hold power alone. Moreover the misguided policy enforced by the left of boycotting the Central Council when it was elected by the congress of councils had prevented the party from taking advantage of Ebert's mistakes in handling the sailors' revolt. To a left wing delegate who argued

---

[1] *Prot. U.S.P.D.* (Berlin, 1919). For a short summary, see Prager, *op. cit.* p. 191.
[2] *Prot. U.S.P.D.* pp. 78 ff.

that the Independents should have resigned when the congress of councils voted for the National Assembly Dittmann replied that they could not disavow parliamentary government. The wrangle between right and left was not resolved. The left blamed the right for compromising it, the right complained that they had not been supported in office. Those who were most incensed by Ebert's behaviour in the Council of People's Commissars were inclined to overlook the co-operation which the two parties had achieved in the Executive Council.

Däumig put forward a draft programme which made workers' councils the sole representative bodies through which the proletariat should exercise power. Their main advantage over the Reichstag, he explained, was that they were executive as well as legislative organs. In answer to the objection that the proletariat had already declared against the abolition of parliament, Däumig said it must think again: the masses must be educated to the council system. But Haase would not agree to give up parliament in the long run, though transitionally proletarian dictatorship was not a contradiction of democracy because 'when the proletariat seizes power the majority of the population will stand behind it'.[1] Haase added that after all parliament had been a cover for the exercise of bourgeois dictatorship, thus showing that he had advanced a long way towards the conception of 'parliamentary cretinism' —a phrase used by Marx—held by Rosa Luxemburg. On the parliamentary issue the Independent party had no clear-cut policy.

In its final shape the party's new programme represented a compromise between the views of Haase and those of Däumig, but weighted in favour of the latter. The most significant passage now read:

The historical task of the U.S.P.D. is to be the standard-bearer of the class-conscious proletariat in its revolutionary struggle for liberation. The...party takes its stand on the council system. It supports the councils in their struggle for economic and political power. It strives for the dictatorship of the proletariat, the representative of the great majority of the nation, as the essential postulate for the realisation of socialism. Only socialism will bring the abolition of all class rule, the elimination of every dictatorship, pure democracy.

To reach this goal, the U.S.P.D. makes use of all political and economic weapons including parliament. It rejects planless acts of violence.[2]

Despite the repudiation of putsches in the last sentence this programme drew protests from the right, especially from Kautsky, who pointed out that it was incompatible with the Berne resolution of the Second International (which Eisner had drafted).[3] But the time was past when Kautsky was listened to as the party oracle. Other warning voices were raised. Now, however, the left was firmly in the ascendant, owing to the growing danger from the nationalist right, and disenchantment with the new republic which left so much unchanged. Yet the inability of the leaders to agree with each other was

[1] *Prot. U.S.P.D.* pp. 95–112.   [2] *Ibid.* p. 3.   [3] *Ibid.* p. 123.

exemplified in the refusal of Haase to sit as chairman with the new co-chairman, Däumig.[1] Däumig thereupon resigned and his place was taken by the less controversial Crispien. But the compromise reached at Berlin had neither convinced the reluctant right nor appeased the ambitious left. The dissension which had nearly led to the break-up of the party in December 1918 continued, and only a common fear of counter-revolution held it loosely together.

VERSAILLES AND WEIMAR: THE SOCIALIST BALANCE SHEET IN THE SUMMER AND AUTUMN OF 1919

Important as the domestic tasks of the coalition government of Germany were in the first few months of its existence, in the spring of 1919 one subject dominated all others—the peace treaty. The Allied terms, presented to the German delegation at Versailles on 7 May, unleashed a storm of indignation when they became known a few days later, and led to a cabinet crisis. Scheidemann, the prime minister, made an emotional speech at a special meeting of the National Assembly in the aula of Berlin University in which he branded the treaty a document of hate and delusion, and declared that any hand would wither which bound Germany in such fetters. It was hoped that the Allies would make concessions, but when they refused to yield on any points of substance, Scheidemann resigned. Bauer, hitherto S.P.D. minister of labour and a trade unionist, succeeded him as prime minister with Hermann Müller as foreign secretary instead of Brockdorff-Rantzau. The new government proposed a conditional acceptance of the treaty: they would sign those parts which were not incompatible with Germany's national pride. But the Allies were adamant, and made it clear that any refusal to sign unconditionally would lead to a renewal of the war with unforeseeable consequences including the probable occupation of the whole country. The socialist Löbe voiced the opinion of most of his party when he told the Reichstag that, harsh and humiliating as the treaty was, the results of its rejection would be even more terrible. Bauer nearly resigned, a step which would have forced the nationalist parties to shoulder the unpopular burden of government; still, the lack of any realistic alternative forced them too to acquiesce in the treaty. The S.P.D. leaders rejected the nationalist argument that national honour demanded refusal to sign, but they showed that they did not feel morally bound by the treaty, which they did not believe could be permanent.[2] In particular the party protested against the exclusion from the Reich of the Germans in Austria and Czechoslovakia and the loss of the colonies. Haenisch, the patriotic socialist who was now minister of education in Prussia, declared:

[1] *Ibid.* p. 254.
[2] Berlau, *The German Social Democratic Party, 1914–21*, pp. 300 ff.

This peace of shame...which represents the temporary victory of Entente capitalism over German socialism is not the last word...In the end the 'ideas of 1914' will yet gain victory over the military and political successes of the western powers and over the ideas of 1789, which are now seemingly victorious...The peace of dishonour of Versailles will ultimately mean nothing more than a scrap of paper.[1]

That a socialist minister of education could denounce the ideas of the French revolution in favour of those of Hohenzollern Germany was a measure of the change that had come over the S.P.D. during the war. Yet even such impeccably nationalist sentiments were not to protect the party from the charge of stabbing Germany in the back. Meanwhile one especially disillusioning feature of the treaty was its failure to maintain the distinction, stressed in the wartime speeches of Wilson and other Western leaders, between the German people and its rulers. By the end of the war this distinction was wearing thin in the western capitals. *The Times* wrote on 20 December 1918: 'The mass of the German people were in fact accomplices in the crimes of militarism because they approved its ends and had no remorse as to the use of its most inhuman means.' The peace as well as the war seemed to fulfil Winston Churchill's earlier prophecy that democracy would be more vindictive than cabinets;[2] popular passions proved harder to assuage than to arouse. In their answer to German complaints about hardships the Allies did not deny the hardships but asserted that the Germans had brought them on themselves.[3] It seemed plain that despite the adoption of a parliamentary regime, the removal of Ludendorff and the Kaiser, and the November revolution, the German people had not gained any alleviation of the peace terms. In the Allied view the majority socialists had failed to protest against the breach of Belgian neutrality and atrocities in the conduct of war or to oppose annexations, while for the German public they bore the stigma of having signed the treaty and announced their intention to fulfil it as far as possible. Neither their previous patriotism nor their genuine revulsion against the treaty, of which Scheidemann's resignation was one example, was to exempt them from Hitler's later strictures as 'November criminals'.

The attitude of the Independent socialists to Versailles was less encumbered by past compromises and current responsibilities. Haase claimed that, in view of his party's consistent opposition to annexations and ruthless methods of warfare, it had the right to have its criticism of the treaty listened to abroad. But in the circumstances he had no doubt that the treaty must be signed; at a time when infant mortality was exceptionally high any other course would be frivolous.[4] In reply to mischievous suggestions that perhaps

---

[1] *Ibid.* p. 305. [2] See p. 84, above.

[3] The Allies 'persisted in regarding the Germany of Ebert and Scheidemann as in no essential regard different from the Junker-dominated Germany of 1914' (Halperin, *Germany tried Democracy*, 1946, p. 152). In a speech in October 1919, for example, Clemenceau, the French prime minister, described the German socialists as allies of the militarist party (*Vorwaerts*, 13 October 1919). [4] Haase, *op. cit.* p. 81.

the Independents might take office, Haase answered that the government would no doubt like them to share an unpopularity which they did not deserve, only to be chased out of office next day. In order to make sure of the U.S.P.D. vote for the treaty in the National Assembly Haase was asked by at least three parties for his support.[1] In the end the Assembly accepted the abhorrent treaty by 237 votes to 138, a sizeable majority.

Meanwhile the majority socialists had held their first post-war conference at Weimar in June 1919.[2] There was a strong undercurrent of discontent. The resolutions from branches all over Germany showed the volume of criticism at the survival of so much of the old regime and the failure to make socialism the inspiring policy on which so many had set their hopes. There were misgivings at the retention of the majority of senior civil servants (it was stated that Prussia had only one socialist *Regierungspräsident* and one socialist *Landrat*); at the use of Freikorps to suppress insurrectionary workers; and at the flagrantly mismanaged trial of the murderers of Liebknecht and Luxemburg. There was considerable demand for reunion with the Independents, provided they did not abandon democracy (which at their Berlin conference they had in fact done). Disappointment was also expressed at the slow progress in socialising industry, which was linked in many minds with some form of workers' control. The democratisation of the officers' corps was called for. In short, the party was asked to put into effect much the same policy as the congress of councils had wanted; but there was more impatience now, for six months had passed. Hermann Müller, who was elected party chairman in succession to Ebert, sought to put some of the blame on the Independents, who had spoiled the chances of an outright socialist victory at the polls by insisting on the postponement of the election of the National Assembly. But Müller was honest enough to admit that his party might not have used its opportunities since 9 November 1918; history, he suggested, would ask if a great movement had not found a small generation.[3] Subsequent events confirmed Müller's judgement. Scheidemann too criticised the Independents for widening the split between the two parties by wishing to disfranchise sections of the population, including such non-proletarians as self-employed farmers, in the election of workers' councils. Wels, now appointed a co-chairman of the S.P.D., dismissed the Independents as no longer a social democratic party but a hotch-potch of divergent opinions. Still, the conference passed a resolution in favour of reunification talks, on terms, with the U.S.P.D.[4]

An important speech was made by Wissell, the S.P.D. economics minister,

---

[1] *Ibid.* p. 182. [2] *Prot. S.P.D.* (Weimar, 1919), is the official report.

[3] *Ibid.* p. 131. Of the S.P.D. leaders Hermann Müller himself bears special responsibility as the Chancellor during the crucial period between the Kapp Putsch and the general election of June 1920.

[4] Representatives of both socialist parties met in conference from 20 to 24 June and agreed to set up committees to consider terms for reunification.

who admitted slowness in applying socialisation but explained the reasons: the absence of a new spirit in government and the civil service, the strength of conservatism in the economy, excessive wage demands which put up costs, and strikes which hindered production.[1] The masses, he complained, lacked the ethical outlook of socialism. David, speaking as another socialist minister, agreed: the incentive of capitalism had been lost and nothing had been found to take its place.[2] Because of the fall of productivity socialised industries would have to be subsidised from taxes, a burden which the economy should not be asked to bear. For this reason, David urged, socialisation must be applied slowly and carefully. This was also the advice of Professor Lederer, a member of the socialisation commission and at the time economics minister in Austria. The S.P.D. leaders were sure that hasty and ill-thought-out socialisation would disrupt industry and impede recovery. They also blamed the Allies for putting shackles on Germany which made it harder to carry out a socialist policy. Whether the majority socialists as a government party were right or wrong in their belief that socialism should follow not precede economic recovery, their lack of initiative disappointed their supporters. Even Wissell resigned as minister of economics when the government rejected a memorandum in which he had advocated far-reaching planning and integration of the economy.[3]

Although some speakers declared that imperialism and militarism in Germany were dead, Scheidemann, who already in February had warned of the dangers facing the young republic, admitted that the old forces were

---

[1] *Prot. S.P.D.* (Weimar, 1919), pp. 363 ff.

[2] *Ibid.* p. 376. David was minister without portfolio in the Scheidemann government, and minister of the interior in the succeeding Bauer government.

[3] Berlau, *op. cit.* pp. 280 ff. The background to Wissell's resignation was as follows. Wissell had been appointed minister of economics in February 1919 on the understanding, which was known to the S.P.D. *Fraktion*, that he would socialise a fairly large sector of the economy, and posters proclaiming 'Socialism has arrived' (*Der Sozialismus ist schon da*) were publicly displayed. This was in accordance with the view the party had come to hold after the experience of 'war socialism' that socialisation should be proceeded with step by step and that post-war Germany should be a mixed economy with a considerable public sector. Then in June 1919 came the crisis caused by disagreement within the government and the S.P.D. over whether or not to sign the peace treaty, and Scheidemann's resignation. The S.P.D. and Centre leaders who advocated signing as the lesser evil had great difficulty in re-forming a coalition government (in which the Democrats refused at the time to share). The Centre agreed to join the new coalition under Bauer only on condition that a halt was called to socialisation. Consequently when in July Wissell presented his socialisation plan to the government, it was rejected, and Wissell resigned. In 1917 a Union for Freedom and Fatherland had been formed of majority socialists, liberal intellectuals and Centre adherents to counteract the *Siegfrieden* propaganda of the Ludendorff–Tirpitz Fatherland party and to prepare for a democratic regime in case Germany lost the war. The group broke up when the terms of the peace treaty became known, and its members found themselves having to defend the much abused Erzberger for insisting that the treaty be signed. In order not to lose any more credit in the eyes of the right, they decided to jettison socialisation, a concession which made the Independent socialists even more disillusioned with the S.P.D. I am indebted to Dr Curt Geyer for this information. Wissell's successor was Robert Schmidt, a right wing socialist.

trying to seize power again,[1] and a woman delegate from Hamburg, Frau Kaemmerer-Leonard, spoke with considerable frankness:

It is not quite incomprehensible that our comrades in other countries, who judge by outward appearances more than we do, should sometimes harbour doubts about the genuineness of a revolution which leaves the old leaders, Hindenburg, Erzberger and others in leading positions in the army, state and parliament, a revolution which reprieves the kings and murders the revolutionaries. (Applause.) There is a danger that socialist Germany will be as much isolated in the Socialist International as capitalist Germany used to be in the old world.[2]

Noske was blamed for having shown too much confidence in the army officers, a criticism which was to have added force after his failure to forestall the Kapp Putsch. The part played by the Baltic Freikorps was also criticised. On the other hand, it was acknowledged that without the Freikorps the government could not have survived, and that the one-sided character of the Freikorps was largely due to the unwillingness of workers to join them. (This was Noske's main defence.) At the end of the conference a more hopeful note was struck by Dr Sinzheimer of Frankfurt, who saw in the workers' councils a means of transforming the much pilloried bourgeois democracy into a socialist one without recourse to dictatorship.[3]

This and other aspirations of the S.P.D. found expression in the new constitution, which was formally promulgated at Weimar on 11 August. Of the twenty-eight members of the National Assembly's drafting committee twelve were socialists. The influence of party thinking on the final result can be seen in such features as the greater powers assigned to the Reich *vis-à-vis* the individual states, the reference to socialisation, the emphasis on social rights and on the duty of property owners to serve the public good. The most novel and most specifically socialist aspect of the constitution was Article 165 which provided for a national system of works councils, headed by a National Economic Council with power both to initiate and to approve in advance social and economic legislation in the Reichstag. This attempt to graft the new concept of councils on to the parliamentary stem was intended to satisfy the left by preserving at least some of the functions claimed by the revolutionary councils, a last salvage from the wreck of the council system. But the Independents, especially those of the left, were not appeased, and described the constitution as an unworkable compromise between capitalism and socialism. The majority socialists claimed that it was the freest in the world; it was, at least on paper, a model of democracy. But by now, under the impact of the peace treaty and of the counter-revolutionary Freikorps, the political atmosphere in Germany had changed radically since the preceding winter, as the government recognised by its decision to elect Ebert president by a vote of the National Assembly in the belief that the alternative

---

[1] *Ibid.* p. 236.   [2] *Ibid.* p. 380.   [3] *Ibid.* p. 406.

of a popular vote would have led to the choice of a right wing candidate.[1] Forebodings about the future of the republic became frequent. On 8 July Haase described his impressions of Berlin after returning from the National Assembly:

I came here from Weimar a fortnight ago. There was a feeling of pogroms in the air...I arrived with the conviction that a military putsch was not imminent and that the flare-up of war in the east had been nipped in the bud, but in Berlin even sober-minded people have got the wind up to such an extent that they have been prophesying a military revolt down to the minutest detail.[2]

The foundations of what later erupted as the Kapp Putsch were already being laid, and it was at this time that the nucleus of the N.S.D.A.P. was being formed in Munich, with Adolf Hitler as its seventh member

Haase's colleague Dittmann disliked the half-measures he found in the constitution but was even more indignant about the spirit in which the laws were administered. He complained that those who were 'democrats' from fear and embarrassment, who lacked any democratic tradition and to whom the notion of popular power, enshrined in the Weimar constitution, was intrinsically alien if not actually repugnant, as well as the old-established officials corrupted and bungled everything that looked democratic. The bureaucrats and legal officials interpreted the democratic rules of the constitution in a purely formal way, and both openly and in secret helped the reactionaries to sabotage the constitution and the laws. Freedom of speech and of the press was abused unscrupulously, and everyone was at liberty to insult and vilify the republic and its leaders. All this happened in the name of democracy. Dittmann described democracy as a charter whereby the reactionaries misused popular rights and liberties to undermine democracy and bring it into contempt among the people.[3]

The old officials had originally stayed in office at the wish of the revolutionary government: they were needed to deal with the urgent problems of demobilisation and food supply and to keep the administrative wheels running smoothly. Thanks to their security of tenure they could also, Dittmann complained, sabotage the Weimar constitution with impunity. That the socialist ministers, who were too kind or easy-going or too dependent on

---

[1] Ebert had been president of the republic since February 1919 under the provisional constitution.

[2] Haase, op. cit. p. 183.

[3] Dittmann, Lebenserinnerungen, ch. 17. Otto Braun, the first socialist minister of agriculture in Prussia, and later prime minister, describes in his memoirs his frigid reception from the civil servants in the ministry of agriculture (Von Weimar zu Hitler, p. 43). 'Hate, dislike and mistrustful inquisitiveness were written on the faces' of the ministerial staff. Friedrich Meinecke, the distinguished German historian, writing from a different point of view than Dittmann, agrees with him in laying the blame for the destruction of the Weimar constitution on the nationalist senior officials, who, in a kind of old boys' conspiracy, carried on an 'open and secret war' against it. (Meinecke, Die deutsche Katastrophe, published in Germany in 1946, English translation by S. B. Fay, Boston, U.S.A., 1950, p. 31.)

their civil servants to dismiss them where they could have done so, did not entirely misplace their confidence is shown by the loyalty to the republic of the majority of civil servants at the time of the Kapp Putsch. Yet not only socialists but also bourgeois intellectuals like Ernst Troeltsch, complained of mistrust and friction caused by retention of monarchist officials who had made no attempt to adjust themselves to the new democratic regime.

The impotence of democrats when faced with hostility in the army, administration, law and industry was the basic reason why in the Independent socialist party the influence of the left continued to grow. Two new secretaries appointed to deal with the increasing work at headquarters, Koenen and Stoecker, both representatives of a younger, more impatient, generation, were in favour of the party merging with the Communists. *Freiheit* refused to print Kautsky's latest pamphlet, an attack on dictatorship entitled *Terrorismus oder Kommunismus*. In Kautsky's view democracy had been violated in practice by the right wing socialists, in theory by the left.[1] Geyer, on the other hand, a left wing leader from Saxony, called for a revision of the party programme so as to authorise revolutionary action by a minority: in the clause demanding proletarian dictatorship the qualifying words 'as representative of the great majority of the people' should be omitted.[2] Geyer regarded parliamentary activity as a waste of time, and wanted the party to adopt the council system without modification and to join the Third International. These proposals were discussed at a *Reichskonferenz* held by the U.S.P.D. in September 1919. Haase opposed them, saying that the people were no longer in a revolutionary temper and would not understand an anti-parliamentary tactic. His arguments prevailed. Hilferding, who had attended the second post-war conference of Second International parties at Lucerne in August, was keen for the party to remain in it. But Stoecker objected that the Second International was dominated by right wing socialists, and urged that if the U.S.P.D. and other European parties, such as those of Norway and Switzerland, joined the new Third International they would prevent it from being a purely Bolshevik body. It was decided to postpone a decision on this highly controversial question until the next party congress.[3]

Meanwhile the majority socialists showed renewed concern at the attacks of Reichswehr officers on the republic, which they insulted in front of their men, and Scheidemann warned the National Assembly in a phrase that became part of the political currency of the Weimar period: 'The enemy is on the right.' Noske too complained of nationalist propaganda in the army against the government parties with its allegation that all Germany's woes started on 9 November 1918. The arrival of Hindenburg in Berlin on 18 November 1919 to give evidence before a Reichstag Committee of Inquiry

[1] Stroebel, *The German Revolution and after*, p. 202.
[2] Prager, *op. cit.* p. 204.　　　　　　　　　　　　　　[3] *Ibid.* p. 205.

into the causes of the German collapse was the signal for an outburst of monarchist and anti-republican feeling; and Hindenburg's refusal to admit the mistakes of the supreme command could only confirm the now widespread belief that the war had been lost because of treachery on the home front. The Independents and Communists held a counter-demonstration in front of the Russian embassy in Unter den Linden. The press of the left blamed the government for not banning the one demonstration, that of the right for not banning the other. Berlin, wrote Noske, was a political madhouse. The republic, he told the Assembly, had to tread a narrow path between precipices.[1]

In a pamphlet published in November 1919 to mark the first anniversary of the revolution, Stroebel, the former editor of *Vorwaerts* who was now a leading member of the right wing of the U.S.P.D., came to a frankly pessimistic conclusion about the political situation:

> Except for a handful of political careerists and a stately swarm of profiteers, who even during the revolution batten on the decaying corpse of our economy like hyenas, the whole country feels greatly depressed by the course and results of the revolution...Today, as the first anniversary of the birth of the republic approaches, not only are the Junkers and upper bourgeoisie simply itching to give it a mortal blow at the first opportunity, not only is it an object of scorn for the small man and the peasant, but it is so even for the proletariat, which feels mocked and cheated and considers democracy simply the façade behind which capitalist exploitation and bureaucratic-military despotism are carrying on exactly as they carried on under the monarchy and the undisguised dictatorship of the sword.[2]

The working class and salaried employees had every reason to be discontented, in Stroebel's view, because while they were still poor and hungry, a minority lived in fantastic luxury. The only hope lay in ending the breach between the socialist parties: 'Either proletarian reconciliation or proletarian self-destruction—there is no other alternative.'

Stroebel's sentiments were shared by many in the majority socialist party, and there was talk of sacrificing Noske, who had become the greatest symbol of discord. *Vorwaerts* of 23 November summed up the situation in much the same terms as Stroebel. There had been the resort to force instead of reliance on the power of ideas (even now the S.P.D. seemed not to understand the problem of power), the waste of revolutionary energy in futile strikes and hopeless street fights, the glaring contrast, unflattering to a socialist government, between the ostentatious wealth of a few and the poverty of the many.[3] (This was the period of Georg Grosz's bitterly ironical cartoons showing legless ex-soldiers begging in the street from pleasure-seeking profiteers and of Brecht's early plays with their harsh, arresting mixture of realism, cynicism

---

[1] *Verhandlungen der Verfassunggebenden Deutschen Nationalversammlung*, vol. 330, 29 October 1919.
[2] Stroebel, *op. cit.* p. 217.
[3] During the first six months of the Republic the number of unemployed rose to one million, about a quarter of whom were in Berlin.

and nihilism against a background (in *Drums in the Night*) of Spartacist gunfire.) The only alternatives seen by *Vorwaerts* were the victory of 'black reaction' or working-class unity which would force the sluggish middle class along the path of progress. Scheidemann, with his usual sensitivity to the political climate, wrote privately to Ebert drawing his attention to the propaganda of the Nationalist party, which he suggested was much more dangerous than that of the frequently banned Independents.[1] The 'nasty experience' of which Scheidemann warned his presidential ex-colleague as the consequence of complacency soon materialised as the Kapp Putsch. But the chances of a reunification of the socialist parties foundered on the intransigence of the left wing Independents who, as has been observed, were more interested in coming to terms with the small but ideologically uncompromised Communist party, though the Communists too were divided at this time and plagued by sectarian quarrels.[2] The ascendancy of the left in the U.S.P.D. was facilitated by the death of Haase, who early in November 1919 succumbed to wounds inflicted by a gunman lying in wait as he was about to enter the Reichstag building. His murderer was found to be insane, but the motive, as in other similar cases, was political. Haase's removal from the scene closed an epoch in the short and stormy life of his party. Though far from being a strong and decisive leader, Haase, thanks to the respect in which he was held for his integrity (as even his political opponents acknowledged) had acted as a bridge between divergent sections of the party though he had not been able to impose the unity which had eluded it throughout. None of his colleagues could fill the gap which he left, the consequences of which were shown at the party's next extraordinary conference held at Leipzig from 30 November to 6 December.

THE U.S.P.D. LEAVE THE SECOND INTERNATIONAL

At Leipzig the U.S.P.D. abandoned the precarious compromise between parliamentary democracy and proletarian dictatorship established at the Berlin conference nine months before. That the party should adopt a more aggressive policy was partly an inevitable reaction to the failure of reformist socialism to satisfy traditional socialist aspirations, partly an act of preparation for the new revolutionary opportunities which were believed to lie ahead. Pessimism and optimism were unevenly balanced. On the one hand, the party had suffered casualties from the civil war; 15,000 were said to have been killed on the socialist side in the street fighting. On the other hand, membership had gone up from 300,000 at the beginning of the year to over 750,000, and the party now published fifty-five daily newspapers, a total

---

[1] Scheidemann, *Memoirs*, II, 331.   [2] See p. 233, fn. 3

never reached before.[1] The influx of recruits was proof that the workers were losing faith in the S.P.D. and encouraged the Independents to pursue a more radical policy.

Däumig as leader of the left reiterated the case he had elaborated before in favour of the substitution of workers' councils for an all-class parliament. It was time to abandon the last remnants of reform socialism, said Däumig, who admitted that the German working class was not revolutionary by tradition or temperament, but believed that the experience of councils would make it so.[2] Other speakers followed in the same vein, contending that, as the example of Soviet Russia showed, workers' councils were the appropriate form for the proletarian dictatorship prescribed by Marx. Clearly the Independents had accepted Lenin's interpretation of Marx but had failed to notice how far the Bolsheviks, by exalting the party over the councils, had contradicted their own slogan of all power to the soviets. Lenin was also invoked to justify the seizure of power by a minority.[3] It was admitted inside the U.S.P.D. that the majority even of the proletariat did not support their policy, but this backwardness, it was explained, was inevitable so long as the proletariat was exposed to reactionary influences in the press and elsewhere. The party's left wing leaders were determined that, should a revolutionary situation recur, they would strike without counting heads first: a forceful and successful minority would soon be followed by the majority. Their purpose should be to make the existence of any party to the left of them unnecessary. The programme of March had demanded the dictatorship of the proletariat 'as representative of the great majority of the people'. Now, at Leipzig, the qualifying phrase was dropped, as Geyer had urged in September. The party had thus abandoned the democratic principle. Crispien, the new chairman, sought to play the role of Haase in resolving conflicts within the party; the new formula, he said, was not really incompatible with the old because in Germany the proletariat was the majority of the nation. But such concessions to the radicals ultimately proved fruitless, as the increasing strength of the right in Germany combined with the magnetic appeal of revolutionary Russia continued to disintegrate the party; while by alienating the moderates

[1] Prager, *op. cit.* p. 207; *Prot. U.S.P.D.* (Leipzig, 1919), p. 86.

[2] *Prot. U.S.P.D.* pp. 236 ff.

[3] *Ibid.* p. 279. Lenin summarised his views on revolution by a minority in the following characteristic passage: 'Now it is this dialectic which the traitors, numbskulls and pedants of the Second International could never grasp: the proletariat cannot conquer without winning over to its side the majority of the population. But to limit this winning over of the population to, or to make it conditional on, "acquiring" a majority of votes in an election *while the bourgeoisie is in power* is impracticable imbecility, or simply cheating the workers.' Lenin clearly believed that in a non-proletarian state the authority and influence of the ruling capitalists would be too strong among the 'non-proletarian labouring masses', by which he presumably meant those workers who were not politically class-conscious. Lenin, *Collected Works* (Russian edition of 1935–7), vol. XXIV, p. 641, quoted in L. Schapiro, *The Origin of the Communist Autocracy* (London, 1955), p. 36.

they made impossible any *rapprochement* with the left wing majority socialists, who were critical of the S.P.D. leadership.

The new emphasis on workers' councils made it essential at last to jettison the Erfurt programme, which, Crispien said, was out of date because it contained no reference to imperialism, failed to state the impossibility of compromise between capitalism and socialism, and did not specify the precise means of establishing a socialist order. Workers' councils must replace parliament, not be grafted on to it. Parliamentary democracy was only a fictitious democracy because real power lay with a minority of capitalists; real democracy would come only through proletarian dictatorship. Like Haase, Crispien wanted this to be temporary and non-terrorist, but the franchise must be such that only socialists would be elected.[1] The party's right wing accepted the new policy with some misgivings: Hilferding warned that so long as they could not set up their own kind of democracy they must be ready to defend the parliamentary one of Weimar.[2] The U.S.P.D., he declared, were in a weaker position than a year before, and if they acted rashly they might suffer the fate of the Paris Commune. In the debate some delegates still hankered after reunion with the S.P.D., but a speaker who urged that the real threat to the party came from the left was received with incredulous laughter. Crispien derided the S.P.D. as 'Noske socialists' in much the same way as during the war they had been known as Kaiser socialists. Ledebour hoped that with their new programme the party need no longer incur the hostility of the Communists, especially as the latter had recently reversed their earlier decision to boycott parliament.[3] Oskar Cohn, the former Independent member of the Reichstag who had been one of the severest critics of the German government's war policy and an early admirer of the Bolsheviks, now, rather surprisingly, rejected the notion of proletarian dictatorship, citing the Austrian *Rote Fahne* in support of his views.[4] For Cohn the example of Russia had become one to avoid not to emulate, for there a minority had been forced to use terror in order to stay in power. Most of the Independents, particularly on the left, were more impressed by the success of Lenin's dictatorship against the counter-revolution than worried by his unscrupulous methods against fellow-socialists. The new U.S.P.D. programme paid lip service to the old humanitarianism by drawing a rather fine distinction between force, which was approved, and terror, which was not;[5] but although parliament was not entirely rejected, the emphasis was firmly placed on workers' councils. It sanctioned, in effect, the revolution by a minority acting in the name of the proletariat.

[1] *Prot. U.S.P.D.* pp. 160 ff.   [2] *Ibid.* pp. 266 ff.
[3] *Ibid.* pp. 297 ff. At its second conference, held at Heidelberg in October 1919, the K.P.D. had split when the syndicalist, putschist and anti-parliamentary left wing (under Laufenberg and Wolffheim) had seceded to form the K.A.P.D. (Communist Workers' party).
[4] *Ibid.* p. 261.   [5] *Ibid.* p. 348.

The other main subject discussed at Leipzig was the party's relation to the Internationals. Opinion was divided into three groups. On the right Hilferding spoke for those who wished the U.S.P.D. to stay in the Second International but to repudiate the mere reformism of the right wing parties. While admitting that the Second International needed changing, he did not want the Independents to cut themselves off from western socialism. For Hilferding as for Kautsky Russia was a backward country even in her revolution. The final decision between socialism and capitalism would be made in the advanced west, to which Germany belonged. Like most of his German Communist opponents at the time Hilferding believed that the Third International had been started prematurely. He also objected to it for splitting the socialist parties of Europe and practising subservience to the Bolsheviks, who used methods of terror and carried out a campaign of slander against centrist parties such as the U.S.P.D. or the British I.L.P. If they joined the Third International, Hilferding declared, they would become a tool in Russian hands. The right policy was to create a genuine International which would include parties of both east and west. Hilferding counted on the survival of the Third International only if the world revolution took place, and this he thought unlikely.[1]

The opposite view was expressed by Stoecker, who said that the Second International had failed through reformism, opportunism and nationalism. Yet the parties of the Second International in their post-war conferences had passed resolutions in favour of bourgeois democracy and the capitalist League of Nations. Any International which tried, as the Second had tried, to combine both reformist and revolutionary policies would collapse when put to the test, as had happened in August 1914. Stoecker conceded that the Third International had been founded too soon and that it was too Russian-orientated, but he claimed that in turning its back on reformism it was right and that its criticism of Kautsky and other right wing Independents was justified.[2] He denied that the U.S.P.D. would put itself under Bolshevik dictation by joining the Third International, for all member parties would rank equally. Stoecker even suggested that through the Third International German socialism would regain its leading position. In reply to Hilferding, who warned of the danger of civil war by imitating the Bolsheviks, Stoecker answered that civil war might in any case be forced on them by the reactionaries. He also defended the use of terror, which Marx had approved. Lenin's vituperative attacks on Independent leaders could be explained if not excused by the desperate situation in which the Bolsheviks found themselves.

A third, intermediate solution of the problem was proposed by Ledebour,

---

[1] *Prot. U.S.P.D.* p. 310.

[2] *Ibid.* p. 328. At the Berne conference of the Second International in February 1919 Bernstein had spoken of the dictatorship of the proletariat as 'the greatest misfortune of humanity'.

whose spirited criticism of the Communists was given weight by the daring and forceful part he had played in the German revolution: originally blamed by them for lacking in revolutionary zeal, he had later been denounced as a 'super putschist', but no one could impugn his revolutionary credentials. The party, said Ledebour, should leave the Second International but join the Third on conditions.[1] He received Crispien's support for a proposal originally made by the Swedish socialist party for a conference of all revolutionary parties of both Internationals. Finally a resolution was passed in favour of the U.S.P.D. resigning from the Second International and negotiating with other left wing parties both inside and outside the Third International with a view to forming a 'reconstructed' International acceptable to all. The resolution was so worded as not to exclude the party's eventually joining the Third International, but on terms that western socialists could accept.[2] However, the Independents were soon to find that whatever conditions they might propose, it was the Russians who decided them. In his speech Ledebour quoted Bukharin as having told him during the war that all along the Bolshevik intention had been to split the Independent party, as the Spartacists had tried to do. He might have added that the Russians aimed at bringing the greater part of the party under their control through the Third International. Both internally and externally the U.S.P.D. was now set on this course, and the split, consummated at Halle ten months later, was already implied by the decisions and attitudes of the Leipzig conference.

Two episodes which occurred at this time are indicative of the divided state of mind inside the party. Leading members of the left, including Stoecker, held secret talks with Levi, the leader of the German Communist party, on the question of joining the Third International: Levi is said to have promised them a seat on the International's executive committee. Signatures of party members were collected as evidence of a widespread demand for this move. When Stoecker was challenged at Leipzig about these talks, he alleged that they were harmless, but not everyone was convinced. The chairman ruled that such an approach to a rival party should not have taken place behind the back of the party leadership.[3] The other episode concerned the attitude of members to the state. When one delegate (Wurm) wanted to introduce a resolution on taxation the left objected on the grounds that socialists should simply refuse to pay taxes to a capitalist state. This was really an anarchist view, and it was significant that Wurm's resolution never reached the conference table.[4]

The picture of the Independent socialists that emerges at the end of 1919 is of a party which was gaining mass support, less through its own merits than the failure of its reformist rival to hold the loyalty of the left wing

[1] *Ibid.* pp. 350 ff.   [2] *Ibid.* p. 42.   [3] *Ibid.* pp. 137 ff.
[4] Prager, *op. cit.* p. 208.

electorate, but which was in an advanced state of dissolution. Prager, the party historian, speaks of a Communist cell in the U.S.P.D. at this time;[1] and clearly the left wing were playing into the hands of Lenin, who at the first meeting of the Third International had passed a resolution in favour of splitting the centrist parties, including the Independents, by undermining the authority of their leaders. The Russians had not forgiven or forgotten the wartime record of Kautsky, Haase, Hilferding and others in supporting national defence, their approval of Joffé's expulsion from Germany, their pro-western orientation since the war, their criticism of Bolshevik methods. Now the Russians saw in the desire of the party majority to join the Third International an opportunity to apply their policy, and to transform an amorphous but undoubtedly proletarian party into an instrument of the International pledged to establish Communist power in central Europe. It is as part of this revolutionary strategy, and not merely in terms of German politics, that the U.S.P.D. must henceforth be seen.

[1] Prager quotes a letter written by a person named Machowski to Bukharin and Chicherin on the tactics to be applied to the U.S.P.D., and recommending that the party should be broken up by an attack on the right wing leaders (Haase and Hilferding) in alliance with the left wing leaders (Däumig and R. Müller). This is in fact what happened (Prager, *op. cit.* p. 202). This letter, which was seized from a courier of the German Communist party on his way to Russia, is adduced by Prager as evidence of the way in which the German Communists incited the Bolsheviks to disrupt the Independent party.

CHAPTER 11

EPILOGUE: THE CLIMAX AND DOUBLE CRISIS OF 1920

We've had a revolution, but we didn't win...
HERMANN MÜLLER in 1920

THE SOCIALISTS AND THE KAPP PUTSCH

The year 1920 saw the climax of the two mutually antagonistic trends which had polarised German politics since the fall of the Kaiser and threatened to overthrow the democratic republic: the military counter-revolution which came to a head in the Kapp Putsch; and the triumph within the Independent socialist party of the revolutionary left, culminating in the Halle congress which split the party and led to the absorption of the majority of delegates into the Communist party on terms dictated by Lenin. Both these trends eroded the Weimar regime, which Scheidemann likened to a candle burning at both ends; and it is no accident that at the first general election since the revolution the republican parties were reduced to a minority in the Reichstag. Extremism on both right and left gained more converts among the politically immature, socially disarrayed and economically desperate German electorate. Nor was it an accident that the year 1920 began with an eruption of violence caused by left wing anger at the government's Works Council bill, for the role of workers' councils was an issue which sharply focused the grievances of the many who had set their hearts on the transformation of German society which they believed that only the councils could achieve.

Ironically, by December 1919 the situation had so far quietened down that the government felt it safe to abolish martial law. This had been in force during most of 1919 in many parts of Germany in order to keep in check the insurrectionary strike movement that had paralysed the country during the early months of the year and had flared up again in the autumn. But, as the anti-Works Council bill demonstration of 13 January showed, the left wing opposition continued its hostility to the policy symbolised by Ebert and Noske. Among the masses discontent was kept alive by the continued unemployment, high prices and shortage of food, by the government's failure to carry out a convincing policy of socialisation, and by the provocative speeches and gestures of the generals and their supporters among the conservative politicians. On the right, the main grievance was the government's proclaimed intention, under extreme duress and on the reluctant advice of the army command, that no other course was a practical possibility, to fulfil

237

the treaty of Versailles with all its disagreeable implications for the military: drastic scaling down in numbers, disbandment of the Freikorps, the punishment of leading generals and politicians as 'war criminals', and abandonment by German troops of the Baltic territories, where many had counted on finding opportunities denied to them in an impoverished and diminished Reich. Those who blamed the government for yielding to Allied pressure showed that, as Noske observed, they did not understand that Germany had lost the war. As we have seen, the stab in the back legend, zealously propagated by the nationalists, was used to exonerate the army from responsibility for the defeat. It was inevitable that the government's prestige should suffer through its acceptance of the peace treaty even though the right wing parties had acquiesced in that decision, but the republican cause suffered a further and unexpected blow early in 1920 when Erzberger had to resign as finance minister after losing a libel action against Helfferich, one of his predecessors in office, and an able if unscrupulous representative of the monarchist regime. The nationalists had never forgiven Erzberger for his part in the July 1917 peace resolution and his leadership of the armistice delegation, and during the trial he was wounded by a revolver shot from a nationalist student. The affair marked the end of Erzberger's political career (next year he was to be murdered). It also exemplified the virulence of the attacks on the republic, which was now permanently on the defensive. Its obvious weakness only encouraged its inexorable enemies.[1]

The episode of 13 January took the familiar form of an anti-government demonstration which got out of hand and led to bloodshed. The Works Council bill, then before the National Assembly, purported to implement Article 165 of the Weimar constitution, whereby factory councils elected by workers were to be empowered to negotiate with employers on wages and working conditions and also on wider matters of management and production. The bill failed to come up to the expectations of the Independent socialists and Communists, who called out their supporters to give vent to their dissatisfaction in a mass demonstration in front of the Reichstag building, where the National Assembly was in session. After the meeting had lasted for several hours and roused considerable excitement, a number of demonstrators tried to force their way into the Reichstag, while a shot was fired, apparently from the crowd. The result was that the troops defending the Reichstag fired machine guns into the crowd, which dispersed in panic, leaving a number of dead and wounded.[2] The Independents were furious and charged the

---

[1] Indeed there is much to be said for the view of Stampfer that the remarkable thing about the Weimar Republic is not that it did not last longer but that it lasted at all (Stampfer, *Erfahrungen und Erkenntnisse*, 1953, p. 235).

[2] Noske, *Von Kiel bis Kapp*, p. 192; Stroebel, *The German Revolution and after*, pp. 217 ff.; Dittmann, *Lebenserinnerungen*, ch. 18. The Central Council, which had handed over most of its powers to the National Assembly in February, gave its last sign of life in

government with using unncessary brutality against an unarmed gathering. They also alleged that the government had actually provoked the demonstration in order to have the opportunity of suppressing it.[1] It is unlikely that the government had such Machiavellian intentions, but its handling of the demonstration was clumsy and ill-considered. When the affair was debated in the National Assembly, the majority socialists accused the Independents of having incited their followers to overthrow the government.[2] It is scarcely credible that the demonstrators were making a serious bid for power, if only because Berlin at the time was full of Noske's troops. But the language of the manifesto calling for the demonstration was ambiguous in the usual inflammatory way, and since the Independents had now abandoned their belief in parliamentary democracy they could more easily be charged with using mob violence to upset a democratically elected assembly. The result of the episode was further to worsen relations between the two socialist parties and to make more difficult the task of those who, like Scheidemann for the S.P.D. and Bernstein for the Independents, sought to bring about reunification in face of their common danger. The Independents bitterly complained that the republican and largely socialist government showed greater readiness to use force against demonstrating workers than the government of William II had done. The only beneficiaries were the nationalists, who profited by the socialists' quarrels and by the reimposition of martial law which followed the revival of revolutionary spirit on the left. The reactionary officers, Dittmann noted, were on top again: the Freikorps leaders were free to send their troops to suppress with bloodshed the protest strikes which broke out in all parts of Germany, to ban Independent and Communist newspapers and occupy their offices, to arrest the workers' leaders and shoot them 'while trying to escape'. In January 1920 several hundred Independent leaders, including 400 in the Ruhr alone, were seized (Däumig was among those arrested in Berlin), and meetings of the left wing parties were forbidden or broken up. In face of the Freikorps chiefs, who felt masters of the situation and knew themselves to be the real power in the state, the government was impotent. The former showed their contempt for the government, and their readiness even to get rid of Noske, who found himself in the position of the sorcerer's apprentice, unable to control the spirits he had conjured up.[3]

In these circumstances, which led the militarists to believe that in a show-

---

October 1919. The more radical Berlin Executive Council was suppressed by Noske in November, but revived in January 1920. (Horkenbach, *Das deutsche Reich von 1918 bis heute*, pp. 85, 91.)

[1] Dittmann, *op. cit.*

[2] *Verhandlungen der Verfassunggebenden Deutschen Nationalversammlung*, 14 January 1920. A more likely explanation is that the provocation came from the Reichswehr, whose leaders, realising that the left was unprepared for a showdown, wished to show their strength. On this view, the episode was a kind of rehearsal for the Kapp Putsch two months later. [3] Dittmann, *op. cit.*

down between themselves and the government the Independent socialists would not support the latter, the conspiracy of Kapp with Lüttwitz and other generals which had originally been conceived in the summer of 1919 came to fruition. An important section of the Reichswehr, in which, after the retirement of Hindenburg and Groener in June 1919, Lüttwitz was the senior commanding officer, had refused to accept the Versailles treaty, the terms of which had come as a shattering blow to an army which prided itself on having survived the revolution and refused to believe that it had been defeated. The reduction of army strength to 100,000 men, as provided by the treaty, affected the Reichswehr personally as well as politically; over 20,000 officers were due to be demobilised.[1] The presentation by the Allies in February 1920 of a list of nearly 900 prominent Germans, including Hindenburg and other national heroes, for trial as war criminals added insult to injury, and stiffened the resolve to resist implementation of the treaty. Seeckt, who had succeeded Groener as head of the *Truppenamt* (the successor body to the forbidden general staff) told his staff officers and departmental chiefs that they should refuse to obey any attempt by the government to comply with this outrageous demand, even if it meant the resumption of hostilities.[2] Noske as minister of defence was well aware of the feelings of the army; he had received several warnings of the generals' plot, and Seeckt's unauthorised action was mentioned in the National Assembly on 1 March. Noske knew, too, that some of the Reichswehr officers were playing with the idea of establishing a military dictatorship with himself as the head;[3] they recognised that to exercise power they needed the support of a representative of organised labour, and Noske, who had long been known as a very moderate socialist, must have seemed an ideal choice. Noske, however, while declining to become a military dictator, remained obstinately trustful of his generals, whose loyalty he believed he had won by his energetic measures against the Communists. He also, according to his own testimony, refrained from taking the advice of his subordinates to act against potential trouble makers, in order not to create bad feeling in the army. In the early months of 1919 Noske had indeed been well liked by the generals, as Maercker had recognized, but since the signature of the treaty his popularity had declined despite his offer at the time to resign, which Ebert had refused. In the later months of the year Noske, who was used to the attacks of the left, came under fire from the right. He was even criticised for his part at the time of the Kiel mutiny; to incorrigible monarchists like Lüttwitz it was not enough that Noske had contained the mutiny, he ought to have reasserted the authority of the old regime.[4] As Noske observed, he was expected to act with a power which the admirals and generals were patently unable to exercise. For Lüttwitz and his friends anyone who had had

[1] Noske, *op. cit.* p. 199.   [2] Wheeler-Bennett, *The Nemesis of Power* (1954), p. 71.
[3] Volkmann, *Revolution über Deutschland*, pp. 322 ff.
[4] Noske, *Aufstieg und Niedergang der deutschen Sozialdemokratie*, p. 145.

anything to do with the events of 9 November 1918 was discredited, including Groener who had told the Kaiser that he could not return to Germany at the head of his troops. In effect Kapp and Lüttwitz, ignoring the military defeat and the parliamentarisation of Germany initiated by Ludendorff, vainly sought a return to the circumstances of 1917.

Seeckt's gesture of defiance could not be overlooked by Noske, who at the beginning of March ordered the Ehrhardt brigade, the immediate source of danger, to be removed from the command of Lüttwitz and put under Admiral von Trotha, who was in charge of what remained of the German navy. On 10 March Lüttwitz, accompanied by several other generals, went to see Ebert and Noske and demanded that the further disbandment of troops be suspended, that General Reinhardt,[1] a republican, be dismissed as head of the *Heeresleitung*, and that the Ehrhardt brigade be put back under Lüttwitz's orders. The demands were, not unnaturally, rejected. When Lüttwitz did not resign as expected he was relieved of his command, while a warrant was issued for the arrest of him and his main accomplices. But the ramifications of the conspiracy were more extensive than Noske realised, for the security police entrusted with the arrests were themselves on Kapp's side. Von Trotha too was a clandestine supporter; and when he was sent by Noske on reconnaissance to Döberitz, the camp of the Ehrhardt brigade to which the other leaders of the plot had fled, he reported that nothing untoward was happening. That very evening, however (12–13 March), news reached the government that the rebels were marching on Berlin, only twelve miles away, and Ehrhardt scribbled a hastily improvised ultimatum which expired at seven the following morning. At a cabinet meeting held in the small hours Ebert and the ministers decided to leave Berlin at once to escape arrest. Although Noske spoke in favour of staying behind and resisting the rebels, he was overruled, mainly from a desire to avoid bloodshed, but also in the knowledge, conveyed to the government by Seeckt, that Reichswehr would not fire on Reichswehr. There was no one to stop Kapp, Lüttwitz and Ehrhardt when, a few hours later, accompanied by their troops and in the presence of the new grey eminence of nationalist radicalism, Ludendorff, they marched through the Brandenburg Gate, and declared the government deposed.[2]

But Kapp and Lüttwitz proved unable to fill the vacuum they had created, and their 'regime' lasted only four days. Apart from denouncing the treaty of Versailles the new masters hardly had a policy, and they had no idea how to use the machine of government which had fallen with such apparent ease into their hands. But the main reason for the failure of the Putsch was

---

[1] The same man who, as Col. Reinhardt, had been made minister of war in the winter of 1918–19 The *Heeresleitung* was the new name of the army high command.

[2] For the Kapp Putsch see Volkmann, *op. cit.* pp. 330 ff.; Stroebel, *op. cit.* pp. 223 ff.; Schüddekopf, *Heer und Republik*, pp. 103 ff.; Noske, *Von Kiel bis Kapp*, pp. 194–211.

the general strike which brought all activity to a standstill. Majority socialists, Independents and trade unionists acted for once in solidarity, and the
strike was joined by white collar employees and civil servants as well as
industrial workers. Altogether twelve million people took part. The man who
now emerged as the key figure was Karl Legien, who for thirty years had
been chairman of the largest trade union organisation, which in 1919 had
been renamed the *Allgemeine Deutsche Gewerkschaftsbund*.[1] Legien, seizing
the initiative in what has been described as the greatest hour of the German
trade unions, refused to call off the strike before the lawful government
accepted an eight-point programme. This said, in brief, that the leaders of the
Putsch must be disarmed and punished, the civil service purged of counter-
revolutionaries, local government democratised, social legislation extended,
counter-revolutionary army units dissolved and replaced by republican
units, food distribution taken out of the hands of profiteers, and the trade
unions consulted on the choice of the new government.[2] Bauer, the Chancellor, and Noske as defence minister were discredited and resigned, though
Ebert tried hard to keep the latter. Noske had been badly let down by the
army, but he also felt that he was being made a scapegoat for the socialists'
reluctance to join the armed forces and defend the republic.[3] The latest example
of this attitude was the refusal of Wels, now chairman of the S.P.D., to
succeed Noske when the post was offered to him, on the grounds that it was
time for another party to take over responsibility for the troublesome
Reichswehr. The socialists were never again to occupy this vital position,
which for the next eight years was held by the Democrat Gessler.

The immediate sequel to the fall of the Bauer government was an attempt
by Legien to form an all-socialist cabinet. The Putsch had given the trade
unions, which were usually, like Legien himself, very moderate in their
socialism, a jolt to the left;[4] and Legien saw that, despite past quarrels, at
this crisis the co-operation of both groups of socialists was a necessity. The
right wing of the Independents were prepared to test Legien's sincerity. They
agreed that he should be Chancellor but asked for a majority in the govern-

---

[1] Membership of the General or 'free' Trade Unions, as they were known to distinguish
them from the Christian (mainly Roman Catholic) and Hirsch-Duncker (left wing
liberal) unions, had risen from 2·5 million in 1912 to 7·3 million by the end of 1919
(Varain, *Freie Gewerkschaften, Sozialdemokratie und Staat*, p. 132).

[2] Dittmann, *op. cit.*; *Illustrierte Geschichte der deutschen Revolution*, p. 473.

[3] Grzesinski (*Inside Germany*, p. 91) defends Noske against the charge that he was merely
a cypher in the hands of his military advisers. Noske was not a weakling, and he might
have been a much more effective minister of defence than his successor during the Seeckt
era. That he showed bad judgement and credulity can hardly be doubted, and he himself
admitted (*Von Kiel bis Kapp*, p. 116) that his choice of soldiers and officers had been
unfortunate. Not without bitterness Noske criticised the socialists for boycotting the
Reichswehr and then complaining of the result.

[4] The *Correspondenzblatt* of the General Trade Unions wrote on 27 March 1920 that it
was a mistake to rely exclusively on parliamentary methods (*Handbuch für die Wähler
der U.S.P.D.* 1. Heft, April 1920).

ment, including certain key posts. Legien accepted; he was anxious to show that, if the Noske wing of Social Democracy was no longer trustworthy, the unions could co-operate with the other wing. Even the small Communist party, which took part in the negotiations, promised 'loyal opposition' to a government headed by Legien. (The Communists had at first refused to join the general strike from dislike of Noske and the majority socialists, but changed their mind a day later.) But at this juncture the left wing of the Independent party, whose suspicions had not been reduced by the Putsch, refused to join a government that contained Legien and the S.P.D. Their argument was simple: the policy of coalition within the S.P.D. had failed in November 1918, therefore it was bound to fail again. They even threatened to split the party if it was tried. For Däumig and his friends the majority socialists were traitors for allying with bourgeois parties. In fact this 'treachery' was forced on them by Independent intransigence. Thus the opportunity, created by Kapp, of forming a solid left wing government pledged to a tough policy, was lost; once again 'principle' had triumphed over 'opportunism'.[1]

And so after a reshuffle the existing coalition of the S.P.D., Democratic and Centre parties continued in office, with Hermann Müller as Chancellor. Under Gessler the Reichswehr did very much as it pleased, especially as the strongly independent and capable Seeckt, despite his equivocal behaviour during the Putsch, was promoted to head of the *Heeresleitung* in succession to Reinhardt, who resigned in solidarity with Noske. Thus, wrote Noske later, the majority socialists bowed out as a power factor in the republic, and none of the lessons of the Kapp Putsch appeared to have been learnt.[2] Nor did those majority socialists who had long regarded Noske as a liability find that on balance his departure brought the party any advantage. In his first speech as Chancellor on 29 March, Müller declared that a republic without democrats was an internal and external danger and he pledged himself to get rid of disloyal elements with an 'iron broom'.[3] These determined words were not followed by deeds. Of the 705 persons officially listed as involved in the Putsch, only one, Kapp himself, received a prison sentence when, after fleeing to Sweden, he returned to Germany two years later. Lüttwitz found asylum in Hungary; Ehrhardt in Bavaria, where, after the S.P.D. had resigned, a nationalist government came to power and Munich became a bastion of anti-republicanism. A general amnesty was eventually granted to the great majority of Kapp's accomplices, to the dismay of the left. Nor were the refractory Reichswehr disciplined. When Dittmann for the Independents reminded the Chancellor of his promise to disarm, Müller

---

[1] This account follows Borkenau (*The Communist International*, 1938, pp. 154 ff.). According to a more recent account, Legien did not accept the offer of the Chancellorship, for reasons he never made public but which can be inferred without much difficulty. See Varain, *op. cit.* pp. 179–81.　　　　[2] Noske, *Aufstieg und Niedergang*, p. 166.

[3] *Verhandlungen der Verfassunggebenden Deutschen Nationalversammlung*, 29 March 1920.

laconically replied: 'Disarm them if you can.'[1] Ehrhardt himself was quoted in the National Assembly as having said that he would like to see the man who dared disarm him.[2] So feeble was the government's authority that political murders continued, and *Vorwaerts* warned of a new right wing revolt. Nor were the government's other promises kept. But under pressure of the right wing parties, which were conscious of having gained support in the country, it agreed to hold new elections early in June.

The Kapp Putsch had also brought to a head the latent crisis in the Ruhr, where the industrial workers were simmering with discontent at the lack of progress in socialisation. In the Ruhr the majority socialist Severing had been given the special post of Reich Commissioner, and found himself holding an uneasy balance between the inflammable Independents and Communists on the one hand and the reactionary General Watter, commander of the seventh army and responsible for martial law, on the other. When, on Kapp's bid for power, Watter seemed to be on his side, the Ruhr workers armed themselves, declared an insurrectionary strike and captured several towns. After the defeat of Kapp by the general strike the Ruhr 'red army' refused to disarm until Severing was able to bring about an agreement through a conference at Bielefeld in which representatives of parties and local authorities took part. By the Bielefeld agreement the red army undertook to give up their weapons in return for political concessions. This satisfied the moderates but not the extremists, who wanted to exploit the crisis to rekindle the revolution and establish a dictatorship of the proletariat, and who continued to resent the presence of Watter. They accordingly ignored the agreement, obliging the government to use troops to 'reconquer' the Ruhr and replace the red terror with a white. In pursuit of the red army the government forces crossed into the part of the Ruhr which was under French occupation, thereby giving the French army an excuse to occupy Frankfurt and other towns in reprisal. The French motive was to further the cause of separatism in the Rhineland rather than to support the Ruhr workers, but its main effect was to strike a blow at the new Müller government and to exacerbate German nationalism, while the use of Senegalese troops to guard the Goethe House at Frankfurt and other cultural monuments excited easily provoked racial susceptibilities.[3] The social forces which lay behind the Kapp adventure remained strong and defiant, and foreign and domestic policies continued to react on each other in a vicious spiral.[4]

---

[1] Dittmann, *op. cit.*

[2] By Henke, an Independent socialist member of the Assembly, speaking 29 March.

[3] Severing, *Mein Lebensweg* (Cologne, 1950), I, 253 ff.

[4] The defeat of armed workers by the Reichswehr, and the concessions made to the latter by the Ebert government in negotiations, signified a loss of power by the left and so weakened Legien's bargaining position. Ostensibly a failure, in reality the Kapp Putsch added to the strength of the right wing nationalists.

The Kapp Putsch and its aftermath threw a revealing light on political attitudes in the Weimar Republic. The right wing parties (the Nationalists and People's party) followed an opportunist policy towards Kapp, with whom they had considerable sympathy. Kapp himself belonged to the governing committee of the Nationalists, and several of his accomplices were also members of the party, including Pastor Traub who sat in the National Assembly. Of the leaders of the People's party Stresemann accepted and even condoned the Putsch as long as it seemed to be succeeding; like many others, he was at this time a fellow traveller on the right.[1] Large sections of the upper bourgeoisie, including intellectuals, also supported Kapp. As for the left wing parties, the failure of Legien's attempt to form an all-socialist government showed that the distrust felt by the left wing Independents had created a gulf which even consciousness of a common danger could not bridge. Short of that, however, the Kapp crisis proved the limited effectiveness of a concerted effort by democrats, socialist and otherwise, in defence of the republic, and the folly of socialist division. It would indeed have been better for the republic if the split in the Independent party, which was still some months ahead, had occurred in March, so that at least the right wing could have formed an alliance with the majority socialists and trade unions; but it was not to be. To become complete, the process of fission needed the catalyst of the Third International.

In April 1920 the campaign for the new elections began, and the Independents issued a manifesto containing eight points which largely coincided with those promised by the Müller government to Legien but also included such additional demands as an end of martial law, the break up of big estates and the establishment of friendly relations with Soviet Russia.[2] Continued disillusion on the left with the majority socialists produced a very encouraging result for the Independents, who received nearly 4·9 million votes and gained eighty-one seats in the new chamber elected in June compared with twenty-two in the old. That most of these gains were at the expense of the S.P.D. was shown by the decline of the latter from 165 seats to 113; indeed the number of votes cast for the S.P.D. was only about 700,000 more than for the Independents. But the total socialist vote had gone down, and even more significant, the votes for the democratic coalition of S.P.D. Centre and Democrats had fallen from nineteen million to eleven million. The main losers were the Democrats, who received less than half the support they had had in January 1919, a sign that the liberal bourgeoisie and intelligentsia were beginning to desert the republic. For, as Eyck pointed out in his *History*

---

[1] H. A. Turner, *Stresemann and the Politics of the Weimar Republic* (1963), pp. 27 ff. The middle-class *Einwohnerwehr* did not take any action against Kapp and in fact recognised his government. In Berlin the rector of the university together with the professors and the majority of students sided with Kapp (Stroebel, *op. cit.* p. 229).

[2] Prager, *Geschichte der U.S.P.D.* p. 217.

of the Weimer Republic, the Democratic party was the only reliable support of republicanism for those who were neither socialists nor Catholics,[1] and its decline proved fatal to the life of the Weimar state. The republican parties were now in the minority in the Reichstag. The electorate had drawn the wrong conclusions from the Kapp Putsch:[2] instead of coming to the rescue of the threatened centre it had given new encouragement to the extremists on both flanks. The left identified the republican regime with capitalism and crypto-militarism; the right with Marxism and defeatism. Many who might have been conservative republicans and had voted for one of the Weimar parties in January 1919 now transferred their support to the monarchist and semi-monarchist parties which they had temporarily abandoned in the crisis of defeat. The historic weakness of German liberalism was once again evident.

The results of the June 1920 election made the problem of forming a new government unusually difficult. The situation seemed to call for a revival of the former coalition enlarged to include another party: the Independent socialists were the obvious choice. Müller, as leader of the S.P.D., was asked by President Ebert to form a government and again, as after the Kapp Putsch, the Independents were invited to join it. He wrote to Crispien, chairman of the U.S.P.D., in the following terms:

In our young German republic it seems to me that the participation of the U.S.P.D. in the government is especially necessary because only by a coalition government strengthened on its left flank can our republican institutions be defended against all attacks from the right; reactionary attacks on the eight hour day and the social-political gains of the postwar period be resisted; and a foreign policy be carried out which accords with the republican and pacifist ideas of the overwhelming majority of the German people.[3]

Crispien's reply, despatched the same day, was a brusque refusal:

The U.S.P.D. cannot join a government which has made its aim the re-establishment of the exploiting capitalist economy which collapsed during the war, and which revives and strengthens militarism in order to hold down the proletariat, as the coalition has done up to now. The entry of the U.S.P.D. into a government of this kind would mean support for the counter-revolutionary policy which it has hitherto fought against on principle.[4]

Crispien went on to say that those who had voted Independent had done so, not to have their interests betrayed but because they wanted a policy of class war and the abolition of capitalism and militarism. In short, the Independents would join only a purely socialist government; as such a government would have fallen far short of a Reichstag majority, Müller's appeal was, in effect, ignored.

---

[1] Eyck, *History of the Weimar Republic* (1962), I, 162. See also p. 273, below.
[2] *Prot. S.P.D.* (Kassel, 1920), p. 94.
[3] Stampfer, *Die ersten vierzehn Jahre der deutschen Republik*, p. 175.
[4] *Ibid.*

This characteristic utterance shows the rigidity with which the Independents clung to their class-war principles and the tenacity with which they maintained the obviously mistaken view that the German economy had 'collapsed' during the war. The S.P.D. approach, on the other hand, appeared realistic and flexible. Unfortunately, Müller's failure to keep his promises of March gave the Independents little reason to take his words at their face value. The result of their inflexibility was the formation of a new coalition under the Centre leader Dr Fehrenbach, including for the first time the People's party (D.V.P.), but not the S.P.D., which promised to 'tolerate' the new government. It was an irony that a cabinet including such confirmed anti-socialists as the D.V.P. should depend on the socialist vote. The positive feature of the change was that it marked the beginning of the reconciliation of the People's party with the republic, of which Stresemann's career was to be an outstanding example. The new government even promised to proceed with socialisation, but such momentum as the movement possessed had gone. In December 1920 Stresemann was to tell his party: 'The time of socialist Germany is past.'[1]

The crisis revealed by the election of June 1920 was one of democracy, for the electorate had given the Weimar regime a vote of no confidence. The majority socialists, the only major party fully committed to democracy, were now out of office after having guided the destiny of Germany for over a year and a half. How much had been achieved during this time, and with what success had the party made use of its unique opportunities? Certain incontestable gains had been made by the working class: equal franchise, collective bargaining, the eight-hour day, unemployment pay. But these were the products of the November revolution, for which the S.P.D. could hardly take much credit. Since then little had been done to realise the party's medium or long term aims, such as socialisation of industry and the land. Laws had been passed for the public ownership of the coal, potash and electric power industries, and a number of regional councils, on which owners, workers and consumers were represented, had been set up under a Reich Coal Council. In fact, however, control remained in the hands of the owners, who profited by the higher prices, and the result was regarded by the left as a travesty of socialism. The reluctance of the S.P.D. to introduce the bold and far-reaching policy of socialisation for which many of its supporters hoped was the subject of much criticism.[2] The main reason for the S.P.D.'s hesitation was its conviction that it would be a mistake to try and socialise industries suffering from lack of capital and raw materials including coal, incessant strikes and low productivity. The first objective was to raise production, and

[1] Turner, *op. cit.* p. 82.
[2] The socialisation commission had ceased to function on 9 April 1919 after a disagreement with Wissell, then Reich minister of economics. See also p. 226, n. 3 above.

the authority of Marx was invoked for the view that socialism should be applied at a time of over-production, not scarcity. The parlous state of the postwar German economy slowly recovering from the blockade, dependent on imported raw materials for which it was difficult to pay, with a falling currency and output reduced by labour disputes, discouraged the socialist leaders from indulging in experiments which in the short run looked like making things worse and depressing the already low standard of living.[1] The bulk of expert opinion, represented by the socialisation commission and including many Independent socialists, advised caution, and thus confirmed Ebert's own unwillingness to endanger order. A further reason for the party's attitude was the lack of thought that had been given to the practical problems involved in running large industrial organisations, and there was no unanimity on the form socialisation should take—state, municipal or some form of workers' control.[2]

While holding back on socialisation the majority socialists had, however, tried to create an economic democracy through the system of workers' councils provided for in the Weimar constitution. That this experiment would not prove successful could hardly be foreseen in June 1920, but the left wing socialists already regarded it as falling far short of their hopes and as amounting to little more than a fig leaf for capitalism. Thus in their social and economic policy, as in their *de facto* dependence on militarism, the majority socialists had lost much credit.[3] That a party which had been obliged, as the S.P.D. had been, to take unpalatable measures against the left and to sign such a humiliating peace treaty should forfeit its popularity was inevitable, as was the ebbing of the enthusiasm that had carried it so near to victory in January 1919. But the loss of so many supporters to its left wing rival at a time when that rival was rapidly becoming a tool of the Third International was ominously significant both for the future of socialism and the stability of the threatened republic.

The results of the June election produced a strangely mixed balance sheet for the U.S.P.D. From the defeat of the Kapp Putsch and the mistakes and pusillanimity of the majority socialists the Independents had gained heavily

---

[1] Some of the difficulties, real or imaginary, that stood in the way of socialisation were set out in *Vorwaerts* of 27 December 1919. See Berlau, *The German Social Democratic Party, 1914–21*, pp. 265–84, An article by N. Osterroth in *Neue Zeit* of 29 August 1919 argued against the bringing of industry under *state* ownership, and pointed out that if coal were nationalised it would have to be subsidised by the taxpayer because the industry was no longer profitable. It was widely believed that socialisation would adversely affect Germany's foreign trade; even Eisner did not consider that socialism in one country (Germany) would work. It was also suggested that the Allies would refuse delivery of raw materials to a socialised Germany. For evidence that some of these fears were exaggerated, see Rosenberg, *History of the German Republic*, pp. 46 ff.

[2] Berlau, *op. cit.*, and article by A. Ellinger in *Neue Zeit* of 13 June 1919.

[3] The Independents also blamed the majority socialists for not having put into effect other reforms in the party programme, such as the election of judges, the separation of church and state and a people's army.

in votes; but their doctrinaire inflexibility prevented them from taking advantage of their success. The eight-point programme on which they had insisted in March was now more or less a dead letter. Dittmann was optimistic enough to believe that the party might still win a majority in the Reichstag; but four months later it was to be in ruins. While the party leaders waited for that further 'radicalisation of the masses' which would sweep them to power, the dissensions within their ranks grew beyond their control. Between June and October the Independent socialists moved from a victory they could not use to a defeat from which they could not recover.

THE U.S.P.D. AND THE THIRD INTERNATIONAL

On 10 December 1919 representatives of the Central Committee of the U.S.P.D. called on Karl Radek to inquire about the probable Russian reaction to the resolution passed by the party's Leipzig conference concerning membership of the Third International. Radek, who was shortly to return to Russia, had served a prison sentence after his arrest in February 1919 for participation in the Spartacist rising, but later under freer conditions had acted as a kind of informal ambassador of the Soviets to a number of leading personalities in German public life. Radek saw in the Independent resolution a favourable basis for negotiations and undertook to support it in Moscow. He thought that a conference with the Russians could be arranged, possibly in Scandinavia.[1] On 15 December the Central Committee wrote to foreign socialists and groups both outside and inside the Third International informing them of the terms of its resolution and suggesting the convening of a preliminary conference to discuss the reconstruction of the Third International. It proposed that the conference should be held in Germany or Austria but that the invitations to it should be sent by the Russians. Replies were received from all the addressees except the Russians, who were ominously silent.[2] In February 1920 the Independents decided to send a commission to talk to the Bolsheviks whom they were anxious not to offend by holding a conference without them. An application for Russian visas for the commission was made to the West European secretariat of the Third International which was in Berlin, but there was still no word from Moscow. Then on 9 April the Russian leader Borodin brought to the headquarters of the U.S.P.D. a letter in the form of a pamphlet signed by Zinoviev, president of the Third International.[3] This was much more than a reply to the Independents' letter; it was a broad and harsh criticism of the party, its past and its

---

[1] *Die U.S.P.D. und die dritte Internationale* (Remscheid, 1920). This pamphlet gives the Independent version of the party's negotiations with the International.

[2] *Ibid.*

[3] Prager, *op. cit.* p. 219. The pamphlet was entitled *Der Leipziger Kongress der U.S.P.D. und die Kommunistische Internationale* (n.p., 1920).

leaders. The propagandist intention of the pamphlet was made plain by its being addressed to 'all the workers of Germany' in the first place, to the German Communist party in the second place, and lastly to the U.S.P.D. The Russians did not give the Independents credit for their belated acceptance at Leipzig of the greater part of Communist policy: if the ideas of Spartacus had been taken over, the process had been only gradual, inconsistent and incomplete. The Bolsheviks declared bluntly that their policy was the only right one even if it involved civil war: it was better for 10,000 workers to be killed than to allow a new imperialist war. The U.S.P.D. was censured for having taken part in the Second International conferences at Berne and Lucerne. The Russians' fear was that if the 'reconstructionists' got their way a fourth International would be created outside their control. They proposed that the Independents should negotiate with them in order to join the Third International, purge themselves of right wing elements and unite with the German Communist party. When Borodin asked what sort of International the U.S.P.D. had in mind, Crispien told him that this must be the subject of negotiations. Further conversations between the Independents and the Bolsheviks took place on 30 April and 7 May, when Shlyapnikov[1] visited Germany. The Russians asked for clarification of the Independent views; Crispien inquired, with some anxiety, whether any of his leading colleagues would have to be included in the proposed purge.[2] That Kautsky was ana-thema to the Bolsheviks had been shown by Lenin's virulent pamphlet against him;[3] and though Kautsky had long ceased to be representative of the Independents, a party which tolerated his views could not be accepted. In June the party decided to send a delegation of four to Russia to attend the second conference of the Third International and to negotiate conditions of entry. The delegation consisted of Crispien and Dittmann, representing broadly the right wing, and Däumig and Stoecker, representing the left. The terms of reference expressly laid down that the party should negotiate as an equal and should in any case keep control of its internal affairs and tactics. The delegates reached Petrograd on 19 July in time for the opening of the conference which next day was transferred to Moscow. The negotiations lasted until 8 August.[4]

Dittmann has left in his Memoirs an account of these negotiations, and also his impressions of Russia and the Bolshevik leaders. It was a time when the latter were buoyant with the success of their war against Poland; and Dittmann was present when the Polish Bolshevik Marchlewski left for the front in the expectation that he would soon set up a Soviet republic in Warsaw. Dittmann discussed the German situation with Chicherin, Commissar for

[1] Shlyapnikov had been Commissar of labour in the first Bolshevik government.
[2] *Die U.S.P.D. und die Internationale.*
[3] *The Proletarian Revolution and the Renegade Kautsky* (1918).
[4] Dittmann, *op. cit.* ch. 19.

foreign affairs, and with Lenin, and found the former much better informed about Germany.[1] In their negotiations with the Russians, the Independents were handicapped by the obvious cleavage between Crispien and Dittmann on the one hand, and Däumig and Stoecker on the other. The Russians had no difficulty in playing the latter off against the former. According to Dittmann, Däumig and Stoecker now agreed entirely with the Russians, though they had signed an official U.S.P.D. reply to Russian criticisms only a month before.[2] The Twenty-One Conditions which were drawn up on Lenin's insistence for acceptance by all parties wishing to join the Third International proved more exacting than had been expected. The sub-committee of the International appointed for this purpose refused to agree to all of them, and another sub-committee had to be specially formed to give them the appearance of legality. Däumig and Stoecker agreed to them secretly; Crispien and Dittmann refused to discuss them and came to the conclusion that they were unacceptable. Yet in the plenary session of the International they were passed with only three dissentient votes, which did not include any of the U.S.P.D.[3]

The four delegates returned to Germany with no illusions as to what membership of the Third International would involve, and reported to a special *Reichskonferenz* held on 1 September.[4] Crispien now denounced the Bolsheviks for encouraging tactics which could only lead to civil war in Germany, for their demoralising charges of treason and insistence on constant purges, their intellectual and moral coercion, and for their attack on the 'yellow' western trade unions. Dittmann, Däumig and Stoecker also spoke. It was decided to refer the decision on the Twenty-One Conditions to an extraordinary general meeting of the party to meet at Halle in October. The *Reichskonferenz* showed the depth of disunity in the party: it was obvious that since the Halle meeting would not produce a unanimous vote a split was now inevitable.

[1] In reply to the Bolshevik charge that the U.S.P.D. were opportunists, Dittmann told Lenin that there were no greater opportunists in history than the Bolsheviks—a reply which must have given Dittmann considerable satisfaction (*ibid.*).

[2] The Independent reply to the Russian charges defended the party's record, especially its participation in the government in November 1918 and in the Berne and Lucerne conferences of the Second International parties, denied that it lacked revolutionary zeal and rebuked the Bolsheviks for trying to apply their methods to the very different conditions of Germany. The Russians were also criticised for failing to appreciate the significant change of policy in the U.S.P.D. since the Leipzig conference of December 1919. But the party was clearly on the defensive (*Antwort an das Exekutivkomitee der III Internationale*, n.p., 1920).

[3] Dittmann, *op. cit.* According to Ruth Fischer, Lenin was so determined to break up the U.S.P.D. that had the Twenty-One Conditions been accepted, he would have invented a twenty-second (Fischer, *Stalin and German Communism*, 1948, pp. 141 ff.). For a summary of the conditions see p. 256, n. 4 below.

[4] Prager, *op. cit.* p. 222.

THE SPLIT IN THE U.S.P.D.: THE HALLE CONFERENCE

The historic conference of the Independent socialist party called to decide on its relation to the Third International, on which its whole future depended, met at Halle in October 1920 and lasted five days. It was preceded by a propaganda campaign conducted by the leaders of the Third International in Russia and their supporters in Germany. All members of the U.S.P.D. received a letter from the Executive Committee of the International explaining and justifying the Twenty-One Conditions and giving the Russian version of the recent negotiations with the Independent leaders. This circular, which was skilfully worded, furthered the Russians' avowed aim of driving a wedge between the rank and file of the party, who were considered ripe for a more revolutionary policy, and their leaders, who were reactionary or compromisers; and enabled the Russians to appeal to the masses over the heads of the bosses.[1] Russian determination to bring the maximum weight to bear on the U.S.P.D. so as to win over as high a proportion of it as possible was underlined by the decision to send Zinoviev, chairman of the Executive Committee of the Third International, as a delegate to the Halle conference. Further evidence of the disloyalty of the left-wingers of the U.S.P.D. to their own party was provided by an article they wrote in the Communist *Rote Fahne* criticising its leadership.[2] That the split already existed *de facto* was made clear when at Halle the pro-Communists or *Neukommunisten* all sat together on one side of the hall.

As the business report by the secretary, Frau Zietz, revealed, the party had made great progress since its last conference.[3] Membership now totalled nearly 894,000, over 200,000 more than in the previous winter. In June they had polled 4·9 million votes. Twice they had been invited to share in the government. On the debit side, said Frau Zietz, 1920 had been a year of hard fighting on two fronts: besides the inevitable struggle against the militarists and the bourgeoisie, they had had to contend with the attacks of the Communists. Recriminations between the two sides of the party came into the open: the left blamed the right for half-heartedness in accepting the policy of proletarian dictatorship and for still hankering after reunion with the majority socialists, the right accused the left of betrayal. The main debate was on the Twenty-One Conditions. Crispien spoke first.[4] He charged the left wing leaders, Stoecker and Koenen, with seeking the alliance of nationalist officers in Germany—a reference to the 'National Bolshevik' trend which was encouraged by the apparent prospect in the summer of 1920 of a Russian

---

[1] *Prot. U.S.P.D.* (Halle, 1920), pp. i–xv. According to Prager, had the Independent party been left to its own counsels and not subjected to a propaganda campaign directed by Moscow with the help of its German allies, the left wing would not have gained a majority at the Halle congress.
[2] Prager, *op. cit.* p. 222.   [3] *Prot. U.S.P.D.* pp. 19–27.   [4] *Ibid.* pp. 36–8, 73–98.

victory over Poland that could unite the Russian and German proletarian armies to fight Entente capitalism. Crispien then criticised the Bolsheviks for having believed that they could win the Polish war despite the evidence, admitted by Zinoviev, that the Polish masses were anti-Soviet; and he ridiculed them for making friends with the notorious Enver Pasha, who had taken a leading part in the Armenian massacres, while regarding Kautsky as untouchable. The Independent socialist party, said Crispien, would never approve the demand in the Twenty-One Conditions that they should break with the Amsterdam International of Trade Unions, which the Bolsheviks denounced as 'yellow'. Däumig, in reply, put the orthodox Communist case, quoting Lenin in support of the view that proletarian dictatorship on the Soviet pattern was a model to be followed in all countries even at the price of civil war.[1] Stoecker spoke of the necessity of proletarian dictatorship even if it involved dictatorship over that section of the proletariat which was in the reactionary camp. He criticised the right wing leaders of the U.S.P.D. for holding back. Some of them, he prophesied, would rejoin the S.P.D.; others would be ground to pieces between the 'counter-revolutionary' Social Democrats and the new revolutionary mass party. Stoecker took the dissolution of the U.S.P.D. for granted.[2]

The most memorable contribution to the congress was made by Zinoviev, who, though using a foreign language, made an eloquent speech lasting several hours.[3] His main thesis was that the dispute inside the Independent party was the German counterpart to that between Bolsheviks and Mensheviks in Russia. The choice was between reformist socialism, which rejected the world revolution, perhaps even for good reasons, such as that it might involve famine, and the revolutionary socialism of which the Bolsheviks were the only true representatives. Already, Zinoviev assured his audience, the revolution was beginning in Italy and in Britain; in Austria a soviet government might be set up at any time, and prospects in the Balkans were promising. Zinoviev then turned to those aspects of Soviet policy which could not be reconciled with Marxism, such as the distribution of land to the peasants, which he explained had been necessary to win indispensable peasant support for the revolutionary government, and the alliance with Enver Pasha, who, despite the blots in his career, was an upholder of Turkish rights against Entente imperialism. Zinoviev stressed the importance of drawing the non-European peoples into the world revolutionary movement and referred to the Baku conference of Asiatic peoples which he had helped to organise. Oppressed nations must be helped even if they were backward and prejudiced. It was not true that the Bolsheviks wanted to push the Germans

[1] *Ibid.* pp. 98 ff.   [2] *Ibid.* p. 131.
[3] *Ibid.* pp. 144–79. Prager describes Zinoviev as being received by his supporters 'like a king by his subjects'.

into war against the Entente, nor did they intend to dictate to other Communist parties; indeed, if they could they would be only too glad to move the headquarters of the Third International to Paris. Coming to the U.S.P.D. programme with its emphasis on workers' councils, Zinoviev reminded them that such councils could not succeed without the Bolshevik party, an essential that had often been overlooked in Germany, where the slogan All Power to the Soviets tended, at least on the left, to be taken at its face value. Even the soviets, he pointed out, had had to be converted to Bolshevism.

The foil to Zinoviev was the Menshevik leader Martov, now exiled from Russia and a bitter enemy of the Bolshevik regime.[1] He declared that recent examples of soviet dictatorship in Finland, Bavaria and Hungary showed that Bolshevism was putschism—a revival of the ideas of Blanqui, the champion of the seizure of power by terrorist minorities. Despite Zinoviev's assurances, Martov insisted that there was Russian dictatorship in the Third International, as the Scandinavian parties had experienced. The use of terror in Russia had caused the shooting of hundreds of innocent people and the taking of hostages; he himself knew what his fate would be if he returned to Russia.

The confrontation between eastern and western forms of socialism at the congress was extended to include Lozovsky, the Bolshevik head of the Red Trade Union International, and the French left wing socialist Longuet (a grandson of Marx) who criticised the Russians for trying to foist their methods on the West. This was also one of the basic objections of Hilferding, who, as often before, threw his weight into the scales against the party's pro-Communist elements.[2] He accused Zinoviev of over-simplifying the differences between right and left and pointed out that, useful as the Russians' experience was, revolutionary policy in Germany could not be just a copy of Russia's. He warned the congress that to stake everything on a successful revolution in the west, as Zinoviev wanted, was a dangerous gamble, which might result in a total loss. The Bolsheviks' failure to attract the Polish masses to Communism during the current war was an illustration of the folly of their methods. As for the despised 'yellow' trade unions, they had, at least, been instrumental in stopping the despatch of arms to the White armies during the civil war. It was dishonest to put right wing trade unionists on the same level as capitalists. Speaking of the land question, Hilferding drew attention to the great difference between Russia and Germany: the German peasants were, on the whole, not land-hungry, and their indifference to the revolution had been shown in the winter of 1918–19. If the Independent party submitted to Communist terms it would have to accept methods of terror which had always been repugnant, and a degree of centralisation which was open to the same objections as those made by Rosa Luxemburg in her famous criticism of Lenin in 1904. Rosa Luxemburg would never have approved the Twenty-

---

[1] *Prot. U.S.P.D.* pp. 208–18.   [2] *Ibid.* pp. 179–204.

One Conditions, the purpose of which was to split the party. Entry into the Third International on these terms would mean loss of the party's independence ,the humiliating exclusion of respected leaders and the destruction of the western trade union organisation. Finally Hilferding foretold the failure of Bolshevik tactics in Germany.

Despite the eloquence of Zinoviev, it is difficult not to agree with Prager, the historian of the U.S.P.D., that in the debate between right and left at Halle the right had the better arguments.[1] But in the highly charged atmosphere emotion counted for more than reason. The Bolsheviks had the prestige of a successful revolution and the propagandist resources of a large if unorganised state. World revolution was an intoxicating idea, and moderate socialism had been thoroughly discredited in Germany by its association with weak government and Freikorps terror. When the congress finally divided 237 votes were recorded for acceptance of the Twenty-One Conditions, 156 against. The minority delegates thereupon left the building and continued the congress by themselves elsewhere. The majority were absorbed into the Communist party at a congress of the latter a few weeks later. For the first time the adherents of Lenin had gained a mass following. The K.P.D. became a major factor in German politics, and the aim which the Spartacists had had from the beginning of destroying their larger and never really united rival had been realised. In the history of German socialism an epoch had ended. The final failure of centrist socialism to reconcile democratic and revolutionary aims was the more significant since it followed so closely on the crisis of democracy four months before.

Among the minority at Halle was the Independent woman socialist Toni Sender, who recorded her impressions:

When, after the vote was taken, and the irrational had triumphed, I left the Halle convention hall with my friends to gather together what was left of a very promising young party, I felt deeply the great catastrophe that had occurred. The splitting and weakening of the only realistic and independent revolutionary party in Germany could lead only to the encouragement of reaction...What did it matter that after a short time those who had led in the surrender to Moscow's dictates became sober and left the Communist party? The damage was done. I knew a new chapter in the history of German labour had begun. The split was worse than a defeat.[2]

Though three-fifths of the delegates at Halle had voted for the Communists the proportion of members who went over was smaller, probably not much

---

[1] Like Prager, Dittmann attributed the result of Halle largely to Russian money and propaganda. Zinoviev's rhetoric counted for something, though only a handful of right wing delegates appear to have crossed the floor. (W. T. Angress, *Stillborn Revolution*, p. 72.) More generally, it may be said that the long attachment to a revolutionary ideology and the magnetism of Lenin's new Communist orthodoxy exacted their price. One Independent who never became a Communist was Ledebour. A born rebel, he was also a born non-conformist. When Hitler came to power he emigrated to Switzerland, where he died in 1947 in his ninety-eighth year.

[2] Sender, *The Autobiography of a German Rebel* (1940), p. 166.

more than a third.[1] The solid rank and file resented the Communist attack on their trade unions, and many of those who quitted were youthful recruits with little experience of politics. Of the eighty-one Independent Socialist members of the Reichstag only twenty changed sides, the remaining sixty-one stayed. But it is estimated that a good many members, perhaps about a third of the pre-Halle total, dropped out of politics in disgust at the internecine quarrel.[2] The rump of the U.S.P.D. rejoined the S.P.D. two years later. Even after the split the party suffered from lack of unity, according to Kautsky, for it still contained people who were Communists rather than Social Democrats but disliked dictation from Moscow. The Leipzig programme became a dead letter as the party gradually realised that the prospect of world revolution was fading and that, instead of preparing for a new November 1918, they must come to terms with reality and defend the republic. Kautsky continued to advocate reunion with the S.P.D. within a party structure that allowed divergences of view,[3] but it was not until the murder of Rathenau in June 1922 produced a fresh wave of alarm and indignation among democrats and socialists that reunion actually took place (at Nuremberg in September 1922) though a tiny remnant which included the doughty veteran Ledebour continued to uphold the U.S.P.D. banner.[4]

[1] The number of Independent socialists who joined the new united Communist party is estimated at about 300,000. The official strength of the K.P.D. before the merger was 78,715, so that the enlarged party had a membership of about 350,000, perhaps rather more (see Angress, *op. cit.* pp. 72–3). Most of the Independent press stayed loyal to the old party.   [2] Borkenau, *op. cit.* p. 200; Dittmann, *op. cit.* ch. 19.

[3] Kautsky, *Mein Verhaeltnis zur U.S.P.D.* pp. 15–19.

[4] Summary of the Twenty-one conditions (as applied to the Independent Social Democratic Party): (1) All party propaganda to be truly Communist and the entire party press to be edited by Communists. (2) All reformists and 'centrists' to be removed from responsible posts in the party and replaced by Communists. (3) An illegal organisation to be created to help the party prepare for revolution. (4) Systematic propaganda to be undertaken in the army, if necessary illegally. (5) Systematic propaganda to be undertaken in rural districts. (6) 'Social pacifism' to be renounced as well as 'social patriotism'. (7) Certain 'centrist' leaders, among them Hilferding, to be excluded. (8) The party to support the movement for colonial liberation. (9) Communist activity to be carried on in trade unions. (10) The party to fight against the Amsterdam Trade Union International. (11) The parliamentary party to be subordinated to the Central Committee. (12) The party to be organised on the principle of democratic centralism. (13) The party to be purged periodically of petty bourgeois elements. (14) The party to give help to the Soviet republics in the Russian civil war. (15) The party to have a new, specifically Communist programme. (16) All resolutions of the Third International to be binding on the party. (17) The party to be renamed a Communist party, section of the Third International. (18) All main documents of the Third International to be published by the party. (19) The party to discuss these conditions within four months of deciding to join the Third International. (20) Two-thirds of the party's Central Committee to consist of comrades who were pro-Communist before the second meeting of the Third International. (21) Party members who in principle reject these Conditions to be excluded from the party. Quoted from *Der Zweite Kongress der Kommunistischen Internationale: Verlauf der Verhandlungen vom 19. Juli in Petrograd und vom 22. Juli bis 7. August in Moskau*, Hamburg, 1921, p. 781, in Ruth Fischer, *Stalin and German Communism*, pp. 141 ff. (abbreviated).)

CHAPTER 12

RETROSPECT AND CONCLUSIONS

Eine Revolution ist ein Unglueck, aber ein noch grösseres Unglueck
ist eine verunglueckte Revolution.   HEINE

The time has come to draw together the main threads in the story and to
consider the whole pattern in perspective.

The two major setbacks of 1920, the electoral reverse suffered by the S.P.D.
and the Independents' split, were both symptoms of growing dissatisfaction
with reformist socialism which, as the last chapter showed, had fateful
consequences for the future of the Weimar Republic. They marked the last
stage of the disintegration of German socialism which, beginning in the war
(though its origins can be traced further back) had been completed by the
Russian and German revolutions. For the Independents the Halle conference was the end of a road that had begun with protests against annexations
and nationalism and ended with demands for proletarian dictatorship and
membership of the Leninist Third International. For the majority socialists
the June 1920 election closed a spell of over a year and a half when, alone or
in coalition, they had held the leading place in the government and had a
unique (but largely wasted) opportunity of reshaping the German state and
society. Although Germany was to remain for some time longer in a condition of latent or overt revolutionary ferment, and the republic was to be
threatened by putsches from right and left for at least three more years,
never again were the socialists to occupy such a commanding position as in
the winter of 1918–19. Nor was there, after October 1920, any prospect of
that reunion on the left which seemed to many people in both parties the only
way of saving democracy as well as socialism. With the absorption of over
a third of the Independents into the Communist ranks (which were thereby
transformed from a struggling sect into a mass party) all such hopes had to be
abandoned: not even the threat of Hitler was to bring together two parties
which both claimed descent from Marx and Bebel. In the post-revolutionary
struggle between reformists and revolutionaries the group which stood, as
the U.S.P.D. did in November 1918, for the retention of both policies in
what amounted to a reconstruction of the Erfurt synthesis, could hardly
survive. Between the *Realpolitik* of Ebert and Noske on the one hand, and
that of Lenin and his German devotees on the other, there was not merely an
impassable gulf, but no room for a genuinely independent party. As the
process of polarisation worked itself out, with the S.P.D. dropping revolutionary aims and becoming dependent on counter-revolutionary forces, the

Independents found themselves driven further to the left until little of their former liberalism remained. Forced to choose between democracy and the revolution, they chose the latter and so abandoned their centrist role. The year 1920 is thus a convenient vantage point from which to review the main stages of this development, by which two parties starting from a common source, but reacting in turn against each other's policy, passed from divergence to irreconcilability.

REFORMIST SOCIALISM FROM BROKEN *BURGFRIEDEN* TO INEFFECTIVE POWER

The S.P.D.'s historic decision on 4 August 1914 to vote for war credits and accept the civic truce offered by the Kaiser determined the course to which the party remained broadly faithful throughout the war. When the government in effect broke the truce by adopting a thinly veiled annexationist policy, the socialists could react to the new situation in one of three ways. They could regard the *Burgfrieden* as null and void and resume the freedom of opposition; they could take a frankly opportunist or nationalist line and say that annexations were justified—thereby abandoning their earlier insistence on pure defence; or they could accept at their face value the Chancellor's assurances that nothing had really changed. The first course was followed, after some initial hesitation, by the party's left wing, which gradually seceded and ultimately established itself as a fully fledged rival, the Independent Social Democratic party. The second course was taken by a small but articulate group of right wing socialists represented by such journalists as Lensch and Haenisch, who came out openly in support of territorial gains and gave a quasi-revolutionary gloss to Pan-German claims. The majority of the party, including most of the leaders, chose the third course, quietening their consciences with the sibylline pronouncements of Bethmann Hollweg and with the reflection that any likely alternative Chancellor would have been a good deal more objectionable.

As the war lengthened and the number of belligerent countries increased it became clear that, whichever side won, the pre-war frontiers were not going to be restored. The Allies' territorial claims against the Central Powers enabled German majority socialists to argue that the war was still defensive. On general patriotic grounds, and because they believed that the working-class standard of living was at stake, the S.P.D. leaders saw a German defeat as the supreme calamity, to be avoided at almost all costs.[1] This was the basic

---

[1] Wolfgang Heine, one of the most right wing socialist politicians, wrote in the Bremen *Bürgerzeitung* of 1 May 1916: 'Even if the present government bore the sole guilt of the war...with the object of subjugating Europe...we could still not act in a manner different from that in which we have acted.' Quoted in Berlau, *The German Social Democratic Party, 1914-21*, p. 136.

reason why they went on voting for war credits despite growing doubts and despite exasperation, particularly marked in the spring and summer of 1917, at the government's refusal to heed their advice on matters of crucial importance such as unrestricted submarine warfare and franchise reform. The degree of opportunism can be measured by the shift of emphasis within the party as the fortunes of war fluctuated. In April 1917, with morale depressed by hunger and war-weariness and a receding prospect of peace (America entered the war before Russia left it) the majority socialists incorporated into their programme the policy of peace without annexations and indemnities which the Petrograd Soviet had taken over from the Zimmerwald conference of anti-war socialists. Then in July the S.P.D. had the satisfaction of seeing the Progressives and Centre party apparently converted to their policy of a 'peace of understanding' and internal reform. But the Reichstag peace resolution had an annexationist loophole, and did not prevent Bethmann Hollweg's successors from making territorial gains, notably at the expense of Russia, or the other parties from approving them. Next year, as Germany's military prospects improved, the S.P.D. accepted the special treaty with the Ukraine and the treaty of Bucharest with Roumania, and abstained from opposing the punitive peace of Brest-Litovsk. The price the S.P.D. paid for this opportunism was two-fold: at home it lost (mainly in the first three years of war) many adherents to the Independents; abroad it alienated the Allied socialists, who henceforth saw in the majority socialists obedient tools of German imperialism, an attitude that was to add to the party's difficulties when it came to power at the end of the war.

Nor was the S.P.D. much more successful in securing the fulfilment by the government of the promised reforms. The reference by Vice-Chancellor Delbrück to a 'reorientation' of domestic policy after the war was made in November 1914, when it was still believed that the war might be short. As this hope faded, losses mounted and hardships pressed with increasing severity, the socialists became more impatient. It was not, however, until news of the Russian revolution alarmed the German government and made change appear a matter of urgency that Bethmann Hollweg persuaded the Kaiser to issue his Easter Message promising franchise reform. This was followed in July by a formal pledge by the Chancellor to introduce the necessary legislation into the Prussian parliament without waiting for the end of the war. The S.P.D. also pressed for an advance towards parliamentary government, an endeavour in which they received some support from their two Reichstag partners of the peace resolution. The few steps taken by the government appeased its critics without changing the balance of power in Germany, now heavily tilted in favour of the military. Hertling's government was rather meaninglessly described as semi-parliamentary because it depended on a Reichstag majority; but the latter did not press their policy on the Chancellor, despite his known dislike of a compromise peace and of a parliamentary regime, and his failure to enforce equal voting rights in Prussia. In both foreign relations (the Papal peace negotiations) and internal policy the S.P.D. had good reason to be dissatisfied with the government, yet there was less sign of discontent in the first three quarters of 1918 than there had been the year before. By refusing to use its vote for war credits as a bargaining counter the S.P.D. had deliberately deprived itself of the principal means of enforcing its will on the government. Some consolation for its lack of success with the Chancellor was found in the party's parliamentary alliance. The new Reichstag majority of which the S.P.D. was a part seemed to open a way for reform in the democratic age which many socialists were convinced would follow the war. They were confident that their party would reap the reward of its moderation and patriotism and would attract many middle-class supporters. Such rosy expectations overlooked the realities of power in wartime Germany. It is hardly conceivable that a victorious Ludendorff would have permitted Germany to become a parliamentary state, or even have sanctioned reform of the Prussian franchise. The S.P.D. had pledged its more or less unconditional support to a government dominated by annexationists and hostile to the party's domestic aims. Max Weber had written before the war that if the revolutionary ardour of the socialists was weakened by concessions made by the state, the state would conquer the party.[1] The concessions made to the socialists during the war did not amount to much, but they were enough, in combination with the S.P.D.'s growing nationalism and fear of defeat, to ensure its loyalty to the Hohenzollern regime.

Yet one important event in the last year of the war seemed to contradict this trend: the participation by the S.P.D. in the great strike of January 1918 against the Brest-Litovsk peace terms and more generally against the prolongation of the war. The motives of the party leaders were to control the strike movement and to prevent it falling into the hands of the Independents; nevertheless they were committing in the eyes of nationalists an unpatriotic if not a treasonable act, for which Ebert at least was never forgiven, and the party lost some of the credit to which its wartime record entitled it. Also, of course, the Marxist ideology which the party still professed but ignored in practice remained, at least in theory, a barrier between it and the middle-class parties. Looked at as a whole, the S.P.D.'s war policy shows it balancing between its two points of reference: the government, to which it gave critical support in the spirit of the new relationship established on 4 August 1914, and its working-class followers, whose allegiance it dared not strain too far for fear of losing them to its left wing rival. The same habit of looking in both directions was to characterise the party during the revolutionary period when it sought to win the confidence of the non-socialist section of the

---

[1] J. P. Mayer, *Max Weber and German Politics* (1944), p. 49.

population while retaining the loyalty of its rank and file. It only partly succeeded in the first, and largely failed in the second: this was, in brief, the experience of the S.P.D. between 1918 and 1920.

When, at the end of September 1918, the Hohenzollern regime faced defeat and the majority socialists were asked, at Ludendorff's instigation, to join a coalition parliamentary government under Prince Max of Baden, they could more or less make their own terms; but no terms could compensate them for taking office at a time when it was more of a liability than an asset. They had to bear the consequences of others' mistakes by signing an unpopular and burdensome armistice and to help govern a country demoralised by defeat and with an exhausted economy. The majority socialists were under no illusions as to the difficulties of their task, which they undertook, despite some initial reluctance, from patriotism and a sense of responsibility. Yet these virtues and the S.P.D. leaders' lack of support for or disapproval of the November upsurge failed to exonerate them from the charge of treason— the libel which, although refuted by an accumulating weight of evidence, was to do the party incalculable harm. According to the legend, which the generals encouraged for obvious reasons, and to which the Kaiser contributed, it was the naval mutiny and insurrectionary strike movement of early November 1918 that forced the German government to abandon its plans for continuing the war in case the armistice terms proved unacceptable. The decision to end the war on what amounted to unconditional surrender was in fact made by Prince Max in his answer to Wilson's Third Note, at the same time as he persuaded the Kaiser to dismiss Ludendorff. This was at least two days before the first signs of trouble at Kiel. Both mutiny and strikes were spontaneous, and came as a surprise to the S.P.D., as they did even to most of the Independents.

In finding themselves on 10 November sitting with the Independents in a cabinet of 'People's Commissars', answerable to the workers' and soldiers' councils which had assumed *de facto* power all over Germany, Ebert and his S.P.D. colleagues were in an awkward and ambiguous situation. They distrusted the councils and wanted to return as soon as possible to the parliamentary regime introduced in October, and they urged that the councils should exercise their authority only until a constituent assembly could be elected. As this was broadly the councils' own decision at their December congress, Ebert was saved from having to accept council government as permanent or lose popular support. But his pact with Groener put him in a false position *vis-à-vis* the councils even in the short run. This pact represented, under very different circumstances, a renewal of the *Burgfrieden* of August 1914. The Hohenzollern monarchy had gone, and all civilian authority was momentarily powerless, but the field army remained. As the party in charge of the state, the S.P.D. could negotiate with the army on equal terms. In theory the army had for the first time been subordinated to the civilian power by the October reforms, but that was under an imperial constitution which no longer existed. The German, and especially the Prussian officer, had been trained to be loyal to the monarchy rather than to the country or even the state.[1] That the army should ally itself with a republican and semi-revolutionary government was a novel and daring step, the result of Groener's quick appreciation of the situation following the Kaiser's abdication, of his confidence in Ebert's personal qualities and political moderation, and, no doubt, of the quasi-legal manner in which Ebert had succeeded Prince Max as Chancellor. Ebert's agreement with Groener was designed to protect the government against an attempt by Liebknecht to seize power, but also against the claims of the councils, which Groener saw, naïvely but understandably, as equivalent to Bolshevism. Noske's use of the Freikorps to crush the 'second revolution' was a desperate yet logical consequence of the pact. But the congress of councils' decision in favour of radical reform of the army and abolition of the officers' authority (the Lamp'l Points) put Ebert in a dilemma: he must either break with the generals or fall foul of the councils. He saved himself by temporising, but at the cost of alienating the Independents, whose resignation from the government precipitated the January rising. In calling on the Freikorps, Ebert became dependent on them to an extent which made impossible a consolidation of socialists from both parties that might have enabled them to play a more positive part in shaping the new republic. Ebert believed, no doubt rightly, that in opposing the attempt of left wing Independents to extend the council regime indefinitely he was preventing civil war; and in suppressing rebels he was doing what any government would have done. But the manner and the effects of the suppression were such as to encourage unbridled militarism on the one hand, left wing extremism on the other. The climax of these two related developments appeared a year later in the Kapp Putsch and the taking over of the Independent party by its revolutionary intransigents. Nor was it only in relation to the army that Ebert shocked and disappointed many of his S.P.D. followers. The socialisation for which the councils had voted at their congress did not materialise as fast as they desired or in a form they approved; and this was another reason for left wing embitterment.

The policy of the S.P.D. leaders during this critical time, and particularly of Ebert in his unique capacity as both Chancellor and chairman of the Council of Peoples' Commissars will always be a matter of controversy.[2] His positive achievement is that he piloted Germany through a transitional

---

[1] Groener, *Lebenserinnerungen*, p. 467; Schüddekopf, *Das Heer und die Republik*, p. 59. One Freikorps officer told his men that, the Kaiser having gone, they had no country. A Nationalist parliamentarian, von Graefe, told the National Assembly on 29 October 1919 that the old army had been the basis of their whole patriotism.

[2] Dittmann in his memoirs makes much of the 'historic guilt' of Ebert and his S.P.D. colleagues for failing to seize their unique opportunities.

period between autocracy and democracy under exceptional difficulties, avoiding large-scale civil war, defeating a Communist bid for power and preventing the Reich, a comparatively new and untried structure, from falling to pieces. His resistance to the Soviet-orientated revolutionaries meant for German foreign relations a decision for the West as opposed to the East, even if reconciliation with the western ex-enemies remained for the time being unattainable.[1] Criticism of Ebert can be made on three counts. First he is blamed for not having carried the democratisation of Germany beyond the formal establishment of the Weimar constitution. This charge is hard to refute. It has long been recognised that the authority of the Weimar Reichstag lacked effectiveness when faced with the hostility of powerful anti-republican elements in the higher civil service, local government and the judiciary, to mention no others. It is significant that Hugo Preuss, the father of the Weimar constitution, afterwards attributed the main weakness of the republic to the disparity between a reformed constitutional system and an unreformed administration.[2] It can hardly be denied that Ebert failed to grasp this problem and to use the most obvious means at his disposal for solving it—the workers' councils. They alone could have injected a democratic spirit into local government; their unique combination of executive and legislative functions was a primitive but effective form of democracy such as Germany needed.[3] That such councils had no place in the philosophy or programme of the S.P.D. (or of the U.S.P.D. either) was no reason why Ebert should not have adjusted himself to the new situation and recognised the councils' potential significance in paving the way for a genuinely democratic society. The majority in the workers' councils, and nearly all the members of the soldiers' councils, were S.P.D. supporters, so that by allowing them greater scope in the transition period Ebert need not have let the situation get out of control. Had the S.P.D. leaders shown a more constructive and imaginative approach to the councils they could have checked the growth of the left wing extremism which was to have such disastrous results for the majority socialists and the republic itself. Ebert's rejection of the rather nebulous and utopian notion that political power might in some way be permanently shared between parliament and councils was no doubt justified by the difficulties that would have arisen from the institutional clash and the differing political composition of the two. But in the short run he might have made more use of the councils to fill the political vacuum before the constituent assembly met, and even perhaps afterwards, as a complementary, not a rival institution. Certainly his initial dislike of the councils was heightened by his experience of the Berlin Executive Council,

[1] As early as 8 January 1919 *The Times* pointed out that the German right wing socialists had turned to the West, although this meant subjection to the Entente, in preference to the alternative policy of renewing the war as an ally of Soviet Russia.

[2] Kolb, *Die Arbeiterräte in der deutschen Innenpolitik, 1918–19* (1962), p. 408.

[3] *Ibid.* p. 404.

which was perpetually interfering in matters within the competence of the People's Commissars, though with its successor body, the all-S.P.D. Central Council, relations were much smoother.[1]

As for Ebert's delay in applying the policy of socialisation for which the congress of councils had voted, he was not alone in believing that caution was the right policy; many Independents and most of the socialist economists agreed with him. The practical problems were formidable.[2] Nor can the S.P.D. be blamed for seeing in the Russian example of war communism a warning, not a model. But although the S.P.D. leaders had a good case for socialising slowly and piecemeal, their lack of enthusiasm contrasted with the eagerness of the masses, with whom emotionally they were not in sympathy. The party was being led from the right, and the rank and file rebelled.

Ebert can hardly be acquitted on the third charge, that he was blind to the dangers of militarism. This was true of the socialists as a whole, including initially the Independents. Although militarism was a problem of German society which the pre-war socialists recognised to the extent of wishing to substitute a militia for the conscript army, it was not given much attention in socialist thinking, except by relative outsiders such as Liebknecht, since it was not a vital part of the Marxist analysis of society. Like imperialism, which had developed since Marx's day and did not figure in his writings, militarism was considered a product of capitalism which would automatically disappear when capitalism was superseded by socialism. Yet Max Weber, a shrewd but not unsympathetic observer of the party, had written in 1906: 'If the S.P.D. seeks political power and yet fails to control the one effective means of power, military power, in order to overthrow the state, its dominance...would only show its political impotence more clearly.'[3] The warning was prophetic. True to their Marxist training the leaders of the S.P.D. always thought of the revolution in terms of a struggle between workers and capitalists, whereas the principal enemy turned out to be the army. Throughout the revolution the strength of anti-militarist feeling was revealed, from the mutiny at Kiel to the Lamp'l Points at the congress of councils. Ebert knew that had he allowed the Points to be put into effect he would have lost the support of the army chiefs and put himself at the mercy of the Spartacists and their allies. The price he paid for using the Freikorps was a high one, both in the growth of militarism and the loss of votes to the Independents. Was there a third alternative? Had the majority socialists been willing to defend the republic,

---

[1] Ebert's marked inclination to leave to the constituent assembly important and urgent decisions, especially on the military side, indicates, as Kolb suggests, that for him the assembly had become not merely a means to a political end but an end in itself. (Kolb, *Die Arbeiterräte in der deutschen Innenpolitik, 1918–19* (1962), p. 182.)

[2] See especially p. 226 n. 3 and p. 248 n. 1. Among those who warned against the pitfalls of hasty socialisation were the trade union leaders. Varain, *Freie Gewerkschaften, Sozialdemokratie und Staat*, p. 137.

[3] Mayer, *op. cit.* p. 65.

either by manning and 'democratising' the Freikorps, or by forming their own units, or even had liberal-minded members of the middle classes played a more active part in public affairs, Ebert and Noske would have been able to avoid their disastrous dependence on the enemies of the republic, and the left wing Independents would have become less intransigent. Behind the refusal of the socialists to fight for their regime lay not only fatigue and apathy —though the physical exhaustion caused by the long war and the blockade should not be underestimated[1]—but a long-standing misconception of the nature of power, the implications of which are discussed below.

A more general criticism of the S.P.D. seniors who governed Germany during the crucial year and a half that followed the Kaiser's abdication is that they failed to provide inspiring leadership, to rouse any revolutionary *élan*, to develop any new ideas. They were lacking, it has often been said, in imagination and boldness. There is no denying that such criticism contains much truth: as even Hermann Müller admitted, a small generation was unequal to its opportunity.[2] Yet there is a good deal to be said on the other side. If the opportunity was great, so were the obstacles to its seizure. Unlike the Romanov and, to a lesser extent, the Habsburg regimes, which perished from a combination of external defeat and internal decay, the Hohenzollern regime, despite its massive miscalculations, its obstinacy and blindness to political realities, remained, within these limits, almost to the last, efficient and vigorous. Only defeat in a world war could pull it down, and the shock of defeat proved a good deal less damaging than first appeared. Under the Weimar regime the social forces which had upheld the state under the Kaiser remained, but in opposition. Ebert and his colleagues found themselves with little room in which to manoeuvre between a suspicious and recalcitrant right and an insurrectionary left, with fresh Allied demands constantly inflaming political passions and a weak economy adding to the instability. Ebert saw that not heroics (of which Germany had had more than enough) but dogged, unspectacular spadework was needed to ensure the country's survival. He regarded himself as a reconciler of classes, not a revolutionary leader, continuing the policy of compromise with the establishment which the S.P.D. had learnt to follow during the war. He had made his way in the party by displaying the virtues of a bureaucrat. In the crisis of November 1918 he showed common sense, a power of decision and great tactical skill. He seemed solid and reliable. On the other hand, he made serious mistakes, as when he unwittingly helped to propagate the stab in the back legend by telling the returning troops at the

---

[1] Wolff, *Through Two Decades:* 'After the four years of war there was no creative energy left' (p. 116).

[2] *Prot. S.P.D.* (Weimar, 1919), p. 131. Compare the judgement of M. J. Bonn (*Wandering Scholar*, p. 200) that the majority socialists knew how to administer but not how to rule. This criticism could be made of many middle-class German politicians; the Bismarckian state had not prepared them for the exercise of power.

Brandenburg Gate that they had not been defeated, and he endangered the republic by placing unjustified confidence in monarchist generals. Nor were his methods always scrupulous.[1] In his defence it might be said that he was faced with a choice of evils. Germany was on the brink of civil war and separatism was a danger. What Ebert and his colleagues could not give either to the revolution or to the republic was glamour, the quality which the Kaiser's regime had possessed, even if much of it was meretricious.[2] The revolution was inseparably connected with defeat. When Scheidemann, in the speech proclaiming the republic from the Reichstag balcony, told his mass audience that with the fall of the old order the people had triumphed all along the line, the fruits of success seemed dearly bought at the cost of a lost war; it is significant that Scheidemann's own account of the German revolution is entitled 'The Collapse', and that in it he writes of the 'guilt' for the 9 November.[3] In the calamity of defeat the revolutionary gains counted for little. Moreover, despite their wartime patriotism the S.P.D. had failed to establish themselves as a patriotic party in the eyes of their critics. Unlike the French left, the German socialists completely lacked the tradition of revolutionary nationalism of which Engels had dreamed, and which might have invested their efforts with a heroic character. More important than the drabness of the S.P.D. leaders was their inability to master events, to hold their enemies in check and guide the bewildered and often truculent working class and the mistrustful middle class into a new relationship to the state. Perhaps only a political genius could have accomplished a task of such magnitude, among such difficulties. There was no socialist leader in Germany who could brilliantly improvise, like Lenin in Russia.[4]

[1] Kolb has shown (*op. cit.* pp. 184 ff.) that when Ebert sent President Wilson a telegram after the armistice asking for food supplies, he added the words 'so long as public order in Germany is maintained and an equitable distribution of food guaranteed'. This qualifying phrase was repeated by the Americans in their reply telegram undertaking to supply food. Landsberg thereupon used 'foreign pressure' as an argument for convening the constituent assembly as soon as possible. Thus the S.P.D. leaders used words they themselves put into the mouths of the Americans as a weapon in their struggle with the Independents. Although the latter suspected some such trick at the time, only the subsequent publication of the American documents (*Papers relating to the Foreign Relations of the U.S., Paris Peace Conference, 1919*, ii, Washington, 1942, pp. 89 ff.) enabled the facts to be known. Another example of Ebert's lack of scruple was his behaviour to his Independent colleagues at the time of the sailors' revolt of 23–24 December 1918, if the Independent accounts of what was said and done are accepted.

[2] Naumann, who as a Democratic member of the National Assembly was present at its opening sessions at Weimar, recorded the general air of disappointment with which the new regime came to birth: the lack of any appropriate mystique, the absence of any legendary qualities. Theodor Heuss, *Friedrich Naumann: der Mann, das Werk, die Zeit* (1937), p. 600.   [3] Scheidemann, *Der Zusammenbruch*, p. 210.

[4] Rosenberg suggests (*History of the German Republic*, pp. 38–9) that one main reason for the failure of the S.P.D. to master the problems of the German revolution was the party's pre-war lack of interest in matters other than social and electoral reform, for which Bebel rather than Ebert or Scheidemann should be held responsible.

THE INDEPENDENT SOCIALISTS: TRIALS OF A
SEMI-REVOLUTIONARY PARTY

If the history of the S.P.D. during our period is that of a reformist party which sought to gain its ends by gradualism and penetration, to use two words characteristic of Fabian socialism, the history of the Independent socialists is that of a party which tried to carry out a revolutionary policy by peaceful methods and found them wanting. The combination of reformist and revolutionary aims for which the U.S.P.D. stood was inherent in the socialist programme of 1891, and the anti-war resolution passed by the Second International, which the S.P.D. helped to draft, had revolutionary implications, if only because a strike in wartime was a very different matter from a strike in peace. The war, by exposing the extent to which the S.P.D. was committed to support an annexationist and militarist government, forced the party's left wing into active opposition, which at first took the form of refusing war credits, asking awkward questions (interpellations) in the Reichstag, and issuing pamphlets attacking the government. Later, as resentment against the war increased and the ineffectiveness of parliamentary criticism became evident, the left turned to a more aggressive policy. The militant language of the manifestos of the Zimmerwald and Kienthal conferences, in which the German left took part, the resolution of the third conference of Zimmerwald parties in favour of an 'international mass struggle for peace' (meaning a strike), and the growing strike movement in Germany with its political demands, culminating in the defiant action of January 1918, all testified to the rise of a revolutionary temper. The objective of the Independents was afterwards summarised by one of their leaders as to end the war as soon as possible on terms which would not involve the violation of any people, and to summon mass support in favour of such a peace.[1] In the choice of tactics the party's right wing (Kautsky) did not want to go beyond constitutional opposition, but on the left two parliamentary militants, Ledebour and Däumig, worked closely with the revolutionary shop-stewards who after January 1918 were preparing for insurrection. When all its internal differences and ambiguities are taken into account, the U.S.P.D. may be described as a semi-revolutionary party. It was criticised for its utopianism by the S.P.D., for its moderation by the Spartacists. The Spartacists were able to abandon the liberal and reformist parts of the socialist programme because they staked everything on revolution and rejected the principle of national defence, whereas the Independents were prepared to back a defensive war but denied that Germany was fighting it. Their opposition to the government's war policy, from the early annexations debates in the Reichstag to Brest-Litovsk and beyond was courageous and consistent, commendably free from

[1] *Reichstag Inquiry*, VII, ii, p. 324.

the opportunism which characterised the other parties. When in October 1918 the S.P.D. joined the government, the Independents held aloof, denounced the reforms as half-measures and demanded a socialist republic. Haase joined, probably not without some misgivings, the shop-stewards' committee which was preparing to lead a revolution in Berlin, but their plans were overtaken by the spontaneous revolutionary wave which started in Kiel.

Although the U.S.P.D. leaders cannot be held responsible for organising the nation-wide outbreak of workers' and soldiers' councils, they were quick to see their significance as guarantees of revolutionary consolidation and progress. Unlike the S.P.D., the U.S.P.D. welcomed the councils and tried to use them to further their policy. Workers' councils had proved their usefulness during the wartime strikes, and in Russia had become the bearers of proletarian dictatorship. But there was little sign in the U.S.P.D. before the revolution that the party might substitute councils for parliament, as the Spartacists planned to do. It is, however, one of the many ironies of the German revolution that the workers' and soldiers' councils gave more support to the majority socialists, who did not believe in them, than to the Independents, who did. As the December congress showed, the councils agreed with the Independents in wanting a radical policy towards the army and the economy, but with the majority socialists in desiring a speedy return to parliamentary government. As democratic socialists, the council delegates did not believe that these aims were incompatible.

Disillusion with parliamentary democracy as practised at Weimar, and with the militarism which simultaneously protected and threatened it, combined with distrust of the S.P.D. leaders, forced the U.S.P.D. into increasing reliance on the workers' councils as the one means of keeping alive the thwarted revolutionary spirit. In the evolution of Independent policy from parliamentary democracy to proletarian dictatorship three stages can be distinguished. In the first stage, beginning in November 1918, the U.S.P.D. wanted to give the councils as much time as possible to complete the revolution (the early success of which had been much exaggerated in the party's manifesto of 12 November) before the election of a constituent assembly, which was seen as inevitable. Tactically this compromise policy matched the Independents' position as colleagues of the S.P.D. in the revolutionary government. After their resignation at the end of December they could revert to a more radical line. The second stage in this process was reached in March 1919 when the party drew up a new programme including a demand for the inclusion of workers' councils in the German constitution and for the first time declared its aim to be the dictatorship of the proletariat. It was decided that, after the revolution, councils should supersede parliament; there was growing sympathy for the view that a bourgeois parliament was, in any case, only a cloak for capitalist dictatorship. Yet the councils were to be elected by a franchise which would exclude non-workers, so that the party was turning away from the democratic principle enshrined in the Erfurt programme and hallowed by long tradition. This was a decisive break with the past, reflecting the Independents' disappointment with their electoral performance in January and growing exasperation with Noske. It also reflected their continuing belief in revolutionary prospects; as Däumig had told the congress of councils, the world war must be followed by a world revolution. The change made any future reunification with the S.P.D. difficult if not impossible. But the left wing, who were now in the ascendant, refused to trim their policy to suit the majority socialists, who appeared to be hand in glove with the counter-revolution.

The third stage came with the adoption at the U.S.P.D.'s Leipzig conference (December 1919) of a programme which authorised revolution by a minority by dropping the qualifying words that the proletarian party must represent the great majority of the nation. Behind this change lay a growing impatience with the 'immature masses', whose fateful preference for a parliamentary regime had cut the ground from under the feet of the revolutionaries. This new twist in the programme, intended to make the party more capable of taking a revolutionary initiative, and influenced by the Bolshevik precedent, together with the parallel decision to seek membership of the Third International made the U.S.P.D. ripe for the Communist take-over that was successful a few months later. Meanwhile the failure of the Kapp Putsch put the party in a tactically favourable position, and the election of June 1920 almost quadrupled the number of its seats in the Reichstag. Again it was prevented from taking advantage of the 'opening to the left' by the stubbornness of its revolutionary wing, which refused the S.P.D.'s offer to join the government. By a final irony, when the party still believed in democracy it lacked the numbers which would have enabled it to be effective; now, when it had gained enough support, it was unable to use it.

The transformation of the U.S.P.D. between 1918 and 1920 might be described as Leninisation. In abandoning parliamentary democracy the party also gave up its aversion to force, its rejection of purges and terror, the semi-pacifism which had underlain its war policy, all of which it had inherited from the Enlightenment and from the humanitarianism of the nineteenth century.[1] Yet organisationally the party remained what it had always been: loose, decentralised, excessively democratic. The paradoxical co-existence within it of authoritarian aims and the fragmentation of power made it an unsuitable instrument for revolution, especially revolution on the Bolshevik model. The

[1] A well-known socialist marching song quoted by Dittmann in his memoirs boasted that socialism would triumph by the 'sword of the spirit', the 'banner of righteousness'.

decision made by the majority at Halle meant the imposition of Leninist organisation and discipline on a party that was already Leninist in ideas. But the party's chronic disunity and weak leadership must throw doubt on its ability to survive even without Moscow's intervention. It never recovered from Haase's tactical error in allowing the left wing to boycott the Central Council in December 1918, which led indirectly to its resignation from the government a fortnight later, the event which triggered off the January rising. Haase failed to prevent the Berlin Independents and the militant shop-stewards from starting a venture which never had any chance of success and unleashed the forces of counter-revolution. As Scheidemann later wrote, without a Ledebour there would have been no Lüttwitz.[1] It could also be said that without Lüttwitz there would have been no Leninisation. The chain of events by which each move by one side provoked a reaction on the other until the U.S.P.D. was destroyed by its own tensions seems to have the fatal inevitability of a Greek tragedy. The only escape from the vicious spiral would have come through a split of the party in the winter of 1918–19, which was nearly provoked by the controversy of parliament versus workers' councils. It has been argued[2] that had Haase, backed by the right and centre of the party, had the courage then to repudiate the putschists and extremists he could have helped to form a powerful centre socialist party which would have included the many S.P.D. supporters who were dissatisfied with Ebert's negative attitude to the revolution and complacency towards the Freikorps. By making concessions to an ultimately insatiable left wing the party's leaders may well have simply postponed a split which they could not avert. Had they been bold and incisive enough to divide the party at a time when such a move could still have affected the fortunes of the German revolution they would at least have prevented the split from being organised by Moscow for reasons based on Russian rather than German needs.

THE GERMAN REVOLUTION AS A PRODUCT OF BISMARCKIAN POLICY AND MARXIST THEORY

The reasons for the failure of the German revolution have been indicated in some detail in previous chapters; the fundamental one was that the three main socialist groups after their wartime split went into it with incompatible aims. The S.P.D. leaders, most of them reluctant revolutionaries, were broadly satisfied with the reforms of October 1918; the Independents wanted a Marxist revolution without bloodshed; the Spartacists a revolution on the Soviet model. The unstable compromise which emerged from the struggle for power in the winter of 1918–19 as the Weimar Republic went some way to fulfilling the aspirations of the S.P.D. while falling short of the expectations

---

[1] Scheidemann, *Memoirs*, II, 667.   [2] See p. 183, note 2 above.

of many of its rank and file, but completely failed to satisfy the Independents and Spartacists. Its inability to win adequate support from the still largely monarchist middle classes was revealed by the results of the elections of 1920, which showed the republic in a defensive minority against the extremists of both right and left. Of all the explanations of revolutionary failure the most misleading and least illuminating is that offered by orthodox Communist historians: 'The tragedy of the 1918 revolution lay in the cleavage between the objectively matured revolutionary circumstances on the one hand and the subjective weakness of the German proletariat, produced by the lack of a purposeful Bolshevik party on the other.'[1] There were many reasons why the objective circumstances in Germany at the end of 1918 were not favourable to revolution: some permanent, such as the strength of the middle classes, the civil service and the industrialists, the conservatism of the peasants and the country's dependence on foreign trade—in all these ways the contrast with Russia could hardly have been more striking; some temporary, such as the conclusion of the armistice, and the Kaiser's abdication, two events which removed much of the dynamism of the situation almost before the revolution had begun. Here again there is a marked contrast with Russia on the eve of the Bolshevik seizure of power. Nor was the absence of a Bolshevik party in Germany an accident; there were valid historical reasons why socialism in the two countries developed on different lines. Had a German equivalent to the Bolsheviks existed (which the Spartacists were not) their seizure of power could only have led to a German version of the Paris Commune or to civil war as occurred in Hungary under Bela Kun. The success of the Bolshevik revolution in Russia, which was Marxist–Leninist, not Marxist in the true sense, was possible for the very reason which differentiated Russia from Germany—its backwardness. The experience of many countries in the last half-century has shown that a revolution of the Leninist (often rather of the Leninist–Stalinist) kind can succeed only in underdeveloped societies, where capitalism, being primitive, produces social tensions such as the West knew during the early industrial revolution, and at the same time is too weak to offer much resistance to a revolutionary party: the existence of an actually or potentially revolutionary peasantry is also essential. Such conditions were not present in the Germany of 1918, which was too advanced for a revolution of the Russian type. The only revolution which appeared to suit Germany was a Menshevik one: this is broadly what the Independent socialists stood for.[2] But the latter did not

---

[1] L. Stern (ed.), *Die Auswirkungen der grossen Sozialistischen Oktoberrevolution auf Deutschland* (1959), I, 201.

[2] For a discussion of this subject, see G. Lichtheim, *Marxism* (1961), especially pp. 393–400. Discussing the prospects of Menshevism in pre-1914 Russia, E. H. Carr (*The Bolshevik Revolution*, I, 41 ff.) refers to the difficulty of applying the Menshevik time-table of two successive revolutions (a bourgeois followed by a proletarian one) in a country such as

then realise that the very factors which, on Marxist premises, made Germany an ideal country for revolution, such as its advanced industry, large proletariat and well organised socialist party (to which at the end of 1918 was added defeat) had thrown up barriers (which Bernstein was one of the first to observe) to the unfolding of the classical Marxist revolutionary scheme.[1] The German left, dazzled by Lenin's success in Russia, were ready to forgive him for deviating from the Marxist text-books, but failed to grasp the extent to which it depended on specifically Russian conditions, and also on a unique combination of circumstances.

For a party as reformist and *embourgeoisé* as the S.P.D. a proletarian revolution on Marxist or Leninist lines was really a chimera.[2] The claims of the Marxist doctrinaires who denied that any proletarian interests could be defended by the war were too one-sided to gain the acceptance of any but a tiny fanatical minority. Liebknecht, whose view this was, admitted that the socialists had over-estimated their power to stop war; it seems not to have occurred to him that in much the same way they might over-estimate their ability to make a revolution. What can reasonably be argued is that had the S.P.D. adopted revisionism in theory as well as in practice and shed its revolutionary objectives it might never have provoked the reaction from the right which proved its ultimate undoing. Bernstein himself had a presentiment of that when he remarked of Liebknecht's demands for proletarian dictatorship on 9 November 1918: 'He will bring us the counter-revolution.'[3] Yet it is possible that in Weimar Germany even moderate socialism, like democracy, could not have withstood the nationalist wave. The forces of nationalism had tamed liberalism a generation before; now, exacerbated by Versailles and determined to reverse the verdict of November 1918, they might have triumphed inevitably in the long run, especially as the long run included inflation and the great depression. What cannot be doubted is that internecine conflict within German socialism immeasurably weakened its powers of resistance.

Russia where the bourgeoisie was not only perhaps incapable of making a revolution, but unwilling to do so if the result would be its own eventual overthrow. Similar considerations apply to Hohenzollern Germany, where, as the first chapter showed, the lukewarm attitude of the middle-class parties to democracy was at least in part due to their fear of the socialism which they believed might follow the introduction of a parliamentary regime. Carr's conclusion that the original Marxist scheme was inappropriate to Russia can thus be extended, *mutatis mutandis*, to Germany.

[1] See pp. 20–26 above.

[2] The bourgeois nature of the S.P.D. came as a shock to foreign observers who went to Germany expecting to see a revolutionary party. The French socialist Hervé recorded this impression when he attended the Stuttgart congress of the Second International in 1907, and Max Weber noted a similar reaction on the part of Russian socialists who were guests at the S.P.D. congress at Mannheim in 1906. See Joll, *The Second International*, p. 134, and Weber, *op. cit.* p. 65.

[3] Bernstein, *Die deutsche Revolution*, p. 34 n.

The full significance of the issues raised by the German revolution can best be seen against a broader historical background. Behind it loom two giant figures: Bismarck, who created its setting, and Marx, who provided its ideology.

Bismarck's achievement had important consequences for German socialism in two ways. First, his defeat of liberalism and consolidation of the authoritarian Prusso-German monarchy placed on the rising socialists rather than on the declining liberals the main burden of taking up the struggle for democracy which an earlier generation of liberals had lost between 1848 and 1866. In Marxist terms, the S.P.D. had to make the running for a bourgeois as well as for a proletarian revolution.[1] But the absence of a sizeable and reliable ally to the right was a grave handicap. Before the war, as was seen in the first chapter, the S.P.D. tried unsuccessfully to gain the support of the National Liberals in their fight for Prussian franchise reform. During the war the middle parties in the Reichstag showed little regard for liberal principles in relation to war aims or internal policy. The smallness of the Democratic party in the Weimar Republic was another symptom of the same weakness.[2] Not until after the second world war did German politics begin to make up for the liberal gap which was the direct result of Bismarck's policy. Max Weber complained in a pamphlet published in 1917 that Bismarck had 'left behind as a political heritage a nation without any political education, far below the level which, in this respect, it had reached twenty years earlier. Above all he left behind a nation without any political will...accustomed to submit...to anything which was decided for it.[3]

Secondly, Bismarck taught the nation to believe in force (successfully tested in three wars) and encouraged a tendency to equate might with right and to underrate moral values in a way that came to be considered characteristic of Hohenzollern Germany. The special status of the army in the Bismarckian Reich was recognised both constitutionally (the chief of the general staff ranked equally with the Chancellor *vis-à-vis* the Kaiser) and socially. Max Weber's comment on the need for socialists to control the army if they were to overthrow the state has already been quoted. This was another case where the liberals' acquiescence in the *status quo* forced the socialists to fight almost single-handed. The war enhanced the political influence of the army chiefs and so made the task more difficult. Even in defeat and dissolution the imperial army was able to play a political role,[4] winning its last battle by defeating the Spartacists in the streets of German towns. Although Marx had

---

[1] The German revolution was once described by Arthur Rosenberg as a middle-class revolution won by the working class in a struggle with feudalism (Anderson, *Hammer or Anvil*, p. 39).

[2] Cf. Bracher, *Die Auflösung der Weimarer Republik* (1955), p. 10. 'Der Weimarer Republik sollte die liberale Mitte schwer fehlen.'

[3] Mayer, *op. cit.* p. 78.

[4] Volkmann, *Der Marxismus*, p. 270.

emphasised that a popular revolution could be successful only if it smashed the bureaucratic–military machine opposed to it, this part of his teaching, like the dictatorship of the proletariat to which it belonged, was taken to heart by few German socialists.[1]

From Marx the socialists drew their analysis of society and their long-term aims. He had little to say about the technique of winning power, but the omission from the S.P.D. programme of the dictatorship of the proletariat to which Marx attached great importance as the transitional form of government between capitalism and socialism was significant, as was the party's ready response to the encouragement given by Engels to the capture of parliamentary seats. This is not the place to attempt an answer to the question which of the two strands in pre-1914 Marxism was the more authentic: proletarian dictatorship with its roots in Jacobinism, Blanquism and the Paris of 1848 and the Commune; or democracy (still a subversive slogan in Hohenzollern Germany) with its revolutionary ancestry of 1789 and 1848, its vital role in the bourgeois revolution that according to the Marxist time-table must precede the proletarian one, and its obvious relevance to the gaining of power in a parliamentary epoch. Marxist texts were quoted in support of both concepts. Kautsky tried to reconcile them by arguing that since the proletariat had become the majority of the nation proletarian rule would be almost synonymous with democracy, a view frequently put forward by the Independent socialists during the revolutionary period. It was only after the war had disproved the assumptions underlying the liberal–Marxist synthesis and Lenin had established a new kind of revolutionary dictatorship that the German left consented to abandon democracy for class rule. And only after the disillusioning experience of 1918–19 did they accept the notion that such a dictatorship might be exercised by a minority of the proletariat, thus reverting to the 'immature proto-Marxism' of 1848–50.[2] The German socialists made

[1] It was significant of the trend in German left wing socialism after the disappointments of 1918–19 that Toni Sender, the Independent leader from Frankfurt, should quote Marx's letter to Kugelmann of 12 April 1871, in which Marx, referring to the last chapter of his *Eighteenth Brumaire*, insisted that the state machine must be shattered, not just taken over. The problem of the German army could also be seen from another angle: Engels often expressed the belief that the growth of socialism among recruits to the Prussian army would ultimately undermine it and make it ripe for revolution. He wrote to Bebel in 1884: 'As things are at present, an impulse from outside can scarcely come from anywhere but Russia. If it does not do so, if the impulse is given inside Germany, then the revolution can start only from the army.' (Quoted in Lichtheim, *op. cit.* p. 262.) Engels was over-optimistic. It took defeat after over four years of war and blockade to revolutionise the German army, and then hardly in a form that Engels would have approved.

[2] *Ibid.* p. 337. For much in this section I am indebted to Mr Lichtheim's book. What the Spartacists were trying to do in the winter of 1918-19 was to revive the 'Jacobin' Marxism of 1848 with its concept of the revolutionary vanguard, in contrast to the 'democratic' Marxism of Marx's own later years, exemplified in his Inaugural Address to the First International (1864) with its recognition of the political role of organised labour.

the same discovery as the French socialists in 1848, that universal suffrage could mean counter-revolution.

Although in their short-term aims and day-to-day thinking the S.P.D. may have been influenced by Lassalle more than by Marx, they inherited from Marx his belief both in the primacy of the economic and in the inevitability of the revolution. As interpreted by the learned but rather pedantic Kautsky, Marxist determinism came to mean that socialists could almost wait passively for capitalism to collapse, and his dictum that the S.P.D. was a revolutionary but not a revolution-making party suggested that the revolution might make itself. Kautsky did not promise that the revolution would not be violent, but he thought it probable that it would be less violent, because of the part to be played by universal suffrage, than previous revolutions.[1] This prognosis fitted in well with the distaste for force which was characteristic of socialists of Kautsky's generation. When Bernstein challenged the Marxist notion of 'collapse' as well as the materialist conception of history he was defeated rather than refuted; but as was seen in Chapter I, the authoritarian state provided little incentive to abandon revolutionary theory, and the crisis of imperialism was adduced by the left as evidence of capitalism's decline. Nevertheless the primacy of the economic and the inevitability of the collapse of capitalism were misleading signposts when the German revolution came. Liebknecht's admission in the *Rote Fahne* of 19 November 1918 that the soldiers were anti-militarist rather than pro-socialist was revealing.[2]

That the Independent socialists should boast in their manifesto of 12 November 1918 that the 'revolutionary people' had broken the 'domination of the capitalist clique in public life' was understandable in the first flush of success; but that the party should go on until 1920 referring to the collapse of the 'exploiting capitalist economy' during the war showed an inability to distinguish between state power and the economic order. The crumbling of state power in Germany in October–November 1918 was the result of defeat, and the capitalist structure survived. The traditional Marxist view that, since capitalism ultimately was to blame for the war and the defeat, the main task of socialists in office would be to socialise the economy was of little immediate help to a party grappling for the first time with the problems of government and Freikorps militarism. As early as 1923 a German historian wrote:

Neither politically nor economically has the bourgeoisie exhausted its powers of action and creation, on the contrary it has gained in influence... The representatives of radicalism in Germany have wrongly seen or wanted to see in the political and military collapse a failure of the social order as well; this false interpretation was the cause of their failure.[3]

[1] Kautsky, *The Road to Power* (1909), p. 50. The sub-title of this book was significantly *Das Hineinwachsen in die Revolution.*
[2] Liebknecht, *Ausgewaehlte Reden, Briefe und Aufsätze*, p. 469 (see p. 163 above).
[3] Stuemke, *Die Entstehung der deutschen Republik* (1923), p. 238.

18-2

The German industrialists, wise in their generation, had, as we have seen, already taken precautions against the approaching storm.[1] The result was the general agreement on wages and other matters between the employers' associations and the trade unions, drawn up during the last weeks of the empire and signed in November 1918, which recognised the unions for the first time as equal bargaining partners. The agreement can be seen as the economic counterpart of the constitutional reforms of October. To militants like Richard Müller it was a stab in the back, an act of treachery comparable to Ebert's sell-out to Groener. It was significant not only in softening the impact of the revolution on industrial relations, but as widening the gap between moderate and revolutionary trade union leaders that was also to be emphasised by their different approach to the problem of workers' councils. Here again the left spoke with a divided voice.

Granted that the revolution occurred in a form unpredicted and in circumstances which prevented the divided socialists from extracting the maximum advantage from it, there remains the final reason for the failure of the German revolution—a misunderstanding of the nature of power. Power or force was traditionally regarded by socialists as a weapon used only by reactionaries, for democracy, being government by consent, would make the use of force unnecessary. Ebert repeated this view at a mass meeting in Berlin on 8 December 1918.[2] The collapse (really temporary paralysis) of the old order and its lack of resistance to the revolution encouraged the belief that the new forceless age had begun. The bloodless revolution, to be brought about by the conjunction of impersonal economic and social forces and the 'revolutionising of minds' of which socialists liked to speak, seemed to have been realised. Under these circumstances, the majority socialists saw no need to defend their republic by arms or to act with more energy against their former or potential opponents in the civil service, the army and elsewhere. Yet that Ebert, who was certainly a realist among socialists, was aware of the need for a power factor is shown by his pact with Groener and by his later use of Freikorps against the insurrectionary left. The Independents at first displayed more consistency. They carried their dislike of force even further than the S.P.D., as their attitude to the war proved, and they prided themselves, as Dittmann wrote in his Memoirs, on having behaved during the revolution with restraint and humanity. Yet a section of them took part in

---

[1] See p. 166 n. 2 above.

[2] Kolb, *op. cit.* p. 174. Scheidemann told the National Assembly on 13 February 1919: 'The times of despotism are over once for all.' In an apt criticism of the S.P.D. leaders Ernst Troeltsch wrote that they failed to understand that the exercise of power was just as necessary in a democracy (or more so) as in a political system based on the army or class privilege, and that they wrongly saw as undemocratic inevitable differences of social function. Troeltsch's article, 'Aristokratie' appeared in *Kunstwart*, 2. Oktoberheft 1919, quoted in Kolb, *op. cit.* p. 407.

the January rising and other acts of violence and ultimately as a party they accepted the 'hard line' of the Third International.

The conflict between a desire to exploit the revolutionary situation and reluctance to betray democratic ideals is nowhere better exemplified than in the later career of Rosa Luxemburg, who, though a Spartacist, shared many of the assumptions of the Independent socialists, including their suspicion of party bureaucracy and their humanitarian approach to politics. Like them, she criticised the Bolsheviks for using terror, for purging and suppressing the opposition, in language which shows a passionate concern for freedom.[1] At the foundation conference of the Communist party she was foremost in resisting the suggestion that they should seize power as a minority. Yet her apocalyptic belief in socialism as the hope of mankind, her revolutionary fanaticism and her conviction that parliamentary democracy would kill the revolution led her to support a policy of incitement to civil war and to direct a campaign of hate against the S.P.D. leaders which found their logical climax in the disastrous January rising (that she backed from a mistaken sense of loyalty) and in her own violent death. Like Marx, who persuaded himself that the revolution would triumph through an alliance between the proletariat and other classes which never took place, she believed that the whole German proletariat would rally to the barricades. She did not live to see the consequences of her miscalculation[2] for the socialist movement. Had she survived, she would no doubt have found, like Robespierre, that the reign of virtue could be secured only through terror.

Thus both socialist parties learnt through bitter experience that force was indispensable. The S.P.D., having none of their own, had to use the Freikorps,

[1] Rosa Luxemburg wrote in the summer of 1918: 'The unheard of acts of violence and cruelties of the Bolsheviks do not let me sleep' (quoted in *Die Zukunft* of 25 January 1919).

[2] There is a revealing parallel between the optimistic predictions of revolutionary prospects made by Marx and Engels in the *Communist Manifesto* and the *Class Struggles in France* (see the third section of ch. 1 above) and the following passage from Rosa Luxemburg's address at the foundation conference of the German Communist party on 31 December 1918: 'With every day that passes this [the Ebert] government is losing more and more the backing of the great mass of the proletariat; besides the petty bourgeoisie, there are only remnants, sad remnants of proletarians which still support it, but it is very uncertain how long they will support Ebert/Scheidemann...The proletariat as a whole has already escaped their grasp, the soldiers too can no longer be used as counter-revolutionary cannon-fodder. What is there left for these poor wretches to do to save themselves?' (Luxemburg, *Ausgewählte Reden und Schriften*, II, pp. 673, 679, quoted in Kolb, *op. cit.* p. 152.) There was no doubt some justification for the opinion that nothing was to be feared from the soldiers, in view of the behaviour of the regular troops in Berlin on 24 December, but Rosa Luxemburg's assessment of the proletariat was wildly at variance with all the evidence. As Kolb points out, the 'poor wretches' of the S.P.D. received 38 per cent of all votes cast in the election of the constituent assembly three weeks later. It was significant that Luxemburg repeated in her generation the kind of miscalculations which Marx had made in the age of Napoleon III, and which Engels had reiterated in 1895.

who, in their short and stormy career, left an indelible mark on the republic. The Independents, at first with hesitation, later in a mood compounded of hope and desperation, sought to follow the Leninist formula for success. Both parties saw that they had overestimated the success of the revolution at first, and underestimated the danger of counter-revolution later—a misjudgement they shared with the Communists. In these and many other ways the revolution failed to conform to any preconceived pattern, and in the new clash of forces that followed the uneasy stalemate of 1919 German politics could find only a temporary equilibrium.

BIBLIOGRAPHY

The following notes may be useful as an introduction to the bibliography (which is not exhaustive) for those who wish to explore the German Revolution of 1918 more thoroughly.

UNPRINTED PRIMARY SOURCES

The minutes of the German war cabinet (*Alte Reichskanzlei 2744: Beihefte zu Kabinettsprotokollen, 1917–19*, Serial No. 9246 H) of which the Foreign Office Library has a photostat copy shed some light on the reactions of members of Prince Max of Baden's cabinet to the crisis of October 1918 and the signs of impending upheaval. The war cabinet met for the last time on 16 November 1918 with Ebert in the chair, when its membership seems to have coincided with that of the Council of People's Commissars. A major source for the revolution is the minutes of the latter (*Protokolle der Kabinettssitzungen*, vols. 1–3, 14 November 1918–8 February 1919, Serial No. 8935 H), also in the Foreign Office Library in photostat, which show how far there was divergence as well as agreement between the two socialist parties and inside the Independent party over controversial issues such as policy towards the generals and relations with Soviet Russia. The minutes are a useful check on Barth's colourful memoirs and Dittmann's more sober record. They confirm that right up to the end of December 1918 the S.P.D. leaders believed the threat of counter-revolution to be virtually non-existent. Matters of exceptional importance were usually discussed by joint meetings of the People's Commissars and the Executive Council (after the middle of December the Central Council), as for example on 20 December when Groener argued his case against 'demilitarisation' embodied in the Lamp'l Points. The minutes of the Central Council (*Protokolle des Zentralrates der Deutschen Sozialistischen Republik*, vol. 1, 8 January–25 January 1919), available at the International Institute of Social History, Amsterdam, are revealing of the sharp criticism of the Freikorps during the suppression of the January rising made by majority socialists, who shared the Independents' fears of the revival of militarism.

Among private sources, the Kautsky Archive (*Nachlass*) at the International Institute of Social History, Amsterdam, contains a very large collection of articles, published and unpublished, press cuttings and letters from Kautsky's long and prolific career as an intellectual leader of central European socialism, only a fraction of which falls within the period 1914–20. It includes a good deal of material on the annexations controversy during the war and on the socialist split which was its main consequence. Kautsky's somewhat tortuous attempts to reconcile socialist attitudes to the war with past pledges and Marxist theory can be traced in some detail. Insight is also given into relations between the rival socialist parties during the critical winter of 1918–19, when Kautsky pleaded the case for their reunion despite difficulties on both sides. The memoirs of Dittmann (*Lebenserinnerungen Wilhelm Dittmanns*), also to be seen at Amsterdam, are important for the history of the Independent Social Democratic party, whose secretary Dittmann was. They contain the author's reflections on the missed opportunities of the German revolution, and his criticism of Ebert in particular, as well as interesting reminiscences of the Kapp Putsch in the Ruhr and of Soviet Russia, which Dittmann visited in 1920 as one of a four-man party delegation to negotiate on membership of the Third International.

An eloquent defence of the Independent socialists, the memoirs reveal at times the party's weakness. They are shortly to be published under the editorship of Professor Georg Kotowski of the Otto Suhr Institute, Free University of Berlin. In contrast, the wartime diary of Eduard David (*Tagebuch Eduard David*) at the German Federal Archive, Koblenz, is illuminating for the reformist group of the S.P.D. of which David was a spokesman, and for its relations with the government. It too is due for publication.

PRINTED PRIMARY AND SECONDARY SOURCES

The policy of both socialist parties can be followed in the socialist press (especially, during the war, *Vorwaerts* and *Die neue Zeit*), in official reports of party conferences, especially those of Berlin, Gotha and Würzburg and the *Reichskonferenz* of 1916, in pamphlets and memoirs, and in the Reichstag and National Assembly debates. For the S.P.D. a handy source for the war years is the minutes of the Council (*Protokolle der Sitzungen des Parteiausschusses der Sozialdemokratischen Partei Deutschlands*)— the representative body which then virtually replaced the annual conference—from 27 September 1914 to 28 June 1917; I have not been able to consult the Council minutes for the period after June 1917 if they are extant. Scheidemann's two-volume *Memoirs of a Social Democrat* and his earlier *Zusammenbruch* (the two overlap) are the most important memoirs for the majority socialists. For the socialist debate on war aims and annexations the contemporary British study, Edwyn Bevan's *German Social Democracy during the War*, is remarkably well informed and still very useful. The cited works of Haenisch and Lensch published during the war give the point of view of the nationalist wing of the S.P.D. For the Independent socialists the standard history is Eugen Prager's *Geschichte der U.S.P.D.*, which has the advantage of including lengthy excerpts from contemporary documents. Published in 1921, it lacks historical perspective, but conveys the spirit of the time as experienced by an *engagé* historian. Much fascinating detail about Germany during the war, and especially about the growth of opposition socialism, the strike movement and the naval mutiny, is contained in the monumental work of the Reichstag Committee of Inquiry into the Causes of the German Collapse (*Die Ursachen des deutschen Zusammenbruches im Jahre 1918*, 12 volumes). Vol. VIII, on the Reichstag during the war, by J. V. Bredt, is particularly enlightening for the attitude of political parties to the main questions of the day. A useful selection from the Report was published in English by Stanford University Press in 1932 under the editorship of R. H. Lutz as *The German Revolution*. For relations between the left wing groups and the armed forces E. O. Volkmann's study, *Der Marxismus und das deutsche Heer im Weltkriege*, written from the point of view of a moderate nationalist, is invaluable. Information about both socialist parties is scanty in the last year of the war, when no major conferences were held and little is recorded in the various memoirs. Dittmann, for one, was imprisoned for his part in the January 1918 strike, which also led to a stricter application of the military censorship. This was especially crippling for the Independent socialists, who lacked a daily newspaper in Berlin to represent their standpoint, though the traditionally left wing *Leipziger Volkszeitung* printed articles by the Spartacists Mehring and Clara Zetkin. In the Reichstag the Independents continued to exercise a right of free speech denied to them elsewhere. After 15 November 1918 the day-to-day policy of the U.S.P.D. can be followed in the party's daily *Freiheit*.

No definitive history of the German revolution exists, but there is no lack of studies by participants and contemporaries representing all points of view. The best general account, well documented, lucid and thoughtful, is Eduard Bernstein's *Die deutsche Revolution*, which, however, only goes up to February 1919. It is written from the angle of a right wing Independent socialist, as is Heinrich Stroebel's narrative, translated into English as *The German Revolution and after*. Stroebel, a former editor of *Vorwaerts*, was a minister in the Prussian revolutionary government of November 1918. His book is less scholarly than Bernstein's but has the advantage of including both the revolution's wartime origins and its post-war sequel up to the Kapp Putsch. Richard Müller's trilogy, *Vom Kaiserreich zur Republik* (two volumes) and *Der Bürgerkrieg in Deutschland*, traces the revolutionary movement with particular emphasis on the part played by the revolutionary shop-stewards whose leader Müller was. The other revolutionary shop-steward leader, Emil Barth, left in *Aus der Werkstatt der deutschen Revolution* a book of memoirs which contains much information, some of doubtful accuracy, about the pre-revolutionary build-up and the quarrels inside the all-socialist government of which Barth was the most controversial figure. Barth's account, deliberately indiscreet and full of the contemporary atmosphere, reflects its author's temperamental braggadocio. Paul Frölich, the biographer of Rosa Luxemburg, told the story of the revolution in his *Zehn Jahre Krieg und Bürgerkrieg* from the point of view of a leader of the Bremen left wing group who became a founder member of the German Communist party. For the January 1919 rising in Berlin the record of the trial of Ledebour (*Der Ledebour-Prozess*), one of the ring-leaders, is important. Some of this and other material about Ledebour is in a memorial volume edited by his widow (Minna Ledebour, *Georg Ledebour, Mensch und Kaempfer*). Of other books on Independent socialists, Ernst Haase's volume on his father *Hugo Haase* includes many letters which reveal Haase's endearing characteristics as a man but is disappointingly sparse on the political side. A recent study of the Bavarian revolution, Fritz Schade's *Kurt Eisner und die bayrische Revolution*, is useful despite its limited approach to the subject but does not deal with the consequences of Eisner's assassination in the soviet dictatorship. *The Autobiography of a German Rebel* by Toni Sender contains interesting reminiscences by a leading Independent woman socialist at Frankfurt. The growing division inside the U.S.P.D. which ultimately destroyed it may be studied in the official reports of the party conferences of Berlin and Leipzig (1919) and finally Halle (1920). For both parties in December 1918 a basic source is the stenographic report of the first congress of workers' and soldiers' councils (*Allgemeiner Kongress der Arbeiter- und Soldatenräte*).

For the majority socialists in the revolutionary and post-war period the official reports of the party conferences of Weimar (1919), and to a lesser extent Kassel (1920) are informative. Books from the S.P.D. point of view include *Die November Revolution*, written with inside knowledge by Hermann Müller, the Chancellor of March 1920. Scheidemann's two books, already referred to, while revealing about the war years are regrettably reticent about the revolution. Ebert's two-volume *Schriften, Aufzeichnungen, Reden* consists largely of public speeches and throws little light on his personal role or motives. Of Kotowki's new biography of Ebert, one volume, going up to 1917, has already appeared. Noske's contemporary *apologia, Von Kiel bis Kapp*, is essential. His later memoirs, *Aufstieg und Niedergang der deutschen Sozialdemokratie*, could be described as emotion recollected in tranquillity if they had not been written under the shadow of the Third Reich. The memoirs of three leading majority socialists who were ministers during the revolutionary period, Grzesinski, Otto Braun and Severing, all contain interesting material. For the revolution 'in the provinces', and indeed for the S.P.D. generally in this period as viewed by a leading reformist socialist in Württemberg, Keil's two-volume *Erlebnisse eines Sozialdemokraten* is worth reading. The first few chapters of Friedrich Stampfer's history, *Die ersten vierzehn Jahre der deutschen Republik*, are a useful introduction to the subject by a man who as chief editor of *Vorwaerts* played an influential part in S.P.D. affairs. Stampfer's later memoirs, *Erfahrungen und Erkenntnisse*, consider German socialism in a perspective stretching from the age of Bismarck to that of Adenauer.

For the Spartacists the main sources are the writings and speeches of Rosa Luxemburg, of which her *Krise in der deutschen Sozialdemokratie* (translated and published in New York as *The Crisis in the German Social Democracy*) is the most notable; the periodical *Die Internationale* of which only one number appeared; the letters, circulars and pamphlets collected and edited by Ernst Meyer as *Spartakusbriefe* and *Spartakus im Kriege* (the former in two volumes); the writings and speeches of Karl Liebknecht collected in *Klassenkampf gegen den Krieg, Ausgewaehlte Reden, Briefe und Aufsaetze* and *Politische Aufzeichnungen aus seinem Nachlass;* the pamphlets and broadsheets edited by Drahn and Leonhard as *Unterirdische Literatur im revolutionären Deutschland während des ersten Weltkrieges;* Mehring's *Kriegsartikel,* some of which appeared in the *Leipziger Volkszeitung;* speeches at conferences of left wing socialists, especially at Berlin and Gotha in 1917; after 10 November 1918 the daily newspaper *Die Rote Fahne;* and the conferences of the German Communist party, especially the foundation conference. Liebknecht's wartime speeches and interpellations are in the Reichstag in the *Verhandlungen* of various dates between 1914 and 1916. The two biographies of Rosa Luxemburg by Frölich and Roland-Holst are sympathetic studies by contemporaries; the first is rather a hagiography. The 'critical biographical sketch' by Fred Oelssner published in (East) Berlin in 1951 restates the stereotyped Leninist view with the Stalinist overtones (especially in the second edition, 1952) of its date. The new two-volume biography of Rosa Luxemburg by J. P. Nettl appeared too late for consultation. A fairly comprehensive collection of material on the German revolution from the Communist point of view is the *Illustrierte Geschichte der deutschen Revolution* (1929). By contrast, the highly selective and slanted collection published as *Zur Geschichte der Kommunistischen Partei Deutschlands* is remarkable for its omissions. Ruth Fischer's *Stalin and German Communism* is a first-hand though unreliable source, with the merits and defects of history written by one who was a committed participant in the events described. The emergence of the Communist party from the Spartacist movement is objectively summarised in O. K. Flechtheim's *Die K.P.D. in der Weimarer Republik*, while the third volume of E. H. Carr's *Bolshevik Revolution* uses Russian sources to elucidate German–Soviet relations. Franz Borkenau's *Communist International* contains some pertinent observations on German socialism.

Of more general works, Arthur Rosenberg's *Birth of the German Republic* admirably summarises the background and origins of the German revolution, while the revolution itself is the main theme of the first few chapters of the sequel, *The History of the German Republic*. Rosenberg was a scholar who combined shrewd judgement with practical experience of politics as a member of the Reichstag, and his work, objective as well as expert, has stood the test of time. Heidegger's *Der deutsche Nationalstaat und die Sozialdemokratie, 1870–1920* is a pedestrian compilation which contains some useful facts. Stuemke's *Die Entstehung der deutschen Republik*, published in 1923, is a perceptive study by a contemporary. Carl Schorske's *German Social Democracy, 1905–17; the Development of the Great Schism*, justly esteemed for its brilliant analysis of pre-war trends in the party, is illuminating for later developments. Another book by an American scholar, A. J. Berlau's *The German Social Democratic Party, 1914–21*, provides much information based on wide reading, somewhat arbitrarily arranged. R. Coper's *Failure of a Revolution: Germany in 1918–19* is excessively subjective, and can hardly be described as a book that succeeded. There is a good summary of the revolution, its causes and consequences, in S. W. Halperin's survey of the Weimar Republic, *Germany tried Democracy*. Allan Mitchell's *Revolution in Bavaria 1918–1919, The Eisner Regime and the Soviet Republic* (Princeton University Press, 1965) came into my hands too late to be consulted.

Special aspects of the revolution and its background are dealt with in a number of monographs, of which the following may be mentioned. Peter Gay's study of Revisionism, *The Dilemma of Democratic Socialism: Eduard Bernstein's challenge to Marx* deals knowledgeably but briefly with the war and the revolution. Klaus Epstein's comprehensive *Mattias Erzberger and the Dilemma of German Democracy* gives the setting of German politics during the war and unravels the constitutional crisis of 1917 and the role of the Centre party. Merle Fainsod's *International Socialism and the World War* is important for the Zimmerwald movement and the Stockholm peace initiative. For relations between the socialist parties and the trade unions H. J. Varain's *Freie Gewerkschaften, Sozialdemokratie und Staat* is indispensable, while Erich Matthias' *Die deutsche Sozialdemokratie und der Osten, 1914–45* discusses German socialist attitudes to Russia at various stages. E. O. Volkmann's *Revolution über Deutschland* is a well-informed account, especially on the military side, in a popular style. O. E. Schüddekopf's collection of documents, with editorial comments, on relations between the republican government and the army (*Das Heer und die Republik*) is a basic work. For Groener's side of the Ebert–Groener relationship there is something, though not much, in the latter's *Lebenserinnerungen*. Two recent works by German scholars on the workers' and soldiers' councils in the revolution are Walter Tormin's *Zwischen Rätediktatur und sozialer Demokratie* and Eberhard Kolb's longer and more searching *Die Arbeiterräte in der deutschen Innenpolitik, 1918–19*.

Memoirs which throw light on one or other facet of the revolution include the *Erinnerungen* of Gustav Mayer, the biographer of Engels, and *Erinnerungen und Erlebnisse* by Angelica Balabanoff, the Russo-Italian socialist who worked in the secretariat of the (Zimmerwald) International Socialist Commission and later became the first secretary of the Third International. *Through Two Decades* by Theodor Wolff contains a vivid description of the revolution in Berlin as seen by the editor of a leading liberal newspaper. Two books by liberal economists are *Wandering Scholar* by M. J. Bonn, which has first-hand information about Eisner and the Bavarian revolution, and *Ein Leben für den Liberalismus* by Eugen Schiffer, the first finance minister of the Weimar Republic. For Germany in the pre-revolutionary period, and for the majority socialist leaders in particular, the *Memoirs* of Prince Max of Baden are essential. An interesting background book is Julius Braunthal's *In search of the Millennium*, based on the author's wide experience of socialist politics in central Europe.

BIBLIOGRAPHY

I. PRIMARY SOURCES

(i) *Unprinted*

David's Diary (*Tagebuch Eduard David*, 29 July 1914–9 March 1919).

Dittmann's Memoirs (*Lebenserinnerungen Wilhelm Dittmanns*).

Kautsky Archive (*Nachlass*), International Institute of Social History, Amsterdam.

Minutes of the Central Council of the German Socialist Republic (*Protokolle des Zentralrates der Deutschen Sozialistischen Republik*, vol. 1, 8–25 January 1919).

Minutes of the Council of People's Commissars (*Protokolle der Kabinettssitzungen*, vols 1–3, 14 November 1918–8 February 1919, Serial No. 8935 H).

War Cabinet Minutes (*Alte Reichskanzlei 2744: Beihefte zu Kabinettsprotokollen, 1917–19*, Serial No. 9246 H).

(ii) *Printed*

(a) *Proceedings of conferences and parliamentary debates*

Allgemeiner Kongress der Arbeiter- und Soldatenräte Deutschlands: Stenographischer Bericht. Berlin, 1919 (first congress, December 1918).

Bericht über den Gruendungsparteitag der Kommunistischen Partei Deutschlands (Spartakusbund) vom 30 Dezember 1918–1 Januar 1919.

Protokoll der Reichskonferenz der Sozialdemokratie Deutschlands. Berlin, September 1916.

Protokolle der Sitzungen des Parteiausschusses der Sozialdemokratischen Partei Deutschlands, Berlin, 27 September 1914–28 June 1917.

Sozialdemokratische Partei Deutschlands: Protokoll über die Verhandlungen des Parteitages der Sozialdemokratischen Partei Deutschlands. Würzburg, 1917.

Sozialdemokratische Partei Deutschlands: Protokoll über die Verhandlungen des Parteitages der Sozialdemokratischen Partei Deutschlands. Weimar, 1919.

Sozialdemokratische Partei Deutschlands: Protokoll über die Verhandlungen des Parteitages der Sozialdemokratischen Partei Deutschlands. Kassel, 1920.

Unabhaengige Sozialdemokratische Partei Deutchlands: Protokoll über die Verhandlungen des Gruendungsparteitages der U.S.P.D. Gotha, 1917 (including, as an appendix, *Bericht über die Konferenz der Arbeitsgemeinschaft und der Spartakusgruppe*. Berlin, January 1917).

Unabhaengige Sozialdemokratische Partei Deutschlands: Protokoll über die Verhandlungen des ausserordentlichen Parteitages der U.S.P.D. Berlin, March 1919.

Unabhaengige Sozialdemokratische Partei Deutschlands: Protokoll über die Verhandlungen des ausserordentlichen Parteitages der U.S.P.D. Leipzig, November–December 1919.

Unabhaengige Sozialdemokratische Partei Deutschlands: Protokoll über die Verhandlungen des ausserordentlichen Parteitages der U.S.P.D. Halle, October 1920.

Verhandlungen des deutschen Reichstags, vols. 306 (1914)–314 (1918).

Verhandlungen der Verfassunggebenden Deutschen Nationalversammlung, vols. 326–333 (1919–20).

(b) *Collections of Documents*

Buchner, E. *Revolutionsdokumente. Die deutsche Revolution in der Darstellung der zeitgenössischen Presse*, vol. 1 (Berlin, 1921).

Drahn, E. and Leonhard, S. (ed.), *Unterirdische Literatur im revolutionären Deutschland während des Weltkrieges* (Berlin, 1920).

Gruenberg, Carl (ed.). *Die Internationale und der Weltkrieg* (Leipzig, n.d.).

Haase, Hugo. *Reichstagsreden gegen die deutsche Kriegspolitik* (Berlin, n.d.).

Meyer, Ernst (ed.), *Spartakus im Kriege* (Berlin, 1927).

Meyer, Ernst (ed.), *Spartakusbriefe* (2 vols, Berlin, 1920–6).

Schüddekopf, O. E. *Das Heer und die Republik: Quellen zur Politik der Reichswehr-führung 1918–33* (Hanover and Frankfurt, 1955).

(iii) *Memoirs, etc.*

This section includes a number of works which, entitled or described as histories of the period, contain first-hand accounts of events in which the writers took part, and which therefore deserve to rank as primary sources.

Balabanoff, Angelica. *Erinnerungen und Erlebnisse*. Berlin, 1927.

Barth, Emil. *Aus der Werkstatt der deutschen Revolution*. Berlin, n.d.

Beckmann, E. *Der Dolchstossprozess in München vom 19 Oktober–20 November 1925*. Munich, 1925.

Bernstein, Eduard. *Die deutsche Revolution*. Berlin, 1921.

Bethmann Hollweg, Theodor von. *Betrachtungen zum Weltkrieg*, 2 vols. Berlin, 1919 and 1921.

Bonn, M. J. *Wandering Scholar*. London, 1949.

Braun, Otto. *Von Weimar zu Hitler*. New York, 1940.

Braunthal, Julius. *In search of the Millennium*. London, 1945.

Bülow, Prince Bernhard von. *Memoirs*, 4 vols. London, 1931–2.

David, Eduard. *Die Sozialdemokratie im Weltkrieg*. Berlin, 1915.

Dittmann, Wilhelm. *Die Marine-Justizmörde von 1917 und die Admiralsrebellion vom 1918*. Berlin, 1926.

Ebert, Friedrich. *Schriften, Aufzeichnungen, Reden*, 2 vols. Dresden, 1926.

Ein Leben für den Sozialismus. Memoirs of Karl Kautsky by various authors. Hanover, 1954.

Froelich, Paul. *10 Jahre Krieg und Bürgerkrieg*. Berlin, 1924.

Groener, Wilhelm. *Lebenserinnerungen*. Göttingen, 1957.

Groener-Geyer, Dorothea. *General Groener—Soldat und Staatsmann*. Frankfurt-am-Main, 1955.

Grzesinski, Albert. *Inside Germany*. New York, 1939.

Haase, Ernst. *Hugo Haase, sein Leben und Wirken*. Berlin, n.d.

Haussmann, Conrad. *Schlaglichter*. Frankfurt, 1924.

Kautsky, Karl. *Mein Verhältnis zur U.S.P.D.* Berlin, 1922.

Kautsky, Karl. *Sozialisten und Krieg: ein Beitrag zur Ideengeschichte des Sozialismus von den Hussiten bis zum Voelkerbund*. Prague, 1937.

Keil, Wilhelm. *Erlebnisse eines Sozialdemokraten*, 2 vols. Stuttgart, 1947–8.

Ledebour, Georg (ed.) *Der Ledebour Prozess*. Berlin, 1919.

Ledebour, Minna (ed.). *Georg Ledebour, Mensch und Kämpfer*. Zürich, 1947.

Lensch, Paul. *Die deutsche Sozialdemokratie und der Weltkrieg*. Berlin, 1915.

Liebknecht, Karl. *Ausgewaehlte Reden, Briefe und Aufsätze*. Berlin, 1952.

Liebknecht, Karl. *Klassenkampf gegen den Krieg*. Berlin, n.d.

Liebknecht, Karl. *Politische Aufzeichungen aus seinem Nachlass, 1917–18*. Berlin, 1921.

Luxemburg, Rosa. *Die russische Revolution, eine kritische Wuerdigung*. Berlin, 1922.

Luxemburg, Rosa. *Letters from Prison*. London, 1946.

Max, Prince of Baden. *Memoirs*, 2 vols. London, 1928.

Mayer, Gustav. *Erinnerungen*. München, 1949.

Merkur, Paul. *Deutschland, sein oder nicht sein*. Mexico City, 1945.

Müller, Hermann. *Die November Revolution*. Berlin, 1928.

Müller, Richard. *Vom Kaiserreich zur Republik*, 2 vols. Vienna, 1925.

Müller, Richard. *Der Bürgerkrieg in Deutschland: Geburtswehen der Republik*. Berlin, 1925.

Noske, Gustav. *Von Kiel bis Kapp*. Berlin, 1920.

Noske, Gustav. *Aufstieg und Niedergang der deutschen Sozialdemokratie*. Zürich, 1947.

Payer, Friedrich. *Von Bethmann Hollweg bis Ebert, Erinnerungen und Bilder*. Frankfurt, 1923.

Prager, Eugen. *Geschichte der U.S.P.D.* Berlin, 1921.

Radek, Karl. *Die russische und deutsche Revolution und die Weltlage*. Berlin, 1919.

Radek, Karl. *In den Reihen der deutschen Revolution, 1909–19*. Munich, 1921.

Renner, Karl. *Karl Kautsky*. Berlin, 1929.

Scheidemann, Philipp. *Memoirs of a Social Democrat*, 2 vols. London, 1930.

Scheidemann, Philipp. *Der Zusammenbruch*. Berlin, 1921.

Schiffer, Eugen. *Ein Leben für den Liberalismus*. Berlin, 1951.

Sender, Toni. *The Autobiography of a German Rebel*. London, 1940.

Severing, Carl. *Mein Lebensweg*, 2 vols. Köln, 1950.

Stampfer, Friedrich. *Die vierzehn Jahre der ersten deutschen Republik*. Karlsbad, 1936.

Stampfer, Friedrich. *Erfahrungen und Erkenntisse*. Köln, 1953.

Stroebel, Heinrich. *The German Revolution and after*. London, 1923.

Wolff, Theodor. *Through Two Decades*, London, 1936.

II. CONTEMPORARY AND LATER STUDIES

(i) *General Works*

Anderson, Evelyn. *Hammer or Anvil: the Story of the German Working Class Movement*. London, 1945.

Angress, Werner T. *Stillborn Revolution: the Communist Bid for Power in Germany, 1921–23*. Princeton Univ. Press, 1963.

Balfour, Michael. *The Kaiser and his Times*. London, 1964.

Baumont, M. *The Fall of the Kaiser*. London 1931.

Benoist-Méchin, *Histoire de l'armée allemande*. Paris, 1964 (first two vols. of ten, covering the years 1918–25).

Berlau, A. J. *The German Social Democratic Party, 1914–21*. Columbia Univ. Press, 1949.

Bergstrasser, Ludwig. *Geschichte der politischen Parteien in Deutschland*, 9th edn. Munich, 1955.

Bernstein, Eduard. *Evolutionary Socialism*. New York, 1961 (reprint of an English version of *Die Voraussetzungen des Sozialismus und die Aufgaben der Sozialdemokratie*, first published at Stuttgart in 1899).

Besson, Waldemar. *Friedrich Ebert, Verdienst und Grenze*. Göttingen, 1963.

Bevan, Edwyn. *German Social Democracy during the War*. London, 1918.

Borkenau, Franz. *The Communist International*. London, 1938.

Bracher, K. D. *Die Auflösung der Weimarer Republik*. Berlin, 1955.

Carr, E. H. *The Bolshevik Revolution, 1917–23*, vols 1–3. London, 1950–3.

Coper, Rudolf. *Failure of a Revolution*. Cambridge Univ. Press, 1955.

Dehio, Ludwig. *Germany and World Politics in the twentieth century*. London, 1959.

Epstein, Klaus. *Matthias Erzberger and the Dilemma of German Democracy*. Princeton Univ. Press. 1959.

BIBLIOGRAPHY

Eyck, Erich. *Bismarck and the German Empire*. London, 1950.

Eyck, Erich. *A History of the Weimar Republic*, 2 vols. Harvard and Oxford Univ. Press, 1962–4.

Fainsod, Merle. *International Socialism and the World War*. Harvard Univ. Press, 1935.

Fischer, Fritz. *Griff nach der Weltmacht*. Düsseldorf, 1965 (2nd edition).

Flechtheim, Ossip K. *Die K.P.D. in der Weimarer Republik*. Offenbach, 1948.

Frölich, Paul. *Rosa Luxemburg*. London, 1940.

Gatzke, Hans W. *Germany's Drive to the West*. John Hopkins Press, Baltimore, 1950.

Gay, Peter. *The Dilemma of Democratic Socialism: Eduard Bernstein's challenge to Marx*. Columbia Univ. Press, 1952.

Gordon, H. J. *The Reichswehr and the German Republic*. Princeton Univ. Press, 1957.

Haenisch, Konrad. *Die deutsche Sozialdemokratie in und nach dem Weltkriege*, Berlin, 1916.

Halperin, S. W. *Germany tried Democracy*. New York, 1946.

Hanke, Kurt (ed.) *Sechzig Jahre Leipziger Vokszeitung*. Leipzig, 1954.

Heidegger, Hermann. *Die deutsche Sozialdemokratie und der nationale Staat, 1870–1920*. Göttingen, 1956.

Horkenbach, Cuno. *Das deutsche Reich von 1918 bis heute*. Berlin, 1930.

Illustrierte Geschichte der deutschen Revolution, various authors. Berlin, 1929.

Joll, James. *The Second International*. London, 1955.

Kautsky, Karl. *Das Erfurter Programm*. Stuttgart, 1892.

Kautsky, Karl. *The Road to Power*. Chicago, 1909.

Kautsky, Karl. *The Dictatorship of the Proletariat*. Manchester, 1920.

Koenigswald, Harold von. *Revolution 1918*. Breslau, 1933.

Kolb, Eberhard. *Die Arbeiterräte in der deutschen Innenpolitik 1918–19*, Düsseldorf, 1962.

Kotowski, Georg. *Friedrich Ebert, eine politische Biographie*, vol. 1 (to 1917). Wiesbaden, 1963.

Kuczynski, Jürgen. *Der Ausbruch des ersten Weltkrieges und die deutsche Sozialdemokratie, Chronik und Analyse*. Berlin (East), 1957.

Laski, H. J. (ed.). *Communist Manifesto, Socialist Landmark*. London, 1948.

Lichtheim, George. *Marxism*. London, 1961.

Liebknecht, K., Luxemburg, R. and Mehring, F. *The Crisis in the German Social Democracy*, English edition. New York, 1918 (first published in German at Berne in 1916 under the pseudonym 'Junius').

Lutz, R. H. *The German Revolution*. Stanford Univ. Press, California, 1932. (This is a translated selection in 2 vols from the 12-vol. work *Die Ursachen des deutschen Zusammenbruches* cited below.)

Matthias, Erich. *Die deutsche Sozialdemokratie und der Osten*. Tübingen, 1954.

Marx and Engels. *Selected Works*, 2 vols. London, 1950.

Mayer, Gustav. *Friedrich Engels: eine Biographie*, 2 vols. The Hague, 1934.

Mayer, J. P. *Max Weber and German Politics*. London, 1944.

Mehring, Franz. *Karl Marx*. London 1936 (1st English edn.).

Mehring, Franz. *Kriegsartikel*. Berlin, 1918.

Oelssner, Fred. *Rosa Luxemburg, eine kritische biographische Skizze*. Berlin (East), 1952.

Roland-Holst, Henriette. *Rosa Luxemburg, ihr Leben und Wirken*. Zürich, 1937.

Rosenberg, Arthur. *The Birth of the German Republic*. London, 1931.

Rosenberg, Arthur. *The History of the German Republic*. London, 1936.

Rünkel, Ferdinand. *Die deutsche Revolution.* Leipzig, 1929.

Ryder, A. J. *The German Revolution, 1918–19.* (Historical Association Pamphlet, G40, 1959.)

Schade, Franz. *Kurt Eisner und die bayrische Sozialdemokratie.* Hanover, 1961.

Schapiro, L. *The Origin of the Communist Autocracy.* London, 1955.

Schorske, Carl E. *German Social Democracy, 1905–17, The Development of the Great Schism.* Harvard Univ. Press, 1955.

Spartakus (pseudonym). *German Communists.* London, n.d.

Stern, L. (ed.) *Die Auswirkungen der grossen Sozialistischen Oktoberrevolution auf Deutschland.* Berlin (East), 1959 (vol. I of four).

Stuemke, Bruno. *Die Entstehung der deutschen Republik.* Frankfurt, 1923.

Turner, Henry Ashby, jr. *Stresemann and the Politics of the Weimar Republic.* Princeton University Press, 1963.

Tormin, Walter. *Zwischen Rätediktatur und sozialer Demokratie.* Düsseldorf, 1954.

Die Ursachen des deutschen Zusammenbruches im Jahre 1918. (Vierte Reihe im Werk des Untersuchungsausschusses der deutschen verfassunggebenden Nationalversammlung und des deutschen Reichstages, 1919–28. 12 vols.) Berlin, 1925–9.

Varain, H.-J. *Freie Gewerkschaften, Sozialdemokratie und Staat.* Düsseldorf, 1956.

Volkmann, E. O. *Der Marxismus und das deutsche Heer im Weltkriege.* Berlin, 1925.

Volkmann, E. O. *Revolution über Deutschland.* Oldenburg, 1930.

Waldman, Eric A. *The Spartacist Uprising of 1919 and the Crisis of the German Socialist Movement: a study of the relation of political theory and party practice.* Milwaukee Univ. Press, 1958.

Wheeler-Bennett, J. W. *Brest Litovsk, the forgotten Peace.* London, 1938.

Wheeler-Bennett, J. W. *The Nemesis of Power: the German army in politics.* London, 1954.

Winnig, August. *Das Reich als Republik.* Berlin, 1928.

Young, H. F. *Maximilian Harden, Censor Germaniae.* The Hague, 1959.

Zeman, Z. A. B. and Scharlau, W. B. *The Merchant of Revolution: the life of Alexander Israel Helphand (Parvus).* Oxford Univ. Press, 1965.

Zévaès, Alexandre. *Le Socialisme en-France depuis 1904.* Paris, 1934.

Zinoviev, G. *Probleme der deutschen Revolution.* Hamburg, 1923.

Zur Geschichte der Kommunistischen Partei Deutschlands (various authors). Berlin (East), 1954.

(ii) *Pamphlets*

Altmaier, Jacob. *Frankfurter Revolutionstage.* Frankfurt, 1919.

Anlauf, Karl. *Die Revolution in Niedersachsen.* Hanover, 1919.

Anon. *Was will die Unabhaengige Sozialdemokratie?*

Dannenberg, Karl. *The Revolution in Germany.* New York, 1919.

David, Eduard. *Wer trägt die Schuld am Kriege?* Berlin, 1917.

Eisner, Kurt. *Schuld und Sühne.* Berlin, 1919.

Fischer, Anton. *Die Revolutionskommandantur Berlin.* Berlin, 1920.

Grimm, Robert. *Zimmerwald und Kienthal.* Berne, 1917.

Handbuch für die Wähler der U.S.P.D. (n.d. but before the 1920 general election).

Icarus (pseudonym). *The Wilhelmshaven Revolt.* London, 1944.

Klarheit in der U.S.P.D., by various authors. Berlin, 1918.

Kuttner, Erich. *Der Siegeszug der deutschen Revolution von Kiel bis Berlin.* Berlin, 1918.

Laufenberg, Heinrich. *Zwischen der ersten und der zweiten deutschen Revolution.* Hamburg, 1919.

Lorenz, Ernst. *Fünf Jahre U.S.P. in Dresden.* Dresden, 1922.

Oehme, Walter. *Sozialismus und Bolschewismus.* Berlin, 1919.

Popp, L. and Artelt, K. *Ursprung und Entwicklung der November Revolution, 1918.* Kiel, 1918.

'Die Revolution.' *Unabhaengiges sozialdemokratisches Jahrbuch für Politik und proletarische Kultur.* Berlin, 1920.

Struthahn, A. (Karl Radek). *Die Entwicklung der deutschen Revolution und die Aufgaben der Kommunistischen Partei.* Stuttgart, 1919.

Die Sozialdemokratische Partei Deutschlands: Sozialismus und Bolschewismus in Stimmen der führenden Männer. Berlin, 1919.

Die U.S.P.D. und die dritte Internationale, Remscheid, 1920.

Westeuropäisches Sekretariat der III. Internationale. *Der Leipziger Kongress der U.S.P.D. und die Kommunistische Internationale.* N.p., 1920.

Zentralkommittee der U.S.P.D. *Antwort an das Exekutivkomitee* (sic) *der III Internationale.* N.p., 1920.

(iii) Articles in periodicals

Broué, Pierre, 'L'Allemagne des révolutions (1918–23). Esquisse d'une analyse des publications depuis 1960', *Revue d'Histoire moderne et contemporaine* (Paris), vol. xii (April–June 1965), 141.

Carsten, F. L., 'Rosa Luxemburg, freedom and revolution', *Soviet Survey* (London), No. 33 (July–September 1960), 93.

Friedlander, Henry E., 'Conflict of revolutionary authority: provisional government vs. Berlin soviet, November–December 1918', *International Review of Social History*, vii (Amsterdam, 1962), 177.

Lowenthal, Richard, 'The bolshevisation of the Spartacist League', *St Antony's Papers*, No. 9 (Oxford, 1960), 23.

Maehl, Wilhelm, 'The triumph of nationalism in the German socialist party on the eve of the first World War', *Journal of Modern History*, xxiv (1952), 40.

Maehl, Wilhelm, 'The role of Russia in German socialist policy, 1914–18', *International Review of Social History*, iv (Amsterdam, 1959), 177.

Meynell, Hildamarie, 'The Stockholm Conference of 1917', *International Review of Social History*, v (Amsterdam, 1960), 1, 202.

Miller, Susanne, 'Zum dritten August 1914', *Archiv für Sozialgeschichte,* iv (Hanover, 1964), 515.

O'Boyle, Lenore, 'The German Independent Socialists in the first World War', *American Historical Review*, lvi (1951), 824.

Schüddekopf, O. E., 'Radek in Berlin', *Archiv für Sozialgeschichte*, ii (Hanover, 1962), 87.

Snell, John L., 'The Russian Revolution and the German Social Democratic Party in 1917', *Slavic Review*, xv (1956), 338.

III. NEWSPAPERS AND PERIODICALS

Der Arbeiterrat (January–April 1919).

Die Freiheit (November 1918 onwards).

Die neue Zeit.

Die rote Fahne (November 1918 onwards).

The Times.

Vorwaerts.

Die Zukunft.

INDEX

Marx, Karl (*cont.*)
  his *Eighteenth Brumaire of Louis Bona-parte*, 18
  Bernstein's adaptation of, 21–2, 31
  and internationalism, 21, 25
  Marxist determinism, 22, 137, 275
  his unawareness of nationalism, 33, 63
  his attitude to war, 33
  his attitude to Russia, 43, 56
  German revolution a product of his theory, 270–8
mass strikes, *see* strike(s)
May Day, 33, 100, 130
Mayer, Gustav, 218
Max, Prince, of Baden, 4, 112, 119–20, 130, 169
  on need of reform, 85
  as Chancellor, 123, 124–5, 135
  and armistice negotiations with President Wilson, 126, 128–9, 149, 261
  and Kaiser's abdication, 126–7, 149–53
  on parliamentary government, 133–4, 154
  resigns, 136, 149–50.
  and naval mutiny, 141, 142
  influence of, 158
Mehring, Franz, 53–4, 77–8, 118, 131–2
Mensheviks, 60, 62, 104, 131
Meyer, Ernst, 95, 97, 138, 195
Michaelis, Georg
  succeeds Bethmann Hollweg, 89–90, 105
  resigns, 91, 108
  ineptitude of, 91, 92, 93, 105
  and naval mutiny, 102
Miliukov, Paul, 84
militarism
  Rosa Luxemburg on, 28
  S.P.D. attitude to, 36–7
  justification for German, 65
  resentment of, 149, 163–4, 275
  in socialist view, a by-product of imperialism, 163, 264
  government accused of favouring, 192–3, 218
  rebirth of, 218–19, 226–7
  see also Freikorps
military tax, 29, 37
Millerand socialists, 12
'Millerandism', 13, 31, 107
Mitteleuropa, 57, 64
Molkenbuhr, Hermann, 157
Moroccan war scare, 27, 34–5
Morocco, 103
Müller, Hermann, 41–2, 75, 143
  warned of emergency by Ebert, 202
  as foreign secretary, 223
  as party chairman, 225
  on the German revolution, 237, 265
  as Chancellor, 243–7

Müller, Richard
  on Spartacus and *Arbeitsgemeinschaft*, 97–8
  leader of revolutionary shop-stewards, 116, 118
  on eve of November revolution, 138–9
  on November revolution, 155
  at Circus Busch, 157
  denounces agreement between industrialists and trade unions, 166–7, 276
  and constituent assembly, 170, 171
  and congress of councils, 180–1
  and January rising, 200, 206–7
  on Bavarian soviet government, 214
Munich, *see* Bavaria, revolution in

Napoleon I, 124
Napoleon III, 25, 34, 43, 277
Narew, river, 114
National Assembly, *see* constituent assembly
nationalisation, 137, 211, 212; *see also* socialisation
National Bolsheviks, 252–3
nationalism, 2, 3
  Marx's attitude to, 21, 25, 33
  effect of, on German socialism, 25–6
  in wartime socialism, 63–5, 80
National Liberals
  support Hohenzollern Empire, 11
  oppose franchise reform, 15, 273
  criticise Peace Note, 76
  demand constitutional change, 88
  oppose peace resolution, 89
  in committee of seven, 90
  not in Prince Max's government, 123
  superseded by German People's party (*q.v.*), 208
national militia, 14, 182, 185, 192
National People's party, 208, 245
Naumann, Friedrich, 1, 57, 120, 161, 266
'navalism', British, compared to German militarism, 65
navy
  abortive mutiny of, summer 1917, 101, 140, 141
  and left wing socialism, 101–2
  Menagekommissionen in, 102
  mutiny of, 1918, 102, 117, 127, 140–2
  sailors' council in Kiel, 140, 141
  sailors' revolt, December 1918, 188–92
Neue Zeit, Die, 20, 44, 64, 77, 99, 109, 248
Niemen, river, 12
Noske, Gustav
  biographical details of, 24
  pre-war career of, 26, 36, 37
  views of, on the war, 45, 80
  and Kaiser's abdication, 129